INNOVATIVE FIRMS IN EMERGING MARKET COUNTRIES

Innovative Firms in Emerging Market Countries

Edited by
EDMUND AMANN
AND JOHN CANTWELL

OXFORD
UNIVERSITY PRESS

Great Clarendon Street, Oxford, OX2 6DP,
United Kingdom

Oxford University Press is a department of the University of Oxford.
It furthers the University's objective of excellence in research, scholarship,
and education by publishing worldwide. Oxford is a registered trade mark of
Oxford University Press in the UK and in certain other countries

British Library Cataloguing in Publication Data
Data available

Library of Congress Cataloging in Publication Data
Data available

ISBN 978-0-19-964600-5

Printed in Great Britain by
MPG Books Group, Bodmin and King's Lynn

Foreword

It was not so long ago that virtually all firms operating at or close to the frontiers of a manufacturing industry had their home bases in North America, Europe, or Japan. Then Korean and Taiwanese firms began to join the club. Then firms in Brazil, China, India . . . Clearly the barriers to the diffusion of the knowhow needed for strong firm competence have eroded significantly. The firms that are competent today to compete on world markets reside in a great number of different places.

What lies behind this momentous change? The evidence presented in this informative book suggests two kinds of developments. One is that general knowledge of advanced technologies and managerial practices has become much more accessible to professionals trained in the art, and good educational programs for training professional engineers, scientists, and business managers and technicians have grown up in a wide range of countries. A second is that the lowering of national barriers to trade in goods, to investment, to the flow of people, and information, has made it much more attractive for firms to establish a worldwide presence, and more difficult to protect their own particular competences from emulation.[1]

Thus firms in countries that were significantly behind the frontiers a quarter century ago have had a variety of sources they might tap to improve their competence to compete, some sources open and some involving interacting with foreign firms. The case studies in this book tell us a lot about both the sources used by firms that have been successful at this endeavor, and more generally about the managerial processes and modes of firm organization involved in successful catching up.

At the same time it is evident that countries have differed greatly in the extent to which they have provided an environment within which world class firms have grown up. To what extent are these differences associated with differences in country policies? This is a question of central interest to both country policy makers and economists and other social scientists studying economic development more generally. This book provides a wealth of information relevant to this inquiry.

Professor Richard R. Nelson
Columbia University

---

[1] This is despite the nominal strengthening of intellectual property protection under the auspices of TRIPS.

Acknowledgements

The genesis of this book lies in an international collaborative project, which was conducted under the auspices of a research program on industrial and technological "Catch Up" initiated by Prof. Richard R. Nelson at Columbia University. The preparation of this volume involved a series of meetings in Manchester, Mexico City, and New York in which the editors and contributors discussed and progressively refined the draft chapters. These important meetings were only possible thanks to the generous funding and support made available through Prof. Nelson and Prof. Jeffrey Sachs, Director of the Earth Institute of Columbia University. We would also like to acknowledge the valuable administrative assistance provided by Ms Feng Zhang at Rutgers University. We would also wish to thank Dr Mamata Parhi of Swansea University for her contributions during the initial stages of this project. Prof. Charles Dhanaraj of the Kelley School of Business at Indiana University provided valuable comments on some of the earlier drafts of the chapters. Finally, we would like to express our appreciation to Mr John D. Cantwell for his preparation of the index.

Contents

Part III: Comparative Conclusions

List of Figures

List of Tables

List of Boxes

Abbreviations

ABDI	Brazilian Industrial Development Agency
ACF	Alpha chlorine-free
AFC	Agrivet Farm Care
ANDA	abbreviated new drug application
ANPCYT	National Agency for Scientific and Technological Promotion
AOX	absorbable organic halogens
ASIC	application-specific integrated circuit
AUO	AU Optronics
AZT	Zidovudine
BNDE	National Economic Development Bank (Brazil)
BNDES	National Economic and Social Development Bank (Brazil)
BOP	balance of payments
CAD	computer-aided design
CadCam	computer-aided design and computer aided manufacturing
CAFMA	Camara Argentina Fabricantes de Maquinaria Agricola
CAM	computer-aided manufacturing
CBU	completely built-up units
CDL	Cheminor Drug Ltd
CEPAL/ECLAC	United Nations Economic Commission for Latin America and the Caribbean
Cipla	Chemical, Industrial and Pharmaceutical Laboratories Ltd
CIS	Community Innovation Survey
CITIC	China International Trust and Investment Corporation
CKD	completely knocked down
CMIC	China Metallurgical Industrial Corporation
CMT	cut, make, and trim
CNC	computerized numerically controlled
CNEGC	China National Erzhong Group
CNPC	China National Petroleum Corporation
CNPq	National Research Council (Brazil)
CSIR	Council for Scientific and Industrial Research
CSMA	Carrier Sense Multiple Access
CTA	Aeronautics Technological Center

DMF	Drug Master File
DOSM	Department of Statistics, Malaysia
DRL	Dr Reddy's Laboratories
DUI	doing, using, and interacting
EBIC	electron beam induced current
ECF	elementally chlorine free
Embrapa	Brazilian Agricultural Research Corporation
ERC	Engineering Research Center
Esalq	College of Agriculture of the University of São Paulo
ESTs	expressed sequence tags
ETRI	Korea Institute for Electronics Technology
FAB	Brazilian Air Force
FDA	Food and Drugs Administration
FDI	foreign direct investment
FERA	Foreign Exchange Related Act
FIE	foreign-invested enterprise
FONTAR	El Fondo Tecnologico Argentino
FTZ	Free Trade Zone
GCRs	Global Competitiveness Reports
GDP	gross domestic product
GDR	global depository receipt
GPN	global production network
GRIs	government research institute
GSK	GlaxoSmithKline
GSP	generalized systems of preferences
HAL	Hindustan Antibiotics Ltd
HR	human resources
IBDF	Brazilian Institute for Forestry Development
IBGE	Instituto Brasileiro de Geografia e Estatística (Brazilian Geographical and Statistical Institute)
IC	integrated circuits
IDPL	Indian Drugs and Pharmaceuticals Ltd
IIA	Investment Incentives Act (Malaysia)
IICT	Indian Institute of Chemical Technology
IJV	international joint venture
ILO	International Labour Organization
IMF	International Monetary Fund

IMP2	Second Industrial Master Plan
IMP3	Third Industrial Master Plan
INDEC	National Statistical Council
IPD	Instituto de Pesquisa e Desenvolvimento
IPEF	Forestry Science and Research Institute (Brazil)
IPO	initial public offering
IPR	intellectual property rights
ISI	import-substitution industrialization
ISO	International Standards Organization
ITA	Instituto Tecnológico de Aeronáutica (Aeronautical Technological Institute)
ITRI	Industrial Technology Research Institute
JIT	just-in-time
JVs	joint ventures
KIET	Korea Institute for Electronics Technology
KSE	Korean Stock Exchange
LCD	liquid crystal display
LCV	light commercial vehicle
LDCs	least developed countries
LSI	large-scale integration
LTPS	low-temperature polysilicon
M&A	merger and acquisition
MBIL	Mercedes-Benz India Ltd
MFA	Multi-Fiber Arrangement
MHRA	Medicine and Healthcare Products Regulatory Agency
MM	Ministry of Machinery (China)
MNC	multinational corporations
MNE	multinational enterprise
MOFTEC	Ministry of Foreign Trade and Economic Cooperation (China)
MPE	Multotec Process Equipment
MRP	materials requirement planning
MRPI	materials resources planning
MRPII	integrated materials resources planning
MSC	Multimedia Super Corridor
MST	minimum stock turnaround
MTMA	Malaysian Textile Manufacturers Association
MUL	Maruti Udyog Ltd

NESTA	National Endowment for Science, Technology, and the Arts
NBER	National Bureau of Economic Research
NDDS	new drug delivery systems
NGO	non-governmental organization
NR	natural resource
NRBP	natural resource-based products
NSI	national system of innovation
NT$	New Taiwan Dollar
NYSE	New York Stock Exchange
OBM	original brand manufacturer
ODM	original design manufacturer
OECD	Organisation for Economic Co-operation and Development
OEM	original equipment manufacturer
OFDI	outward foreign direct investments
PDA	personal digital assistant
PINTEC	Pesquisa de Inovação Tecnológica
PITCE	Industrial, Technological, and Foreign Trade Policy Initiative (Brazil)
PCB	printed circuit board
PDC	Penang Development Corporation
POSCO	Pohang Iron and Steel Company
POSEC	POSCO Engineering and Construction
PPC	production, planning, and control
PSDC	Penang Skills Development Center
PT	process technology
PV	photovoltaic
QCCs	quality control circles
R&D	research and development
RDE	R&D expenditure in sales
RDP	R&D personnel
SASAC	State-owned Assets Supervision and Administration Commission
SEZ	special economic zone
SIC	standard industrial classification
SGA	small group activities
SI	skills intensity
SIAM	Society for Indian Automobile Manufacturers
SMEs	small and medium-sized enterprises

SOE	state-owned enterprise
SPC	statistical process control
SPRU	Science Policy Research Unit
SQC	statistical quality control
STI	science, technology, and innovation
SUV	sports utility vehicle
TACO	Tata Autocomp Systems Ltd
TAG	technology absorption group
TCF	totally chlorine-free
TE	training expenditure in sales
Telco	Tata Engineering and Locomotive Company
TFP	total factor productivity
TFT	thin film transistor
TIC	technical information centre
TNC	transnational corporation
TPM	total preventive maintenance
TQC/M	total quality control/management
TQM	total quality management
TRIPS	Agreement on Trade-Related Aspects of Intellectual Property
TSMC	Taiwan Semiconductor Manufacturing Corporation
UMC	United Microelectronics Company
UNCTAD	United Nations Conference on Trade and Development
US-CBC	US-China Business Council
USFDA	United States Food and Drugs Administration
USPTO	United States Patent and Trademark Office
VCP	Votorantim Celulose e Papel
WEF	World Economic Forum
WOFE	wholly owned foreign enterprise
WTO	World Trade Organization
ZT	zero tillage

List of Contributors

Edmund Amann is Reader in Development Economics at the University of Manchester, Manchester, UK.

Martin Bell is Emeritus Professor at SPRU (Science and Technology Policy Research Unit) at the University of Sussex, Brighton, UK.

John Cantwell is Distinguished Professor (Professor II) of International Business at Rutgers University, Newark, New Jersey, USA.

Paulo N. Figueiredo is Professor of Innovation Management at the Brazilian School of Public and Business Administration (EBAPE) at the Getulio Vargas Foundation (FGV), Rio de Janeiro, Brazil.

Dinar Kale is Lecturer in International Development and Innovation at the Open University, Milton Keynes, UK.

Keun Lee is Professor of Economics at Seoul National University, Seoul, Korea.

Huiping Li is Associate Professor at Anisfield School of Business, Ramapo College of New Jersey, Mahwah, New Jersey, USA.

Anabel Marin is a Researcher at SPRU (Science and Technology Policy Research Unit) at the University of Sussex, Brighton, UK and at Conicet, Buenos Aires, Argentina.

John A. Mathews is Professor of Strategic Management at the Macquarie Graduate School of Management at Macquarie University in Sydney, Australia and Eni Professor of Competitive Dynamics and Global Strategy at LUISS, Guido Carli University, Rome, Italy.

Rajah Rasiah holds the Khazanah National Chair of Regulatory Studies and is Professor of Technology and Innovation Policy at the University of Malaya, Kuala Lumpur, Malaysia.

Part I

The Theoretical and Empirical Context

1

Innovative Firms in Emerging Market Countries: An Introduction

Edmund Amann and John Cantwell

1.1. INTRODUCTION

This book forms part of a wider program of research on technological and economic catch-up which has been coordinated by Professor Richard Nelson at Columbia University, New York. Two volumes in this series have already emerged. One, edited by Franco Malerba and Sunil Mani, focuses on sectoral innovation systems and catch-up.[1] The other, edited by Hiro Odagiri, Akira Goto, Akira Sunami, and Richard Nelson, examines intellectual property rights and catch-up.[2] These volumes concern the wider industrial systems within which firms operate and the overall policy and regulatory environment for technological change in emerging market countries. In contrast, this book is preoccupied with capability formation at the firm level. While much of the catch-up literature in the past has focused on aspects of the wider environment within which firms operate, we wish to bring firm-level capabilities to the forefront of the story. In our view, the formation of capabilities at the firm level is a critical feature of all successful technological and economic catch-up experiences, yet one which has been little studied.

We believe that the firm-level orientation of this book speaks to a wider audience interested in the role of business transformation and entrepreneurship in late industrializing countries. Numerous entrepreneurial and innovative businesses have lately been emerging and growing in late industrializing economies such as China, India, and Brazil. In tandem with this, a number of recent books have examined institutionally driven and market-driven innovation in the context of different emerging market countries. Khanna and Yishay (2007) discuss the growth of entrepreneurship in China and India in the

---

[1] Malerba and Mani (2009).   [2] Odagiri et al. (2010).

context of their institutional environments, while Prahalad and Lieberthal (1998) discuss how the particular characteristics of some emerging markets have given rise to many new entrepreneurial opportunities. Our volume examines another dimension of this unfolding set of processes: the building of technological capabilities in these firms in late industrializing countries. We argue that such capability building is unleashing the potential for accelerating enterprise development, so in turn giving rise to an increased role for late industrializing country firms on the global stage.

In the second half of the 20th century the global concentration of industrial innovation in the world's advanced industrial economies, having been extended to include Japan during the middle decades of the century, was further extended to encompass another generation of new entrants to the club of producers of the world's industrial technology. These newcomers consisted of a small number of economies, and among these greatest attention has been concentrated on three in East Asia (Korea, Taiwan, and Singapore), though others such as Israel were also involved. The East Asian part of this change has been extensively documented—for example by Amsden (1989, 1997), Ernst (2002), Hobday (1995, 2000), Kim (1997), Kim and Nelson (2000), Mathews (2006) Mathews and Cho (2000), Nelson and Pack (1999), Wong and Ng (2001), and many others.

This wealth of case-study material and broader synthesis tells a story of cumulative deepening of technological and related capabilities and activities at the firm level. A growing sub-set of firms across these countries had moved from technological imitation and adaptation, through innovative reverse engineering and incremental improvement to more "fundamental" modes of technological innovation that were close to, or even pushing forward, the international technological frontier. Recognition of the importance of these processes across several industries in Korea, Taiwan, and Singapore gave rise during the 1990s to views about the emergence of a new international technological division of labor. But the significance of this was sometimes questioned by those who emphasized the limited number and size of these economies, together with the historically specific conditions under which they had made this progression from imitation to innovation.

The contours of this change in the international distribution of innovative effort have been mapped more broadly in a recent study (Athreye and Cantwell, 2007). This demonstrates that with reference to the most advanced kinds of technological innovation (as measured by patenting in the US) there was actually further consolidation, not reduction, in the degree of concentration across countries from around 1970 through to the early 1990s. However, lower-level kinds of innovation of the sort that rely on simpler and more basic capability development were already dispersing during this period, as measured by the total international licensing receipts earned by the firms of countries for their intellectual property creation, and this was partly accounted for by new entrant countries. Then, in a transition since the early 1990s, the more sophisticated kinds of innovative effort have become more geographically dispersed across countries too—with the well-known East Asian new entrants being significant among the contributors to this shift.

But two other new entrants were also important contributors to this transition—India and China. Wider recognition of the emergence of significant innovative activity in these large economies at the dawn of the 21st century adds to a palpable scent of change in the air. Combined with the further deepening and spread of innovative activity among firms in the new entrant economies of the previous decade or two, this suggests that a redistribution of global innovative activity may be under way on an unprecedented scale. This appears to be reinforced by the deepening of firms' innovative capabilities in industrializing economies such as Brazil, Argentina, and perhaps Malaysia—suggesting a further cohort of potential entrants to the global industrial innovators' club. This transformation is likely to have far-reaching consequences, not only for patterns of industrialization and development in the developing world, but also, more generally, for the future global balance of economic, political, and military power. This intriguing set of circumstances, and the critical role within it of the technological upgrading and geographical restructuring of the activities of firms, provides the background for this volume.

This emerging transition is shaped by numerous trends and forces. Three are central to the issues addressed in the book. First, it has been argued that the catch-up in basic levels of innovative capacity has been strongly encouraged especially since the early 1980s by the rapid growth of arm's length markets for intellectual property trade, which has created an opportunity for the emergence of new players (Arora et al., 2001). Second, the rapid growth of foreign direct investment (FDI) has brought with it a global redistribution of not only the direct production activities of multinational corporations (MNCs) but also of their innovative activities, as branches of MNCs have evolved from being purely competence-exploiting to becoming locally competence-creating (in the terminology of Cantwell and Mudambi, 2005). Third, the combination of outsourcing and offshoring via global production networks and value chains has further reinforced the global dispersion of innovation in two ways: technology development capabilities have been deepened by supplier firms in the globally dispersed locations of production (most strikingly in East Asia—e.g. Hobday, 1995; Ernst, 2002), and firms in the advanced countries have increasingly outsourced and offshored elements of their innovative activities themselves (Teece, 2006; Chesbrough, 2003).

Given these different routes to developing innovative capabilities, several types of firm have been at the center of the emergence of innovation activities in new global locations. Some have been indigenous firms—usually exploiting the opportunities to acquire technology in different forms through arm's length transactions in international markets, and sometimes deepening their capabilities as suppliers within global value chains, perhaps progressing from OEM, via ODM to OBM positions within those chains (Hobday, 1995). Some have been branches of foreign-owned MNCs, whose shift toward dispersed competence-creation has increasingly been prompted by the availability of newly developed competences in host economies—particularly in Singapore, China, and India. Yet others have involved cooperative ventures between indigenous firms and multinationals.

One of the aims of the book is to get a better feel for the landscape that is emerging from the interaction between the forces fostering the dispersion of innovative competence and the types of firm that are the key actors in the new locations of innovative activity. We aim to understand better where—in what countries, and in what sectors—innovative firms of different types have in the past, and may in the future, evolve and emerge. However, that is a challenging task because there is little consensus around most of the issues involved. In particular, the influence of the three trends noted above is far from clear.

First, although the accessibility of technology through arm's length market transactions may be increasing, many would argue that the current international intellectual property rights (IPR) regime raises, rather than reduces, the barriers faced by at least some kinds of firms in developing countries in actually accessing substantial parts of the international stock of knowledge.

Second, the capability-enhancing role of participation in global value chains has been questioned. The significance of knowledge flows from advanced country firms to support technological upgrading in developing country suppliers seems to be contingent on several issues—e.g. the governance of the value chain (Schmitz, 2004). In particular, knowledge flows to facilitate upgrading of the functions of supplier firms toward, for instance, design, marketing, and R&D functions involved in deeper innovation activities often seem limited, so contributing little to firms' progression from OEM to ODM and OBM positions in global chains (Schmitz, 2004; Giuliani et al., 2005). Indeed, rather than global value chains acting as key conduits of knowledge and capabilities for developing country firms, it may be that local investment in creating and cumulatively deepening knowledge resources provides the necessary basis for participating in such chains and networks (Ernst and Kim, 2002).

Third, the extent to which MNC subsidiaries enhance innovative capabilities in developing countries is also far from clear. They evidently do so in some circumstances—e.g. in many subsidiaries in Singapore (Amsden and Tschang, 2003) or in some firms in the automobile industry in Brazil (Quadros and Queiroz, 2001). However, three kinds of qualification arise: (i) there seems to be considerable variation between subsidiaries and circumstances—as among subsidiaries in Argentina where significant innovative activity was undertaken in only a minority of cases in quite narrowly defined local and corporate situations (Marin, 2006), (ii) even in "favorable" circumstances there may be limits to the deepening of their innovative capabilities beyond which subsidiaries will rarely go—as suggested for Singapore by Amsden and Tschang (2003), and (iii) wider knowledge spillovers from subsidiaries to other firms have only rarely been identified (e.g. Gorg and Greenaway, 2004).

More generally, as with the relationship between knowledge accumulation and participation in global value chains, there may be an issue about sequence and causation in the case of FDI. The story of the contribution to local innovative capacity being made in some cases by MNCs has to be matched by the story of the pull on MNCs to become involved in or associated with enterprise activity in emerging market economies where innovative capabilities already exist—as shown in the study by Athreye and Cantwell (2007). This found that, on average across countries, inward FDI since 1950 had not preceded the emergence of lower levels of innovative activity in countries catching up. Indeed, the increased geographical dispersion of competence-creating innovative efforts across existing MNC subsidiaries (often located in other centers of excellence abroad) appears to have reinforced the position of the most established technology-producing countries. However, the extension of such networks to new locations that had already built up sufficient absorptive capacity in the form of basic levels of innovative capability has on average facilitated the catch-up of countries in more sophisticated kinds of innovation since the early 1990s. (Of course, these are merely the average tendencies—we know that there have been important variations in the role of FDI in technological capability development across countries, it being substantial in (say) Singapore or China, but of much less significance in (say) Korea or India (Hobday, 2000; Lall, 2001).)

Thus, the picture seems complex. Different types of firm have played different types of role (including none at all) in the emergence of progressively deeper levels of innovative activity across different situations in industrializing economies over recent decades. It may be that they have played different roles at different stages in that process, and also that the capability-building efforts of the different types of enterprise have interacted in different ways at different times. Then, cutting across that diversity, the key characteristics of some of the types of firm have changed over time—in particular the corporate strategies and structures of many MNCs at the start of the 21st century are totally different from those of the 1970s. In this volume, the central aim will be to develop a much greater depth of understanding of how and why that diversity of innovative activity in enterprises has emerged as part of the past and evolving global redistribution of innovative activity. We are also interested in advancing our understanding of the potential impact upon corporate innovative capabilities of the interactions between firms of different types. These inter-firm relationships include, although they are not limited to, those between foreign-owned MNCs and indigenous firms.

1.2. THE ROLES OF TRADE, MARKET LIBERALIZATION, AND FDI

In accounting for increased geographical dispersion of innovation, the distinctive roles of falling barriers to trade and investment on the one hand, and rising FDI on the other, cannot be overlooked. Regarding the former, the past 20–30 years have seen a number of important countries across Asia and Latin America consciously pursue a strategy of opening up their economies as they sought to dismantle the policy structures laid in place by import-substitution industrialization (ISI). ISI as a policy regime first emerged in the 1930s but was rapidly expanded and formalized in the 1950s and 1960s. Its key objective was to overcome the external constraint, boost growth, and ultimately to facilitate a change in an economy's position in the international division of labor. This was to be achieved by selective protection of key sectors, notably those associated with the manufacture of consumer goods (Baer, 2008). As these new sectors expanded, so it was hoped, growth would be lent impetus while the need to import would be diminished.

As time went by, the expansion of the industrial sector under ISI led to the development of indigenous technological capabilities in some of the larger economies which adopted the strategy. As will be seen in Chapters 4, 7, and 8, these included India, Argentina, and Brazil. Successful though ISI may have been in effecting rapid structural change and a short-term increase in trend growth rates, the strategy was associated with considerable shortcomings. In particular, economies that adopted it remained heavily dependent upon key imported inputs such as fossil fuels, capital goods, and, significantly, technology (whether embedded in goods or transferred through FDI or licensing agreements). Given an export sector rendered uncompetitive by the effects of protection and exchange rate overvaluation, the ISI strategy became, by the 1970s, increasingly compromised by external disequilibrium and a consequent need to accumulate foreign debt. By the emergence of the debt adjustment crisis in the early 1980s, it had become clear that the pursuit of ISI was simply no longer viable (Cimoli et al., 2009). This was due both to the adverse external funding environment and to the strategy's distinctly patchy track record on trade performance and growth. As a consequence, for a decade from the mid-1980s onwards, ISI was progressively abandoned in a range of Asian and Latin American economies, some of which, of course, feature in this volume. In the case of China (though not by any means an economy which had implemented Indian or Latin American-style ISI), the period from the late 1970s on has, too, witnessed a marked reduction in barriers to trade and investment. Stemming from this, China has been integrating itself into the global economy at an astonishing pace.

The embracing of trade and market liberalization—whether in place of ISI or the pre-1978 Chinese model—represents a profound transition in *policy regime*. This, as shall be seen, has had important consequences for the emergence and behavior of innovative firms in a number of countries featuring in this book. In particular, it will be argued that the transition to greater openness in trade and investment has exercised a significant influence on firms' capability accumulation paths. This influence has been exercised as openness to trade and investment has affected the sources of technology to which firms have turned, as the role and scope of inward and outward FDI has expanded, and as firms have found themselves increasingly exposed to the forces of international competition. However, as later chapters argue, the fact that inward-orientated industrialization strategies were swept away should not imply that they had no redeeming features or favorable enduring legacies. In fact, as the cases of Argentina, Brazil, China, and India make clear, considerable technological capabilities *were* accumulated under the previous policy regime. These capabilities, as it turns out, were to provide a vital springboard to further capability building in the liberalization period.

Despite the change in the policy environment, the path dependency associated with capability building has meant that the specific form of implementation of liberalization has varied to reflect those inherited capabilities. One key aspect of this is that the nature and the composition of established capabilities of indigenous firms affects their interaction with foreign-owned multinational companies and this therefore sets the parameters for the impact of FDI on local firms and thus the way in which opening up to FDI has occurred across different countries. Consequently, while in every case the general theme is a greater degree of integration between domestic and foreign firms, as a condition for effective catch-up, the organizational form of this association between domestic and international business has varied dramatically between countries. Some countries, such as Korea and India (at least until recently), have adopted relatively closed approaches toward FDI and are characterized by more arm's length and contractual relationships between domestic and foreign firms.

Conversely, countries such as Singapore and in recent times China have adopted increasingly open approaches to FDI which has become the locus of integration between domestic and foreign-owned firms. In the case of Latin America, attitudes and policy toward FDI have tended to sit between these two poles, allowing for distinctive modes of integration of multinational subsidiaries into local knowledge networks. Therefore, it is very difficult to generalize about the context for FDI in emerging market economies and the nature of its impact on capabilities building in indigenous companies. We can note a number of different industrial policy models or frameworks for FDI each of which may potentially be successful within a given setting of national institutions and industrial structures inherited from the past.

This helps to explain why in this book we have adopted a country-based approach in which we examine some of the most interesting national cases in separate chapters. One of the purposes, therefore, of each chapter is to illustrate the relationship between indigenous firms and foreign companies in the context of the development experience of the country in question. Moreover, what we do in this book is to focus in individual country chapters on those types of enterprises that have been the most innovative in a given national setting. In some cases, such as China and Malaysia, this means that we have a great deal to say about the role of innovative foreign-owned firms in those countries. In other cases, such as Korea or Brazil, we have less to say about innovative foreign enterprises since they have played a less substantial role in firm-level capability building in those economies. There has been a debate which is often set in very general terms about the role of FDI and foreign multinationals in national economic development. While those such as Amsden have argued that domestic firm capability building has to proceed in a relatively protected environment in order to create an independent national technological base, others writing about knowledge spillovers in China have stressed how relationships with foreign multinationals may enhance independent economic development. In our book, we have aimed for a more balanced view in which we recognize first a range of interdependencies between domestic firms and foreign multinationals. Second, as just described, we wish to emphasize that the nature of this relationship between domestic and foreign business varies greatly across different countries. We will return to this issue in Chapter 9 in drawing upon the evidence in the country chapters to produce some cross-country comparisons about the role of FDI and foreign firms.

1.3. THE FOCUS: ENTERPRISE LEARNING AND INNOVATIVE CAPABILITY BUILDING

To accomplish its task the book will draw on the substantial and growing body of empirical literature which has begun to emerge concerning emerging market enterprise innovation in the new global context. Part of the motivation for the book is that much of the established literature on catch-up has focused on the roles of government policy and societal institutions (see Fagerberg and Godinho, 2005). These writings generally acknowledge the role of dynamic local firm capabilities in technological and economic catch-up, but tend to focus on the environmental context in which such capabilities are fostered, rather than on the firm itself as the locus of such development (Teece, 2000). Here instead we focus on the micro-foundations of enterprise capability formation, and place firms at the center of our study. A critical set of issues raised by the centrality of firms to capability development is what types of firms have been most involved in catch-up processes, the conditions under which different types of firms become more innovative, and the role of the interaction in innovation (knowledge spillovers) between different types of firms. Our authors share a common starting point in recognizing the following six observations or stylized facts about the development of technological capabilities in firms (adapted from Lall, 2000).

First, firm learning is primarily a conscious, purposive, and costly process, rather than an automatic and passive one. It relies on the deliberate building of capabilities that have strong tacit elements, rather than learning by doing through the continued practice of established processes which entail little risk or directed effort. Second, learning tends to be path-dependent and cumulative, and so firms tend to move incrementally along specific or localized trajectories, and build upon their established capabilities and organizational routines (Nelson and Winter, 1982; Dosi, 1988; Bell and Pavitt, 1993). Firms usually cannot make swift transitions or optimal selections of technology, but they engage in experimental technological search processes. In the earlier stages of capability development, firms may have to learn how to learn, to establish effective search processes, and to better recognize how they may be able to build up the most relevant capabilities needed to master more advanced technologies. Third, the learning process is highly technology-specific and sector-specific, and different technologies require different learning costs, risks, and duration of effort. This is especially relevant when considering the scope for paths that upgrade technological effort, since, for example, learning garment assembly may be "easier" than textile manufacture, which in turn is "easier" than making textile machinery, and so on (Lall, 2000).

Fourth, capability development involves efforts at all levels of the firm. In the earliest stages of the more simple or basic capability building, it relies relatively more on organizational innovation such as the introduction and improvement of technical functions like quality management and maintenance. As the technologies mastered become more complex and sophisticated, then distinct processes of search and experimentation come increasingly to the fore, and formal R&D becomes necessary, especially in larger firms.

Fifth, the progression from basic to sophisticated capabilities can also be described as a transition from the attainment of operational capabilities (know-how) to a deeper understanding of the principles of the technology used (know-why). This transition is far from automatic, and many firms do not progress beyond the achievement of efficient process engineering, quality control, and maintenance routines. Yet the emergence of know-why allows firms to develop the more autonomously driven innovative capabilities (based on knowledge interdependencies rather than pure dependencies) that are needed to move up the technology scale, to diversify their technological base, to better deploy existing know-how, and to cope with unanticipated technological shocks or opportunities. Technological upgrading in this sense need not be about operating at some notional world frontier; even good "follower" strategies require good know-why capabilities.

Sixth, technological learning in a firm does not take place in isolation, but is rife with knowledge-centered externalities and linkages with other actors (Nelson, 1995; Stiglitz, 1996). These include linkages with other firms (locally and internationally), local universities and public research institutes, consultants, industry associations, regulatory bodies, and training institutions. Many such linkages are informal in character, and some depend upon the geographical proximity associated with the clustering of industries or certain types of activity.

1.4. THE FRAMEWORK FOR ANALYSIS

Throughout this book, the examination of the phenomenon of innovative firms in late industrializing countries makes use of a simple conceptual framework. This has two main dimensions:

(i) A set of *"levels" of innovative activity and capability* through which firms may (or may not) evolve over time—moving at differing rates and over different "distances," perhaps in differing sequences.

(ii) A set of *firm categories* (e.g. MNC subsidiaries or large indigenous firms) between which firms may (or may not) move over time in differing ways.

Within the combination of those two dimensions, each country chapter will address two *core* questions about the firms covered:

(1) How have firms evolved through different "levels" of innovative capability and activity toward a more innovative type of enterprise, and what factors have facilitated and constrained these learning trajectories?

(2) How, if at all, have these paths of learning within firms influenced, or been influenced by, the development of innovative capabilities in other firms (especially those in other firm categories), and have changes in innovative capability been associated with the movement of firms between firm categories?

This book also addresses a question surrounding the *consequences* of the learning trajectories followed by enterprises in their selected firm types and sectors:

(3) What kinds of economic, environmental, or other outcome have followed from the paths of learning and innovative capability building in the selected enterprises?

Each country chapter addresses these questions with reference to selected firm categories and sectors that reflect the availability of relevant material and the importance of the different categories in the country or region covered. Therefore, each country chapter also addresses a question concerning the *broader context* of their core analysis of selected firm types and sectors:

(4) Across a wider range of industries than those covered in the core analysis (questions 1 and 2), what levels of innovative activity and capability do we find in the country or region in question, and what do we know about the distribution of these different types of innovative enterprise across firm categories and sectors?

It is recognized that addressing questions (3) and (4) may have had to rest on types of data or analysis that are more limited than those drawn on in addressing questions (1) and (2). Nevertheless, these are important issues about which the book aims to contribute original understanding.

In order to elaborate on these four questions it is necessary to define what we mean by (a) "innovation," (b) "levels of innovative activity/capability," and (c) "firm category."

First, innovation is regarded as the introduction of products or processes that are new to the context of the location, and not necessarily new to the world as a whole. Thus, innovation is not defined here relative to (best practice at) some notional world technology frontier. Innovation consists essentially of a continuous process of problem-solving in and around production (Rosenberg, 1982), and so, as argued above, it relies upon learning of a localized kind in firms (Nelson and Winter, 1982). This approach follows on from several streams of work—in particular: (i) the perspective adopted in the literatures on national and regional systems of innovation (by those such as Freeman, 1987, Nelson, 1993, Cooke, 2001, or Asheim and Gertler, 2005), and (ii) the long stream of work on enterprise learning in developing countries which, following the pioneering studies of Jorge Katz and colleagues in the 1970s (Katz, 1987), includes such contributions as Bell et al. (1982), Dahlman et al. (1987), Kim (1997), Ernst et al. (1998), Dutrenit (2000), Figueiredo (2001), and Rasiah (2005). It is also embedded in the work on innovation survey methods in successive vintages of the Oslo Manual that have drawn distinctions between innovations that are new to the world, new to the market, and new to the firm (OECD, 2005).

Second, with innovation defined in this broad way, it is evident that one can observe in any economy an array of different types of innovative activity, or different types of innovative firm, drawing on different "levels" of innovative capability. Some activities or firms rely mainly on basic capabilities and simpler forms of knowledge, while others require more sophisticated capabilities and more complex kinds of knowledge, the generation of which draws upon a wider dispersion of prior knowledge sources (and so relies on a wider range of knowledge interdependencies between the focal firm and other actors, both locally and internationally). In the context of "catching up" in industrializing economies, we can think of firms' capabilities as potentially progressing through levels associated with these different kinds of innovative activity. Some firms may move quite limited distances through these levels, perhaps remaining essentially as relatively imitative adopters of other firms' innovations—albeit with the technological complexity of the adopted technologies perhaps rising over time. Others may move much longer distances to higher levels of innovative activity that build upon know-why, and ultimately come to rely on search through R&D that depends on a more intensive exchange of knowledge with others.

So we propose that innovative activities can be divided into a hierarchical ordering of the type proposed by Lall (1992), Bell and Pavitt (1995), and recently operationalized by Figueiredo (2001). Such hierarchical conceptual structures can take many forms (Bell, 2007, Annex 2). In particular, apart from various structures of differentiated "levels," there are differences in the key enterprise behaviors or functions that are taken into account in defining those levels. For example, (i) in distinguishing between categories on the OEM to OBM spectrum, Hobday (1995) highlighted two dimensions (technological and marketing-related); (ii) Figueiredo (2001, Table 3.1, pp. 28–30) provides a full description of five different functions associated with a seven-level hierarchical structure; and (iii) in their assessment of the innovativeness of Korean firms, Hobday et al. (2002) used nine enterprise activities to distinguish between four levels of innovative firm in a hierarchy running from Type A firms ("unaware" of the need for technological improvement and "passive" in implementing change) to Type D firms (highly "aware" of the competitive importance of technology and "creative/proactive" in helping to define the international technological frontier). Leaving aside the diversity of functions involved, such a hierarchical schema is represented in illustrative, summary form below.

We aim to address question (1) by using a scheme along these lines in order to examine how firms progress (or fail to progress) from lower-end kinds of innovative activity and capability that are more characteristic of early stages of development toward "higher end" innovative activities and capabilities that reflect transition to more fundamental kinds of innovative effort. By "a more innovative type of enterprise" in question (1), we mean a firm that has successfully moved higher up the ladder toward more complex and sophisticated kinds of innovative capability.

Third, as an initial guide, we distinguish between seven main categories of enterprise, as in Figure 1.2 below. Within their selected sectors and firm types some chapters have focused on MNC subsidiaries or foreign-indigenous firm interaction, while others have concentrated more on the evolution of business groups or state-owned enterprises (SOEs). Putting together the two key organizing dimensions of our study—the levels of innovative activity/capability (Figure 1.1) and the categories of firms (Figure 1.2)—an analytical matrix emerges which can be used to address the four central questions. These are now elaborated a little further. Whatever the case, each country chapter aims to explain why the chosen categories of firms have evolved successfully in the specific context of the domestic institutional and business environment.

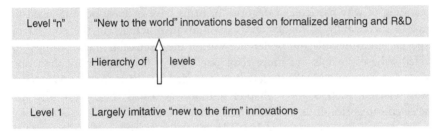

Fig. 1.1. Illustrative schema of levels of innovative activity and capability

1.	MNC subsidiaries (competence-exploiting and competence-creating)
2.	Joint ventures
3.	Subcontractors, licensees, OEM, ODM, local MNE suppliers, etc.
4.	OBM, and other large, independent indigenous firms
5.	Business groups
6.	(Former) State-Owned Enterprises (SOEs)
7.	SMEs, including venture capital supported start-ups

Fig. 1.2. Illustrative schema of categories of enterprise

Question 1: What learning trajectories and why?

The matrix enables us to better understand the evolutionary paths of enterprises through different levels of innovative activity and perhaps also between firm types. This allows us to tractably address a series of complex issues about differences across firms in technological capability development. The chapters also, of course, do not ignore the sectoral dimensions of the story, for example, enabling a view to be taken of which sectors were most dynamic or of which firm types within a given sector were most likely to be most (or least) ambitious in their innovative scope. However, to stress again, for the purposes of coherence and comparability, the key analytical optic in our study is *firm type*.

As explained above, authors of country chapters were invited to select their own focus on firm types and sectors. Because we aim to advance our understanding of why particular categories of firms have or have not managed to evolve successfully to higher levels of innovative activity in the context of specific environments, our preference was for the discussion in each context to refer—where possible—to more than one type of firm and more than one sector, so as to provide the variety that is needed for a rich analysis. Whatever was selected, each country chapter author was asked to explain why the selected categories of firms had been chosen.

Of course, the chapters seek to do much more than simply present a descriptive portrait of firm (or even sector) types and their associated innovative patterns. That is only the first part of question 1. The key issues that the chapter authors seek to address center around *why* particular patterns have established themselves (the second part of the question). Chapters also reflect on the likely evolution of observed innovative patterns over the medium to long term. In seeking to explain why some types of firms have become more innovative than others, the chapters have needed to make reference to a range of potentially relevant "environmental" factors. These include, but are not limited to, the policy setting and the internal technological logic of the products or processes concerned for a given sectoral specialization.

Subject to the same health warning as for firm categories, with regard to an acknowledgement of important differences between countries, the environmental factors that may influence firm evolution include the following:

- the degree of firm internationalization and external orientation (in terms of trade and/or investment)—which in turn depends on country size, but which we know already to be crucial (see e.g. Pack, 2000; Lall, 2001);
- the general level of educational attainment (which again is uncontroversial, and a robust finding in many studies);
- the macro and trade policy environment;
- the role (if applicable) of institutional reform and policy change affecting the degree of openness to external knowledge and ideas;

- the role of knowledge spillovers and access to specific skills and training through universities and public research institutes;
- the role of geographically localized clustering of firms;
- the role of the IPR regime;
- the role of capital markets, including venture capital, and corporate governance structures;
- the role of appropriate learning mechanisms affecting particular functional areas in firms, in terms of the capacity to move between specific levels of innovative capability (what is needed to accomplish one phase of transition may not be the same as in another);
- the capacity to develop such learning mechanisms in the course of development.

Given the motives of the book, when discussing policy impacts, reference is made to policies that have affected certain firm types more than others (whether intentionally or otherwise). For example, it is interesting to determine whether implicit or explicit policy designs tended to favor small and medium-sized enterprises (SMEs) above MNC subsidiaries or domestic business groups, or indeed whether (the other way round) institutions and policies have been adapted in recognition of the dominance of some particular brand of innovative enterprise, which may have cumulatively reinforced the successful evolution of that firm type. It is also interesting to determine whether there existed any systematic differences between firm types regarding the likelihood of their engagement with local providers of technological services such as research institutes or university departments. Equally, an attempt has been made to determine, within particular firm types, what relationship (if any) exists between the policy/external research environments and firms' ability to progress along the hierarchy of innovative effort.

While, of course, the policy environment features in the discussion in the manner suggested, we have avoided chapters becoming descriptive surveys of individual policy regimes or national systems of innovation (NSIs). To repeat, ours is an enterprise-focused discussion and not a comparative review of NSIs. As outlined earlier, there are already many studies of catch-up that focus on wider macro factors, and the intention of this book is not to duplicate these studies, but to take account of these considerations in the background, while the business firm is in the foreground.

Question 2: What learning-related interactions between firms?

Although the issue about inter-firm knowledge flows (e.g. spillovers) is included as a possible "input to" (or influence on) learning in enterprises, the chapters also address more extensively questions concerning such inter-firm knowledge flows as "outputs from" enterprise learning. In particular, questions addressed include to what extent and in what ways learning in one category of firms has been a basis for learning in others (e.g. learning in large indigenous firms or state-owned enterprises as a basis for learning in their suppliers; or learning in MNC subsidiaries as a basis for spillovers to locally owned firms in the same sector). More generally, learning and the evolution toward higher-level innovative capabilities may have various kinds of influence on other firms.

Question 3: What outcomes from the paths of innovative capability building?

A common criticism of some of the literature about innovation in industrializing countries has been that it sets up innovating as an objective in its own right—and one that is extremely costly in contrast to simply borrowing and imitating. We therefore hope that the book helps to throw light on issues about the returns to building up innovative capabilities. Some explorations in this direction have focused *within* the firm, examining aspects of firm performance. Others have concentrated more on *external* effects, tracing beyond knowledge spillovers themselves to identify consequences of those knowledge flows. Cutting across these internal and external explorations it is important to try and identify not just consequences in terms of efficiency (as in the analysis of productivity growth in most spillover studies), but also consequences concerned with change in the composition of output. Such change might arise, for example, within learning firms via product diversification or outside the learning firms via knowledge spillovers leading to new firm start-ups. Micro-level analyses of these issues can be linked, for example, to the kind of macro debate addressed in Nelson and Pack (1999) or to the recent discussions about learning ("self-discovery") and change in the composition of output in emerging market countries in Hausmann and Rodrik (2003 and 2006).

Question 4: What broader distribution of innovative enterprise across firm categories and sectors?

In places the chapters go beyond the particular scope of their selected focus and sketch out a broader mapping of where in the particular country or region (in terms of sectors and firm types) one finds more and less innovative firms. Thus, for a selected range of developing countries, we have been able to develop an overview of which firms have followed what paths of innovative development. However, where this has been possible, the chapters go beyond a mere description to try and explain why that specific pattern (rather than others) emerged in each context. To enable meaningful analysis and comparisons to be made, countries were chosen which not only possessed a sizeable population of innovative firms but also shared common features, especially in regard to industrial structure and institutional contexts. As has already been made clear, a further point of comparison emerges from a varied experience of liberalization in all the countries considered. The selection of comparable countries allows conclusions to be drawn surrounding how capabilities are built in varying policy, sectoral, and institutional environments.

1.5. THE BOOK STRUCTURE

Bearing in mind the considerations outlined in the previous section, it was decided to focus on the experiences of firm-level capability building in some of the most important emerging market countries of Asia and Latin America. In the case of Asia, the book begins (in Part IIA) with a review of the Chinese and Indian experiences, which are at the forefront of contemporary discussion and the subject of some controversy. As in the case of Brazil and Argentina (reviewed in Part IIB), both countries have undergone profound, though distinctive, episodes of liberalization which have set the scene for substantial local firm-level capability building. Additionally, the experiences of the longer-standing export-orientated industrializers, Malaysia and South Korea, are analyzed (see Part IIA). Having reviewed developments in Asia, Part IIB reflects on firm capability formation in Brazil and Argentina, both examples of late industrializing economies conventionally viewed as "lagging behind" their Asian counterparts. Both cases, in their admittedly distinctive ways, nevertheless turn out to possess several features in common with comparable emerging market economies. Not least, as already highlighted, such common features emerge in relation to shifts in the policy regime.

In Part III of the book, Chapter 9 draws comparisons between individual national experiences and shows how such comparisons provide the foundation for the further development of our evolutionary framework for the analysis of firm level innovative capability building across an increasing variety of environments. It will already be clear that this book is attempting to address a broad array of issues relating to the complex phenomenon of firm capability building. In order to provide an appropriate context for this, Chapter 2 sets out the theoretical and empirical background on which the subsequent country case studies rely.

Having established the objectives of the book, what of its structure? The book is divided into three components, Parts I, II, and III. Part I of the book sets out to supply the broad theoretical and empirical context, while Part II consists of a series of country studies. In Part III, comparative conclusions are developed in the light of the discussion featured in the previous two parts.

REFERENCES

Amsden, A. H. (1989), *Asia's Next Giant: South Korea and Late Industrialization*, New York and Oxford: Oxford University Press.

—— (1997), "South Korea: Enterprising Groups and Entrepreneurial Government," in A. Chandler, F. Amatori, and T. Hikino, *Big Business and the Wealth of Nations*, Cambridge: Cambridge University Press.

—— and Tschang, F. T. (2003), "A New Approach to Assessing the Technological Complexity of Different Categories of R&D (with examples from Singapore)," *Research Policy*, 32: 553–72.

Arora, A., Fosfuri, A., and Gambardella, A. (2001), *Markets for Technology: The Economics of Innovation and Corporate Strategy*, Cambridge, Mass.: MIT Press.

Asheim, B., and Gertler, M. S. (2005), "The Geography of Innovation: Regional Innovation Systems," in J. Fagerberg, D. C. Mowery, and R. R. Nelson (eds.), *The Oxford Handbook of Innovation*, Oxford and New York: Oxford University Press.

Athreye, S., and Cantwell, J. A. (2007), "Creating Competition? Globalisation and the Emergence of New Technology Producers," *Research Policy*, 36(2): 209–26.

Baer, W. (2008), *The Brazilian Economy*, Boulder, Colo.: Lynne Rienner.

Bell, M. (2007), "Technological Learning and the Development of Production and Innovative Capacities in the Industry and Infrastructure Sectors of the Least Developed Countries: What Roles for ODA?," paper prepared for UNCTAD Division for Africa, Least Developed Countries and Special Programmes, SPRU, University of Sussex, Brighton, UK.

—— and Pavitt, K. L. R. (1993), "Technological Accumulation and Industrial Growth: Contrasts between Developed and Developing Countries," *Industrial and Corporate Change*, 2(2): 157–210.

———— (1995), "The Development of Technological Capabilities," in I. ul Haque (ed.), *Trade, Technology and International Competitiveness*, Washington, DC: World Bank.

—— Scott-Kemmis, D., and Satyarakwit, W. (1982), "Limited Learning in Infant Industry: A Case Study," in F. Stewart and J. James (eds.) (1982), *The Economics of New Technology in Developing Countries*, London: Frances Pinter and Boulder, Colo.: Westview Press.

Cantwell, J. A., and Mudambi, R. (2005), "MNE Competence-Creating Subsidiary Mandates," *Strategic Management Journal*, 26(12): 1109–28.

Chesbrough, H. (2003), *Open Innovation: The New Imperative for Creating and Profiting From Technology*, Boston, Mass.: Harvard Business School Press.

Cimoli, M., Dosi, G., and Stiglitz, J. (eds.) (2009), *Industrial Policy and Development*, Oxford: Oxford University Press.

Cooke, P. (2001), "Regional Innovation Systems, Clusters, and the Knowledge Economy," *Industrial and Corporate Change*, 10(4): 945–74.

Dahlman, C., Ross-Larsen, B., and Westphal, L. E. (1987), "Managing Technological Development: Lessons from the Newly Industrializing Countries," *World Development*, 15(6): 759–75.

Dosi, G. (1988), "Sources, Procedures, and Microeconomic Effects of Innovation," *Journal of Economic Literature*, 36(4): 1120–71.

Dutrenit, G. (2000), *Learning and Knowledge Management in the Firm: From Knowledge Accumulation to Strategic Capabilities*, Cheltenham, UK: Edward Elgar.

Ernst, D. (2002), "Global Production Networks and the Changing Geography of Innovation Systems: Implications for Developing Countries," *Journal of the Economics of Innovation and New Technology*, 12: 1–27.

—— Ganiatsos, T., and Mytelka, L. (1998), *Technological Capabilities and Export Success in Asia*, London and New York: Routledge.

—— and Kim, L. (2002), "Global Production Networks, Knowledge Diffusion and Local Capability Formation," *Research Policy*, 31(8–9): 1417–29.

Fagerberg, J., and Godinho, M. M. (2005), "Innovation and Catching-Up," in J. Fagerberg, D. C. Mowery, and R. R. Nelson (eds.), *The Oxford Handbook of Innovation*, Oxford and New York: Oxford University Press.

Figueiredo, P. N. (2001), *Technological Learning and Competitive Performance*, Cheltenham, UK: Edward Elgar.

Freeman, C. (1987), *Technology Policy and Economic Performance: Lessons from Japan*, London: Frances Pinter.

Giuliani, E., Pietrobelli, C., and Rabellotti, R. (2005), "Upgrading in Global Value Chains: Lessons from Latin American Clusters," *World Development*, 33(4): 549–73.

Gorg, H., and Greenaway, D. (2004), "Much Ado About Nothing? Do Domestic Firms Really Benefit from Foreign Direct Investment?" *World Bank Research Observer*, 19: 171–97.

Hausmann, R., and Rodrik, D. (2003), "Economic Development as Self-Discovery," *Journal of Development Economics*, 72: 603–33.

———— (2006), "Doomed to Choose: Industrial Policy as Predicament," John F. Kennedy School of Government, Harvard University, Cambridge, Mass.

Hobday, M. (1995), *Innovation in East Asia: The Challenge to Japan*, Aldershot, UK: Edward Elgar.

—— (2000), "East versus Southeast Asian Innovation Systems: Comparing OEM- and TNC-led Growth in Electronics," in L. Kim and R. R. Nelson (eds.), *Technology, Learning and Innovation: Experiences of Newly Industrializing Economies*, Cambridge and New York: Cambridge University Press.

—— Rush, H., and Bessant, J. (2002), "Firm-Level Innovation in the Korean Economy," Report to the World Bank, SPRU, University of Sussex, UK.

Katz, J. (ed.) (1987), *Technology Generation in Latin American Manufacturing Industries*, Basingstoke: Macmillan Press.

Khanna, T., and Yishay, Y. (2007), "Business Groups in Emerging Markets: Paragons or Parasites?" *Journal of Economic Literature*, 45(2): 331–72.

Kim, L. (1997), *Imitation to Innovation: The Dynamics of Korea's Technological Learning*, Boston, Mass.: Harvard Business School Press.

—— and Nelson, R. R. (eds.) (2000), *Technology, Learning and Innovation: Experiences of Newly Industrializing Economies*, Cambridge and New York: Cambridge University Press.

Lall, S. (1992), "Technological Capabilities and Industrialisation," *World Development*, 20(2): 165–86.

—— (2000), "Technological Change and Industrialization in the Asian Newly Industrializing Economies: Achievements and Challenges," in L. Kim and R. R. Nelson (eds.), *Technology, Learning and Innovation: Experiences of Newly Industrializing Economies*, Cambridge and New York: Cambridge University Press.

—— (2001), *Competitiveness, Technology and Skills*, Cheltenham, UK: Edward Elgar.

Malerba, F., and Mani, S. (2009), *Sectoral Systems of Innovation and Production in Developing Countries: Actors, Structure and Evolution*, Cheltenham, UK: Edward Elgar.

Marin, A. (2006), "Technologically Active Subsidiaries and FDI-Related Spillover Effects in Industrialising Countries: Evidence from Argentina in the 1990s," PhD thesis, SPRU, University of Sussex, UK.

Mathews, J. A. (2006), "Catch-up Strategies and the Latecomer Effect in Industrial Development," *New Political Economy*, 11(3): 314–35.

—— and Cho, D. S. (2000), *Tiger Technologies: The Creation of a Semiconductor Industry in East Asia*, Cambridge: Cambridge University Press.

Nelson, R. R. (ed.) (1993), *National Innovation Systems*, Oxford and New York: Oxford University Press.

—— (1995), "Co-evolution of Industry Structure, Technology and Supporting Institutions, and the Making of Comparative Advantage," *International Journal of the Economics of Business*, 2(2): 171–84.

—— and Pack, H. (1999), "The Asian Miracle and Modern Growth Theory," *Economic Journal*, 109: 416–36.

—— and Winter, S. G. (1982), *An Evolutionary Theory of Economic Change*, Cambridge, Mass.: Harvard University Press.

Odagiri, H., Goto, A., Sunami, A., and Nelson, R. R. (2010), *Intellectual Property Rights, Development and Catch Up: An International Comparative Study*, New York: Oxford University Press.

OECD (2005), *Oslo Manual: Guidelines for Collecting and Interpreting Innovation Data*, Paris: Organisation for Economic Co-operation and Development.

Pack, H. (2000), "Research and Development in the Industrial Development Process," in L. Kim and R. R. Nelson (eds.), *Technology, Learning and Innovation: Experiences of Newly Industrializing Economies*, Cambridge and New York: Cambridge University Press.

Prahalad, C. K., and Lieberthal, K. (1998), "The End of Corporate Imperialism," *Harvard Business Review*, 76(4): 68–78.

Quadros, R., and Queiroz, S. (2001), "The Implications of Globalisation for the Distribution of Design Competences in the Auto Industry in Mercosur," *Actes du Gerpisa*, 32: 35–45.

Rasiah, R. (2005), "Learning and Innovation: The Role of Market, Government and Trust in the Information Hardware Industry in Taiwan," *International Journal of Technology and Globalisation*, 1(3–4): 402–32.

Rosenberg, N. (1982), *Inside the Black Box: Technology and Economics*, Cambridge and New York: Cambridge University Press.

Schmitz, H. (2004), *Local Enterprises in the Global Economy: Issues of Governance and Upgrading*, Cheltenham, UK: Edward Elgar.

Stiglitz, J. E. (1996), "Some Lessons from the East Asian Miracle," *World Bank Research Observer*, 11(2): 151–77.

Teece, D. J. (2000), "Firm Capabilities and Economic Development: Implications for the Newly Industrializing Economies," in L. Kim and R. R. Nelson (eds.), *Technology, Learning and Innovation: Experiences of Newly Industrializing Economies*, Cambridge and New York: Cambridge University Press.

—— (2006), "Reflections on the Hymer Thesis and the Multinational Enterprise," *International Business Review*, 15(2): 124–39.

Wong, P. K., and Ng, C. Y. (eds.) (2001), *Industrial Policy, Innovation and Economic Growth: The Experience of Japan and the East Asian NIEs*, Singapore: Singapore University Press.

2

Building Innovative Capabilities in Latecomer Emerging Market Firms: Some Key Issues

Martin Bell and Paulo N. Figueiredo

2.1. INTRODUCTION

The aim of this chapter is to provide an analytical framework that acts as a bridge between the introductory overview of the book in the previous chapter and the empirical subject matter in subsequent chapters. This bridging role takes two forms. On the one hand it helps to illuminate and pave the way for the analyses of aspects of enterprise learning that *are* examined in the six country chapters that follow. On the other hand, some issues noted here *are not* examined in those chapters, or not examined sufficiently fully, and this chapter therefore paves the way for the discussion in the final chapter about remaining challenges for work in this field.

We start this introductory section by clarifying some of the basic ideas that frame what follows in the rest of the chapter: the notion of the latecomer firm, the linked ideas of catching up and accumulating innovation capability, the distinction between rates and directions of change generated by those capabilities, and the "stages" of development to which all this relates. We then outline the remaining sections of the chapter.

2.1.1. Some Framing Perspectives

Latecomer firms

As emphasized in the previous chapter, this book is centrally concerned with innovation and catching up at the level of individual firms, and the process of building innovation capabilities is placed at the center of those interests.

Among other things, therefore, it is about the field of study concerned with what have been called "latecomer firms." Such firms have been defined as those which meet four conditions (Mathews and Cho, 1999; Mathews, 2002): not only (i) the *dis*advantages about dislocation from technology sources and advanced markets stressed by Hobday (1995), but also (ii) the existence of initial competitive *advantages* such as low costs, as well as (iii) the historically determined, rather than strategically chosen, position of late entrant, and (iv) the strategic intent of catching up. The approach taken here requires at least two kinds of qualification to that perspective.

First, being dislocated from technology sources may once have been a characteristic of industrial firms in developing/emerging economies. However, over recent years such firms have become embedded in increasingly pervasive international networks that at least provide *potential* access to numerous sources of technology. Consequently, their key technological disadvantage is much less about their intrinsic dislocation from technology sources and more about their initially limited internal capabilities for exploiting available sources in order to implement innovation in their own production activities. Consequently, we use the latecomer firm idea only in a very general sense of an *"initially imitative"* firm, regardless of how dislocated it may be from markets and technology sources—and also regardless of any particular rate at which it may in practice "catch up" by moving toward more innovative patterns of behavior.

Second, the latecomer firm concept has typically been applied only to firms that are domestically owned. However, we do not identify the category here in terms of any particular form of ownership, and hence for instance we specifically include the subsidiaries of multinational corporations. This is consistent with perspectives on the MNC subsidiary that have been developed in the international business literature over the last decade or so. These approaches have identified subsidiaries not simply as strategically passive components of hierarchical corporate structures, but as potentially active enterprises in their own right that may significantly shape their own paths of development at the interface between local economies and global corporate networks (Birkinshaw, 1997; Birkinshaw and Hood, 1998; Cantwell and Janne, 1999; Birkinshaw et al., 2005). Like locally owned firms, they do not start out being intrinsically dislocated from technology sources, but typically have limited internal capabilities for exploiting available sources of technology to implement innovation in their own activities. But, again like locally owned firms, they may move from such "initially imitative" positions to others where they pursue significantly more innovative patterns of behavior, and there is also considerable heterogeneity among them in terms of the extent to which they do so and the rate at which that occurs (Cantwell and Mudambi, 2005; Marin and Bell, 2006; Boehe, 2007).

Our central interest is about that trajectory of change: about how firms of all kinds move along it and why. That matches the two components of the first of the *core questions* set up in the previous chapter—about firms' learning trajectories and the factors that affect them.

Catching up and local capability building

Our interest in firms' *technology-related* catch-up trajectories is closely linked to broader ideas about *economic* catch-up—or its absence (Abramovitz, 1986; Baumol, 1986; Verspagen, 1991). But a further distinction is important. The idea of technological catch-up has been commonly discussed in terms of the narrowing (or widening) of gaps between the "*technological capabilities*" of firms and economies. But the notion of a gap in technological capabilities has often been used in a way that combines two different kinds of gap. These correspond to the distinction made by some scholars between firms' *production* capabilities and their *innovation* capabilities (e.g. Bell and Pavitt, 1993, 1995).

On the one hand, the capabilities of firms may catch up with global industry leaders with respect to the technologies they *use* in production. Their products may come to incorporate technical and design specifications and performance features that are progressively closer to those of the most advanced in the global market, perhaps eventually matching products that are on, or close to, the international product technology frontier. Similarly, the production processes they use may come to embody increasingly advanced technological features, reflected in rising productivity and other aspects of competitive performance, and again these may come to match those that are on or close to the international technology frontier. Such narrowing of technological gaps between current practice and the international frontier constitutes one form of "catch-up"—catching up in production capabilities. This is often represented by trends in the ratio between productivity in follower firms, industries, or economies and the productivity of international leaders such as the US.

On the other hand, firms may catch up in terms of capabilities to generate and manage *change* in their technologies, moving from positions of technology imitation on the basis of very limited innovative capability to deeper levels of capability that enable them to undertake modest forms of innovation, perhaps proceeding further to engage directly and creatively in innovation activities at the international frontier. In other words, this second kind of technology-related catch-up is the process that Linsu Kim analyzed in his book about Korea's path of capability development *Imitation to Innovation* (Kim, 1997).

These two kinds of capability are commonly thought of as closely linked, with their accumulation proceeding hand-in-hand as latecomer firms both (i) narrow the gap between the technological characteristics of their *production activities* and those of technologically "advanced" firms at the international technological frontier, and (ii) increase the level of their *innovative capability*. However, they may not always be closely linked. The production capabilities of technology-using firms may move considerable distances along catching-up trajectories, with very limited input from their own innovative activities. In the extreme, a firm may acquire a fully operational, new production system embodying "advanced" technology by contracting an array of external consultant designers, process engineers, and project managers to define and bring into operational use on its behalf a new set of product, process, and organizational technologies. This may be repeated through several generations of advancing technology, enabling the technology-using firm to narrow the gap between its *production* capabilities and those of other firms that are closer to the technological frontier. But through such sequences there may have been little or no change in the low level of *innovative* capability in the technology-using firm. For instance, this pattern was followed during the rapid expansion of the pulp and paper industry in Indonesia over a decade from the mid-1980s (van Dijk and Bell, 2007).

In different cases of technology catch-up, the degree to which indigenous local capability building is engendered may differ. Our central interest is in catching up to generate and manage innovation as such. We explore questions about how firms accumulate these capabilities, perhaps moving to levels of capability that enable them to engage creatively in innovation activities at the international frontier. We also stretch that kind of catching-up idea to encompass "overtaking." Former technology "followers" may deepen their innovative capabilities to the point where they are used to develop products and processes that are more "advanced" than those of the former leaders at the previous international frontier.

The direction of innovation and the international frontier

In discussions of technological catch-up, the idea of the international frontier has usually been very narrowly conceived. It has been associated with the idea of following the same technological path (or direction of technological advance) as that previously followed by the global technology leaders. From that perspective, therefore, success in catching up means arriving at the same end-position as the industry leaders in terms of *the kinds of* technology used and produced. However, that is largely about catching up in terms of production capability.

Here, however, by focusing specifically on innovation capability, we stretch the idea of the frontier much wider. We envisage the possibility that the progressive deepening of firms' innovative capabilities may enable them to follow *different directions* of technological development from those already pursued by the global industry leaders. Such deepening capabilities need not be used to arrive only at predetermined technological end-points on established trajectories. Instead, they may enable firms to develop different kinds of product, process, and organizational configuration from those already developed by industry leaders. These would then widen the diversity of frontier production technologies. For example, as demonstrated by Zheng and Williamson (2007), numerous Chinese firms have been pursuing paths of what the authors describe as "cost innovation" to capture important positions in global markets. Also described as "frugal innovation" (*The Economist*, 2010), this has not been just about using established techniques to produce existing types of product at low costs based on low factor prices in China. As in India, it has been about using innovation capabilities to create unique competitive positions in low-income markets on the basis of "new" products that are *less* technologically complex than equivalent products produced by firms in advanced economies—for example, the Nano automobile designed and developed by Tata. In other words, firms in these countries have used their deepening innovative capabilities to create novel positions in the frontier array of competitive technologies. With reference to Korean firms developing Carrier Sense Multiple Access (CSMA) cellular phone technology, Lee and Lim (2001) described this kind of route to the international frontier as "*path-creating*" catching up, in contrast to "*path-following*." We elaborate on this issue about path creation and the direction of latecomer innovation when we discuss the nature of innovation in Section 2.2.

Innovation capabilities and "stages" of economic growth

One influential view about the global spread of innovative capabilities suggests that the importance of innovation activities varies with stages of economic growth. Indeed, in its simplest form, the argument is that innovation only becomes relevant at all in developing countries once they have reached relatively late stages—roughly equivalent to the top-most tiers of the middle-income economies. Before that, innovation is largely irrelevant since technological advance can be achieved by acquiring already available technology from the more advanced economies.

This view was elaborated in a particularly influential form in the annual Global Competitiveness Reports (GCRs) of the World Economic Forum (WEF) during the early 2000s. The view built on the tripartite classification of the world's economies in Porter's widely read *Competitive Advantage of Nations* (Porter, 1990). This distinguished three stages through which economies progressed (pp. 545–56): the *factor-driven stage*, the *investment-driven stage*, and the *innovation-driven stage*—when "firms not only appropriate and improve technology and methods from other nations but *create* them."

In this framework, the identification of the third stage as the one where innovation (technology "creation") occurred was a little fuzzy. Porter also noted that at the investment-driven stage: "foreign technology and methods are *not just applied but improved upon*" (emphasis in original) as firms begin developing their own refinements including their own product models. Increasingly, skilled workers are therefore needed not only to operate sophisticated facilities but also to provide the "internal capability to assimilate and improve technology" (pp. 548–9).

However, that blurring of the boundary between innovation and routine production was almost entirely lost, when the framework was transferred into the WEF's Global Competitive Reports—e.g. the GCR 2001–2 (McArthur and Sachs, 2002; Porter et al., 2002). Instead, a sharp, innovation-related divide was drawn between the first two and the third of Porter's categories. This rests on the distinction between: (a) creating a "truly new technology," and (b) "adopting (and adapting)" a technology that has been developed abroad. The first process was defined as "technological innovation" and the second as "technological diffusion" (p. 29). Economies that engaged in the former were identified as the world's "core economies" and those engaged in the latter as "non-core economies"—a distinction that was used to highlight what the report described as: ". . . the critical division in today's world economy between the *innovating* and *non-innovating* economies" (p. 30).[1] Crossing that division was described as a "transition from technological adoption to innovation" (p. 38), and very few developing/emerging economies—only Taiwan, Iceland, Ireland, Hong Kong, Singapore, and Korea—had made that transition between 1990 and 2000.

The later chapters in this book concentrate on such economies—two that had made the McArthur-Sachs type of transition by 2000 (Taiwan and Korea) and five others that might be considered to have made it since then or to be close to doing so (Argentina, Brazil, China, Malaysia, and India). It might be thought that this country focus endorses that McArthur-Sachs-type perspective on the irrelevance of innovation at earlier stages of development. That is not the case—for two reasons.

First, the recent experience of innovation capability accumulation that is examined in our later chapters is only the recent phase of a much longer process. In very important ways, the processes by which those countries developed their current levels of innovation capability have their roots in activities that occurred several decades ago. As we emphasize later, even in firms in Korea and Taiwan that have been particularly successful in following a "fast track" of innovation capability accumulation, the transition process from imitation to significant innovation consisted of a cumulative sequence of

---

[1] This framework, with its separation of the world's economies into innovators and non-innovators, has become widely held in communities concerned with overall development policy. For example, it pervaded the analysis and conclusions of the influential report of the Commission on Growth and Development (2008).

linked activities that ran through 20–30 years, and this had its origins at a time when the firms existed in low-income or lower-middle-income economies.

Second, as we will also stress later, the early phases of such long processes of capability accumulation are not simply innovation-inactive. They are not "dormant" stages leading to a later flowering of firms' innovative activities when their economies reach the requisite income levels. Instead, the progressively deepening capabilities play *creative* technological roles at all stages. These roles involve much more than merely selecting and adopting existing technologies within a process by which they are diffused among a growing number of user firms in supposedly non-innovating economies. Indeed, the simplistic distinction between innovation and diffusion that lies behind the McArthur-Sachs-type separation of the world's economies (and firms) into innovative sheep and imitative goats reflects a misunderstanding of the micro-level resources and activities that are involved—a point that was illuminated many years ago in the insights of the economic historian Nathan Rosenberg (1972, 1975), and re-emphasized more recently by Nelson and Pack (1999).

In other words, the issues about accumulating innovation capabilities that we outline in this chapter relate to latecomer firms at *all* stages in their own development and in the development of their economies.

2.1.2. The Structure of the Chapter

The rest of the chapter covers two basic sets of questions—one about the paths that firms may follow as they progressively deepen their innovative capabilities, the other about factors that may help to explain differences in how they do so.

We deal with the first set of questions about corporate technological paths in three sections. We start in Section 2.2 with comments about the kinds of innovative activity we are discussing. We emphasize the importance of innovation in the "organizational" aspects of production; we examine different types of innovation, emphasizing the significance of "incremental" forms; and we explore the incidence of some of these different types. In Section 2.3 we turn to the paths of capability accumulation followed by latecomer firms, covering questions about the levels and types of capability they may develop, together with the pathways and sequences they may follow through these levels and types. Then we examine in Section 2.4 the mechanisms and processes firms use to acquire and create their successive levels of innovative capability. We describe these as "learning" processes—somewhat distinct from other uses of the term that refer more to the activity of actually undertaking (particular kinds of) innovation.

We deal with the second set of questions—about explanation of differences in firm capability building—in Section 2.5. This briefly reviews the factors that may influence the depths of innovation capability accumulated and the rate at which this occurs.

2.2. INNOVATION IN LATECOMER FIRMS

We have distinguished above between capabilities for undertaking unchanging production activities on the one hand and, on the other, capabilities for designing and implementing change in those activities—i.e. innovation capabilities. Three further questions immediately arise about the latter. What aspects of production are encompassed by the idea of innovation adopted here—in particular, is innovation concerned solely with the physical components of productions systems? Among the innumerable types of innovation, which types are included here and how do we differentiate among them? What is the relative importance of those different types? We address these questions below. We also elaborate on what we mean by the "direction" of innovation.

2.2.1. Innovation: Change in Organizational as well as Physical Aspects of Production

There was a time, roughly between the 1960s and 1980s, when the study of innovation focused very largely on "hardware." Attention centered on product and process innovations, and both were seen in terms of artifacts—the techno-physical components of production systems. But the importance of change in the organizational aspects of production, or "organizational innovation,"[2] has been given much more attention in recent years. In particular, a useful distinction has been made by Nelson and Sampat (2001), who emphasize that a firm's production activities (or routines) do not consist solely of physical technologies, but also incorporate "social technologies"—essentially, forms of division of labor and modes of coordination. Correspondingly, innovation (change in production systems) embraces change in these social technologies

---

[2] Some care is needed to distinguish between at least two notions that are described as "organizational innovation." On the one hand, the term is used to refer to organizational change as an *output from* innovative activity. For example, the use of this term in the latest round of EU Community Innovation Surveys refers, as here, to innovative activity that results in change to the organizational dimensions of production activities. On the other hand, the same term is also used to refer to organization as an *influence on* (or input in) innovative activity. For example, Lam (2005) discusses "organizational innovation" with reference to the influence of broad aspects of organization on the innovativeness and adaptability of firms.

as well as the more commonly discussed changes in physical technologies of products and processes.

However, change in the social or organizational dimension of production activities has not been prominent in studies of innovation in latecomer firms. In Latin America, for example, there was a little research in this area during the period of import-substituting industrialization, but significant attention was not given to organizational innovation until the phase of liberalization, when it came to be seen as part of the necessary restructuring process (Humphrey, 1993, 1995; Kaplinsky, 1994; Bessant and Kaplinsky, 1995). For the most part, these studies concentrated on issues about management and production efficiency, but some focused on wider social dimensions, including gender-related issues (Posthuma, 1990; Meyer-Stamer et al., 1991; Mitter, 1993).[3]

At least two important themes emerged from this work. First, organizational innovation is frequently tangled up with innovation in the physical characteristics of products and processes such as computer-aided design (CAD) and computer-aided manufacturing (CAM), and studies emphasized the importance of the organizational dimensions of innovation if substantial gains were to be achieved from introduction of electronics-related hardware (Hoffman, 1989; Mody et al., 1992). Second, particular types of organizational change cannot simply be replicated as ready-made, standard models, but require dynamic adaptation to local circumstances (Humphrey, 1995).

However there were also several limitations. In particular, research concentrated on the more easily observable types of change that were identified by clear labels—JIT, TQC/M, MRP, SPC, and so forth, and less attention was given to more informal and "unlabeled" types of organizational change that may be just as important—less hierarchical management structures, integration of production with quality control and maintenance functions, multi-tasking and so forth. It also concentrated on aspects of organization that were internal to the firm, what Edquist et al. (2001) describe as "*organizational* process innovations." Much less attention was given to "external" organizational innovation, including such things as changes in the organization of links with suppliers or logistics and distribution arrangements to deliver products to customers.

But that imbalance was reversed about a decade ago. The emphasis on "internal," process-type organizational innovation ceased to be prominent in research about innovation in industrializing countries, and much greater attention was given to changes in the "external" aspects of firms' organizational arrangements as an integral aspect of wider types of innovation. We argue in Section 2.3 below that it is important for issues about internal

---

[3] There are several studies on innovation in production organization and industrial relations conducted under the auspices of the International Labour Organization (ILO) during the 1980s and early 1990s. These have evolved into the current ILO's concern with the "Regulating for Decent Work and Globalization" project.

organization to be much more central to the analysis of innovation in catching-up firms. But this is not about returning to the earlier interests in organizational aspects of *production capabilities*; it is about organizational aspects of the innovation process, and hence about the importance of organizational elements of *innovation capability* that have to be developed and accumulated as an integral aspect of deepening overall innovation capabilities.

2.2.2. Innovation: Differing Types of Change

Beyond the difference between innovations involving physical and organizational (social) technology, numerous other kinds of distinction have been drawn between different types of innovation. Most of these have focused on differences in the following characteristics: the "inputs" used, the technological "novelty" of the outputs, or the "impact" of the innovation once the outputs have been introduced and diffused. These kinds of distinction may overlap, e.g. science-based innovation may also be relatively novel—though the reverse does not necessarily hold.

Among the input-based distinctions, most have focused on differences in the kinds of knowledge input used in innovation—for example, between innovations that draw on recent scientific research (science-based innovation) and those that draw primarily on established engineering knowledge plus experience of technology use. For example, Jensen et al. (2007) have distinguished between two different modes of innovation: the science, technology, and innovation (STI) mode and the doing, using, and interacting (DUI) mode; showing that, in Denmark, firms that combined both modes were more likely to innovate new products than firms that relied primarily on one or the other. Differences based on the impact of innovations have, for example, distinguished between innovations with relatively minor effects on the individual innovating firm and its competitiveness and those that have much more pervasive effects across whole industries, perhaps even leading to the creation of new industries.

We focus here on distinctions in terms of the technological/market "novelty" of the innovation—the extent to which it differs from existing technologies, ranging from innovations that are close to being pure imitations to those that are fundamentally different from anything currently existing. This kind of differentiation has been widely used, especially in analyses of innovation in latecomer firms.

Some of the important ways of identifying differences in novelty were made in the 1960s and remain particularly useful today. For example, with reference to the history of process innovation in petroleum refining, Enos (1962) distinguished between what he called the alpha phase of innovation (the initial invention and commercial innovation of technologically novel processes based on new technological principles) and the beta phase (successive improvements to novel processes that had been created in a preceding alpha phase). Hollander (1965) examined aspects of Enos's beta-phase innovation, using the example of technical change in rayon production by DuPont over a period of about 30 years during which the company built a succession of new plants.[4] He demonstrated that process innovation did not necessarily depend on substantial investment in new plant that embodied technological advances. Instead, a succession of small improvements could also be "engineered into" existing plants during their lifetimes. He also showed that a considerable proportion of such innovation could be based on the firm's existing stock of knowledge by engineering departments and technical groups closely associated with production, not on the development of new knowledge via formally organized research and development.

A major contribution of these two studies was their estimates of the relative economic importance of the various kinds of change—a valuable aspect of analysis that has been surprisingly rarely undertaken in recent years. Both cases demonstrated the considerable economic significance of minor/incremental forms of innovation. Enos demonstrated that the cumulated economic gains from successive improvements to existing processes (the beta phase of technological progress) were as significant in their economic effects as the step-jump gains following initial commercial innovation of novel processes (the alpha phase). Hollander demonstrated similar patterns in the case of "minor" technical changes in rayon production by DuPont.

In numerous subsequent studies, a broad amalgam of such typologies of innovation types came to be summarized in the simple distinction between innovations that were "incremental" and "radical." But use of this distinction typically lost sight of operational definitions and meaningful differentiation, and "incremental" and "radical" became vague categories with very limited value for cumulative and comparative analysis. Yet, the distinction has been widely used in discussions about innovation in latecomer firms and late industrializing economies. As we note later, such evidence-lite discussions have had an unfortunate influence on policy by typically identifying incremental with trivial and radical with important.

Two approaches have sought to add a least a little more rigor into the empirical analysis underlying such discussions. First, the OECD's Oslo Manual, providing guidelines for undertaking innovation surveys, has aligned several of these kinds of distinction in a scale of innovation novelty running from "new to the firm," via "new to the market,"[5] to "new to the world" (OECD, 2005). We use this approach later in this section in discussing the

---

[4] DuPont initially entered the rayon industry by licensing technology from the original alpha-phase innovators in Europe.

[5] A market is defined somewhat ambiguously as being either a firm and its competitors in general or those existing in a particular geographical region.

incidence of different types of innovation. Second, several studies of firms' technological capabilities in developing countries have identified levels of capability in terms of the kinds of innovation firms undertake (e.g. Lall, 1987, 1992; Figueiredo, 2003; Ariffin and Figueiredo, 2004). These have used detailed methods of classification to distinguish levels of innovation (or innovation capability) that run in slightly differing ways from "simple" to "advanced." We use this approach here, distinguishing between four levels of novelty—"basic," "incremental/intermediate," "advanced" and "world leading." We use this later in Section 2.3 to discuss the associated level of progressively deeper innovation capability.

It is important to stress that this spectrum is about the novelty of innovations, not about their technological sophistication or complexity. Thus, "world-leading" simply means that the innovation incorporates features that are globally novel within the area of technology concerned. It does not necessarily imply that the innovation is also "science-based" or "high-tech" in its knowledge inputs or potentially disruptive in its consequences for existing industries. Thus, firms may engage in world-leading innovation in areas such as semiconductors, flight simulators, stem-cell therapeutics, or intelligent materials, but as illustrated in Box 2.1, they may also be world-leading innovators in toothbrushes.

Box 2.1 World-Leading Innovation: The Case of Toothbrushes

Following the introduction by DuPont during the late 1930s of the manual toothbrush based on nylon bristles, which replaced the pig hair toothbrush that had been invented in China, the firm Oral-B developed, during the 1950s, the multi-tufted, flat-trimmed, end-rounded nylon filament brush which became a kind of dominant design for further new generations of toothbrushes. However, limitations in terms of users' brushing techniques and brushing time led to radical changes in bristle patterns to improve performance. As a result, contemporary toothbrushes have varied from high-performance manual to novel oscillating/rotating/reciprocating electric toothbrushes. These have involved intense product development efforts involving detailed studies of the tooth-brushing process, using advanced scientific and ergonomic research methods. For instance, to develop novel models under the toothbrush project "Whole Mouth Clean," the Colgate-Palmolive Technology Research Center has conducted basic and applied research involving PhDs in organic, inorganic, and physical chemistry, biochemistry, and chemical engineering. This new product development process sought to identify specific insights leading to the development of several features not previously seen in commercial toothbrushes. To achieve this, new product development teams were formed with specialized professionals from multiple functional areas, including marketing, product development, and advanced technology, as well as clinical, engineering, manufacturing, and intellectual property areas, with these drawn from several geographical locations.

Source: Hohlbein et al. (2004); *The Boston Globe* (2005), *CNN.Money and Fortune 500* (2005).

2.2.3. The Relative Importance of Different Types of Innovation: A Brief Overview

It would be useful for analytical and policy purposes to be able to say something about the relative "importance" of different types of innovation. In principle, that might be seen as requiring information about a combination of two things: (i) the typical social or economic "significance" of particular types of innovation (for example, along the lines of the earlier studies by Enos and Hollander), and (ii) the typical frequency with which these types occur— i.e. their incidence. But in practice it is impossible to provide such a picture, even in the most sketchy form. Despite the frequent use of distinctions between types of innovation for many years, information about their relative "significance" is rare. There has not even been much information until recently about the incidence of the different kinds of innovation.

This is important because it has left a gap to be filled by speculation. Unfortunately, such speculation has been influenced by the imbalanced orientation of academic research. Much of the literature about innovation in advanced economies has focused on the "higher-level" types of innovation ("radical," "new to the world," and so forth), and it has also concentrated attention on the particular kinds of industries where these types of innovation are seen to be concentrated—typically "high-tech" industries like pharmaceuticals or semiconductors. Much less attention has been given to the lower end of the spectrum ("incremental," "minor," and similar types of innovation). These, and the industries in which they are thought to be concentrated, came to be seen as much less important.[6] The attention of policy-makers was aligned with such views.[7]

Similar perspectives have been influential in developing countries, and these were typically associated with views about a clear-cut structural divide between innovation in developed and developing countries—the former being responsible for the world's "radical" innovation and the latter undertaking at best only incremental and other "inferior" kinds of innovation at the other end of the spectrum.[8] Not surprisingly, large parts of the policy agenda for

---

[6] However, as we note later, there has recently been some work that begins to redress this imbalance—e.g. Von Tunzelmann and Acha (2005) and a special issue of the journal *Research Policy* (Volume 38, Issue 3, 2009).

[7] Studies of "innovation gaps" and "hidden innovation" by the National Endowment for Science, Technology, and the Arts (UK) have sought to redress the imbalance in policy orientation (NESTA, 2006, 2007)

[8] As one among numerous examples, Viotti (2002) highlighted such a distinction. Defining innovation strictly in Schumpeterian (new-to-the-world) terms, he noted (p. 656) that this was "at the core of the processes of technical change" in advanced industrial countries, but had only "a secondary role, possibly, no role at all, in the process of technical change" in late industrializing or developing economies since that process depended on the absorption and incremental adaptation and improvement of technologies developed earlier in the advanced economies. We

technology and innovation came to be focused on changing this structural divide—primarily by seeking to establish a greater presence in the "more important" kinds of innovation. This has been seen as requiring a considerable concentration of public resources on building the particular kinds of organizational, institutional, and human capabilities thought necessary. Much less attention is typically given to strengthening capabilities for innovation at the other end of the spectrum, and for cumulatively deepening capabilities on that base. This difference in emphasis matters because it involves different kinds of organizational, institutional, and human resources. For the most part, the first approach has been seen as requiring substantial resource allocation to building innovation capabilities in centralized public organizations like research institutes and universities. In contrast, the second calls primarily for building innovation capabilities on a much more dispersed basis in firms. This is not a contrast between policy alternatives. It is about an imbalance in complements. In particular, among the various forms of complementarity, the dispersed, firm-centered locus for accumulating deep capabilities for "radical" types of innovation is a necessary complement to the accumulation of such capabilities in centralized and largely public organizations.

Fortunately, it has recently become possible to look at least a little more closely, though still very inadequately, at aspects of the importance of different kinds of innovation and the associated balance of complementary policy emphases. While we can still say little about the "significance" of different types of innovation, the growing body of data from innovation surveys allows us to do a little better than merely speculating about their relative incidence.

Among such surveys, the Canadian is particularly useful in this respect because the survey questions focus intensively on specific innovations in firms—their "most important" during the survey period. Table 2.1 shows the resulting picture for Canadian manufacturing firms in the period 1997–9. First, it shows that, although an "innovation" was defined fairly comprehensively to cover most of the spectrum of different types discussed above, as many as one-fifth of the firms had *not* introduced any kind of product or process innovation within that spectrum during the three-year survey period. Second, among the 80 percent of firms that *had* done so, about half reported that their "most important" innovation was only new to the firm itself—neither new to Canada nor new to the world. Only 12 percent had produced "world-first" innovations. Thus, around 60 percent of *all* Canadian manufacturing firms had either not innovated at all, except perhaps in very minor ways, or had produced as their most important innovations only those

suggest below, however, that this preoccupation with "radical" innovation (perhaps roughly synonymous with "new-to-the-world" innovation) loses sight of a very large and important part of the innovation activity of firms in the advanced economies, as well as undervaluing its role in developing economies.

Table 2.1. Incidence and types of innovation among Canadian firms

Manufacturing firms, 1997–1999					
	Whether firms were product or process "innovators" during 1997–1999*				
Percentage of:	NO	YES			
All firms	20%	80%			
		Among innovator firms (i.e. "Yes" above), the novelty of their "most important" innovation			
		New to firm	New to Canada	New to world	Don't know
Innovating firms	–	51%	20%	12%	18%
All firms	20%	41%	16%	10%	14%

* An innovating firm was one that had implemented a new or significantly improved product or process. Aesthetic/minor modifications of products, and minor/routine changes to processes were excluded.
Source: Statistics Canada (2002).

Table 2.2. Incidence of innovative activity—selected EU countries (2002–2004)

Selected countries	GDP per capita (average over the 2002–4 period)	Enterprises with innovation activities	Enterprises with new to the market product innovations
	USD	As a proportion of all enterprises	
Germany	26,134	65%	18%
Sweden	27,782	50%	26%
Finland	27,586	43%	21%
Italy	26,240	36%	11%
Portugal	18,849	43%	21%
Poland	11,608	25%	11%
Romania	7,193	20%	5%

Source: Eurostat, CIS 4.

that were new to the firm. In other words, nearly two-thirds of Canadian firms had engaged only in the kinds of incremental innovative activity that have commonly been considered the preserve of firms in developing countries, while only one-tenth of them claimed that even their most important innovation was a "world first."

There are, however, considerable differences between countries in such aggregated national pictures of the incidence among firms of different kinds of innovative activity. This is illustrated in Table 2.2 for a cross-section of selected EU countries at different levels of GDP per capita. This uses indicators of the incidence of only two types of innovation for the survey period (2002–4): (i) the proportion of enterprises "with innovation activity,"[9] and

[9] Defined as firms that had introduced new or significantly improved products or processes—i.e. similar to the Canadian product or process "innovator" category.

(ii) the proportion of all enterprises that introduced new or improved products that were new to the market.[10] The incidence of both categories rises more or less in line with GDP per capita—from 20 percent and 5 percent respectively in Romania to around 50 and 26 percent in Sweden and 65 and 18 percent in Germany.

The notion of "catching up" in innovative activity might therefore be seen as movement upwards through differing incidence levels for various types of innovation along the lines of Table 2.2—in this case, from Romania-type patterns of incidence toward Swedish-German-type patterns But that is too simple because, behind such inter-country (inter-income level) differences in the incidence of different types of innovation there are considerable intra-country differences between industries.

This is illustrated in Table 2.3, which focuses again on Canada. Differences are especially pronounced with respect to new-to-the-world innovations. In some industries, mainly mature industries like sawmilling and the manufacture of clothing or furniture, only around 3–7 percent of firms introduced such innovations. But at the other end of the spectrum in industries like industrial machinery, instruments, or computer equipment, the proportion of firms that were first-to-world innovators was five or six times greater. The incidence of new-to-Canada-type innovations also differed widely. Consequently, only around 10–20 percent of firms in the more mature industries introduced either of these two kinds of innovation, whereas 40–50 percent of the firms did so in the industries at the other end of the spectrum.

Broadly similar patterns of inter-industry difference in the incidence of different types of innovation are evident in other countries. However, it is important to be wary of drawing unduly sharp distinctions between supposedly "low-tech" industries like those toward the top of Table 2.3 and so-called "high-tech" industries toward the bottom. It is becoming clear that behind such aggregate generalizations there is considerable diversity within both types of industry. In particular, hidden behind their average "low-medium tech" characteristics, such sectors include firms with considerable innovative capabilities that undertake new-to-market and new-to-the-world types of innovation (Von Tunzelmann and Acha, 2005).[11] Developing innovative

---

[10] This is based on definitions and categories that are different from those in the Canadian survey and cannot be compared with the Canadian data in Table 2.2 above.

[11] This point is also stressed by several papers in the recent special issue of *Research Policy* on low- and medium-technology industries (Volume 38, Issue 3, 2009). In particular, in a study of German manufacturing industry, Kirner et al. (2009) note: ".... we observe significant and substantial intra-sectoral heterogeneity regarding the R&D intensity of firms. There is a significant discrepancy between the sectoral classification and the firm-level reality as regards R&D intensity ... Only around half of the firms (between 43 percent and 55 percent) actually match their respective sectoral classifications, while others are either more or less R&D-intensive" (p. 449).

Table 2.3. Incidence of innovation: Canadian firms by selected manufacturing industries

Selected manufacturing industries*	Proportion of all firms in each industry (1997–1999)			
	That were	Whose "most important" innovation was new to		
	"Innovators"**	Canada	The world	Either
	%	%	%	%
Sawmills and wood preservation	73.6	4.6	3.0	7.6
Clothing manufacturing	69.7	7.0	4.2	11.2
Furniture and related products manufacturing	81.9	13.2	6.6	19.7
Primary metal manufacturing	75.7	16.3	5.7	22.0
Food manufacturing	80.5	17.7	4.5	22.2
Paper manufacturing	77.9	19.5	5.1	24.6
Veneer, plywood, and engineered wood products	64.8	15.1	12.5	27.6
Motor vehicles, bodies/trailers, and parts	78.6	19.4	10.8	30.3
Machinery manufacturing	86.9	18.5	14.2	32.7
Chemical manufacturing (excl. pharmaceuticals)	87.7	19.6	13.3	32.9
Textile mills	85.8	23.8	11.6	35.3
Agriculture, mining, and industrial manufacturing	88.0	16.8	26.0	42.8
Communications equipment manufacturing	91.5	17.1	27.1	44.2
Instruments, magnetic, and optical media	91.3	14.7	30.8	45.5
Computer and peripheral equipment	95.6	22.2	27.4	49.6
Total manufacturing industries	**80.2**	**16.3**	**9.6**	**25.9**

* Selected to *illustrate* the types of industry involved in different segments of the wide inter-industry diversity in the incidence of innovation.
** An innovating firm was one that had implemented a new or significantly improved product or process. Aesthetic/minor modifications of products, and minor/routine changes to processes were excluded.
Source: Statistics Canada (2002).

capabilities in such low-tech industries may be extremely important as part of the catch-up process.

Nevertheless, the idea of "catching up" in innovative activity at the country level should not be seen only as a matter of generally raising the incidence of innovation *within* firms and industries in the existing structure of the economy. It is also about *changing the structure* of the economy toward an increasing proportion of economic activity in sectors that are typically associated with relatively high levels of innovative activity.

The combination of these two components is illustrated in Table 2.4 with reference to a cross-section of EU countries and industries, using only one

Table 2.4. Incidence of innovation: selected EU countries by income level and selected industries

	Poland		Portugal		Italy		Sweden		Germany	
GDP per Capita $ppp[1]	11,608		18,849		26,240		27,782		26,134	
Selected Industries	EIA[2]	VAM %[3]	EIA	VAM %	EIA	VAM %	EIA	VAM %	EIA	VAM %
(A) With typically falling VA share in manufacturing										
Wearing apparel, etc.	13%	3.9	25%	5.8	12%	3.3	55%	0.2	34%	0.5
Textiles	27%	2.5	31%	5.8	32%	4.0	67%	0.6	72%	1.0
Food products and beverages	24%	17.9	39%	13.2	32%	31.3*	50%	7.0*	64%	7.2
(B) With variable VA share in manufacturing										
Wood, wood products, and cork	17%	4.6	46%	4.5	33%	2.4	44%	4.3	61%	1.4
Pulp, paper, and paper products	27%	2.4	43%	4.3	38%	2.0	67%	6.8	70%	2.1
Basic metals	40%	4.0	55%	2.5	40%	4.9	58%	6.2	62%	4.7
(C) With typically rising VA share in manufacturing										
Machinery and equipment n.e.c.	37%	7.3	52%	6.1	52%	14.3	59%	13	81%	15.4
Electrical (inc. electronic) and optical equipment	38%	8.2	56%	7.2	53%	9.5	64%	14.9	85%	14.9
Machinery and electrical/optical equipment		15.5		13.3		23.8		27.9		30.3

1 Average of GDP per capita in PPP (constant 2000 international USD) over the reference period
2 Number of enterprises "with innovation activities" over 2002–4 as a proportion of all enterprises in each industry
3 Each industry's share of value added in all manufacturing: 2000 (Poland, 2006)
* Also includes tobacco products

Source: Eurostat, CIS 4.

kind of indicator—the proportion of all firms that were innovators (shown in the columns headed EIA—Enterprises with Innovation Activities). This indicates that, *between* economies, the incidence of innovation increases fairly regularly in all the selected industries as income levels rise (i.e. along the rows across the spectrum of selected countries).[12] But it also increases *within* each country between mature and more modern high-tech industries (i.e down the columns). These different kinds of industry are shown in three illustrative groups: (A) those whose share in total manufacturing value added (the VAM column) typically falls with rising GDP per capita, (B) those whose shares may remain constant or vary with rising income levels—frequently natural resource-based industries, and (C) those with shares that typically rise.

So, to catch up with the aggregate innovation intensity of the leading European innovators in manufacturing, as shown earlier in Table 2.2, Poland, for instance, would need to move through two kinds of process: (i) raising the proportion of innovative firms in all industries toward the levels in countries like Sweden and Germany, and (ii) changing the structure of the manufacturing sector toward the composition that exists in those countries— i.e. reducing the share of Group A-type industries and raising the share of Group C types.

We are mainly concerned in this chapter with the first of those processes (with how firms increase the innovativeness with which they produce what they produce). But two important qualifications should be made.

The first is a caution about the way we explore that issue. In the remainder of the chapter, we will give increasing attention to issues about accumulating capabilities for closing in on existing technological frontiers, for overtaking them, and for opening up new directions of frontier development. In other words, we will give increasing emphasis to the accumulation of capabilities for "new-to-market" and "new-to-the-world" types of innovation. As we do so, it will be important to bear in mind one of the main points highlighted here: that even in the advanced economies such "higher-level" types of innovation are a fairly small proportion of the total. Correspondingly, the low incidence of incremental, "new-to-the-firm" types of innovation are likely to be as much a part of lagging behind in developing countries as is the low incidence of new-to-the-world-type innovation. The latter may be more glamorous and more written about in academic studies; but changing the incidence of the former may do more to raise average incomes. In connection with that, it may be opportune still to recall after more than 30 years the insight of the economic

---

[12] The selection of countries and industries for illustrative purposes has suppressed considerable noise around the two trends. For example, the Commuinty Innovation Survey (CIS) survey responses about the types of innovation in firms are highly subjective and there are apparently anomalous inter-country patterns suggesting the existence of country-specific biases in modes of response. Also, numerous other factors, for example firm size, influence the incidence of particular types of innovation.

historian, Nathan Rosenberg, as he commented on the relative roles of natural scientists and economists in considering the significance of different kinds of technical knowledge:

> The factors which influence the productivity of resources in economic activity are numerous and prosaic. It is time to recognize that the intellectual division of labour has given the economist a subject matter in which relatively grubby and pedestrian forms of knowledge play a disconcertingly large role. (Rosenberg, 1976: 62)

The second qualification is that the two processes discussed as neatly separable in connection with Table 2.4 are actually closely interlinked: the existence of innovation capabilities in latecomer firms, and their cumulative deepening over time, are centrally important in the process of structural change in the economy. This arises in two ways: (i) via the "internal" diversification of output in the firms that accumulate the capabilities, and (ii) via the initiation of new-to-the-economy lines of production on the basis of spillovers of innovation capabilities from the firms in which they were originally accumulated.

The role of innovation capabilities in the internal diversification of output is well recognized in the context of firms that are close to the international innovation frontier—most clearly in Chandler's classic studies of the long-run dynamics of industrial enterprises in the US and Europe (Chandler 1962, 1990).[13] However, this role is much less clearly recognized in the context of technology-following, latecomer firms which, it is often argued, need only select and adopt existing technologies from the advanced economies in order to enter new lines of business. But this misrepresents the "nuts and bolts" realities of the experience of diversifying latecomer firms. In particular, dynamic and competitive firms in East Asia during the 1970s and 1980s typically used substantial bodies of in-house engineering, design, and managerial competence as a basis for their acquisition of foreign technology to enter markets and technologies that were new for the economy. The role of this technological basis for such entrepreneurial innovation was elaborated most explicitly in Amsden's analyses of the importance of "project executing capabilities" that enabled Korean firms to diversify into new markets and technologies (Amsden, 1989, 1997, 2001; Amsden and Hikino, 1994).

This kind of innovation-supported diversification underpinned the structural change in East Asian industrial economies that was a central feature of their growth experience over the last four decades of the 20th century, as emphasized by Nelson and Pack (1999). Those authors also emphasized that such diversification had little in common with the influential idea that, in

---

[13] Though Chandler emphasized that it was not necessarily the initial, leading innovators that succeeded in such diversification, but often the close followers.

order to enter new industries, the only thing firms in developing countries had to do was select and import the required technologies from advanced economies as part of the global process of technology diffusion. As had been stressed already by Rosenberg in the 1970s, the kinds of knowledge, search, experimentation, and learning needed for such new-to-the-firm and new-to-industry innovation during the diffusion of technology were not fundamentally different from the kinds of knowledge, search, and experimentation needed for new-to-the-world innovation at the international frontier. Indeed, when technology importing occurs in areas that are relatively close to the international technology frontier, the kinds of knowledge base and search/learning activity required for such so-called "imitation" are virtually indistinguishable from those needed for new-to-the-world innovation. This has been demonstrated for instance in Chuang's recent research on the electronics industry in Taiwan where diversification by firms into the large-scale TFT-liquid crystal display business was based on technology licensing from Japanese firms—preceded by extensive R&D and experimentation undertaken to create the basis for technology acquisition (Chuang, 2009).

Beyond these few studies, the role of firms' innovation capabilities in such internal diversification of firms' output is poorly understood.[14] But the initiation of new-to-the-economy lines of production via the spillover of capabilities to other firms is even less well documented. The conventional spillover literature, whether about FDI or R&D, fails to distinguish between the effects of spillovers on (i) the productivity of established firms in lines of business that already exist in the economy and (ii) the initiation of new-to-the-economy lines of production, either by existing firms or new start-ups. At the same time, the majority of the literature about new start-up firms in developing countries seems to have been preoccupied with the emergence of these from, or in association with, universities and research institutes, not via spillovers from existing firms. Nevertheless, there is a scattering of anecdotal information suggesting that inter-firm spillovers are important in underpinning the innovation-based initiation of new-to-the-economy lines of business.

Such spillovers may take the form of new enterprise creation by more or less formally organized spin-off mechanisms. These might involve a sequence like the creation of internal "units" of new activity that are transformed into subsidiaries and then spun off as independent firms—as in the case in Box 2.2, where internal innovation capabilities in the Korean firm, POSCO, led to the creation of new kinds of economic activity spanning a considerable technological distance from a starting point in the steel industry with supposedly

---

[14] For instance, it is interesting that, among the numerous studies of innovation capabilities in highly diversified Korean firms, those examining the cumulative deepening of capabilities within individual business lines, such as automobiles or semiconductors, far exceeds the number that examine the process by which such firms changed the composition of their lines of business.

Box 2.2 Innovation Capabilities and Change in the Composition of Output: Diversification from Steel to Knowledge-Intensive Services and Software—The Case of POSCO in Korea

---

In Korea through the 1970s and 1980s the Pohang Iron and Steel Company (POSCO) invested heavily in building up its own in-house engineering capabilities as the key "reservoirs" for absorbing and assimilating technology. The company used these capabilities in its upgrading, expansion, and new plant development activities that drove it to become one of the largest and most efficient steel producers in the world. In 1994 it consolidated these knowledge assets into a subsidiary company—POSCO Engineering and Construction (POSEC)—which began to provide engineering services to third-party clients in Korea. By the end of the decade, POSEC was operating in the international market and, as POSCO E&C since 2002, it is now a significant international engineering contractor.

In turn, this trajectory of diversification, from innovation-supporting capabilities in the production of steel to the production of knowledge-intensive services, led further to the internationally competitive production of specialized software. POSEC's engagement with engineering software led first to its own in-house, innovative software development, and then to the formation of a distinct subsidiary (Modeling, Integrated Design and Analysis Software Co.). This was then spun off as MIDAS IT—a software and services company operating in the international market.

---

mature technology to the production of knowledge-intensive services and software. In other cases, the spillover mechanism may be more involuntary as, for instance, individuals or small teams who have built up a base of technological and/or market competence leave a firm to start up firms based on new-to-the-economy innovations. These often seem to have been concerned with supplying inputs to the firms that had initially been responsible for creating and accumulating the spilling-over capabilities.

At the same time, in contrast to the preoccupation with "science parks" and similar initiatives as vehicles for fostering new enterprise creation by spillovers from R&D in research institutes and universities, it seems to be the case that such facilities in late industrializing economies frequently support spillovers from innovation capability that has been accumulated in firms. In South Africa, for example, in 2001 the provincial government of Gauteng established the Innovation Hub in Pretoria, close to a major complex of government R&D institutes and also to a strong center of academic research. This science park was intended to contribute to narrowing the so-called "innovation chasm" in the country—the large gap between public R&D and the application of its results in innovation. However, it was activities originating in firms' innovation capabilities that came to play the leading role. The first anchor tenant was the large South African paper company, Sappi, which established one of its major technology centers there in order to pursue areas of its technology development that were particularly diversification-oriented. By 2005 most of the other 50 tenant companies had their origins in some form of spin-out from other, usually fairly large, businesses—not from the nearby universities or research institutes.

In other words, alongside the relationship between firms' deepening innovation capabilities and their catching up in existing lines of business like steel, automobiles, or semiconductors, there also seems to be an important but poorly understood relationship between firms' innovation capabilities and changes in the composition of output in late industrializing economies. This leads into discussion of the broader issue about the "direction" of innovation.

2.2.4. The Direction of Innovation

We highlighted earlier the idea that latecomer firms might pursue innovation in directions that were different from those already mapped out by the past trajectories of leaders at the moving international innovation frontier. Questions about such differences in the *direction* of innovation can be distinguished from questions about its *rate*. In the context of this chapter, the latter are about the rate at which latecomer firms accumulate progressively deeper innovation activities and catch up with global leaders by moving more or less along the prior paths of frontier-moving, new-to-the-world innovation—though possibly skipping over steps and phases on the way (Lee and Lim, 2001).

This distinction between rate and direction has long been drawn in the analyses of invention and innovation. It was, for example, the framing idea for one of the most important books in the early development of the field—the NBER volume on *The Rate and Direction of Inventive Activity* (Nelson, 1962). This was concerned almost entirely with questions about invention at the technological frontier in advanced economies, and in that context the idea of direction was used in two ways. First, it referred to changing patterns in the distribution of inventive activities between different purposes or fields of potential application—for example, its shifting distribution between industries, or the rising/falling level (or share) of inventive activity associated with particular objectives such as defense or health. Second, it was used to refer to aspects of the outcomes of invention, in particular its productivity effects. Direction was identified in terms of the influence of innovation on the relative factor saving composition of overall productivity growth, with a focus on labor and capital saving and the consequences for trends in wage rates and returns on investment.

Here, in the context of latecomer firms, we follow both those approaches, though with more emphasis on revealed *ex post* outcomes and consequences of innovation than on the *ex ante* distribution of innovative activity between purposes or fields. We comment briefly on three illustrative examples of such directionality: (i) the orientation of factor saving, with a focus on its implications for employment and the environment, (ii) the orientation of innovation toward low-income consumers and their needs, with its implications for poverty reduction; and (iii) the orientation of innovation toward the diversification of output rather than in existing lines of business.

The scope for developing capabilities in environmentally friendly technologies

In the 1960s and 1970s, a large amount of research on technology in developing countries was undertaken on this aspect of the direction of technical change. Particular interest centered on the relative use of labor and capital and the consequences for employment growth and the distribution of income (Stewart, 1972, 1978; Kaplinsky, 1990). Having been seen initially as primarily a problem about the *choices* firms made among alternative available techniques, it came to be seen much more clearly as a matter of the direction of *change* in technology. At the same time, though, it also became clear that the direction of technological change, when not locked into historically determined paths, was less an influence on the distribution of income than a consequence of it and the associated composition of demand and structures of political power. Since then, the issue has virtually disappeared from the research agenda, and interest in catching up has focused much more on the rate of growth of productivity—partial and total—relative to leading firms and economies.

However, in recent years questions about innovation and the direction of factor use and factor saving have re-emerged with an emphasis, not on capital and labor, but on energy, materials, and other environmental/natural resources. Initially, the growing attention given to innovation and the environmental impact of technology focused heavily on end-of-pipe solutions, and these were typically highly capital-using technologies to reduce environmentally damaging outputs. But attention shifted toward the importance of "win-win" technologies—new product and process configurations that reduce both costs and environmental damage. Although this raised the attention given to issues about innovation and the environment, debate tended to concentrate on only a part of the spectrum of different types of innovation—"radical" innovation (along the lines of Enos's alpha phase and the Oslo Manual's new-to-the-world innovations). One consequence was a view that saw such innovation as heavily concentrated in advanced countries, with the technology being transferred to latecomer firms, not created and shaped by them. But that is much too narrow. As Enos demonstrated in the case of the petroleum industry, incremental beta-phase innovation can play a large role in reducing the intensity with which fuel and materials are used in production. Michael Rock and colleagues have similarly highlighted the importance of engineering-based, incremental innovation in contributing to more sustainable directions of technical change—for example, an energy-saving direction in a cement plant in Thailand and a waste-reducing direction in an electronics cluster in Malaysia (Rock and Angel, 2005; Rock et al., 2009). In other words, progressive deepening of the innovation capabilities of latecomer firms may contribute in important ways to relatively "green" directions of industrial development.

Orientation toward low-income consumers and its implications for poverty reduction

An important thread in the analysis of "appropriate" directions of technical change in the 1970s was concerned with the appropriateness of products, not just the relative capital and labor intensity of processes. This was about the design of products and their consequent features and functions. The issue was seen as important for two reasons. First, product specifications frequently determine process specifications, and hence contribute to shaping the employment intensity of production. Second, the specifications of products influence their prices; and directions of product innovation can be pursued to simplify "excessive" complexity, reduce prices, and hence raise the real income of consumers—in particular, low-income consumers.

These ideas have recently been rediscovered. In particular, Prahalad (2006) has again identified the "inappropriate" nature of product technology for consumers at the bottom of the pyramid:

> During the last decade, many MNCs have approached BOP markets with an existing portfolio of products and services. Because these product portfolios have been priced and developed for western markets, they are out of reach for potential customers in BOP markets. More important, the feature-function set has often been inappropriate. (p. 23)

What is called for is a new direction of innovation to meet the needs of low-income consumers. Examples of such redirection of innovation have been identified by Zheng and Williamson (2007) in what they describe as the patterns of "cost innovation" pursued by Chinese firms.

2.3. PATHS OF INNOVATIVE CAPABILITY BUILDING IN LATECOMER FIRMS

We elaborate here on three issues about the paths of innovation capability building pursued by latecomer firms: (i) the types of capability involved, and taxonomies of "levels" or "stages" in their accumulation by firms, (ii) the rates at which firms move through these sequences, and (iii) possible discontinuities in the accumulation process.

2.3.1. Innovative Capability Building: Types, Levels, and Stages

The boundary we have emphasized between *production* and *innovation* capabilities is obviously blurred in practice. Nevertheless it has been found useful in several studies, albeit with differences in terminology. It was emphasized some time ago in a broad analytical overview by Bell and Pavitt (1995),[15] and has subsequently been used in various empirical studies: for example by Cimoli (2000) with reference to firms in the Mexican innovation system,[16] and by Choung et al. (2000) with reference to Korean semiconductor firms.[17]

It has become common practice to differentiate further "levels" *within* the category of innovation capabilties. In some cases, this involves relatively simple distinctions, such as "minor" and "major" change capabilities or "improvement" and "generation" capabilities. Other studies have developed more detailed typologies of different levels of capability corresponding roughly to different levels of novelty in innovation, as discussed earlier in Section 2.2.2. We elaborate on this kind of typology here. First, we focus on the technologically creative human resources, skills, and knowledge bases needed to undertake different levels of innovation. We refer to this as the "technological" dimension of innovative capability. Second, we outline what we refer to as the "organizational" dimension, a less well-developed perspective in the context of late industrializing economies. We then illustrate how these two perspectives might be integrated. Finally, we comment briefly on the way firms seem to move through these "levels" of capability as they make their transition from imitation to innovation.

(i) The technological dimension of innovative capability

Various methods of classifying levels of innovative capability have been used since the earliest studies by Jorge Katz and colleagues in Latin America and by Sanjaya Lall in India and then more generally for developing countries (Katz, 1987; Lall, 1987, 1992). Others have subsequently followed similar approaches. Although these use varying terms and concepts, they usually involve sequences that start with levels of production capability and run into levels of

---

[15] Those authors used the more general term "technological capability" to refer to what we describe here as "innovation capability."

[16] He distinguishes production capacity from the ". . . resources needed for the generation and management of technological change . . .".

[17] They refer to technology-*using* capabilities and technology-*generating* capabilities as two components of general technological capability.

innovative capability. Some have distinguished four levels (e.g. Hobday et al., 2004; Tsekouras, 2006). Others have developed more detailed schema running to six or seven levels (e.g. Figueiredo, 2003; Ariffin and Figueiredo, 2004).

In most cases, the typologies have been based on what one might call a "revealed capability" approach. Rather than specifically identifying levels of capability in terms of particular quantities and qualities of human resources, skills, knowledge bases, and so forth, they have identified levels of increasing novelty and significance of innovative *activity*, along lines discussed earlier in Section 2.2.2, and then inferred that different levels of capability lie behind the different types of innovative activity.

As a basis for later discussion, we link these two approaches in an illustrative framework in Table 2.5. This first shows in the left-hand column the four levels of innovation activity as discussed earlier in terms of different levels of novelty (from "basic" to "world leading"), and these are associated with different kinds of capability identified in terms of human resources and knowledge bases. Clearly though, the precise kinds of human resources needed for particular levels of innovative activity will vary across different situations and the suggested association should be seen as involving considerable flexibility.

In line with previous studies, this framework highlights capabilities that are internal to the firm, but it also recognizes that a substantial part of a firm's capability to innovate lies in other organizations outside the firm itself—in suppliers, lead users, specialized consulting firms, research institutes, competitors, universities, and so forth. Consequently, a significant part of the firm's internal capabilities for developing and implementing innovation consists of human resources and knowledge bases needed to interface with external capabilities. These are not simply capabilities to *acquire* external knowledge, but also capabilities to *integrate* it into the firm's internal knowledge bases and to *coordinate* different stakeholders in the timing and nature of knowledge generation. Although identified by Cohen and Levinthal (1990) specifically as R&D resources, the nature of these interfacing, absorptive capabilities naturally varies with different levels of innovative activity—an issue we will note again later.

Box 2.3 provides an illustrative example of a firm's progress through most of these levels of innovative capability. The innovative activity of this medium-sized, South African mining equipment manufacturer was at one stage limited to minor product improvements and problem-solving undertaken as part of its customer support operations. It gradually deepened and expanded its internal engineering, design, and R&D capabilities, also developing links with universities and a public research organization. On this basis, it came to generate innovative products at the international technological frontier, building a strong export business in the global mining industry.

Table 2.5. Levels of innovative capability: the "technological" dimension

Levels of innovative activity	Illustrative elements of capability (focusing on human capital, knowledge bases, etc.)
World leading Overtaking incumbent innovators at the international frontier by cutting-edge innovation in products, production, and organizational processes and systems	A substantial and varied body of internationally recognized R&D personnel with a number of teams of highly specialized engineers and related professionals working on cutting-edge research, design, and development of products/services, production processes, new materials, and new sources of raw materials that are likely to push the world innovation frontier forward. Some teams may be engaged in pre-competitive forefront research. Large incidence of people with sophisticated cognitive skills for generating imaginative and original innovations. These are distributed across different organizational units in the firm and also work on a collaborative basis with professionals from other organizations (e.g. suppliers, competitors, lead users, research institutes, specialized consulting firms, and universities). Consequently substantial numbers of professionals are engaged in external knowledge acquisition, knowledge leveraging, and knowledge internalization.
Advanced Catching up with the international technological frontier and closing in on leading global incumbents, perhaps with differing directions of innovation	Various types of design and development engineers, researchers, and other specialized professionals in different functional areas within and outside the firm. Among these are those with additional skills for new knowledge sharing and external knowledge screening/searching and leveraging (e.g. "T-skilled"/"A-skilled" people, knowledge-bridging people, "multi-lingual managers," project champions, team-work boosters, technological gatekeepers). These professionals implement applied research, design, and development of complex products/services and production systems that are *close to the international innovation frontier*. They work either within the firm's boundaries or in collaboration with professionals from other organizations (e.g. suppliers, competitors, lead users, research institutes, specialized consulting firms, and universities). There is high preference for people with strong cognitive skills (for complex problem framing) and with ability to generate new ideas and advanced innovation activities implementation.
Incremental/intermediate Relatively complex improvements and modifications to products, processes organization, and systems	Increased number of specialized engineers and technicians allocated in different and dedicated organizational units involved in product development, product re-design, process engineering, and automation systems. Expanded number of management professionals trained in advanced management techniques/practices for problem-solving and problem-framing and also in marketing, logistics, and finance. These professionals work on activities such as duplicative and/or creative imitation to advanced modifications to products (including product re-design), large-scale production systems, software, and equipment systems to meet local demand and raw materials characteristics. Firms tend to give preference to

Continued

Table 2.5. *Continued*

Levels of innovative activity	Illustrative elements of capability (focusing on human capital, knowledge bases, etc.)
	professionals with good technical skills and some cognitive skills (problem-solving and framing) for creative imitation.
Basic Minor adaptations and improvements, close-to-imitation adoptions	Groups of engineers and qualified technicians working informally on experiments and incipient or informal R&D activities. Dedicated groups of engineers and qualified technicians and well-trained operators working on the implementation of minor adaptations in products, production processes, and organizational and/or automated systems, equipment components and related software. To carry out such activities, firms demand people with good functional skills and technical skills.

⇧   ⇧

Innovation capabilities

⇧

FUZZY BOUNDARY

⇩

Production capabilities

Typically the kinds of "ladders" of capability accumulation outlined in Table 2.5 and illustrated in Box 2.2 have been applied to different functional areas within the firm. Lall (1992), for example, identified capability levels in firms' investment and production functions, distinguishing within the latter between product- and process-related engineering functions. More recently, Figueiredo (2003) and Ariffin and Figueiredo (2004) have applied close variants of that approach.

Such studies have relied heavily on a rather narrow range of data sources involving the direct acquisition of information about the technological activities of firms via interviews and/or questionnaire-based surveys. Data from secondary sources have rarely been useful in tracing out paths of capability building in latecomer firms because, although commonly used in advanced economies, the types of available information (e.g. about R&D or patenting) are irrelevant for large parts of those paths in developing countries. They only become useful once firms have built up their innovative capabilities to the point where they involve measurable R&D activities or recorded patenting. In Korea, for example, measures based on domestic patenting only started to become useful in tracing innovative activities from about the early 1990s—as

Box 2.3 Deepening the Knowledge Base for Innovation: The Case of Multotec Process Equipment, South Africa

Multotec Process Equipment (MPE), a Johannesburg firm employing about 75 people, manufactures cyclones and spirals for the separation of materials in mining gold, platinum, diamonds, and coal. They are the world's largest and second largest supplier of coal spirals and heavy mineral spirals, respectively. Turnover grew by about 60 percent between 1999 and 2004. The firm has an 85 percent share of the local market, and exports, mainly to Australia, Russia, and Norway, have been built up to account for 30 percent of output. The company is part of a larger group, with majority ownership held by a German firm employing 700 people globally.

The manufacture of its products does not require especially advanced manufacturing capabilities, and historically the firm's senior managers did not see themselves as pursuing an R&D-centered strategy. But in the 1990s they decided to provide a strong service function to customers. This required an engineering capability to provide support and problem-solving, and this led the firm into a stream of incremental innovations to meet the specific needs of customer industries, and then to more radical redesigns of their range of cyclones. MPE emerged as the leader in making innovative products to order rather than "off-the-shelf" products. This requires a combination of advanced computer modeling together with experimentation and testing of different designs.

Innovation became increasingly integral to the business in order to build the firm's domestic market position. Only by maintaining ongoing improvements could MPE stay ahead of local and international firms that sought to copy its products, and this was critical in building its export markets. The innovation-centered strategy contrasts with competitors, which, as licensees or local subsidiaries of international firms, have a fixed range of products and do not undertake the same level of in-house design and ongoing development in South Africa.

Behind this strategy lay a cumulative deepening of the human capital and knowledge bases of the firm—both accumulated internally and accessed via links to other organizations. It built up a team of in-house design engineers to support its service support strategy, and was able to develop an experience-intensive engineering team unusually rapidly in the late 1990s because of retrenchments in the big upstream industries. Recruitment included, for example, the lead process engineer who until 1994 had been head of R&D in the country's largest steel company. This deepening of the company's innovative capability has been supported by the existence in South Africa of considerable "computing power," mainly skills and capabilities of people employed in modeling and product design that was both readily available and cheap. With this strong base of human capital, the team was able to move forward rapidly with development and design improvements. Building on this, the company also reached out to interact with universities and to collaborate with a public industrial research organization (The Council for Scientific and Industrial Research—CSIR) in computational fluid dynamics modeling. Together with the acquisition in 2003 of a full-scale rig for testing innovative prototypes, this base of internal human resources and external links to knowledge resources enabled Multotec to develop a new generation of more efficient cyclones.

Until recently MPE did not identify R&D as a separate function, and even in 2004 R&D expenditure was only about 1.5 percent of turnover, and it employed seven qualified process engineers. But several innovative design and engineering activities were not accounted as R&D—including the costs of staff responsible for ongoing product development and customization. The costs of the full range of innovative activity rooted in its design and engineering resources were clearly several multiples of the formally recorded expenditure on R&D.

Source: Adapted from original research reported in Roberts (2005).

in the analysis of Korean business groups by Choo et al. (2008); and measures based on patenting in the US became useful only for the period since the late 1990s—as in the study of Korean semiconductor firms by Choung et al. (2000) or in the comparison between Korea and Taiwan in Park and Lee (2008).

Despite the need to acquire original information at firm level, empirical applications of frameworks like the one in Table 2.5 have used a variety of study designs. Some have used intensive interview designs to reconstruct historical paths of capability accumulation over considerable periods of time (around 30–60 years), but with limited numbers of firms—for example, Dutrénit's (2000) study of a single Mexican glass firm, Figueiredo's comparative study (2003) of two Brazilian steel firms, or the study by Dantas of Petrobrás's offshore oil operations in Brazil (Dantas, 2006; Dantas and Bell, 2009). However, other study designs have covered histories of capability accumulation, usually over shorter periods, in much larger numbers of firms—for example, 53 firms in the electronics industry in Malaysia (Ariffin, 2000; Ariffin and Bell, 1999), later matched with 29 firms in Brazil (Ariffin and Figueiredo, 2004); 25 firms across seven industries in South Korea (Hobday et al., 2004); and 80 firms in the Mexican electronics industry (Iammarino et al., 2008). Such relatively large samples have permitted meaningful comparative analysis—for example, between locally owned firms and MNC subsidiaries in Malaysia and Brazil, or between sub-regional clusters in Mexico. But even with relatively small sample sizes, careful research design has allowed illuminating comparative analyses—for example, in Tsekouras's (2006) two-stage design for his study of food-processing firms in Greece.

The studies in the later chapters of the book have all followed variations on these kinds of method and design. However, data from innovation surveys are beginning to open up opportunities for research using new kinds of firm-level indicator that reflect a wider range of innovative activities and capabilities than the conventional R&D- and patent-based indicators. Once such data become available from repeated (and comparable) surveys over meaningful periods of time, there will be opportunities to develop imaginative methodological approaches that integrate quantitative analyses for relatively large samples with the examination of complementary qualitative information for smaller sub-samples.

(ii) Organizational dimension of capability

We highlighted earlier the importance of the organizational dimension of a firm's *production* activities. Correspondingly, there is also an important organizational dimension to a firm's *innovative* activities and hence an organizational dimension to its innovation capabilities. Two largely disconnected strands of research have discussed this dimension. One has been about latecomer firms in developing economies and the other about highly innovative and world-leading firms in the technologically advanced economies.

The first strand was already evident in the early studies of innovative capability in latecomer firms. Both Katz and Lall recognized the importance of the organizational dimension of that capability—though they gave it less emphasis than the kinds of capability we have described above as "technological."[18] These studies focused primarily on the emergence of innovative capabilities at the lower end of the range in Table 2.5, and the important organizational issues were usually identified as being about *organizational specialization and differentiation*—i.e. they were about developing distinct components within the organizational structure of the firm for undertaking emerging activities and capabilities concerned with innovation rather than with ongoing production operations. Such organizational "homes" for emerging components of innovative capability include such things as:

- off-line quality management centers that engage in product adaptation and design instead of routine quality monitoring;
- the consolidation of technical customer support activities into groups undertaking incremental product adaptation and design improvement— as in the case of Multotec in Box 2.3 above;
- the establishment of process engineering sections that go beyond routine maintenance and engage in adapting and improving process technologies;
- the creation of formally structured technology development units or R&D sections that establish these activities on a permanent rather than intermittent basis.

Parts of such organizational specialization may also deal with the firm's interfaces with external knowledge sources—for instance, the development of specialized teams to undertake the process of technology acquisition for new projects, or the development of customer service teams that acquire information from users in order to inform product improvement engineering. Such arrangements seem to have been especially important among catching-

---

[18] For example, in setting up the taxonomic framework for his study of capability development in India, Lall noted: "The above classification has dealt with strictly technical aspects of an enterprise. However, organizational capabilities have to accompany technological ones" (Lall, 1987: 17).

up firms in East Asia in the 1970s and 1980s. For example, Amsden and Hikino (1994) and Amsden (1989) describe how large Korean firms built up strong specialized units of "project execution capabilities" in order to acquire technology from external sources in order to initiate new lines of production within their diversification strategies.

A number of subsequent studies gave less attention to issues about specialization and differentiation in discussing the organizational basis of innovation capability. Instead, they attached more importance to *integration and coordination*. This shift in emphasis seems to have reflected a change in focus from relatively low levels of innovation capability accumulation to more advanced levels. For example, in her study of a Mexican glass firm, Dutrénit (2000) highlighted the emergence of organizational challenges centered on integrating its internal knowledge resources as its capability-building path moved beyond the level of organizationally dispersed incremental innovation. Several other studies have also emphasized the importance of organizational mechanisms for effectively integrating externally acquired knowledge—as demonstrated for example by Kim (1998) in the case of Hyundai's development of innovative capabilities in the automobile industry.[19] In the case of the Korean semiconductor industry, Choung et al. (2000) showed how the technological scope of inventive activity widened as firms moved through increasingly advanced vintages of product technology, and as they diversified their product portfolios; and Mathews and Cho (1999) noted how this diversification of the firms' knowledge bases increased the importance of the firms' "combinative capabilities" to integrate not only the different areas of knowledge but also the knowledge acquired from different external sources and their own R&D activities. Tsekouras (2006) made the same point in his study of the transition toward innovation-based competition by firms in the Greek food industry. In seeking to shift from adaptive innovation toward the creation of unique innovation-based competitive advantages, firms had to draw on increasingly diverse knowledge bases, both inside and outside their own organizations; and the more successful among them were those that demonstrated greater effectiveness in integrating those areas of knowledge.

The second strand of research about the organizational dimension of firms' innovative capabilities has focused on firms in the advanced economies that have already accumulated substantial capabilities to innovate—world-leading firms that are already located at the top of Table 2.5, not somewhere lower down trying to deepen their innovative capabilities and move upwards. Consequently, the discussion has largely been about how firms use their *existing* innovative capabilities to re-build and re-create new distinctive positions of strategic competitive advantage, perhaps even by changing, or at least adding to, the

---

[19] This experience is elaborated later in Section 2.4.1.

areas of technology within which they innovate. Within this strand of work, even greater emphasis has been placed on managerial-cum-organizational issues about *integrating* the complex diversity of technologies and competencies required to innovate at the international frontier[20]—for example in cardiovascular drug discovery in the US (Henderson, 1994), in automobile and computer innovation in Japan (Iansiti and Clark, 1994), or as Japanese and European firms moved from competitive positions in electronics and materials to establish new bases of competence for innovation in optoelectronics (Miyazaki, 1994). In part, the problem of integration is about bringing together knowledge that already exists within the firm. But, as stressed in such studies, it also encompasses the integration of internal knowledge with knowledge acquired from outside the firm.

These ideas about the importance of integration became a key element in the concept of "dynamic capabilities," with its emphasis on "coordinating and combining" as the core process in developing new, innovation-centered competitive advantages (Teece et al., 1997). In Teece's further development of these ideas (Teece, 2007a, 2007b), he argued that "excellence in these 'orchestration' capacities undergirds the enterprise's capacity to successfully innovate...." (2007a: 1320). These capacities are identified at a highly aggregated level as capabilities for (i) "sensing" opportunities and threats, (ii) "seizing" opportunities, and (iii) "reconfiguring" (or transforming) assets and organizational structures. Taken together, these constitute a firm's dynamic capability—a "meta-competence" that "... enables a firm ... to innovate profitably" (p. 1344). Although that meta-competence is identified almost entirely in organizational and managerial terms, technological aspects are not absent altogether. They are clearly evident in Teece's elaboration of the detailed micro-foundations of dynamic capability, but the key point is that they are identified more in managerial and organizational terms than in technical.

In summary, different literatures have thrown light on different aspects of the organizational dimension of firms' innovative capabilities, suggesting that different kinds of organizational capability are important in different levels of innovative activity and capability.

(iii) Integrating the technological and organizational dimensions of capability

Gabriela Dutrénit was perhaps the first to connect the two dimensions of innovative capability outlined in the preceding sections—(i) the "*technological*," centered on human resources, skills, and knowledge bases (as in Table 2.5

---

[20] This complexity became increasingly well recognized, for example, in studies of "multi-technology" firms and their distributed technological competencies (Patel and Pavitt, 1997; Granstrand et al., 1997).

above), and (ii) the "*organizational*," centered on different forms of organizational specialization/differentiation, integration/coordination, and meta-level "orchestration." We develop that insight further here. The basic idea is that the relative importance of different kinds of organizational issue seems to vary with different levels of innovative activity. This is illustrated in Figure 2.1—adapted from Dutrénit's original.

Initially, as firms move through the lower levels of capability building to support more systematic forms of incremental innovation, the main emphasis is on creating the key "technological" elements of capability—i.e. moving "vertically" upwards in Figure 2.1 (equivalent to Table 2.5 earlier). At this initial stage, the associated organizational issues are about organizational specialization and differentiation. However, as firms reach more advanced levels of innovative activity, Dutrénit suggested that firms move through a "transition phase" in which they not only continue moving "upwards" to achieve more advanced and then globally leading levels of capability in technological terms, they also had to move "horizontally" to address increasingly important issues about building organizational capabilities for integration and coordination. Then, if firms successfully negotiated that transition, they would enter the domain discussed by Teece and colleagues where a "meta competence" for orchestrating diverse activities and knowledge resources

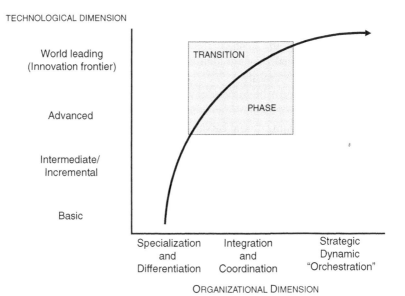

Fig. 2.1. Innovation capability accumulation: changing emphasis on "technological" and "organizational" dimensions

becomes the core of "dynamic capabilities" needed to create and re-create areas of strategic competitive advantage at the global innovation frontier.

We should emphasize that study of the organizational dimension of innovative capabilities in latecomer firms has been limited, and the kind of association we outline in Figure 2.1 between that dimension and the technological dimension is somewhat speculative. Nevertheless, this path of shifting emphasis on the two dimensions of innovative capability is not only consistent with the experience of the Mexican firm examined in Dutrénit's study, it also maps well onto the experience in the studies noted above (Mathews and Cho, 1999; Choung et al., 2000; Tsekouras, 2006). In both the Korean semiconductor industry and the Greek food industry, it was at the point when firms were moving into relatively advanced kinds of technological activity close to the global innovation frontier that they encountered increasingly complex issues about integrating diverse areas of knowledge and about coordinating different innovative activities inside and outside the firm.

(iv) The cumulative nature of capability deepening

Studies using variations of the framework in Table 2.5 to identify stages of innovative capability building have emphasized the cumulative characteristics in the paths followed by firms. In particular, prior accumulation of deep operational capability plays a critical role in accumulating and sustaining subsequent levels of innovative capability. For example, Figueiredo (2001) showed that in one firm in the Brazilian steel industry, USIMINAS, strong production-based operating capabilities for ensuring consistent high product quality were a necessary basis for successful product development (developing high specification steels for the automobile industry). In contrast, in its competitor, CSN, shallow and incomplete accumulation of routine operating capability contributed to the firm's slow and inconsistent accumulation of product development capability.

Also, as they move through the accumulation of successive levels of innovative capability, some firms have attempted to move to higher levels without having completed the accumulation of previous levels. These "holes" left in their capabilities have negative implications for the effectiveness of the subsequent innovative activities (Ariffin, 2000; Figueiredo, 2001; Figueiredo et al., 2008). At the same time, as higher levels of capability are added to existing ones, previously accumulated levels of capability may also need to be strengthened and renewed to prevent new "holes" emerging as the complexity of existing technologies increases. In other words, in the overall process of accumulation, the continuous strengthening and renewal of existing levels of innovative capability may be just as important as shifting upwards to higher levels. This is illustrated by the case of the Chinese heavy equipment maker, CNEGC (Box 2.4). The firm developed a path toward increasingly novel

Box 2.4 Stages in the Accumulation of Innovation Capability: The Case of the China National Erzhong Group (CNEGC)

The heavy machine builder CNEGC is a large state-owned company that was created in 1958 and started up in the early 1970s. Its *first stage* (early 1970s to late 1980s) was marked by the building of initial levels of production-based capability in association with basic to intermediate levels of innovative capability. CNEGC began by introducing new foreign manufacturing technologies and machinery through licensing agreements with Japan and the US. The firm also began to engage in minor innovative activities such as imitation of mature products and minor adaptation to foreign technologies. To assure quality of production processes and products, the firm implemented standards used by foreign industrial leaders as it began to establish its own product-standard system. These activities were carried out by the newly created Standards Committee and Office and by the Total Quality Management Office. Additionally, drawing on its basic and initial intermediate capability, the firm began to implement incremental innovations based on the redesign of some mature products to match local market needs. These were carried out under the Heavy Machinery R&D Unit and Large-size Casting and Forging Research Unit.

During its *second stage* (early 1990s–2000), CNEGC accumulated innovation capability in between the intermediate and advanced levels. In parallel, the company upgraded its production-based capabilities. Increased competition from privately owned firms led CNECG to strengthen its R&D Center to focus on imitation of foreign technologies to make large castings and forgings. It also set up its Technology Center to take charge of the company's innovation management and collaborations with Chinese universities and research institutes. The firm also sought to absorb and learn the latest technological information through joint design and collaborative manufacturing. By 1998 CNECG had accumulated advanced innovation capability to independently design, produce, and install a longitudinal shearing unit for Baoji Petroleum Steel Plant. This involved the *integration* and *coordination* of different types of expertise and skills and specialized areas within and outside the company such as mechanical, electric, and hydraulic engineering, R&D, production areas, and related supporting units. To improve its process technology and design capability, the firm also formulated a series of protocols to ensure scientific, programmed, and standardized processes management. In parallel, in 2000 the firm restructured its Quality Department as a means of improving its production-based activities.

During its *third stage* (2001–6), CNECG moved into the accumulation of advanced to world-leading capability as it strengthened its basic to intermediate innovative capabilities and renewed its production-based capabilities. The company integrated its dispersed research units (process technology, measurement, heavy equipment design, and information technology) under the Technology Center. It also created new research units in high-tech heavy pressure vessels and nuclear power products. By 2005 CNECG had become a major exporter of complete-set metallurgical equipment to multinational firms from Europe, Japan, and the US. By the end of 2006 CNECG had over 1,200 R&D personnel. In parallel to its research-based activities, the firm constantly improved its own production standards and processes for machinery manufacturing and revised its 11-volume technological standards. Strong emphasis was given to its intellectual property management and the setting-up of its first patent incubator. In 2004 its key "coreless coil box" technology was granted the Chinese Excellent Patent Award. The company also patented a series of new products such as the low carbon upper rim castings for the Three Gorges turbine and the 600 MW supercritical steam turbine cylinders.

Source: Adapted from Xiao et al. (2008).

---

innovation activities, moving through three stages that combined the upgrading of both the technological and organizational dimensions of its innovation capability. As it moved into higher levels of innovative capability, it also renewed and strengthened both lower innovative levels and production-based levels that had been previously accumulated.

However, the cumulative nature of the capability-building process does not mean that there is any kind of "automatic" progression up successive steps on the innovation capability "ladder" once previous capability levels have been mastered. Such mastery of particular levels constitutes merely a necessary condition for movement to subsequent levels, and in many firms the capability-building process may stop, or at least pause for long periods, at particular stages—an issue we explore a little more fully in the next two sections.

2.3.2. Rates and Depths of Innovation Capability Building

Surprisingly little attention has been given to the temporal dimension of the process by which latecomer firms move from *production* capabilities toward various forms of *innovative* activity (Bell, 2006). We know little about how long firms take to move through these steps and stages under different circumstances. Nor do we know much about how smoothly firms make the transitions between qualitatively different kinds of innovative capability. In other words, we have a rather poor basis for assessing the performance of firms in terms of the rate and continuity/discontinuity of capability accumulation.

There are, however, a number of studies that provide glimpses of information about these issues. We draw on these, in particular a number of studies in Brazil and Malaysia (Ariffin, 2000; Figueiredo, 2008; Ferigotti and Figueiredo, 2005; Miranda and Figueiredo, 2010; Tacla and Figueiredo, 2006; Figueiredo, 2003; Figueiredo et al., 2008), to throw a little light on two issues: (i) the high degree of variability in the time periods involved in accumulating innovative capabilities and (ii) the considerable differences in the depths of capability achieved.

Building innovative capabilities is a slow process. Some observations indicate that around 20 years has been required to move from start-up to a capability level *close* to the international innovation frontier—around the level of advanced innovative capability in Table 2.5. This was the case on average for electronics firms in Malaysia and firms producing capital goods, software, and motorcycles in Brazil. It is also roughly consistent with some of the descriptions of successful East Asian electronics firms provided in Hobday (1995). For example, a bicycle manufacturer (Anam) entered the electronics industry (chip packaging) in 1968 and, having passed through several capability-building phases concerned with engineering and design, the firm entered a phase of increasingly intensive, research-based product innovation around 1988—a capability-building trajectory from industry entry to "advanced" innovation capability that lasted around 20 years. Similarly, Samsung entered the electronics industry in 1969—assembling simple products in a joint venture with Sanyo. Having passed through various capability-building stages concerned with engineering and design, the company entered into research-based innovative activities *close* to the international frontier in the late 1980s. Again the capability accumulation path from industry entry to the initiation of advanced innovation was around 20 years, and the firm went on to emerge as a global innovation leader *at* the innovation frontier by the early 1990s.

But this rate of accumulation seems to vary widely. In other situations, firms traveled roughly the same "distance" from industry entry or start-up to "advanced" innovation at much slower rates. For instance, a Brazilian steel firm took 35 years and firms in the forestry, pulp, and paper industries in Brazil took around 55, though moving to a higher innovative capability level closer to the innovation frontier. In other cases, for instance, some Brazilian electronics, motorcycle, and bicycle firms, it took around 20 years to reach only lower ("intermediate") innovative capability levels. There were also situations in Brazil in which firms took nearly twice as long to reach that kind of intermediate capability level—e.g. a steel firm and a firm manufacturing refrigerators.

There is no clear pattern of inter-industry differences in these rates of capability accumulation. Indeed there seems to be considerable variability between firms in similar industries (and in similar wider contexts). For example, a study of automobile component firms in Thailand (Scott-Kemmis and Chitravas, 2007) showed that different types of firm took widely varying time periods to move from basic production capabilities to OEM suppliers with significant design and engineering-based innovative capabilities. Wide differences in the rate of capability accumulation were also shown in Figueiredo's (2001) study of two steel firms in Brazil.

Behind such differences between firms in the time periods taken to move through levels in Table 2.5, there are also considerable variations in the "depths" of innovative capability they reached. Not all firms moved through all levels, and behind the averages for groups of firms, many had not moved very far at all. For example, although the Brazilian steel producers USIMINAS and CSN were in roughly the same market over more or less the same time period, USIMINAS built up an "advanced" level of innovative capability in about 35 years, while CSN spent nearly 40 years stuck at a production-based capability level. Also, although USIMINAS built up its capabilities relatively rapidly to an "advanced" level close to the established innovators, it did not move beyond that to achieve a world-leading position as the South Korean POSCO did. Similarly, within the Malaysian electro-electronics industry, Ariffin (2000) showed that only 85 percent of the firms had deepened their capabilities beyond the purely production-based level; and only around one-third had moved beyond that to build more advanced, R&D-based innovative capability.

Such differences in the depths of capability accumulated, or at least the existence of "pauses" in building deeper levels of innovation capability, raise broader questions about whether there are general and systematic discontinuities in the accumulation process.

2.3.3. Discontinuities in Capability Accumulation

Studies of innovative capability building in developing and emerging economies have typically emphasized continuity. Firms have typically proceeded fairly smoothly through successive stages of increasingly deep innovative activity over long periods running for two, three, or more decades. This has been especially so in the case of the large body of firm-level studies in Asian contexts—for example: Amsden (1989) or Kim (1997) about firms in Korea from the 1960s and 1970s; or Hobday (1995) and Mathews (1997, 1999) covering electronics firms in Singapore, Taiwan, and Korea over a 20–30-year period. More recent studies have followed a similar perspective— e.g. Lee and Lim (2001) or Choung et al. (2000).

Behind these micro-level paths, fairly continuous evolution and relative stability have also characterized broad macro-level policy and the institutional contexts of firm behavior in the relatively small number of Asian countries where most of our understanding about long-term technological behavior in industrial firms has been generated. There have been shifts and changes in important emphases of policy, as well as wider disruptions and crises in political and economic environments. But, these have not been so disruptive that existing innovative capabilities were destroyed and dispersed—as happened, for example, in the socialist/centrally planned economies of Central and Eastern Europe, and also in much of Latin America. Consequently, the main trajectories of technological development were rarely disrupted in substantial ways, let alone truncated or reversed. Even the Asian financial crisis of

1997 was, after a very short setback, relatively benign in technological terms. It had far-reaching effects on the ownership of enterprises and on the diversity of their production activities, especially in countries like Korea, Thailand, and Indonesia. But where they had existed before the crisis, most of the main trajectories of technological learning and innovation remained in place. Indeed, in several areas the crisis seemed to have the effect of intensifying the investment made by Asian firms and governments in strengthening their innovative capabilities and activities.

In these macro contexts, the large body of Asian research emphasizing cumulative continuity in the micro-level accumulation of innovation capabilities has given very limited attention to investigating *dis*continuity. Yet there are important broad questions in this area—for example, are there generally observable "breaks" in the micro-level capability-building process? If so, where do they arise and why?

One perspective, mainly about experience in Latin America, has focused on the influence of macro-level conditions that have disrupted micro-level paths of capability accumulation. Two kinds of macro-generated discontinuity have been noted. One has focused on broad policy regimes and their change—in particular, the influence of the import-substituting industrialization (ISI) regime and its subsequent replacement by liberalized regimes. It has been argued on the one hand that the ISI regime constrained the depth of innovative capability at "intermediate" levels of incremental innovation, based largely on various forms of design and engineering—in effect, setting up a pervasive and long-lasting discontinuity in the deepening of innovation capability in the region. On the other hand, it is also evident that the reform process that ended ISI regimes in the region was massively destructive of even the constrained level of innovative capability that had been built up previously. Beyond that, it has been argued, the various dimensions of reform, together with some of its consequences such as the structural change in the economy toward primary and natural resource-based production, established in most countries a persistent obstacle to deepening innovative capabilities. Thus, it was argued, this change in regime imposed a persisting discontinuity on accumulation, perhaps at a lower level of capability than that set by the preceding ISI regime (for instance, Reinhardt and Peres, 2000; Ocampo, 2004, 2005; Cimoli and Katz, 2003). A second perspective has focused on more narrowly defined forms of economic instability in Latin America economies—the succession of financial and trade and macroeconomic crises that have characterized most Latin American economies *within* both the ISI and post-ISI regimes. It has been shown that these also have had a disruptive effect on what might have been more continuous paths of capability deepening.

We do not explore further such macro-imposed discontinuities. Instead we focus on those that may be more intrinsic to the process at the micro-level. Some studies have suggested, for instance, that firms face inherent difficulties in making the distinct qualitative transition from technology-using, copying, and operating activities into any form of innovative behavior. Other perspectives have suggested there is an inherent discontinuity at a higher level—at the transition from "incremental" forms of innovation to more "radical" ("advanced") forms. Such discussion is particularly common in Latin American literature (e.g. Viotti, 2002). However such arguments are hard to nail down to empirically based distinctions, and it is difficult to claim that any observable discontinuities are "inherent" in the sense of constituting persisting obstacles to capability deepening that are independent of macro-level contextual factors.

Somewhat more systematic is a small amount of work on discontinuity at the upper end of the scale of capabilities in Table 2.5. Perhaps the clearest and most explicit is the study by Amsden and Tschang (2003) about R&D in Singapore. This carefully distinguished different kinds of "R" as well as different kinds of "D," identifying aspects of inherent complexity in the different categories. Based on analysis of the intrinsic characteristics of those more and less complex activities, they suggested there was a clear qualitative transition as one moved from "from exploratory or advanced development to applied research." Then, drawing on detailed interviews with firms in Singapore, they concluded that there was:

> . . . a sharp division as R&D moved from exploratory and advanced development to applied research. Moving into applied research was a hurdle in the case of a late-industrializing country . . . Overcoming this hurdle, we would predict, is the major challenge that other latecomers will also face. (p. 571)

It is difficult to map that distinction very precisely onto the categories of capability level we have used above in Table 2.5. However, it is obviously somewhere around the "advanced" level, perhaps associated with the combined technological and organizational transition suggested in Figure 2.1.

Hobday et al. (2004) develop a slightly different perspective on a "transition phase" in their study of Korean firms as they approach the innovation frontier. This is about firms shifting from follower and catch-up innovation to positions of innovation-based leadership in their industries. The study highlights two interesting points. First, it is too simple to see this issue in terms of a comprehensive shift for the whole firm. Instead, several firms followed a range of strategies across their product portfolio, involving a mix of latecomer, follower, and leader innovation. Second, they discussed transition at the upper end of this spectrum primarily as a matter of strategic choice for the firm—not so much as an issue about inherent complexities and qualitative discontinuities.

There is, however, enough scattered information to suggest that the transition from follower innovation to innovation leadership involves more than just managerial choice on the part of firms. It may actually be much harder to make this step than other steps and stages in the innovation capability-building process.[21] This takes us back to Figure 2.1. In part the difficulties *may* involve issues that are specifically associated with the *technological dimension* of innovation capabilities—in the sense suggested by Amsden and Tschang and reflected in the vertical axis of Figure 2.1. But there are also grounds for thinking that considerable difficulty is involved in building the *organizational dimension* of innovation capability needed to close in on the innovation frontier—as reflected, for instance, in the insights of Dutrénit about the reasons why the Mexican glass firm she studied failed to sustain its capability building through the transition to strategic innovation and leadership.

2.4. LEARNING PROCESSES IN BUILDING INNOVATIVE CAPABILITIES

The most proximate variables that contribute to explaining variation in the rate, depth, and continuity of innovative capability accumulation are concerned with the specific efforts firms make to create those capabilities— i.e. they are about the intensity, persistence, and effectiveness with which firms specifically manage and invest in acquiring and creating the human resources, knowledge bases, and organizational capabilities they need to conceive and implement innovation. We refer to that investment as "learning" and, to reiterate, we use that term to refer specifically to the creation of capabilities *to* innovate—not to refer to particular kinds of innovative activity themselves.

This section therefore rests on a very simple argument: if firms make limited efforts to invest in acquiring and creating the resources required to innovate, they will deepen their innovative capabilities only slowly, if at all; they will have difficulties crossing whatever discontinuities exist between different levels of capability; and in particular they are likely to remain locked into forms of "follower" innovation rather than innovating as leaders—either by "overtaking" at existing points on the international frontier or by opening up new segments.

We explore here what these "efforts" may actually consist of. This obviously takes us into the well-trodden assertion that learning in the sense of building and deepening capabilities to innovate is conscious, purposive, and costly rather than automatic and passive (e.g. Lall, 1992). We try here to unpack that idea and to illustrate a little of the concrete activities that may be involved. We do so in two steps. First (Section 2.4.1), we focus on learning in individual

---

[21] Even Hobday et al. (2004) note that firms do face relatively complex problems at this stage: "... the substantial additional costs and difficulties of increased R&D and original new product development. They may also risk challenging their traditional sub-contracting partners ... (that) ... may force Korean firms to invest in additional marketing and distribution channels ... adding further risk, cost and uncertainty to their business strategies" (p. 1434).

firms. Then (Section 2.4.2), we turn to ways in which the development of innovative capabilities in individual firms may be influenced by the development of such capabilities in other firms—one of the broad questions addressed in this book.

2.4.1. Learning in Individual Firms

Internal and external learning

Building innovative capabilities in firms involves learning processes and activities of two broad types: those that are internal to the firm, and those that involve acquiring knowledge skills and other elements of capability from external sources. Internal learning activities involve such things as the following:

(i) Various kinds of training to acquire innovation-related skills—e.g. training in product design routines and know-how.

(ii) Various kinds of intra-firm communication of knowledge—e.g. the "socialization" of what may have been tacit or located only in isolated parts of the organization.

(iii) Various forms of experience acquisition. Some may be "passive," in the sense that skill or knowledge is acquired as a by-product of simply undertaking particular activities. But others, usually more important, depend heavily on formally managed processes of exposure to experience-rich opportunities, as well as explicit measures to "capture" and embed what is only potentially available in such opportunities.

(iv) Deliberate knowledge-creation via reverse engineering of products, process equipment, or software.

(v) Knowledge creation by R&D. This may not be undertaken in order to provide elements of the knowledge needed to implement internal technology development and design, but to provide a knowledge base for acquiring existing, but relatively inaccessible, knowledge from external sources—perhaps knowledge that provides a basis for understanding what to search for, or knowledge to use as a negotiating "lever" for licensing designs from other firms.

(vi) The development of internal organizational arrangements for doing all these things, often via deliberate organizational experimentation, redesign, and refinement. As noted earlier, these may be arrangements that develop elements of organizational specialization in particular kinds of innovative activity, or arrangements for integrating knowledge across different parts of the organization, across different fields and technologies—and also, as we emphasize below, across the boundaries of the firm.

Externally mediated learning involves such things as the following:

(i)   Various kinds of training—e.g. training in the design and development department of supplier or customer firms, or short training courses in overseas organizations to build up core competence in engineering routines and their underlying knowledge bases.

(ii) Types of experience acquisition that require the "practice" of innovative activities in other organizations, perhaps necessitating negotiation and expenditure to secure access and support that borders on more formally organized training—e.g. the simulated design of "not-for-construction" chemical process plants under supervision of contracted engineering companies.

(iii) The acquisition of codified knowledge as a basis for developing new products or processes—e.g. the search of patent documentation to identify specifications as a basis for innovation (for instance, data about impending out-of-patent pharmaceutical products as a basis for engineering the necessary process), or the acquisition of design algorithms for undertaking process design and development.

(iv) The acquisition of ready-made specifications for new products that can be brought into production with very limited original design, development, and engineering—e.g. the acquisition of full design details of products from customers, perhaps with process data as well, or the licensing of product designs from third parties.

(v)   The hiring of "ready-made" innovative human capital—e.g. the "poaching" of experienced development engineers from other firms, perhaps from leaders in advanced economies.

(vi) The establishment via FDI of R&D facilities in knowledge-rich locations in other countries, perhaps by acquisition of existing advanced country firms, in order to tap into state-of-the-art know-how and techniques.

(vii) The development of organizational mechanisms and procedures for undertaking these kinds of learning from external sources.

Frameworks for discussing such learning mechanisms are provided in several sources (e.g. Bell, 1984; Malerba, 1992; Kim, 1997; Figueiredo, 2001). Also, numerous fragments of information about specific mechanisms are scattered across the literature on latecomer learning. Usually these merely indicate the presence and perhaps basic characteristics of particular mechanisms that contributed to capability building in specific situations—for example, the use of outward foreign direct investment as a knowledge acquisition mechanism by Korean firms (Sachwald, 2001). Consequently there are numerous limitations in available understanding in this area. We will touch briefly on two—one about the relative importance of different learning mechanisms, the other about effectiveness in their implementation. Both of these are centrally important issues in connection with developing meaningful insights about the management of learning.

The relative importance of learning mechanisms

We know little about the relative importance of different mechanisms, and even less about whether and how this varies as firms deepen their innovative capabilities. Without this understanding, the field lacks even a rudimentary basis for offering insights about the practicalities of managing learning in latecomer firms. This is important because there are some risks that the development of such insights may be shaped more by fortuitous developments in the types of data that become available than by more open exploration of what is involved. The growing attraction and availability of data from innovation surveys may raise such a risk, for example, in connection with the relative importance of augmenting capabilities in latecomer firms by acquiring disembodied information and by investing in people.

Having been developed for use in the advanced economies, innovation surveys focus their questions much more heavily on aspects of how innovation occurs than on the prior process of creating and accumulating capabilities to undertake such innovation. So, for example, even when surveys are adapted for application in developing countries, questions about the "knowledge sources" used by firms are usually questions about the sources of knowledge for implementing innovations, and not about sources of knowledge and skill for building the firms' capabilities to innovate. This orients attention toward the role and sources of disembodied information inputs to innovation. Subsequent academic analysis of such survey data is inevitably much more about how such information is used by firms' *existing* capabilities in undertaking specific instances of innovation than about how *new and deeper* capabilities to innovate are created by firms in the first place.

In contrast to studies that focus on learning as *information* acquisition, studies of learning as an input to building innovation capabilities in latecomer firms have highlighted the importance of people and human capital. For example, studies of innovative capability development at relatively low levels in Table 2.5 have frequently emphasized the importance of various kinds of training—the development of design and engineering capabilities in a Korean chemical firm (Enos and Park, 1988); the development of similar capabilities ("project execution capabilities") in several other kinds of Korean firm (Amsden, 1989, 2001; Amsden and Hikino, 1994); or the development of initial levels of design capability in the Brazilian oil company, Petrobrás (Dantas, 2006; Dantas and Bell, 2009).

But this people-centered perspective also seems important at higher levels of capability development, as illustrated in Box 2.5 about Taiwanese firms

Box 2.5 Learning by Hiring: Accumulating the "People Base" of Innovation Capabilities for Taiwan's Entry to the Large-Size TFT-LCD Industry

In the late 1990s a number of firms in Taiwan entered the production of large-size, thin film transistor-liquid crystal displays (TFT-LCDs). For most of the main entrants this involved considerable diversification from their previous activities in other areas of the electronics industry and, although they had undertaken R&D in the new area, none of them had the full suite of operational technologies required to initiate competitive production. At the same time, collaborative projects involving firms and ITRI (a public sector R&D institute) had not resulted in the necessary product and process technologies. Consequently, firms entered the industry on the basis of licensed technology from Japanese and US producers. However, in advance of that entry, they had to create a substantial array of innovative capabilities as a basis for both acquiring the licenses in the first place and for engaging almost immediately in their own innovation in the new area of rapidly advancing technology.

Two features of this base of innovation capability were striking. First, although an important contribution was made by knowledge derived from the firms' own R&D activities, from collaboration with other firms and from the R&D projects with ITRI, the core of the firms' new areas of innovative capability seems to have been people. Second, the key sources of this people base of innovation capability were other firms, supplemented by the flow of experienced R&D engineers from ITRI. These features can be illustrated by the experience of two of the entrants—AU Optronics (AUO) and Chi Mei Optoelectronics (CMO).

AUO was formed by the merger of Unipac Electronics and Acer Display Technologies (ADT), subsidiaries of two large electronics groups—UMC and Acer respectively. Hence, it was the capability building in the two subsidiaries that initially created the base of capability for AUO's entry to the large-size TFT-LCD business.

In the case of Unipac the roots of the capability building lay in strategic decisions made nearly a decade before entry to the industry. In 1990 the firm recruited as its President Dr Tuan, who had been a senior R&D manager at Xerox USA, where he had worked on the development of TFT-LCD technology. It also recruited as Vice-President of Product Research Dr Su, who had been responsible for TFT-LCD projects with General Electric USA. Then later in 1996 Dr Luo, with 30 years' experience in TFT-LCD research at Westinghouse, Xerox, and General Electric was recruited as Vice-President for Technology Development. These key individuals were supplemented by a team of skilled engineers who already had extensive experience in related areas of semiconductor technology at United Microelectronics Company (UMC), the parent company. Finally, a considerable number of skilled engineers were recruited from other smaller firms in related areas of the Taiwanese electronics industry.

Starting somewhat later, ADT followed a similar path. In 1996 it recruited as R&D Director Dr Hsiung, formerly a senior researcher at DuPont Central Research. A year later he was joined by Dr Lu, who had worked at Bell Laboratories for more than ten years, and then at ITRI as Deputy Director of Display R&D. These leading managers were not only supplemented by a number of experienced engineers from ADT's parent company (Acer), but also by a complete R&D team of five to six people who were transferred from ITRI. Again, as with Unipac, recruitment of skilled engineers and other professionals from other smaller firms in Taiwan also contributed a major part of the firm's innovative capability as it entered the new industry.

A similar pattern was followed by CMO, a subsidiary of the Chi Mei Group, primarily a petrochemicals company. The key strategic leader of the initiative, Dr Wu, was recruited from Prime View—a Taiwanese producer of small and medium-sized TFT-LCD products that was reluctant to enter the large-scale business. Once at CMO, he recruited a technology development team by drawing experienced engineers from Prime View and also from ITRI, where he had previously been responsible for several TFT-LCD R&D projects. In addition, several members of the team were drawn from other firms in Taiwan, often with prior overseas R&D experience—for example, the Vice-President of manufacturing came from Unipac's TFT-LCD activities; and Dr Hsu came from Taiwan Applied Materials, with prior experience as a research engineer with Motorola semiconductors.

Source: Chuang (2009).

---

deepening and re-orienting their already considerable innovative capabilities in order to enter the large-size thin film transistor-liquid crystal displays (TFT-LCD) industry during the 1990s. In this case, though, the emphasis was more on learning by hiring than learning by training. This emphasis on creating capabilities by hiring perhaps illustrates one way (one of many?) in which the relative importance of different mechanisms changes as firms deepen their innovative capabilities. But see also Box 2.3 earlier, describing how the recruitment of an experienced, senior-level R&D manager in a mining equipment firm in South Africa was a critically important step in developing capabilities at a lower level in Table 2.5—capabilities for intensified engineering-based product development as a step toward deeper more research-based innovation.

Effective implementation—the importance of integrating internal and external learning

There are, of course, innumerable studies of the management of innovation, mainly in innovative firms in advanced economies, but also in latecomer firms. But these are almost entirely about managing innovation in firms where most or all elements of the capabilities for innovation already exist, not about how firms manage the process of building up those capabilities in the first place—though in some cases insights can be gleaned from them to illuminate the management of capability building (e.g. Nonaka and Takeuchi,

1995). In contrast, there have been hardly any systematic analyses that focus specifically on how latecomer firms manage more or less effectively the kinds of learning mechanisms reviewed here, or about how differences in the effectiveness of that management may affect the capability accumulation process. There are, however, a few exceptions—for example, (i) the examination by Figueiredo (2001) of how differences in the comprehensiveness, intensity, and functioning of a wide array of learning mechanisms contributed to differences in the paths of capability accumulation in two Brazilian steel firms; (ii) the analysis by Dutrénit (2000) of a single firm in Mexico; and (iii) Marcelle's (2004) study of technological learning in 26 telecommunications operating firms in four African countries.

Such studies highlight one aspect of management in this area that seems generally important—the *integration* of different forms of knowledge and capability: people-embodied and disembodied capabilities (Marcelle), knowledge in different parts of the organization (Dutrénit) or capabilities created by different kinds of learning mechanism (Figueiredo). We focus here on the importance of managing the integration of what we listed separately above as internal and external learning mechanisms. The importance of integrating internal and external learning has been widely discussed with respect to the management of innovation being undertaken by firms in advanced economies that have already accumulated significantly deep innovative capabilities. Much of this analysis followed key contributions in the 1990s such as Cohen and Levinthal (1990), Iansiti and Clark (1994), Nonaka (1994), and Nonaka and Takeuchi (1995). The issue has attracted much less attention in studies about how such capabilities are created and accumulated in the different context of latecomer firms in emerging market countries. Indeed, especially in studies that asymmetrically emphasize the importance of such firms being open to external knowledge, it is glossed over with a cursory reference to the importance of "absorbing" such knowledge, without much (or any) reference to the internal processes by which that might be achieved.

An important exception is the work of Linsu Kim—in particular, his analysis of the learning path followed by Hyundai in automobile production over three decades from the 1960s to the 1990s (Kim, 1998). Kim showed how Hyundai organized major steps of learning in a circular sequence of four activities (Figure 2.2): (i) internal preparation for the acquisition of external knowledge, (ii) the acquisition of that knowledge, (iii) its effective assimilation, and (iv) its subsequent improvement—so creating a higher knowledge base for the preparatory phase of another cycle of learning.

This four-step cycle played the key role in taking Hyundai through a succession of qualitative discontinuities in the cumulative development of its design, engineering, and innovative capability. Starting from its position as an assembler of Ford automobiles on a CKD basis, the first discontinuity was the transition in the mid-1970s to the development and launch of a locally

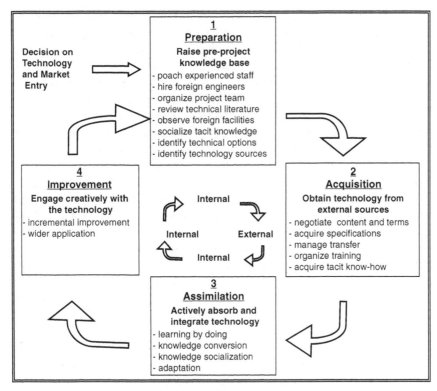

Fig. 2.2. Integrating internal and external learning: Hyundai 1960s–1990s
Source: Adapted from Kim (1998).

designed "Korean" model of a simple vehicle drawing on a wide range of licensed technology from multiple sources. The second in the early 1980s involved the deepening and extension of capabilities in order to develop a more advanced vehicle with the licensing of technology for selected key components but without any external engineering assistance. The third in the early 1990s involved the transition to fully independent development, design, and introduction of a sub-compact car for the international market.

Access to external knowledge and skill was a key issue at each of these discontinuities. But three of the four steps in each cycle were concerned with internal learning efforts that played two key roles in complementing external knowledge acquisition in the overall learning process: (a) creating *ex ante* the necessary knowledge base for acquiring external technology, and not merely (b) ensuring *ex post* the effective absorption of whatever had been acquired externally.

This appears to have been a "success story" in deepening innovative capabilities at a rapid rate in a developing country firm. Moreover, the process seems to have been based on a clear recognition that deepening the firm's innovative capabilities did not proceed smoothly along a linear path. It involved a series of qualitative discontinuities in the types of capability needed to undertake successively more complex kinds of innovative activity. Transition through these discontinuities called for the mobilization of resources on a large scale to launch new cycles of preparation, acquisition, assimilation, and improvement. Behind each of these cycles, senior management set the challenges for capability building at a high level—deliberately constructing what Kim described as a succession of "crises" for the organization.

A much more mixed picture emerges from the few other studies of this and other kinds of integration in emerging market economies. For example, in his study of the development of innovative capabilities in the food-processing industry in a European industrializing country (Greece), Tsekouras (2006) showed considerable differences between firms in the effectiveness of their integration of knowledge across the borders of the firm (as well as in other forms of knowledge integration), and he demonstrated how these differences were associated with the differences in the firms' success as emerging innovators. Similarly, Marcelle (2004) highlighted wide variation in the integration of different learning processes in African telecommunications firms, variation that contributed to differences in the systemic character of the firms' capability building.

This variability in the effectiveness of firms' knowledge integration activities adds to the variability of their investment in specific internal and external learning efforts on their own, and sets up a dual source of variability in the rate at which firms accumulate innovation capabilities.

Our emphasis on the potentially wide variation of explicit investment in, and management of, efforts to accumulate capabilities contrasts with views that see learning arising more or less automatically as a by-product from undertaking other activities in the economy. Such views can be seen as falling into two groups. The first is about learning as a consequence of undertaking production—the "learning-by-doing" idea that underpinned arguments about the need for (temporary) trade protection for infant firms and industries to enable them to catch up with established firms in other economies. It has long been argued that this is an unhelpful perspective, but it continues to attract adherents—for example among those who argue for renewed attention to infant industry protection as a basis for learning. Consequently, brief comment may be useful: (i) catching up is not just a matter of catching up with static levels of higher efficiency in established firms; it is about catching up in a technologically dynamic world, and hence about creating capabilities to innovate in latecomer firms (Bell et al. 1982, 1984); (ii) simply doing routine production provides little basis for learning to do the qualitatively different activities involved in innovation (Bell, 1984), and the gap between the first kind of doing and the second kind of learning has widened in historically

successive phases of late industrialization (Bell and Pavitt, 1993); (iii) consequently, explicit and active investment, not just passive "doing," is required to
create the particular kinds of capability needed for innovation—as argued in
almost every study by close observers of innovation capability building in
developing countries since the early work in the 1970s and one of the first
syntheses (Dahlman et al. 1987).

The second group of views is slightly different and has emerged more
recently. This argues that additions to capabilities for absorbing and improving technologies arise more or less automatically from doing other kinds of
economic activity such as FDI or importing knowledge-intensive goods and
services. However, our emphasis here on the importance of variability in the
investment firms make in learning to innovate suggests, for example, that
innovation-related spillovers from imports (in particular, from importing
capital goods) depends not simply of the volume of imports but also on the
intensity of efforts to reverse engineer knowledge out of those goods and to
integrate it with other knowledge in the accumulating capabilities of firms.
Similarly, innovation-related spillovers from inward FDI will depend not
simply on its volume but on two related sets of investment in creating,
acquiring, and accumulating knowledge assets: (i) efforts in subsidiaries themselves to accumulate a *potential* base of knowledge that *may* spill over to local
firms (Marin and Bell, 2006; Marin and Sasidharan, 2008) and (ii) efforts in
local firms to acquire and absorb elements from that potential knowledge
resource.

2.4.2. Innovation and Learning Relationships between Firms and other Organizations

It is now well known that a firm's own inputs to its innovation activities are
typically complemented by innovation inputs from other firms and organizations. But it is important to distinguish between two kinds of relationship here.
One is about interdependence in *undertaking innovation* among firms and
other organizations that have already developed significant levels of capability
to innovate, and hence to collaborate effectively in doing so. The second is
about the role of inter-firm and firm-university links in contributing to the
prior development of innovation capabilities in those firms and other organizations. These raise different issues and we discuss them separately.[22]

---

[22] See Brundenius et al. (2009) for an excellent and well-balanced recent review of these dual
roles of universities in developing country innovation systems—though using somewhat different language.

Interdependence in undertaking innovation: firms, universities, and public research institutes

The importance of interactions among firms in undertaking innovation is well recognized, but the importance of interactions with other organizations like universities and public research organizations is much less clear. On the face of it, one type of evidence suggests that, relative to inter-firm linkages, the role of universities and public research organizations is quite minor. Across a wide range of developing and advanced economies, information from innovation surveys shows that on average firms draw primarily on other firms for knowledge inputs to their innovative activity, and that only small proportions of them (around 3–8 percent) draw on universities and public research organizations—see for instance Table 11.3 in Brundenius et al. (2009) for a cross-section of data about links specifically with universities.

But one might expect that the relative importance of these different kinds of relationship would change as firms build up progressively deeper levels of innovative capability. As they undertake increasingly novel forms of innovation (moving toward the top of Table 2.5), they are likely to generate greater demand for new, research-based knowledge and this may translate into demand for such knowledge from universities and public research organizations. Also, as Mazzoleni and Nelson (2007) have argued, this appears to have become more important in the contemporary catching-up process, and is likely to become increasingly so. This is primarily for two reasons. First, because of the growing scientific basis for many technologies, advanced training in those fields—provided primarily by universities and sometimes by public research organizations—"has become a prerequisite for ability to understand and control those technologies" (p. 1515). Second, and possibly more important, under prevailing international agreements (particularly under WTO and TRIPS), support policies for latecomer industries and firms "will have to be subtler, and focus on supporting the development of sectoral infrastructures, training and research systems" (p. 1515).

It seems likely that both these arguments carry greater significance for individual firms as their capability-building processes deepen over time, becoming increasingly centered on capabilities beyond those needed for incremental-type innovation. We are not aware of longitudinal evidence for this, but various types of cross-sectional data are highly suggestive. In particular, although data from innovation surveys show that *on average* only small proportions of firms draw on universities and public research organizations for inputs to their own innovation, that generalization hides at least one important type of variation: the greater importance of such links for firms with deeper levels of innovation capability and more intensive innovative activity. For example Arundel and Geuna (2004) show that, compared with European firms in general, these sources of inputs to innovation are much more important for relatively large, R&D-intensive firms that already have deep innovative capabilities. Similarly, Giuliani and Arza (2009) show that among wine firms in both Italy and Chile, the strength of innovation-centered links with universities and public research organizations were greatest for firms with the strongest internal knowledge bases for supporting their own change and innovation.

Thus, perhaps universities and public research organizations come to play an increasingly important complementary role in firms' innovation as the latter move into deeper levels of innovation capability toward the top of Table 2.5.

But care is needed in drawing conclusions from this type of data. This is partly because the data are cross-sectional and our basic interest is in change over time in latecomer firms. But it is also because such data tell us only about one kind of complementary relationship—about interactions that contribute to *undertaking* innovation on the basis of *capabilities that already exist*. Much less seems to be known about inter-organizational complementarities in *building new capabilities* for innovation.

Interdependence in creating capabilities for innovation

A very large part of the research about accumulating innovation capabilities in latecomer firms has focused on "internal" learning activities within individual firms, as in Linsu Kim's studies of transitions from imitation to innovation in Korean firms—highlighted in part in Figure 2.2 above. Clearly however, universities play at least a foundation role in providing the initial, often research-based, training for skilled scientists, engineers, and managers who later contribute to internal capability accumulation processes in firms. In effect, universities provide much of the "raw material" for creating innovative human capital, and firms themselves then transform that base into effective capabilities for innovation. But universities, and also public research organizations, may also play an important role in that subsequent transformation as well. For example, at key steps in its cumulative deepening of innovation capabilities, the oil company Petrobrás in Brazil drew very heavily on specialized engineering and research training provided for the firm's personnel by universities—though these were located throughout the world and not only in Brazil (Dantas and Bell, 2009).

But, the case of Petrobrás also demonstrates the importance of *other firms* as contributors to that cumulative learning process: much of the know-how and detailed expertise needed to build its innovative capabilities were acquired through interactions with other firms in the global oil industry. However, we know surprisingly little about the relative roles of other firms and other external organizations in the learning processes of latecomer firms. Nevertheless a few glimpses of what is involved hint that the role of other firms may be much more substantial than often suggested. For example, the study cited earlier about Taiwanese firms entering the liquid crystal display industry throws a little light on one experience of this type—the development of these firms' innovative capabilities during the 1990s as a basis for their catch-up entry into this advanced area of electronics technology (Chuang, 2009). As emphasized earlier in Box 2.5, flows of people were centrally important in this process. Within that, however, it is striking that, although a public R&D organization (ITRI) played a major role as a source of such people (mainly highly experienced R&D engineers), people flows from other *firms* were at least as important in the capability-building process.

More generally, important features of this inter-firm dimension of the capability-deepening process in these Taiwanese firms matched three broad patterns that are prominent in our current understanding of the accumulation of innovation capabilities in latecomer firms. Since these patterns may be changing in important ways, they merit some emphasis.

- First, a very large part of our understanding about this process is based on studies of the experience of latecomer firms that were, or rapidly became, large multi-functional and often multi-product, Chandlerian-type organizations—Samsung, Hyundai, POSCO, Acer, USIMINAS, Petrobrás, Embraer, Ranbaxy, Wypro, and the like. The four Taiwanese firms fitted this pattern—all involved large multi-product firms that were deepening their capabilities across a range of technology-intensive functions. Very large parts of the learning process that built up innovative capabilities in liquid crystal display technology occurred in departments and subsidiaries that drew on capabilities accumulated previously in other departments and subsidiaries of the parent companies.

- Second, a very large part of our understanding about inter-firm learning relationships emphasizes the complementary importance of similar Chandlerian-type firms on the "supply side" of the relationships. Although latecomer firms have often drawn on multiple sources of external inputs in building up their innovation capabilities, the heart of the process has often been identified primarily in terms of dyadic relationships between the latecomers and single, technologically advanced suppliers of know-how and learning opportunities—e.g. partners in joint ventures, suppliers, and their customers in global (or local) value chains, MNC parent companies and their subsidiaries, licensors and their licensee partners, plant suppliers, and user firms.

- Third, these dyadic relationships have been seen in much previous research as fairly comprehensive in covering the necessary technological scope of a latecomer's emerging innovation capability. For example, global buyers in value chains have been seen as actual or potential sources of both product design knowledge and production and process technology.

Or attention has focused on parent companies as potential sources of, or at least mediating channels for, a comprehensive array of technology to enhance innovation capabilities in subsidiaries. Such observations have shaped our view of the interactive capability-building process.

Thus, research about the accumulation of innovation capabilities in latecomer firms, albeit mostly in manufacturing which has been the focus for almost all research on the subject, has suggested that the dominant processes and opportunities for inter-firm capability building involve these kinds of dyadic interaction between Chandlerian-type firms on both sides of the relationships.

However, these processes and opportunities for inter-firm learning may be fundamentally shifting away from these kinds of dyadic relationships. In a wide range of ways ("open" innovation, "distributed" innovation, and so forth), the process of innovation is being substantially disintegrated—or organizationally decomposed[23]—and, as firms adopt a variety of different post-Chandlerian forms, integrated innovation activities that used to be undertaken in-house and on a highly centralized basis are being increasingly subdivided into specialized segments, many of which are decentralized in various ways. This organizational decomposition may be largely internal to the firm—as in the decentralization of innovation activities to subsidiaries within large and usually multinational corporations, with innovation shifting to take place on a corporate network basis rather than centrally within hierarchical structures. Alternatively, the decomposition may be inter-organizational—the focus of a considerable body of research that preceded and followed Chesbrough's (2003) popularization of the "Open Innovation" concept. This can take many forms. For example, when firms subcontract manufacturing of their products to specialized supplier firms within modular production networks, they often leave process and production innovation largely to the specialized suppliers, concentrating their own attention on product innovation (Sturgeon, 2002). Alternatively, producers of relatively complex products may collaborate in various kinds of network with other firms that undertake innovation with respect to specialized components and subsystems of final products. Or firms may engage independent suppliers of knowledge-intensive services to undertake aspects of particular innovation projects.

Schmitz and Strambach (2009) have raised questions about whether and how these changes in the organization of innovation in the advanced economies will affect the development of innovation capabilities in latecomer firms. We return to these questions in the next section where we discuss how these and other changes in the global context facing latecomer firms will influence their creation and accumulation of innovation capabilities.

---

[23] We take this term from Schmitz and Strambach (2009).

2.5. EXPLAINING INNOVATION CAPABILITY ACCUMULATION IN LATECOMER FIRMS

Over the last two or three decades, research about innovation capability building in latecomer firms has been particularly weak in addressing questions about explanation. There are two aspects to this. First, the specification of what needs explaining has been poorly elaborated. Second, attention has focused on a narrow range of explanatory variables. We explore these two issues in this section.

2.5.1. Innovation Capability Accumulation—What Needs Explaining?

In previous sections of the chapter we have sought to develop a simple framework within which this question might be addressed. As summarized in Figure 2.3, it includes three linked components—two concerned with "inputs" to innovative activity (A and B) and one (C) focused on "outputs." We have tried to illustrate how each of these seems to differ widely between situations (across firms, industries, economies, etc.), and also, though with much less evidence, how they change over time within such contexts. Explaining such differences and change seems important.

The first component—(A)—is concerned with firms' investment in creating and building capabilities for innovation. This investment may involve explicit financial outlays—e.g. on specific kinds of training and knowledge acquisition or on taking over firms that already have relevant capabilities. But a large part also involves investment of managerial and organizational effort to address both intra-firm and external learning mechanisms and processes—as discussed in Sections 2.4.1 and 2.4.2 above. Inter-firm and inter-industry differences in the intensity and continuity of these financial and managerial investments seem to be important in contributing to differences in the other components in Figure 2.3, as do changes over time in their intensity. Such variability therefore appears to constitute an important focus for micro-level and management-oriented research. But only a few studies have sought to explain such variability in latecomer firms—for example, the longitudinal case studies by Kim (1997, 1998) and Dutrénit (2000); and the combination of longitudinal and inter-firm comparative analysis by Figueiredo (2001, 2002).

The second component—(B)—is concerned with the "results" of the investments under (A): the paths of achieved capability accumulation that have been followed by firms through different levels and types of capability. In principle, the focus here might be on explaining differences in the rates at which firms move through particular "distances" on a scale of innovation capabilities

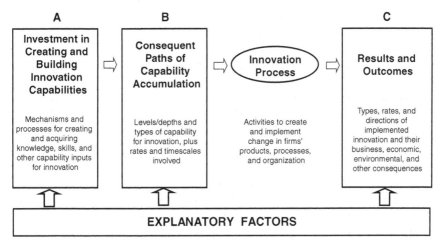

Fig. 2.3. Innovative capability accumulation in latecomer firms: what needs explaining?

(e.g. as illustrated in Table 2.5). Or interest might center on the levels (or "depths") of innovation capability reached by firms at comparable stages in their own development or in the development of industries or economies. Interest might also center, for instance, on inter-firm differences in their success in negotiating transitions through particularly significant discontinuities between levels of innovation capability.

Some approaches to examining such variability have sought to use conventional measures of R&D activity as a proxy for the scale of innovation capabilities in firms. But, as is well known, this reflects only a fraction of a firm's innovative capability; and it reflects none of it in the case of firms that have only non-R&D-based innovative capabilities. This limitation has been overcome by studies using qualitative assessments of a wider range of capabilities—as in several of the studies reviewed earlier in Section 2.3, using variations around the scale of capability levels in Table 2.5. As illustrated in the recent work of Esin Yoruk (2011), this kind of approach can be simplified to provide data that allows quantitative analysis of inter-firm differences in paths of capability accumulation over considerable periods of time. In addition, Oslo Manual-type innovation surveys capture data about a much wider range of "inputs" to innovation than merely R&D. As the quality, number, and accessibility of such surveys increase in developing and emerging economies, they should permit increasingly meaningful analyses of variability in the paths of capability accumulation in latecomer firms. As yet, however, much of the research in this area does not focus on variability in the capability inputs to innovation per se, but on indicators of the outputs from it—the last component of the framework in Figure 2.3.

This third component—(C)—is concerned with the results and outcomes of implemented innovation—or, more indirectly, with the outcomes from prior investment in creating and accumulating capabilities to undertake such innovation. The main issues here are about the types of innovation (e.g. "new-to-the-firm" and "new-to-the-world" types, as discussed earlier in Section 2.2.3), or about the rate of innovation and its direction—as reflected in a wide variety of different indicators.[24] Research about such innovation outcomes in latecomer firms and industries has given increasing attention to framing the analysis explicitly in terms of "catching up," and two important developments in that kind of analysis merit much more attention.

First, as noted earlier, there is a growing interest in bringing questions about the *direction* of innovation, not just its rate, into the discussion of catch-up. This then leads to the important distinction between path-following and path-creating forms of catching up. Arguably, the latter poses greater demands for deeper levels of innovation capability, something that seems to be increasingly important in an age that faces rising pressures to generate much greater diversity in the directions of innovation in order to address the challenges of persisting poverty and rising sustainability.

Second, increasing attention is being given to an important distinction in the general idea of catching up: between "intra-national" and "inter-national" catching up. These concepts are not defined consistently in different studies, but essentially they involve improvements in performance by latecomer firms relative to (i) benchmarks that are within latecomer firms' domestic economies, and (ii) performance benchmarks outside those economies that constitute some form of international "best practice" or "frontier" (Jung and Lee, 2010; Iacovone and Crespi, 2010). This distinction is important because different kinds of explanatory variable seem to be important with respect to the two kinds of catching up. However, the evidence about how they differ appears to be at least partially contradictory. In examining catch-up between Korean and Japanese firms, as reflected in their total factor productivity (TFP), Jung and Lee (2010) distinguish between sector-level and firm-specific characteristics that may be important in influencing catch-up paths—with the latter including among other things "innovation capabilities" along the lines

---

[24] This range spans across: (i) indirect reflections of purely technical performance such as patents (Joo and Lee, 2009, is a recent example); (ii) more direct measures of technical/physical performance of products and processes (for example, the "coke rate" in blast furnaces, as used in the analysis of Brazilian steel companies by Figueiredo, 2002); (iii) the combination of such physical performance measures with economic data to form, for example, unit-cost trends for processes (as in the classic case studies by Enos, 1962, and Hollander, 1965), trends in price-performance ratios for products, or trends in the energy-intensity or carbon-intensity of overall production paths; (iv) a wide range of economic indicators such as partial or total factor productivity ratios or export performance indicators; and (v) various measures of business performance relating to finance, market shares, or simply long-term growth.

of component (B) in Figure 2.3 above. They suggest that: "... the sector-level variables only affect international TFP catch-up, whereas the *firm-level variables* only determine *intranational catch-up*" (p. 23, emphasis added). In examining catch-up in Mexican firms, Iacavone and Crespi (2010) also identify a set of firm-specific variables, and among these they emphasize various "technological capabilities." However, instead of contrasting these with industry-level variables, they focus on the more general issue of variation in openness to trade—albeit reflected in firm-specific differences in trade integration with international markets. With respect to the firm-level variables, they reach different conclusions from Jung and Lee: "In summary, our results suggest that building *firm level technological capabilities* is important for catching-up *with the global frontier*." In contrast, policy focused only on trade "will help with the convergence toward the best technological practices available locally but it will run short of encouraging convergence with the global frontier" (p. 13, emphasis added).

2.5.2. A Framework for Explanation: Extending the Range of Variables

We turn here to review types of analysis that seek to explain one or more of the components of innovation capability accumulation that were summarized in Figure 2.3 above.[25] Our broad view is that these have focused quite narrowly on a limited range of explanatory variables, while giving much less attention to others that seem no less interesting or important. Our approach here involves a different balance. We comment only briefly on the areas of explanation that are already well-trodden, and give more emphasis to some that are relatively neglected.

We start by extending the still useful framework for explanatory analysis in this area that was outlined by Sanjaya Lall nearly 20 years ago (Lall, 1992). Lall's explanatory interest centered on "the development" of firm-level technological capability and, as we have done in this chapter, he emphasized that the primary driving force for this was investment undertaken by firms—in other words, he highlighted the importance of Component (A) in Figure 2.3. However, he saw such investment as a response to external and internal stimuli. This led him to distinguish between firm-specific factors and factors that are common to countries, distinguishing between "incentives" and

---

[25] Some forms of explanatory analysis examine relationships *among* the kinds of variable summarized in Figure 2.3. For example, as noted above, Iacavone and Crespi (2010) and Jung and Lee (2010) examined the relationships between aspects of innovation capability (Component B) and of firms' catch-up performance (Component C)—though in both cases the selected aspects of catch-up performance were not seen as exclusively determined by innovation capabilities, and other explanatory variables were included.

"institutions" at the country level (p. 169). However, he had little to say about industry-specific and global-level factors. As these are also important, we add them to Lall's framework and organize this discussion around the following five areas of explanation: (i) firm-specific factors, (ii) industry-level factors, (iii) economy-wide incentives, (iv) economy-wide institutions, and (v) the implications of global production networks.

Firm-specific factors

Several characteristics of firms have been considered quite often as providing explanations of, or at least correlates with, the innovative capabilities of firms: age, size, ownership, and market orientation.

Among these, perhaps the most commonly examined are the age and size of firms—e.g. Westphal et al. (1990) on Thai firms; Romijn (1999) in a similar study in Pakistan, Wignaraja (1998) on garment and engineering firms in Sri Lanka; Wignaraja and Ikiara (1999) on similar firms in Kenya; Deraniyagala and Semboja (1999) on engineering firms in Tanzania; and Wignaraja (2002) on garment firms in Mauritius. Given their common cross-sectional design, such studies have said little about dynamic aspects of innovation capability creation and accumulation, but they nevertheless suggest considerable heterogeneity. On the one hand, large firms, or older more established and experienced firms, appear in some circumstances to be particularly important vehicles for building significant depths of innovation capability, and also for using those capabilities to catch up in existing lines of business or to diversify production—either within the firms themselves or more widely in the economy via the spillover effects they generate. On the other hand, large and/or experienced firms do not play these roles. What probably matters more than size or experience per se are other mediating variables.

Considerable emphasis has also been placed on the influence of firm ownership on firms' innovation capabilities or innovation performance, in particular the difference between foreign and domestic (national) ownership.[26] Again, most studies of this have been cross-sectional and unable to say much about the dynamics of capability building. When that has not been the case and the creation of innovation capabilities in MNC subsidiaries has been examined over time, almost all studies have been about subsidiaries in advanced country contexts (e.g. Cantwell and Mudambi, 2005). Indeed, until fairly recently the dominant opinion was that MNC subsidiaries simply did not develop such capabilities in any significant way in the context of

---

[26] Despite the fact that the question addressed is inherently comparative, a surprising feature of many studies that address it is that they are not comparative. Many examine MNC subsidiaries alone, and conclusions suggest, at least implicitly, the existence of difference from what would happen under domestic ownership.

developing or emerging economies. However, as demonstrated in several more recent studies (e.g. Athreye and Cantwell, 2007) and elaborated more extensively in Chapter 1 of this book, this has been changing. This has been especially evident in the case of MNC subsidiaries in the large and knowledge-rich economies of India and China, but has also been demonstrated by a growing number of studies in other late industrializing economies—e.g. in Brazil (Quadros and Queiroz, 2001; Boehe, 2007; Quadros and Consoni, 2009); in Argentina (Marin and Bell, 2006, 2010); and across a range of countries in Africa, Asia, and Latin America (Rasiah, 2004). However, in all these studies the picture is one of considerable heterogeneity. A substantial proportion of MNC subsidiaries, though usually a minority, have developed considerable depths of innovation capability, and these capabilities seem to be increasingly used to play significant roles both within the innovation systems of their parent corporations and within the innovation systems of their host economies. But there are also substantial proportions that demonstrate none of these characteristics, or only weak forms of them. As yet, explanation for this heterogeneity is poorly developed, not least because of the scarcity of work that is designed to be both comparative between different types of ownership and longitudinal to capture the dynamics of capability deepening over time.

Considerable attention has also been given to the relationship between latecomer firms' innovation capabilities and their market orientation, specifically their degree of engagement in export markets. Some studies have focused primarily on the role of innovative capabilities in sustaining export performance—e.g. Ernst et al. (1998) on the textile and electronics industries in Asia. However, many have addressed the reverse relationship to that examined here: the role of firms' export intensity as a factor contributing to the explanation of change in their innovative capabilities. As examined by Hobday (1995) via case studies of the electronics industry in Asia between the 1960s and early 1990s, the argument about that relationship is that it involves a dual effect. First, involvement in export markets exposes firms to competitive pressures that induce greater investment in creating and deepening innovation capabilities; and second, it provides latecomer firms with opportunities to acquire the kinds of knowledge, skill, and experience needed for such capability deepening—primarily via interactions with customers in global value chains.

The significance of this dual effect has been examined in studies with larger samples of firms—for example, by Rajah Rasiah and colleagues covering several countries in Asia, Africa, and Latin America (Rasiah, 2004, 2006). More broadly, the relationships have been examined in the "learning by exporting" literature—e.g. Girma et al. (2004) and Greenaway et al. (2005); and country-specific studies by Arne et al. (2004) on countries in Sub-Saharan Africa; Isgut (2001) on Colombia; Clerides et al. (1998) on Colombia, Mexico, and Morocco; Delgado et al. (2002) on Spain; and Aw and Hwang (1995) on Taiwan and Korea. But widely differing results emerge from such analyses.

One issue contributing to this heterogeneity is the self-selection problem: the difficulty of untangling whether positive associations between indicators of exporting and firm capabilities reflect (i) the occurrence of learning as a result of exporting or (ii) relatively high levels of exporting by firms that have already accumulated capabilities to be efficient and competitive in international markets. Some recent studies have suggested that both may be important, as reflected in the higher capabilities of exporting firms before their entry into export markets and their continuing capability accumulation subsequently. Such a combination perhaps indicates the importance of mediating factors that shape the relationship between the intensity of firms' exporting and the creation and accumulation of their innovative capabilities.

One such mediating factor has been suggested by studies of the governance of global value chains (Humphrey and Schmitz, 2002; Gereffi et al., 2005). These have argued that exporting in global markets involves engaging with types of value chain that differ, among other things, in their governance structures. Some of these may facilitate the deepening of innovative capabilities, as in Hobday's East Asian case studies; but others may constrain it. Much of the evidence points toward the latter. For example, Humphrey and Schmitz (2004) suggest that, under the most common forms of chain governance, firms in developing countries may incrementally upgrade their products and process, but their "functional upgrading" (i.e. their deepening of design, innovation, and marketing activities) may be severely restricted over long periods. Similarly D'Costa (2002) has argued that high levels of export-orientation have locked Indian software firms into dependent non-innovative growth paths; and Bazan and Navas-Alemán (2004) show that Brazilian shoe producers were for a long period merely design-taking producers locked into "captive" relationships with global buyers. Indeed, some types of exporting relationship may not merely constrain the positive deepening of suppliers' capabilities but induce explicitly negative effects—as demonstrated for instance by Rabellotti (2004) in the case of Italian shoe producers whose engagement in some kinds of export value chain led to functional "downgrading" as producers were pushed to abandon design and marketing activities and to focus only on production. But two aspects of research design and method commonly limit the usefulness of such studies in understanding the relationship between exporting and the accumulation of capabilities to innovate.

One aspect is the propensity to focus observations of innovation capability on only the most visible dimensions of such capability, such as R&D—often drawing negative conclusions from observations of its absence, while neglecting significant elements of less visible capability accumulation, often associated with various kinds of design and engineering. This may be combined with underestimation of the time required to develop elements of innovative capability, leading to misleading negative conclusions from short-term studies that cover periods of time that are inadequate to reveal trends of change. Lema

(2010) suggests that this combination accounts for a succession of studies of the Indian software industry, like those of D'Costa (2002), that have reached negative conclusions about the learning effects of exporting rather than illuminating the role of exporting in contributing to the "slow" paths of cumulative, incremental deepening of innovation capabilities that *have* taken place.

The second methodological limitation has been the scarcity of comparison. For example, analyses of global value chains may compare learning patterns associated with global chains with different governance structures, but they rarely compare those with the capability deepening that is associated with *domestic* (non-global) value chains. However, in one exception, Bazan and Navas-Alemán (2004) show how some Brazilian shoe producers broke out of their long-standing "captive" relationships with global buyers and deepened their capabilities in design and marketing as a result of learning opportunities that emerged when they turned to *domestic* markets. There has also been limited comparison between export-linked learning and learning by importing. Yet Marcelle (2004) notes the importance of capability building in African telecommunications firms in association with their imports of equipment, engineering services, and project management services for investment projects. However, in contrast with common arguments about the general incidence of such learning effects, she showed that they were present and strong in only a few of the 26 cases and absent or weak in most.

Thus, cutting across the studies of learning-by-exporting, it is hard to resist a broad interpretation that there is nothing *inherent* in exporting that either supports or constrains the development of firms' innovative capabilities. Instead, it seems that one or more other factors differentiate firms that more or less effectively exploit their market positions in ways that contribute significantly to a cumulative deepening of their innovative capabilities. The opportunities for such active, capability-building strategies may often be particularly great for firms that engage in export markets. But such opportunities may also be there for firms that engage in domestic markets—for example, Brazilian shoe producers (Bazan and Navas-Alemán, 2004) or African telecommunications operators (Marcelle, 2004). They may also be significant for firms that engage in *both* kinds of market, such as the South African producer of mining machinery noted in Box 2.3 earlier.

Thus the key issue seems to be not about the learning implication of market orientations per se, but about factors that influence the effectiveness with which firms actively seek to exploit the potential learning opportunities that are latent in, not automatically delivered by, their market positions and transactions.[27] Indeed, that may be the lesson to draw with respect to all the

---

[27] Our emphasis on this learning-related exploitation of market relationships seems to be very similar to John Mathews's stress on the role of "leveraging" their (mainly international) linkages by East Asian latecomer firms in order to achieve cumulative learning effects (Mathews, 2006).

firm-level characteristics reviewed above. Age (i.e. experience), size, and (at least some types of) foreign ownership all hold latent opportunities for deepening the innovative capabilities of firms, but other factors seem to shape how effectively those opportunities are exploited. While some of these arise at other levels, the range of relevant firm-level variables must surely be wider than the few that are most commonly examined.

For example, scattered observations suggest that greater attention should be given to one such variable—firms' "leadership." As pointed out by Pavitt (1990, 2005) with respect to innovation leaders in advanced economies, technology strategies and innovation processes involve many professions, functional tribes, and political forces, and hence the effective development and implementation of strategies and processes also involves advocacy, battles, and negotiation. Consequently, an important role in building firms' techno-logical capabilities is played by leadership—not only at the top management level but also among managers at other levels in the firm and among the groups and coalitions that shape its strategic options. Leonard-Barton (1995) stresses similar issues with respect to building, nurturing, and sustaining core technological capabilities (p. 265).

The same issue has surfaced in several studies of innovation capability building in latecomer firms. For example, Kim (1997, 1998) showed that, in the Korean firms Hyundai and Samsung, leadership played a critically impor-tant role in designing strategies for external knowledge leverage and in periodically constructing an internal "sense of crisis" that helped to push these firms through important capability transitions on the basis of intensive knowledge acquisition and internal absorption (as in Figure 2.2 earlier). In the case of the Brazilian steelmaker USIMINAS, Figueiredo (2001) showed the importance of similar types of leadership behavior that both shielded the then state-owned firm from external vested interests and political interference and created the internal power coalitions that were crucial to implement consistent strategies for innovation capability building. As in Hyundai and Samsung, USIMINAS' leadership was able to set challenging targets and instill into the firm a long-term and company-wide value and commitment to innovation capability building. Marcelle (2004) notes the importance of similar leadership issues as an influence on capability building in African telecommunications firms. Such insights are, however, merely tantalizing glimpses of the possible importance of a multi-dimension concept that seems to be important but remains largely unexplored in even a moderately systematic fashion.

Industry-level factors

There has been little systematic analysis of how inter-industry differences influence the paths of capability deepening in latecomer firms. This is a little surprising because, since the work of Pavitt (1984) on sectoral differences in patterns of innovation, the analysis of such differences has become a major field of enquiry. At the heart of this has been the work of Malerba and colleagues on sectoral systems of innovation, with their emphasis on differences in the technological regimes and knowledge bases of industries, as well as on differences in sectoral innovation actors, networks between them, and institutional contexts in which they operate (Malerba and Orsenigo, 1996; Malerba et al., 1997; Malerba, 2002, 2004, 2005). From the perspective of this book, however, two constraining features of this body of work have been important. First, it has been concerned almost exclusively with differences between sectors *within manufacturing.*[28] Second, until very recently it has focused almost exclusively on experience in *the context of the advanced economies.*

The first issue is important because it leaves out patterns of innovation in industries that account for very large segments of emerging market economies—not just the obviously important cases of agriculture and health care services, but also (i) other primary sectors like mining and petroleum; (ii) infrastructure sectors like energy supply, transport, water, sanitation, and telecommunications services, as well as (iii) the construction and engineering services industries supplying both those groups of industries. Moreover, it seems arguable that the differences across such sectors, and between them and manufacturing, may be much greater than sectoral differences within manufacturing.

Nevertheless, for the moment we focus here on the second feature—the focus on advanced economies. This is important because one consequence is that the research has been concerned with sector/industry systems in which firms (among other actors) have already accumulated significantly deep innovation capabilities—i.e. they are already located toward the top of Table 2.5 earlier. Consequently, the issues addressed are primarily about how sector differences influence how innovation is executed at differing rates and in different directions, not about how capabilities to innovate are created and accumulated in the first place. In other words, differences between technological regimes and sectors are examined as providing possible explanations for only component (C) in Figure 2.3 above, not Components (A) or (B). Nevertheless one might expect sector/industry differences to have a significant influence on the capability-creating processes in latecomer firms. Two strands of research have begun to move in that direction, but they still shed limited light on the issue.

First, a body of research on sectoral innovation systems in developing and emerging economies has begun to emerge (e.g. Malerba and Mani, 2009; Joseph, 2009). However, such work is still preoccupied with the basic task of

---

[28] There has been a little work on some service industries, but this also has been quite narrowly focused.

seeking to understand the main characteristics of sectoral systems in these contexts and how they emerge and evolve over time. Very few studies are systematically comparative across different types of system and, when they are, this is undertaken in order to illuminate patterns of system difference, not to consider such differences as independent variables that might influence the creation and accumulation of innovation capabilities by firms as the core actors in the systems.

However, a second strand of work, centered on the catch-up experience of Korea and Taiwan, has moved a little further in that direction (Lee and Lim, 2001; Amsden and Chu, 2003; Kim and Lee, 2003; Park and Lee, 2006; Jung and Lee, 2010). Focusing heavily on key features of technological regimes as developed by Malerba and colleagues (technological opportunity, cumulative-ness of innovation, appropriability, and other features of the knowledge base),[29] this has sought to explain technological dimensions of catching up at the level of firms and industries in Korea and Taiwan between the 1980s and early 2000s. However, while this work explores important aspects of this relatively late stage of catching up in those economies, it sheds limited light on the accumulation of capabilities at earlier stages. Hence, for example, it cuts into the East Asian catch-up story only *after* one of the most important phases of structural transformation in sectoral innovation systems had been largely completed—the shift from structures in which governments played the domi-nant role in funding and even performing R&D to one where firms played the dominant role.[30]

But stretching this strand of work to explore such earlier stages of capability accumulation in East Asian or other contexts would involve more than just a re-orientation toward different time periods. It would require quite funda-mental change in at least two core aspects of the approach. One is methodo-logical: regarding the pervasive reliance on patent data. This involves the use of such data as a basis for both (i) measures of the rate and direction of catching up—one of the dependent variables in the analysis, as in component (C) in Figure 2.3 earlier; and (ii) measures of key features of the sectoral technological regimes—the key explanatory variables. But such patent data are simply not generated by industrial innovation systems before they reach stages when internationally patentable inventions become significant forms of inno-vative activity—i.e. stages that are roughly comparable to those in Korea and Taiwan by around the 1980s. The second need for change is more conceptual and theoretical: the focus on characteristics of "technological regimes" as the

---

[29] Other variables considered particularly relevant to the catch-up context were also included.

[30] In Korea, for example, the ratio of public/private expenditure on R&D had reversed from around 70:30 in the early 1970s to about 30:70 by the mid-1980s. Taiwan also was well on its way through a similar transition, though somewhat less pronounced because of the different organi-zational structure of industrial production.

key explanatory variables. This theoretical framework was developed to help understand the kinds of formally organized and R&D-intensive innovative activity undertaken close to the international frontier by firms in the advanced economies. It seems highly likely that differences in other kinds of sectoral characteristic will be more important in influencing investment in capability creation and accumulation at earlier stages of the catch-up process. For example, even if one considers only inter-sectoral differences *within* manufacturing, fairly simple distinctions between heavy process-type industries and those producing discrete products may involve important differences in the types of knowledge needed for innovation; in how it is appropriated in the international economy—in both organizational and legal terms; in the learning processes and mechanisms needed to acquire it; and in the kinds of organizational arrangement within which it is effectively accumulated in latecomer firms and industries. These differences may have important implications for the rate of capability accumulation, and for management and policy. Even within the discrete products industries, there may be differences along these lines between standardized and customized (high volume/low volume) production.[31]

There is, therefore, a major challenge in this area. It seems inherently likely that inter-industry differences have important influences on the ways in which latecomer firms create and accumulate innovation capabilities at all stages of the catch-up process. It also seems plausible that such differences will have important implications for managing capability creation and accumulation at firm level, and probably also for defining policy frameworks within which that management is undertaken. In other words, there are strong reasons for generating much greater understanding about this issue than is currently available. But addressing this challenge will call for new theoretical and methodological bases for research, not simply for its reorientation.

Economy-wide incentives

A central thread of emphasis through this chapter has been that a very large part of the process of creating and accumulating capabilities to innovate is an investment activity that necessarily takes place in enterprises. It requires firms to commit explicit financial outlays and considerable managerial effort—as at (A) in Figure 2.3 earlier. But returns to the assets created by that investment are usually uncertain and difficult to appropriate. This is partly because,

---

[31] Much more attention might also be given in the context of latecomer firms to the interesting distinction drawn by Jensen and colleagues between two modes of learning and innovation in Danish firms—STI (science, technology, and innovation) and DUI (doing, using, and interacting) modes (Jensen et al., 2007). Although, strictly speaking, this distinction was used to summarize *firm-level* characteristics in the original development of the idea, it seems also to reflect generalizations that characterize industries.

especially in the early stages of the cumulative process, a large proportion consists of human capital—a highly mobile type of asset for which the social returns are likely to be much greater than the returns to the private asset-creating investor. Also, compared with investment in the innovation process itself (i.e. investment that *uses* existing innovation capabilities to undertake and implement innovation activities), the *prior* investment in creating capabilities for innovation is more distant in time from realizing returns from the results of innovation—so further diminishing private incentives.

Thus, as occurs with many other forms of knowledge asset, the process of creating and accumulating innovation capabilities involves a considerable divergence between the social and private incentives for making the necessary investment. Sanjaya Lall, among many others in this field, attached considerable importance to this issue, and highlighted in his framework of influences on the rate of capability accumulation three economy-wide factors that influenced private investment in these kinds of knowledge asset: (i) macroeconomic incentives, (ii) incentives from competition, and (iii) incentives from factor markets (Lall, 1992). Despite the importance of the first, we focus here on the other two.[32]

Incentives from competition are usually discussed, as in Lall (1992), primarily with reference to the degree or form of competition that arises from differences in trade policy, primarily with respect to trade protection versus openness. The basic argument with respect to trade protection and learning is well known—though not always accepted.[33] In some circumstances, a degree of protection from trade competition may be an important condition for initial stages of technological learning by latecomer firms, but high levels and prolonged periods of protection will usually reduce incentives to invest in capability creation. Consequently, as in the experience of East Asia, even short periods of protection need to be matched by incentives for performance and efficiency. However, managing this balanced and controlled form of protection requires demanding levels of bureaucratic competence combined with particular political structures and relationships. Unless these conditions can be met, the effect of restricted trade competition can be negative with respect to both short-term efficiency and longer-term investment in cumulatively deeper capabilities.

But, despite the extensive discussion of these issues over many years, trade policy has an inherently limited influence on the accumulation of innovation

---

[32] This is not for the same reason as Lall who noted that the impact on investment and capability building arising from growth, stability, sensible balance-of-payments, monetary, or fiscal policies was "obvious and need not be discussed in detail" (p. 171). Instead, we pass it by here because the issue has attracted little systematic analysis—though an exception is the work of Valeria Arza (Arza 2005a, 2005b) who has demonstrated the negative effect of macroeconomic instability on firms' expenditure on R&D and fixed capital in Argentina.

[33] For one strongly dissenting view, see Pack and Saggi (2006).

capabilities since it is primarily designed to influence *production* capacity, not *innovation* capabilities. Protectionist policy is intended to alter the composition of production by influencing the entry of firms into new industries and their survival in existing ones; and open trade policy is intended to ensure the allocative efficiency of production. At best, therefore, trade policy has only a partial and indirect influence on the development of innovation capabilities.

On the one hand, the influence of protection on capability accumulation can impinge on only a narrow range of capabilities. The conventional argument is that by fostering firms' entry into new kinds of industry, while also supporting a period of continuing survival, protection enables "learning-by-doing" to occur in those firms. But the only kind of learning opportunity that is directly attributable to trade protection is the more or less passive form of learning from "doing *production*." Hence the conventional argument about protection and learning applies only to the strengthening of *production* capabilities and perhaps relatively simple kinds of innovation capability. It is not relevant to the kinds of innovation capability whose accumulation depends much more heavily on learning by *actively investing* in the creation of capabilities.[34] Indeed, by reducing the competition-derived incentives for firms to undertake such investment, protection for the continuing existence of production may have a negative effect on the accumulation of innovation capabilities.[35]

On the other hand, the influence of trade openness on capability accumulation can only be relatively indirect. The conventional argument is that the competitive pressures from openness will stimulate firms to raise efficiency and improve other dimensions of competitiveness, and this will lead to the intensification of innovative activity by firms. However, this does nothing directly to address the divergence between private and social incentives for explicit investment in capability deepening.

At the same time, in addition to those limitations, trade policy involves large costs as a means of fostering the development and accumulation of innovation capabilities. On the one hand, trade protection is likely to reduce efficiency in production across the whole economy; while on the other trade openness is likely to result in only slow structural change in production, with persisting specialization in areas of *existing* comparative advantage.

---

[34] Learning by "doing *innovation*" is a different issue. It can indeed contribute to the deepening of innovation capabilities, but it depends heavily on prior investment in creating capabilities to undertake innovation in the first place. Such investment-driven learning seems to be particularly important in connection with capability deepening that involves crossing qualitative discontinuities in the cumulative process.

[35] It is sometimes argued that trade policy can and should be aligned to foster the development of particularly "technology-intensive" types of industry and that this will carry with it an inherently high level of localized "innovation intensity." However, there is little that is *inherently* innovation-intensive about so-called "technology-intensive" industries. The extent to which, and the rate at which, latecomer firms develop innovation capabilities alongside their production activities in such industries varies, just as it does for other kinds of industry.

These limitations are partly recognized in the conventional discussion of trade policy where it is argued that subsidies specifically focused on the relevant "market failure" are much more efficient than "second-best" protection-type measures. This shifts the discussion from economy-wide competition-centered incentives to Lall's third set of economy-wide incentives: those associated with factor markets, and in particular with the private underinvestment in human-resource-intensive innovation capabilities that is likely to arise from the gap between private and social returns.

Within that framework, subsidies specifically focused on "learning" are commonly seen as the most appropriate means of addressing that kind of market failure. But the argument then usually centers on one or other of two kinds of subsidy that are largely irrelevant to issues about investment in the cumulative deepening of technological capabilities.

- The first is about subsidies for investment in production capacity and its continued existence over a significant learning period. But, as discussed above, this argument rests on misplaced beliefs about what can be achieved through "learning by doing" *production*. It also leads to erroneous views about the magnitude of the costs involved—the costs of subsidizing production, rather than the much more narrowly focused costs of subsidizing investment in creating innovation capabilities.
- The second is about subsidies for "R&D." But this fails to recognize that R&D is just the tip of a deep capability iceberg, and that a long and costly process of capability deepening needs to have taken place before capabilities are in place to make effective use of R&D subsidies.

In other words, the most common focus of discussion about policy responses to the gap between private and social returns to investment in innovation capabilities has very limited relevance for the situation facing latecomer firms.

Economy-wide institutions

Increasing attention has been given to the relationship between technological advance and "institutions"—mainly in the context of the more developed economies. As yet however, "there remains a significant gap between aspirations and achievements" (Nelson, 2008: 1). Much the same can be said about the efforts of scholars in examining the relationship between "institutions" and technological capability accumulation in latecomer firms.

A large part of the difficulty in this area stems from the fact that the term "institution" means significantly different things to different authors: "... the notion of institutions itself is not yet a coherent concept, at least not across the various users of the term ..." and "... we believe it is a mistake to try and make the term 'institutions' cover too much conceptual ground" (Nelson and

Sampat, 2001: 32 and 39). As a step toward greater clarity, Nelson and Sampat peel off part of the excessive scope by identifying what they call "social technologies"—the complement to physical technologies that make up production routines. This still leaves "institutions" as "a diverse lot of things" that support social technologies (Nelson, 2008: 3).

As a very rough distinction, studies of the influence of institutions on capability accumulation in latecomer firms might be seen as covering three categories within that "diverse lot of things."[36]

(i) Institutions as specifically knowledge-related institutes and organizations surrounding latecomer firms—such as those concerned with education, training, standards, research, and so forth;

(ii) Institutions as complex regimes of interconnected segments of implemented public policy within which firms operate—for example as the main focus of the discussion in Lall (1992) or Rasiah (1996);

(iii) Institutions as aspects of the political and bureaucratic relationships and structures that underpin particular kinds of policy regime.

The first of these areas is addressed extensively in the growing body of work on innovation systems in developing and emerging economies (for recent overviews, see Malerba and Mani, 2009; Lundval et al., 2009). We have also already touched more specifically on the role of universities in Section 2.4.2. We therefore comment here only on the shifting structure of relationships associated with some current trends in the evolution of global production networks.

The implications of global production networks

We can ask whether the fragmentation of production, the emergence of global production networks (Ernst and Kim, 2002) and a new division of labor between firms in more open innovation systems will alter the process of creating and accumulating innovation capabilities in latecomer firms. This issue seems to be potentially important because the organizational decomposition of innovation constitutes a major element in the breakdown of Chandlerian-type firms in the advanced economies, and hence also makes a large contribution to breaking down the dyadic relationships between such firms that have underpinned not only a large part of our understanding about accumulating innovation capabilities in latecomer firms, but probably also a large part of the reality of what has actually occurred. Consequently, to the extent that the fragmentation and modularization of production takes place as one element in the shift toward a post-Chandlerian world and the breakdown of those kinds of dyadic relationship, there are likely to be quite fundamental

---

[36] These do not constitute an attempt to provide a comprehensive definition of "institutions"—merely a list of three areas of work in this field of interest.

changes in the processes of creating and accumulating innovation capabilities in latecomer firms. That possibility can be sketched out with reference to both the "supply" and "demand" sides of the learning relationships.

On the supply side in the advanced economies, individual firms will have available much less comprehensive sets of knowledge and skill. This is likely to arise in two ways. On the one hand, with a much greater degree of vertical disintegration of *production* activities, individual firms will know about much narrower areas of technology. On the other hand, with a much greater decomposition of innovative activities, they will have internally available much "thinner slices" of innovative capability. In both respects, they are likely to retain minimal competences to ensure their own internal integration of outsourced production and outsourced innovation, but these coordination capabilities are unlikely to be a basis from which latecomer firms can learn about the kinds of technology or the kinds of innovation that mostly lie outside the boundaries of the individual firms. Consequently, instead of connecting into the kinds of dyadic inter-firm learning relationship that seem to have been important in contributing to effective capability deepening in latecomer firms over the last four or five decades, those firms, whether they are subsidiaries of MNCs or independent firms trying to leverage other kinds of relationship, may have to engage in much more complex networked learning relationships with a much wider range of firms (and other organizations) in order to develop an adequately comprehensive base of capability for effective innovation. At the very least, this magnifies the demands on managing the process of learning and integrating the components of much more organizationally decomposed learning mechanisms.

This type of learning process has been evident in some industries, such as petroleum, where considerable organizational specialization in different areas of the industry's technology has existed for a long time, alongside the outsourcing by oil companies of substantial elements of their innovative activity. Consequently, for example, since the late 1960s Petrobrás in Brazil has had to draw on knowledge from a wide range of different firms as it progressively deepened its innovation capabilities in offshore oil technologies (Dantas and Bell, 2009). It is striking that this was achieved in a classic Chandlerian-type latecomer firm. Petrobrás was a multi-product diversified firm with a considerable depth of innovation capabilities, and it had developed strong internal capabilities for managing its "open learning process," and for integrating the component elements of capability that it acquired from different sources. The nucleus of that capability was an R&D facility that was for many years at least as much a vehicle for acquiring and accumulating *existing* knowledge and innovation skills across the organization's multi-product and multi-technology portfolio as it was a center for creating *new* knowledge and developing *novel* technologies. In these ways, Petrobrás had many similarities with the Chandlerian-type firms that played such a significant role in the accumulation of innovation capabilities in latecomer firms in Japan, Korea, and Taiwan.

But that raises questions about whether latecomer firms on the "demand side" of such international learning relationships will continue to have the same kinds of Chandlerian characteristics. At least two kinds of consequence might follow.

- First, individual latecomer firms will have limited internal abilities and resources to support and manage learning relationships across the multiple sources likely to be involved in more "open learning" organizational structures. Moreover, if effective innovation by the latecomer requires geographically close networks of similarly specialized innovators in the latecomer economy, the effectiveness of a firm's own efforts to create and accumulate its capabilities for innovation will depend on similar capability-creating efforts in the other firms and organizations. This raises questions about interdependence in the process of building up complementary sets of capabilities both in and around latecomer firms, and resolving problems of "system failure" will become much more prominent alongside the problems about market failure.

- Second, this in turn might make more significant a particular kind of threshold and discontinuity in the process of deepening innovation capabilities. A significant jump may be needed to move from (i) narrowly focused, innovative production of components, subsystems, and specialized services to (ii) the achievement of competitive positions in markets for the complete, integrated final goods. In the case of the commercial aircraft industry, for example, Japanese producers seem to have been unable to cross such a threshold (Kimura, 2007).

In considering these possible consequences of the disappearance of Chandlerian firms in both the advanced and latecomer economies, one should bear in mind the multi-dimensional transforming role that they have played in the latter case. Not only have they acted as vehicles for deepening innovative capabilities with respect to specific lines of production—as in the case of Embraer for aircraft, Hyundai in automobiles, or Samsung in semiconductors. They have also played the critically important economic role of fostering the bases of capability for changing the structure of production in the economy. This was, for example, very important in Korea where the ability of the *Chaebol* to enter a succession of new industries depended on their accumulation of internal innovation capabilities in the form of design, engineering, technology acquisition, and investment management capabilities—what Amsden and Hikino (1994) described as "project execution capabilities." The same pattern was evident in aspects of the diversification of firms in Taiwan. In addition, in some situations, capability accumulation within Chandlerian-type firms has been the basis for structural change in the economy not only via the internal diversification of multi-product firms, but also via the "incubation" of capabilities that spilled over or spun off to open up new lines of production.

This discussion about the possible implications of transition to a post-Chandlerian world is almost entirely a matter of speculation. But behind this lies a growing body of argument that at least some form of fundamental transition away from Chandlerian types of firm may be an emerging reality. Langlois (2003), for example, has argued that the "visible hand" of the Chandlerian firm is vanishing, while Lazonick (2005) has argued that:

> The hierarchical and functional division of labor that, when integrated into learning organizations, generated innovation in the past cannot necessarily be expected to do so in the future when faced with changes in technology, markets and competition . . . (p. 50)

Subsequently (Lazonick, 2010), he has taken the argument further:

> In the 2000s it can be fairly said that the Chandlerian corporation has ceased to exist. (p. 345)

Our concluding observation is therefore that this apparent global transition, together with its possible implications for accumulating innovation capabilities in latecomer firms, merits considerable further attention. If even partially valid, that combination of current speculations may force us to change considerable parts of what we have learned about the processes and mechanisms of capability accumulation in latecomer firms over the last 40–50 years. Beyond that, the practice of management and policy with respect to capability accumulation in latecomers may have to change dramatically—just as we have begun to get a better grasp on these practicalities with respect to capability accumulation in such firms in the Chandlerian age.

REFERENCES

Abramovitz, M. (1986), "Catching up, Forging Ahead, and Falling Behind," *Journal of Economic History*, 66(2): 385–406.

Amsden, A. H. (1989), *Asia's Next Giant: South Korea and Late Industrialization*, New York: Oxford University Press.

—— (1997), "South Korea: Enterprising Groups and Entrepreneurial Government," in A. Chandler, F. Amatori, and T. Hikino, *Big Business and the Wealth of Nations*, Cambridge: Cambridge University Press.

—— (2001), *The Rise of "The Rest": Challenges to the West from Late-Industrializing Economies*, Oxford and New York: Oxford University Press.

—— and Chu, W.-W. (2003), *Beyond Late Development: Taiwan's Upgrading Policies*, Cambridge, Mass.: MIT Press.

—— and Hikino, T. (1994), "Project Execution Capability, Organizational Know-How, and Conglomerate Corporate Growth in Late Industrialization," *Industrial and Corporate Change*, 3(1): 111–47.

—— and Tschang, F. T. (2003), "A New Approach to Assessing the Technological Complexity of Different Categories of R&D (with Examples from Singapore)," *Research Policy*, 32: 553–72.

Ariffin, N. (2000), "The Internationalisation of Innovative Capabilities: The Malaysian Electronics Industry," unpublished PhD thesis, SPRU, University of Sussex, Brighton, UK.

—— and Bell, M. (1999), "Firms, Politics and Political Economy: Patterns of Subsidiary-Parent Linkages and Technological Capability-Building in Electronics TNC Subsidiaries in Malaysia," in K. S. Jomo, G. Felker, and R. Rasiah (eds.), *Industrial Technology Development in Malaysia*, London: Routledge.

—— and Figueiredo, P. N. (2004), "Internationalisation of Innovative Capabilities: Counter-Evidence from the Electronics Industry in Malaysia and Brasil," *Oxford Development Studies*, 32(4): 559–83.

Arne, B., Collier, C., Dercon, S., Fafchamps, M., Gauthier, B., Gunning, J. W., Oduro, A., Oostendorp, R., Pattillo, C., Söderbom, M., Teal, F., and Zeufack, A. (2004), "Do African Manufacturing Firms Learn from Exporting?", *Journal of Development Studies*, 40(3): 115–41.

Arundel, A., and Geuna, A. (2004), "Proximity and the Use of Public Science by Innovative European Firms," *Economics of Innovation and New Technology*, 13(6): 559–80.

Arza, V. (2005a), "The Impact of Business Confidence and Macroeconomic Uncertainty on Firms' Investment Behaviour in Argentina During the 1990s," DPhil thesis, SPRU, University of Sussex, Brighton, UK.

—— (2005b), "Technological Performance, Economic Performance and Behaviour: A Study of Argentinean Firms during the 1990s," *Innovation: Management, Policy and Practice*, 7(2–3): 131–51.

Athreye, S., and Cantwell, J. (2007), "Creating Competition? Globalisation and the Emergence of New Technology Producers," *Research Policy*, 36: 209–26.

Aw, B. Y., and Hwang, A. (1995), "Productivity and the Export Market: A Firm Level Analysis," *Journal of Development Economics*, 47: 313–32.

Baumol, W. (1986), "Productivity Growth, Convergence and Welfare: What the Long-Run Data Show," *American Economic Review*, 76(5): 1072–85.

Bazan, L., and Navas-Alemán, L. (2004), "The Underground Revolution in the Sinos Valley: A Comparison of Upgrading in Global and National Value Chains," *Local Enterprises in the Global Economy*, Cheltenham, UK: Edward Elgar, 110–39.

Bell, M. (1984), "Learning and the Accumulation of Industrial Technological Capacity in Developing Countries," in K. King and M. Fransman (eds.), *Technological Capability in the Third World*, Basingstoke: Macmillan.

—— (2006), "How Long Does it Take? How Fast is it Moving (If At All)? Time and Technological Learning in Industrialising Countries," *International Journal of Technology Management*, 36(1–3): 25–39.

Bell, M., and Pavitt, K. (1993), "Technological Accumulation and Industrial Growth: Contrasts between Developed and Developing Countries," *Industrial and Corporate Change*, 2(2): 157–211.

—— —— (1995), "The Development of Technological Capabilities," in I. ul Haque (ed.), *Trade, Technology and International Competitiveness*, Washington, DC: The World Bank.

—— Scott-Kemmis, D., and Satyarakwit, W. (1982), "Limited Learning in Infant Industry: A Case Study," in F. Stewart and J. James (eds.), *The Economics of New Technology in Developing Countries*, London: Frances Pinter.

Bessant, J., and Kaplinsky, R. (1995), "Industrial Restructuring: Facilitating Organisational Change at the Firm Level," *World Development* (Special Issue), 23(1): 129–41.

Birkinshaw, J. M. (1997), 'Entrepreneurship in Multinational Corporations: The Characteristics of Subsidiary Initiatives,' *Strategic Management Journal*, 18(3): 207–29.

—— and Hood N. (1998), *Multinational Corporate Evolution and Subsidiary Development*, Basingstoke: Macmillan.

—— —— and Young, S. (2005), "Subsidiary Entrepreneurship, Internal and External Competitive Forces, and Subsidiary Performance," *International Business Review*, 14: 227–48.

Boehe, D. M. (2007), "Product Development in MNC Subsidiaries: Local Linkages and Global Interdependencies," *Journal of International Management*, 13: 488–512.

Brundenius, C., Lundvall, B.-Å., and Sutz, J. (2009), "The Role of Universities in Innovation Systems in Developing Countries: Developmental University Systems—Empirical, Analytical and Normative Perspectives," in B.-Å. Lundvall, K. J. Joseph, C. Chaminade, and J. Vang, *Handbook of Innovation Systems in Developing Countries: Building Domestic Capabilities in a Global Setting*, Cheltenham, UK and Northampton, Mass.: Edward Elgar, Chapter 11.

Cantwell, J. A., and Janne, O. E. M. (1999), "Technological Globalisation and the Innovative Centres: The Role of Corporate Technological Leadership and Locational Hierarchy," *Research Policy*, 28: 119–44.

—— and Mudambi, R. (2005), "MNE Competence Creating Subsidiary Mandates," *Strategic Management Journal*, 26: 1109–28.

Chandler, A. D. (1962), *Strategy and Structure: Chapters in the History of the Industrial Enterprise*, Cambridge, Mass.: The MIT Press.

—— (1990), *Scale and Scope: The Dynamics of Industrial Capitalism*, Cambridge, Mass.: The Belknap Press of Harvard University Press.

Chesbrough, H. (2003), *Open Innovation: The New Imperative for Creating and Profiting from Technology*, Boston, Mass.: Harvard Business School Press.

Choo, K., Lee, K., Ryu, K., and Yoon, J. (2009), "Changing Performance of Business Groups over Two Decades: Technological Capabilities and Investment Inefficiency in Korean Chaebols," *Economic Development & Cultural Change*, 57(2): 359–68.

Choung, J.-Y., Hwang, H.-R., and Yang, H. (2000), "Transition of Latecomer Firms from Technology Users to Technology Generators: Korean Semiconductor Firms," *World Development*, 28(5): 969–82.

Chuang, Y.-S. (2009), Personal communication, based on doctoral research at SPRU, University of Sussex, on the development of absorptive capacityin latecomer firms in the liquid crystal display industry in Taiwan.

Cimoli, M. (2000), "A Note on Networking Activities and Innovation System: The Case of Mexico," *El Mercado de Valores: An Update on Mexico's Economy and Finance* (English edition), Year VII(1), January–February.

—— and Katz, J. (2003), "Structural Reforms, Technological Gaps and Economic Development: A Latin American Perspective," *Industrial and Corporate Change*, 12(3): 387–411.

Clerides, S. K., Lach, S., and Tybout, J. R. (1998), "Is Learning by Exporting Important? Micro-dynamic Evidence from Colombia, Mexico, and Morocco," *Quarterly Journal of Economics*, 113: 903–47.

CNN.Money and *Fortune 500* (2005), "Gillette Unveils 5-bladed Razor," September 14.

Cohen, W. M., and Levinthal, D. A. (1990), "Absorptive Capacity: A New Perspective on Learning and Innovation," *Administrative Science Quarterly*, 35: 128–52.

Dahlman, C., Ross-Larsen, B., and Westphal, L. (1987), "Managing Technological Development: Lessons from the Newly Industrializing Countries," *World Development*, 6(15): 759–75.

Dantas, E. (2006), "The Development of Knowledge Networks in Latecomer Innovation Systems: The Case of PETROBRAS in the Brazilian Offshore Oil Industry," DPhil thesis, SPRU, University of Sussex, Brighton, UK.

—— and Bell, M. (2009), "Latecomer Firms and the Emergence and Development of Knowledge Networks: The Case of Petrobras in Brazil," *Research Policy*, 38(5): 829–44.

D'Costa, A. P. (2002), "Software Outsourcing and Development Policy Implications: An Indian Perspective," *International Journal of Technology Management*, 24(7–8): 705–23.

Delgado, M. J., Farinas, C., and Ruano, S. (2002), "Firms' Productivity and the Export Markets," *Journal of International Economics*, 57: 397–422.

Deraniyagala, S., and Semboja, H. (1999), "Trade Liberalisation, Firm Performance and Technology Upgrading in Tanzania," in S. Lall (ed.), *The Technological Response to Import Liberalisation in Sub-Saharan Africa*, Basingstoke: Macmillan, 57–111.

Dutrénit, G. (2000), *Learning and Knowledge Management in the Firm: From Knowledge Accumulation to Strategic Capabilities*, Cheltenham, UK: Edward Elgar.

Edquist, C., Hommen, L., and McKelvey, M. (2001), *Innovation and Employment: Process versus Product Innovation*, Cheltenham, UK: Edward Elgar.

Enos, J. L. (1962), *Petroleum Progress and Profits*, Cambridge, Mass.: The MIT Press.

—— and Park, W. H. (1988), *The Adaption and Diffusion of Imported Technology: The Case of Korea*, London: Croom Helm.

Ernst, D. (2002), "Global Production Networks and the Changing Geography of Innovation Systems: Implications for Developing Countries," *Economics of Innovation and New Technology*, 11(6): 497–523.

—— Mytelka, L., and Ganiatsos, T. (1998), "Technological Capabilities in the Context of Export-Led Growth—A Conceptual Framework," in D. Ernst, L. Mytelka, and

T. Ganiatsos (eds.), *Technological Capabilities and Export Success in Asia*, London: Routledge, 5–45.

Ferigotti, C., and Figueiredo, P. N. (2005), "Managing Learning in the Refrigerator Industry: Evidence from a Firm-Level Study in Brazil," *Innovation: Management, Policy and Practice*, 7(2–3): 222–39.

Figueiredo, P. N. (2001), *Technological Learning and Competitive Performance*, Cheltenham, UK: Edward Elgar.

—— (2002), "Does Technological Learning Pay Off? Inter-Firm Differences in Technological Capability Accumulation Paths and Operational Performance Improvement," *Research Policy*, 31: 73–94.

—— (2003), "Learning, Capability Accumulation and Firms Differences: Evidence from Latecomer Steel," *Industrial and Corporate Change*, 12(3): 607–43.

—— (2008), "Industrial Policy Changes and Firm-Level Technological Capability Development: Evidence from Northern Brazil," *World Development*, 36(1): 55–88.

—— García, C., Cohen, M., and Gomes, S. (2008), "Acumulação de Capacidades Tecnológicas, Inovação, Estratégias de Aprendizagem e Performance Competitiva: Evidências de Empresas dos Setores Florestal, de Celulose e de Papel no Brasil (1950-2006)," Programa de Pesquisa e Aprendizagem Tecnológica e Inovação Industrial no Brasil; EBAPE/FGV (Final Report).

Gereffi, G., Humphrey, J., and Sturgeon, T. (2005), "The Governance of Global Value Chains," *Review of International Political Economy*, 12(1): 78–104.

Girma, S., Greenaway, D., and Kneller, R. (2004), "Does Exporting Increase Productivity? A Microeconometric Analysis of Matched Firms," *Review of International Economics*, 12(5): 855–66.

Giuliani, E., and Arza, V. (2009), "What Drives the Formation of 'Valuable' University-Industry Linkages?: Insights from the Wine Industry," *Research Policy*, 38(6): 906–21.

Granstrand, O., Pavitt, K., and Patel, P. (1997), "Multi-technology Corporations: Why they have Distributed rather than Distinctive Core Competencies," *California Management Review*, 39: 8–25.

Greenaway, D., Gullstrand, J., and Kneller, R. (2005), "Exporting may Not Always Boost Firm Level Productivity," *Review of World Economics*, 141: 561–82.

Henderson, R. (1994), "The Evolution of Integrative Capability: Innovation in Cardiovascular Drug Discovery," *Industrial and Corporate Change*, 3(3): 607–30.

Hobday, M. (1995), *Innovation in East Asia: The Challenge to Japan*, Aldershot: Edward Elgar.

—— Rush, H., and Bessant, J. (2004), "Approaching the Innovation Frontier in Korea: The Transition Phase to Leadership," *Research Policy*, 33: 1433–57.

Hoffman, K. (1989), "Technological Advance and Organizational Innovation in the Engineering Industries," World Bank IED Working Papers, Industry Series Paper, no. 4, Washington, DC: World Bank.

Hohlbein, D. J., Williams, M. I., and Mintel, T. E. (2004), "Driving Toothbrush Innovation through a Cross-Functional Development Team," *Compendium of Continuing Education in Dentistry*, October 25, 10(Suppl. 2): 7–11.

Hollander, S. (1965), *The Sources of Increased Efficiency: A Study of DuPont Rayon Plants*, Cambridge, Mass.: MIT Press.

Humphrey, J. (1993), "Quality and Productivity in Industry: New Strategies in Development Countries," *IDS Bulletin*, 24(2): 1–86.

—— (1995), "Introduction," *World Development*, 23(1): 1–17.

—— and Schmitz, H. (2002), "How Does Insertion in Global Value Chains Affect Upgrading in Industrial Clusters?" *Regional Studies*, 36(9): 1017–27.

————H. (2004), *Local Enterprises in the Global Economy*, Cheltenham, UK: Edward Elgar.

Iacovone, L., and Crespi, G. A. (2010), "Catching Up with the Technological Frontier: Micro-Level Evidence on Growth and Convergence," *Industrial and Corporate Change*, 19(6): 2073–96.

Iammarino, S., Padilla-Perez, R., and von Tunzelmann, N. (2008), "Technological Capabilities and Global-Local Interactions: The Electronics Industry in Two Mexican Regions," *World Development*, 36(10): 1980–2003.

Iansiti, M., and Clark, K. (1994), "Integration and Dynamic Capability: Evidence from Product Development in Automobiles and Mainframe Computers," *Industrial and Corporate Change*, 33: 557–605.

Isgut, A. (2001), "What's Different about Exporters? Evidence from Colombian Manufacturing," *Journal of Development Studies*, 37(5): 57–82.

Jensen, J. D., Bauer DuMont, V. L., Ashmore, A. B., Gutierrez, A., and Aquadro, C. F. (2007), "Patterns of Sequence Variability and Divergence at the Diminutive Gene Region of Drosophila Melanogaster: Complex Patterns Suggest an Ancestral Selective Sweep," *Genetics*, 177(2): 1071–85.

Joo, S.-H., and Lee, K. (2010), "Samsung's Catch-Up with Sony: An Analysis Using US Patent Data," *Journal of the Asia Pacific Economy*, 15(3): 271–87.

Joseph, K. J. (2009), "Sectoral Innovation systems in Developing Countries: The Case of ICT in India," in B.-A. Lundvall, K. J. Joseph, C. Chaminade, and J. Vang, *Handbook of Innovation Systems in Developing Countries: Building Domestic Capabilities in a Global Setting*, Cheltenham, UK and Northampton, Mass.: Edward Elgar, Chapter 7.

Jung, M., and Lee, K. (2010), "Sectoral Systems of Innovation and Productivity Catch-Up: Determinants of the Productivity Gap between Korean and Japanese Firms," *Industrial and Corporate Change*, 19(4): 1037–69.

Kaplinsky, R. (1990), *The Economies of Small: Appropriate Technology in a Changing World*, London: Intermediate Technology Publications.

—— (1994), *Easternisation: The Spread of Japanese Management Techniques to Developing Countries*, London: Frank Cass.

Katz, J. (1987), *Technology Generation in Latin American Manufacturing Industries*, Basingstoke: Macmillan.

Kim, C. W., and Lee, K. (2003), "Innovation, Technological Regimes and Organizational Selection in Industry Evolution: A 'History Friendly' Model," *Industrial and Corporate Change*, 12(5): 1195–221.

Kim, L. (1997), *Imitation to Innovation: The Dynamics of Korea's Technological Learning*, Boston, Mass.: Harvard Business School Press.

—— (1998), "Crisis Construction and Organisational Learning: Capability Building in Catching-Up at Hyundai Motor," *Organization Science*, 9: 506–21.

Kimura, S. (2007), *The Challenge of Late Industrialization: The Global Economy and the Japanese Commercial Aircraft Industry*, Basingstoke: Palgrave Macmillan.

Kirner, E., Kinkel, S., and Jaeger, A. (2009), "Innovation Paths and the Innovation Performance of Low-Technology Firms: An Empirical Analysis of German Industry," *Research Policy*, 38(3): 447–58.

Lall, S. (1987), *Learning to Industrialise: The Acquisition of Technological Capability by India*, Basingstoke: Macmillan.

—— (1992), "Technological Capabilities and Industrialization," *World Development*, 20(2): 165–86.

Lam, A. (2005), "Organizational Innovation," in J. Fagerberg, D. Mowery, and R. R. Nelson (eds.), *The Oxford Handbook of Innovation*, Oxford: Oxford University Press.

Langlois, R. N. (2003), "The Vanishing Hand: The Changing Dynamics of Industrial Capitalism," *Industrial and Corporate Change*, 12(2): 351–85.

Lazonick, W. (2010), "The Chandlerian Corporation and the Theory of Innovative Enterprise," *Industrial and Corporate Change*, 1: 317–49.

—— and Prencipe, A. (2005), "Dynamic Capabilities and Sustained Innovation: Strategic Control and Financial Commitment at Rolls-Royce plc," *Industrial and Corporate Change*, 14(3): 501–42.

Lee, K., and Lim, C. (2001), "Technological Regimes, Catching-Up and Leapfrogging: Findings from the Korean Industries," *Research Policy*, 30(3), March: 459–83.

Lema, R. (2010), "Adoption of Open Business Models in the West and Innovation in India's Software Industry," Research Report No. 62, Institute of Development Studies, Brighton, UK.

Leonard-Barton, D. (1995), *Wellsprings of Knowledge: Building and Sustaining the Sources of Innovation*, Boston, Mass.: Harvard Business School Press.

McArthur, J. W., and Sachs, J. D. (2002), "The Growth Competitiveness Index: Measuring Technological Advancement and the Stages of Development," in M. E. Porter, J. D. Sachs, P. K. Cornelius, J. W. McArthur, and K. Schwab, *The Global Competitiveness Report 2001–2002*, World Economic Forum, New York and Oxford: Oxford University Press.

Malerba, F. (1992), "Learning by Firms and Incremental Technical Change," *The Economic Journal*, 102(413): 845–59.

—— (2002), "Sectoral Systems of Innovation and Production," *Research Policy*, 32: 1031–54.

—— (ed.) (2004), *Sectoral Systems of Innovation: Concepts, Issues and Analyses of Six Major Sectors in Europe*, Cambridge: Cambridge University Press.

—— (2005), "Sectoral Systems: How and Why Innovation Differs Across Sectors," in J. Fagerberg, D. C. Mowery, and R. R. Nelson (eds.), *The Oxford Handbook of Innovation*, Oxford and New York: Oxford University Press, 380–406.

—— and Mani, S. (eds.) (2009), *Sectoral Systems of Innovation and Production in Developing Countries: Actors, Structure and Evolution*, Cheltenham, UK and Northampton, Mass.: Edward Elgar.

—— and Orsenigo, L. (1996), "Schumpeterian Patterns of Innovation are Technology Specific," *Research Policy*, 25(3): 451–78.

—— —— and Peretto, P. (1997), "Persistence of Innovative Activities, Sectoral Patterns of Innovation and International Technological Specialization," *International Journal of Industrial Organization*, 15: 801–26.

Marcelle, G. (2004), *Technological Learning: A Strategic Imperative for Firms in the Developing World*, Cheltenham, UK: Edward Elgar.

Marin, A., and Bell, M. (2006), "Technology Spillovers from Foreign Direct Investment (FDI): An Exploration of the Active Role of MNC Subsidiaries in the Case of Argentina in the 1990s," *Journal of Development Studies*, 42(4): 678–97.

—— —— (2010), "The Local/Global Integration of MNC Subsidiaries and their Technological Behaviour: Argentina in the Late 1990s," *Research Policy*, 39(7): 919–31.

—— and Sasidharan, S. (2008), "Active MNC Subsidiaries and Technology Spillovers in Late Industrialising Countries: The Case of Argentina and India," paper presented at Globelics 2007, Saratov, Rússia.

Mathews, J. A. (1997), "A Silicon Valley of the East: Creating Taiwan's Semiconductor Industry," *California Management Review*, 39(4): 26–54.

—— (1999), "A Silicon Island of the East: Creating a Semiconductor Industry in Singapore," *California Management Review*, 41(2): 55–78.

—— (2002), "Competitive Advantages of the Latecomer Firm: A Resource-Based Account of Industrial Catch-Up Strategies," *Asia Pacific Journal of Management*, 19(4): 467–88.

—— (2006), "Catch-Up Strategies and the Latecomer Effect in Industrial Development," *New Political Economy*, 11(3): 313–35.

—— and Cho, D.-S. (1999), "Combinative Capabilities and Organizational Learning by Latecomer Firms: The Case of the Korea Semiconductor Industry," *Journal of World Business*, 34: 139–56.

Mazzoleni, R., and Nelson, R. R. (2007). "Public Research Institutions and Economic Catch-Up," *Research Policy*, 36(10): 1512–28.

Meyer-Stamer, J., Rauh, C., Riad, H., Schmitt, S., and Welte, T. (1991), "Comprehensive Modernisation on the Shop Floor: A Case Study on the Brazilian Machinery Industry," Berlin: GDI.

Miranda, E. C., and Figueiredo, P. N. (2010), "Dinâmica da acumulação de capacidades inovadoras: evidências de empresas de software no Rio de Janeiro e em São Paulo," *Revista de Administração de Empresas*, 50: 75–93.

Mitter, W. (1993), "Education, Democracy and Development in a Period of Revolutionary Change," *International Review of Education*, 39(6): 463–71.

Miyazaki, K. (1994), "Search, Learning and the Accumulation of Technological Competences: The Case of Optoeletronics," *Industrial and Corporate Change*, 3(3): 631–55.

Mody, A., Suri, R., and Sanders, J. (1992), "Keeping Pace with Change: Organisational and Technological Imperatives," *World Development*, 20(12): 1797–816.

Nelson, R. R. (ed.) (1962), *The Rate and Direction of Inventive Activity: Economic and Social Factors*, Princeton: Princeton University Press.

—— (2008), "What Enables Rapid Economic Progress: What are the Needed Institutions," *Research Policy*, 37(1): 1–11.

—— and Pack, H. (1999), "The Asian Miracle and Modern Economic Growth Theory," *The Economic Journal*, 109: 416–36.

Nelson, R. R., and Sampat, B. N. (2001), *Recent Developments in Institutional Economics: International Library of Critical Writings in Economics*, Cheltenham, UK: Edward Elgar.

NESTA (National Endowment for Science, Technology and the Arts) (2006), *The Innovation Gap: Why Policy Needs to Reflect the Reality of Innovation in the UK*, London: NESTA.

—— (2007), *Hidden Innovation: How Innovation Happens in Six "Low Innovation" Sectors*. London: NESTA.

Nonaka, I. (1994), "A Dynamic Theory of Organisational Knowledge Creation," *Organisational Science*, 5(1): 15–37.

—— and Takeuchi, H. (1995), *The Knowledge Creating Firm: How Japanese Firms Create the Dynamics of Innovation*, New York: Oxford University Press.

Ocampo, J. A. (2004), "Latin America's Growth and Equity Frustrations during Structural Reforms," *Journal of Economic Perspectives*, 18(2): 67–88.

—— (ed.) (2005), *Beyond Reforms: Structural Dynamics and Macroeconomic Theory*, Stanford, Calif.: Stanford University Press.

OECD (2005), *Oslo Manual*, Paris: European Commission/Eurostat.

Pack, H., and Saggi, K. (2006), "Is there a Case for Industrial Policy? A Critical Survey," *World Bank Research Observer*, 21(2): 267–97.

Park, K.-H., and Lee, K. (2006), "Linking the Technological Regime to the Technological Catch-Up: Analyzing Korea and Taiwan Using the US Patent Data," *Industrial and Corporate Change*, 15(4): 715–53.

Patel, P., and Pavitt, K. (1997), "The Technological Competencies of the World's Largest Firms: Complex and Path-Dependent, but Not Much Variety", *Research Policy*, 26: 141–56.

Pavitt, K. (1984), "Sectoral Patterns of Technical Change: Towards a Taxonomy and a Theory," *Research Policy*, 13: 343–73.

—— (1990), "What We Know about the Strategic Management of Technology?" *Californian Management Review*, 32: 17–26.

—— (2005), "Innovation Process," in J. Fagerberg, D. C. Mowery, and R. R. Nelson (eds.), *The Oxford Handbook of Innovation*, Oxford and New York: Oxford University Press, 86–114.

Porter, M. E. (1990), *The Competitive Advantage of Nations*, Basingstoke: Macmillan.

—— Sachs, J. D., and McArthur, J. W. (2002), "Executive Summary: Competitiveness and Stages of Economic Development," in M. E. Porter, J. D. Sachs, P. K. Cornelius, J. W. McArthur, and K. Schwab, *The Global Competitiveness Report 2001–2002*, World Economic Forum, New York and Oxford: Oxford University Press.

Posthuma, A. (1990), "Japanese Production Techniques in Brazilian Automobile Components Firm: A Best Practice Model Basis for Adaptation," Conference on the Organization and Control of the Labour Process, Birmingham, Aston University.

Prahalad, C. K. (2006), *The Fortune at the Bottom of the Pyramid: Eradicating Poverty through Profits*, New Jersey: Wharton School Publishing.

Quadros, R., and Consoni, F. (2009), "Innovation Capabilities in the Brazilian Automobile Industry: A Study of Vehicle Assemblers' Technological Strategies and

Policy Recommendations," *International Journal of Technological Learning, Innovation and Development*, 2(1–2): 53–75.

—— and Queiroz, S. (2001), "The Implications of Globalisation for the Distribution of Design Competencies in the Auto Industry in Mercosur," *Actes du Gerpisa*, 32: 35–45.

Rabellotti, R. (2004), "How Globalization Affects Italian Industrial Districts: The Case of Brenta," in Hubert Schmitz (ed.), *Local Enterprises in the Global Economy*, Cheltenham, UK: Edward Elgar, 140–73.

Rasiah, R. (1996), "Institutions and Innovations: Moving towards the Technology Frontier in the Electronics Industry in Malaysia," *Industry and Innovation*, 3(2): 79–102.

—— (2004), *Foreign Firms, Technological Intensities and Economic Performance, Evidence from Africa, Asia and Latin America*, Cheltenham, UK: Edward Elgar.

—— (2006), "Ownership, Technological Intensities, and Economic Performance in South Africa," *International Journal of Technology Management*, 36(1–3): 166–89.

Reinhardt, N., and Peres, W. (2000), "Latin America's New Economic Model: Micro Responses and Economic Restructuring," *World Development*, 28(9): 1543–63.

Roberts, S. (2005), "Resource-Based Technology Innovation in South Africa: Multotec Process Equipment—Dense Medium Cyclone for Materials Separation," Employment-Oriented Industry Studies, Human Sciences Research Council, Pretoria, South Africa.

Rock, M. T., and Angel. D. P. (2005), *Industrial Transformation in the Developing World*, Oxford: Oxford University Press.

—— Murphy, J. T., Raiah, R., van Seters, P., and Managi, S. (2009), "A Hard Slog, Not a Leap Frog: Globalization and Sustainability Transitions in Developing Asia," *Technological Forecasting and Social Change*, 76(2): 241–54.

Romijn, H. (1999), *Acquisition of Technological Capability in Small Firms in Developing Countries*, Basingstoke: Macmillan.

Rosenberg, N. (1972), "Factors Affecting the Diffusion of Technology", *Explorations in Economic History*, 10(1): 3–33. Also published as Chapter 11 in Rosenberg (1976).

—— (1975), "Problems in the Economist's Conceptualization of Technological Innovation," *History of Political Economy*, 7(4): 456–81. Also published as Chapter 4 in Rosenberg (1976).

—— (1976), *Perspectives on Technology*, Cambridge: Cambridge University Press.

Sachwald, F. (2001), *Going Multinational: The Korean Experience of Direct Investment*, London: Harwood Academic Publishers.

Schmitz, H., and Strambach, S. (2009), "The Organisational Decomposition of Innovation and Global Distribution of Innovative Activities: Insights and Research Agenda," *International Journal of Technological Learning, Innovation and Development*, 2(4): 231–49.

Scott-Kemmis, D., and Chitravas, C. (2007), "Revisiting the Learning and Capability Concepts: Building Learning Systems in Thai Auto Component Firms," *Asian Journal of Technology Innovation*, 15(2): 67–100.

Stewart, F. (1972), "Choice of Technique in Developing Countries," *Journal of Development Studies*, 9(1): 99–121.

Stewart, F. (1978), "Inequality, Technology and Payments Systems," *World Development*, 6(3): 275–93.

Sturgeon, T. J. (2002), "Modular Production Networks: A New American Model of Industrial Organization," *Industrial and Corporate Change*, 11: 451–96.

Tacla, C. L., and Figueiredo, P. N. (2006), "The Organisational Basis of Learning and Technological Capability Building: Firm-Level Evidence from the Capital Goods Industry in Brazil," *International Journal of Technology Management*, Special Issue, 36(1–3): 62–90.

Teece, D. J. (2007a), "Explicating Dynamic Capabilities: The Nature and Micro-Foundations of (Sustainable) Enterprise Performance," *Strategic Management Journal*, 28: 1319–50.

—— (2007b), "The Role of Managers, Entrepreneurs and the Literati in Enterprise Performance and Economic Growth," *International Journal of Technological Learning, Innovation and Development*, 1(1): 43–64.

—— Pisano, G., and Shuen, A. (1997), "Dynamic Capabilities and Strategic Management," *Strategic Management Journal*, 18(7): 509–33.

The Boston Globe (2005), "And Then there were Five: Gillette Unveils Fusion, Taking Back Bragging Rights from Schick," September 15.

The Economist (2010), "The World Turned Upside Down," Special Report on Innovation in Emerging Markets, April 15.

Tsekouras, G. (2006), "Gaining Competitive Advantage through Knowledge Integration in a European Industrialising Economy," *International Journal of Technology Management*, 36(1–3): 126–47.

Van Dijk, M., and Bell, M. (2007), "Rapid Growth with Limited Learning: Industrial Policy and Indonesia's Pulp and Paper Industry," *Oxford Development Studies*, 35(2): 149–69.

Verspagen, B. (1991), "A New Empirical Approach to Catching Up or Falling Behind," *Structural Change and Economic Dynamics*, 2(2): 359–80.

Viotti, E. B. (2002), "National Learning Systems: A New Approach on Technical Change in Late Industrializing Economies and Evidences from the Cases of Brazil and South Korea," *Technological Forecasting & Social Change*, 69(2002): 653–80.

von Tunzelmann, N., and Acha, V. (2005), "Innovation in 'Low Tech' Industries," in J. Fagerberg, D. C. Mowery, and R. R. Nelson (eds.), *The Oxford Handbook of Innovation*, Oxford: Oxford: Oxford University Press, 407–32.

Westphal, L. E., Kritayakirana, K., Petchsuwan, K., Sutabutr, H., and Yuthavong, Y. (1990), "The Development of Technological Capability in Manufacturing: A Macroscopic Approach to Policy Research," in R. E. Evenson and G. Ranis (eds.), *Science and Technology: Lessons for Development Policy*, London: Intermediate Technology Publications.

Wignaraja, G. (1998), *Trade Liberalization in Sri Lanka: Exports, Technology and Industrial Policy*, London: Macmillian and New York: St Martin's Press.

—— (2002), "Firm Size, Technological Capabilities and Market-Oriented Policies in Mauritius," *Oxford Development Studies*, 30(1): 87–104.

—— and Ikiara, G. (1999), "Adjustment, Technological Capabilities and Enterprise Dynamics in Kenya," in S. Lall (ed.), *The Technological Response to Import Liberalisation in SubSaharan Africa*, Basingstoke: Macmillan.

Xiao, Y., Tylecote, A., and Liu, J. (2008), "Thirty Years' Evolution of Technological Capabilities and Competitive Advantage in a Chinese State-Owned Equipment Manufacturer: A Corporate Governance Perspective," paper presented at the VI Globelics Conference, Mexico City, September 22–4.

Yoruk, E. E. (2011), "The Influence of Technological Capabilities on the Knowledge Network Component of Innovation Systems: Evidence from Advanced Materials in Turkey," *International Journal of Technological Learning, Innovation and Development*, 4: 330–62.

Zheng, M., and Williamson P. J. (2007), *Dragons at your Door: How Chinese Cost Innovation is Disrupting the Rules of Global Competition*, Boston, Mass.: Harvard Business School Press.

Part IIA

Innovative Firms in Emerging Markets Country Experiences (Asia)

3

China

Huiping Li and John Cantwell[1]

3.1. INTRODUCTION

China's economic reform—started in 1979 under the new leadership of Deng Xiaoping—began a gradual movement from a centrally planned to a market economy. In the ensuing quarter century, the private business sector, including small businesses, township enterprises, and foreign-owned or connected firms, has become the driving force behind China's economic renaissance. Many of these local businesses have become highly innovative. This chapter focuses upon the accumulation of technological capability by these firms, both domestic and foreign-invested enterprises (FIEs), in China.

Section 3.2 describes the evolution of foreign direct investment (FDI) in China, and the types of investment vehicle used at different stages of China's economic reform. Section 3.3 describes the types of innovative firms in China, treating separately those that derive from state-owned enterprises (SOEs), and those that are derived from FDI. The section examines the typology of innovative firms in China, and reveals the relevance of our focus here on international joint ventures (IJVs). Section 3.4 explains the details of our study of IJVs, in terms of methods and a description of the survey sample. Section 3.5 addresses how Chinese firms have evolved through different "levels" of innovative capability and activity toward a more innovative type of enterprise, and what factors have facilitated these learning trajectories. Section 3.6 examines how, if at all, these paths of learning within firms have influenced, or been influenced by, the development of innovative capabilities in other firms (especially those in other firm categories). Section 3.7 concludes with a discussion of what kinds of economic or other effects have followed from the paths of learning and innovative capability building in the selected enterprises.

[1] The authors wish to express their thanks to Martin Bell for his valuable comments.

3.2. THE EVOLUTION OF FDI IN CHINA

Over the last 25 years, FDI in China has evolved through several stages: incorporating sequentially the representative office, the joint venture, the wholly owned foreign enterprise, and the China holding company. Table 3.1 offers a brief description of the characteristics of each stage.

3.2.1. Stages of FDI

The representative office was a useful and inexpensive way for MNCs to establish an initial presence in China. Before making any investment, many MNCs opened representative offices in a major city such as Beijing, Shanghai, and Guangdong. An application by the foreign company to set up a representative office triggered a bureaucratic process. A government organization was required to sponsor the representative office. A business license had to be obtained and renewed annually. A representative office was supposed to facilitate trade between foreign companies and business entities based in China. It might conduct market research or facilitate purchasing activities for its MNC. However, this kind of office was not permitted to sign contracts or directly invoice sales in China. In essence, the representative office was a bridge between the foreign company and local enterprises, acting as a point of liaison in matters relating to negotiation and sales administration.

International joint ventures (IJV) between foreign companies and Chinese enterprises were first entered into as a way to circumvent policy restrictions imposed on foreign investors in many Chinese industries. Those restrictions arose in part as an ideological response to the foreign commercial and military interventions the country suffered from the mid-19th century onward (Rosen, 1999). From 1980 until 1998, over 70 percent of FDI in China took the form of

Table 3.1. The stages of foreign presence in China

Timeline	Type of investment	Characteristics
Early 1980s	Representative office	Liaison office No investment
1980s–mid-1990s	Joint venture	Minority–majority Learning curve
1990s–present	Wholly owned foreign enterprise	100% ownership Control
Late 1990s–present	China holding company R&D center Purchasing center	Consolidation Scope

Source: Authors.

joint ventures. The growth of such ventures, however, has slowed in recent years. With the dismantling of policy restrictions in the wake of China's entry into the WTO, more options were presented to foreign companies to gain access to Chinese markets and Chinese export bases using other vehicles, such as merger and acquisition and/or wholly owned foreign enterprises.

Also, as foreign companies have amassed a greater understanding of Chinese consumers, Chinese markets, and the Chinese business system, many have opted to choose wholly owned foreign enterprises as the preferred method to enter, or expand their presence in, China. Wholly owned foreign enterprises (WOFEs) have become the investment vehicle of choice for foreign companies wishing to manufacture, process, or assemble in China, as WOFEs eliminate the necessity for a Chinese partner. Manufacturing WOFEs that intend to export their product can also obtain significant tax and other incentives if they operate in Free Trade or Export Processing Zones.

In 2000, the volume of business transacted by wholly owned foreign businesses exceeded that of Chinese-foreign joint ventures for the first time. According to figures published by the Ministry of Foreign Trade and Economic Cooperation (MOFTEC), wholly owned foreign enterprises accounted for fully 45 percent of total FDI in China in that year. The increasing number of WOFEs in the last few years reflects China's willingness to open its economy and the more prominent position China has in the global strategies of foreign companies.

As their investments increased, some foreign companies established research and development (R&D) centers to facilitate their growth in China. MNCs seeking market access, market share, or government relationships are more likely to find them in the form of equity-based R&D centers. By February 2009, 920 MNCs have established 1,100 R&D centers in China. MNCs originating in the US and Europe are the biggest R&D investors in China to date, while cities like Shanghai and Beijing collectively account for more than half of the R&D establishments. Some of these global firms have established large R&D centers in China, with 53 percent of them having more than 150 R&D personnel at these centers, thus "offshoring" key aspects of knowledge development. By 2009, the total investment in R&D centers in China was US$ 6.4 bn.

It should also be noted that many of these R&D centers are not of cutting-edge design. They are sometimes referred to as PR&D centers due to the public relations benefits they bring—but their potential integration into global research and design networks also should not be ignored or underestimated. Delphi, for instance, uses its 34 technical centers around the globe to implement "24/7 engineering." Diesel engine technology is a specialty of its European center, and it collaborates on projects with design centers in the US and Asia that have complementary expertise.

As of the end of 2002, Shanghai was home to 70 regional headquarters and 37 international purchasing centers of foreign companies. These are encouraged by the preferential policies of the Chinese government. In Shanghai, transnational procurement or logistics centers set up by regional headquarters are eligible to trade internationally; those with R&D functions in the high-technology sector are also eligible for preferential treatment. In addition, Shenzhen and Beijing are witnessing a surge in the establishment of regional headquarters, purchasing and logistics centers.

Traditionally multinational corporations formed joint ventures in China to achieve localized status. More recently, many MNCs are trying to gain greater control over these joint ventures, and to integrate their sprawling businesses, so as to cut operating costs and improve efficiency. They are using consolidation as the means to achieve these objectives.

China, as a late industrializing country, has made tremendous progress in economic development using an open-door policy to attract FDI. The US \$60.64 bn in FDI that China received in 2004 is an impressive achievement. And with much of it devoted to developing China's export sector, this investment foreshadows the country's increasingly important position in the global economy. Foreign affiliates account for 23 percent of China's industrial production, 18 percent of its tax revenues, and 48 percent of its total exports, playing an important role in China's economy. UNCTAD statistics show that in 2000–1, one-third of China's FDI was accounted for by foreign affiliates reinvesting their earnings. FIEs generated nearly one-fifth of the total tax revenues and 23.5 million job opportunities, and employed about one-tenth of China's urban workers, accounting for between one-quarter to one-third of the growth of China's gross domestic product (GDP) at that time (see Tables 3.2 and 3.3).

3.2.2. The Geographical and Sectoral Distribution of FDI

Although initially FDI was permitted only in a few regions and only in select sectors of the economy, the number of regions and sectors has rapidly expanded. To gain entry into the WTO, China committed to open its market to foreign investors. As the result of entry into the WTO, all industries were opened up to FDI except for the automobile industry.

The patterns of FDI across China show a great disparity among regions: for the period from 1983 to 1998, FDI in the eastern region accounted for 87.8 percent, while the central region attracted just 8.9 percent and the western region recorded only 3.3 percent. This inequality stems in part from the FDI policies of the Chinese authorities. The open-door policy began with the creation of special economic zones (SEZs) and preferential regimes for 14 coastal cities. This has resulted in an overwhelming concentration of FDI in the east. With the adoption of more broadly based economic reforms and open-door policies for FDI in the 1990s, FDI inflows into China have now started to spread to other provinces (OECD, 2000).

Table 3.2. FDI in China (in US$), 1979–2004

	1979–89	1990	1991	1992	1993	1994	1995	1996	1997	1998	1999	2000	2001	2002	2003	2004
Total Foreign Direct Investment (FDI)																
No. of contracts	21,776	7,273	12,978	48,764	83,437	47,549	37,011	24,556	21,001	19,799	16,918	22,347	26,139	34,171	41,081	43,664
Amt. contracted ($ bn)	32.36	6.60	11.98	58.12	111.44	82.68	91.28	73.28	51.00	52.10	41.22	62.38	69.19	82.77	115.07	153.47
Amt. utilized ($ bn)	18.47	3.41	4.37	11.01	27.52	33.77	37.52	41.73	45.26	45.46	40.32	40.72	46.85	52.74	53.51	60.63
US direct investment																
No. of contracts	959	357	694	3,265	6,750	4,223	3,474	2,517	2,188	2,238	2,028	2,609	2,594	3,363	4,060	3,925
Amt. contracted ($ bn)	3.95	0.36	0.55	3.12	6.81	6.01	7.47	6.92	4.94	6.48	6.02	8.00	7.51	8.20	10.16	12.17
Amt. utilized ($ bn)	1.73	0.46	0.32	0.51	2.06	2.49	3.08	3.44	3.24	3.90	4.22	4.38	4.86	5.40	4.20	3.94
US share of contracted investment	12.20%	5.40%	4.60%	5.40%	6.10%	7.30%	8.20%	9.44%	9.68%	12.44%	14.59%	12.83%	10.85%	9.91%	8.83%	7.93%

Source: Authors, based on data provided by Ministry of Commerce (MOFCOM) and US-China Business Council (US-CBC).

Table 3.3. FDI by investment vehicle, 2007 and 2008

	Number of projects			Utilized FDI value ($ bn)		
	2007	2008	% Change	2007	2008	% Change
Total FDI	37,871	27,514	−27.4	$74.8	$92.4	23.6
Equity JVs	7,649	4,612	−39.7	$15.6	$17.3	11
Non-equity JVs	641	468	−27.0	$1.4	$1.9	34.4
WOFEs	29,543	22,396	−24.2	$57.3	$72.3	26.3
Foreign-invested shareholding ventures	38	38	0	$0.5	$0.9	74.7

Notes: EJVs = equity joint ventures; WOFEs = wholly foreign-owned enterprises.
Source: Authors, based on data provided by MOFCOM and US-CBC.

In terms of sectoral distribution, the majority of FDI is in manufacturing industries. In the year 2003, 70 percent of the total contracted FDI was in manufacturing. The industries in which foreign-owned firms account for the highest percentage of local valued added in China are: electronic and communication equipment, professional and scientific instruments, and then articles for culture, education, and sports activities. Table 3.4 shows by sector the percentage of value added for which FIEs were responsible between 1997 and 2003.

3.2.3. Contribution of FIEs

FDI projects and the operations of FIEs have helped to improve China's access to advanced technologies, to management practices, and to a wide range of skills. FIEs have therefore served as a major channel for technology imports (OECD, 2008). A number of scholars have demonstrated empirically that FDI can promote innovative capability and facilitate technological capability accumulation in China through spillover channels such as reverse engineering, skilled labor turnover, demonstration effects, and supplier-customer relationships (Cheung and Lin, 2004; Liu, 2001; Hu and Jefferson, 2004; Wei and Liu, 2006).

3.2.4. Types of Foreign-Related Firms

Since the mid-1990s, China began to allow foreign firms to have wholly owned ventures in China. Some of the foreign investing firms started to take more equity, and some converted from IJVs to become wholly owned foreign

Table 3.4. Proportion of local value added accounted for by FIEs by industry (%)

Sector	1997	2000	2003	Sector	1997	2000	2003
Food processing	19	20.7	26.3	Medical and pharmaceutical products	24.7	24.6	23.9
Manufacture of foods	35.5	41.9	41.4	Manufacture of chemical fibers	15.8	39.3	22.9
Manufacture of beverages	24.4	27.9	32.3	Manufacture of rubber	20.1	35.6	37.8
Manufacture of tobacco	0.6	0.5	0.4	Manufacture of plastics	31.6	44.3	44.1
Manufacture of textiles	18	20.7	24.2	Non-metal mineral products	10.7	17.3	16.9
Garments and other fiber products	43.7	48.8	47.1	Smelting and processing of ferrous metals	2.9	4.7	7.3
Leathers, furs, down, and related products	23.2	28	26.2	Smelting and processing of non-ferrous metals	9.9	11.2	11.4
Timber processing, bamboo, cane, palm fiber, and straw products	43.7	54.6	50.7	Manufacture of metal products	22.9	34.8	33.6
Cultural, educational, and sports goods	42.1	59.5	60.3	General purpose machinery	13.7	22.2	27.4
Manufacture of furniture	24.3	43.9	48.6	Special purpose machinery	10.4	14.9	21
Papermaking and paper products	17.9	28.8	31.7	Manufacture of transport equipment	23.9	30.8	44.6
Printing, reproduction of recording media	17.3	29.4	32.2	Equipment	49.4	34.2	35.2
Petroleum refining and coking	3.1	5.7	11.6	Electronic and telecommunications	61.3	65.4	69.6
Manufacture of raw chemical materials and chemical products	14.9	21.5	25.1	Instruments, meters for cultural and office work	39.3	49.4	64.3

Source: Compiled by authors from Zhang and Gan (2006); *China Industry Economy Statistical Yearbook* (2002 and 2005).

enterprises. As a consequence of these changes in permitted ownership structure, foreign-owned businesses in China can now be divided into five different categories: (i) joint ventures majority owned by foreign parties; (ii) joint ventures majority owned by the Chinese partner; (iii) foreign firms that have bought out their Chinese partners, becoming wholly owned foreign subsidiaries; (iv) large SOEs that have evolved from joint venture partnerships with foreign firms to become stocklisted companies in China; and (v) wholly owned subsidiaries that have otherwise been newly established since 1995.

Since 1995, when the Chinese government relaxed its rules to allow foreign investors to establish wholly owned foreign enterprises, the number of IJVs has fallen relative to the number of WOFEs. However, the IJV remains a very important category of innovative firm in China. All subsidiaries of foreign parent companies including IJVs have experienced pressures from the Chinese government to provide technology to support local capability building. Given the economic conditions, the local institutional environment, and the target markets, many IJVs realized that they have had to substantially adapt their technology for Chinese operations, and hence to build suitable local capabilities. Therefore, this chapter focuses especially on an analysis of learning in IJVs.

3.2.5. Relationships between Foreign-Owned/IJV Firms and their Environment

MNCs that command sophisticated technologies wish to produce in China in part to exploit their technological advantages by gaining access to potentially substantial Chinese domestic markets. However, small firms from some other newly industrialized economies such as Hong Kong use more mundane technologies. They are more interested in using low-cost inputs, such as labor and land in China, so that they can continue to export manufactured goods to third countries, thus avoiding rising input costs in their own domestic economies. The following are some of the issues involved in the scope for inter-firm and inter-unit transfer of technological knowledge by foreign-owned firms operating in China.

Absorptive Capacity of Local Partners

Absorptive capacity refers to the ability to identify, access, and utilize know-how for economic gain (Cohen and Levinthal, 1990). Prior research reveals that the influx of FDI does not necessarily always generate a technology spillover effect. Whether FDI advances the host country's industrial technology and stable economic growth will depend upon the host country's absorptive capacity (Blomstrom and Kokko, 2001; Borensztein et al., 1998). Cantwell (1989) suggested that in a host country environment in which local technological absorptive capacity is weak, foreign investors may not engage in technologically sophisticated production, but may concentrate instead on simpler assembly-type activities. Klevorick et al. (1995) argued that only when accumulated know-how and technological capability have reached a certain level can FDI begin to contribute to an innovative local industry.

In his paper, Fu (2008) found that FDI has a significant positive impact on the overall regional innovation capacity in China. The strength of this positive effect depends, however, on the availability of the absorptive capacity and the presence of innovation-complementary assets in the host region. Increased regional innovation and the assimilation of technological capabilities through FDI have contributed to further regional economic growth in China's coastal regions, but not in the inland regions.

Attracting and Training Local Talent

China has long been known as a source of inexpensive labor. Although this may still be the case for the country's unskilled labor market, companies that are looking to hire for finance, technical, or managerial openings have a difficult time finding and retaining employees. The competition for talent means that turnover rates are high and wage levels are rising. From 2001 to 2005, average employee turnover rates in China rose from under 9 percent to around 14 percent. In 2006, according to Hewitt Associates, average salary rates increased by 7–9 percent in first-tier cities such as Beijing, Shanghai, and Guangzhou, and by 7.5–10.6 percent for second-tier cities such as Chengdu, Sichuan; Hangzhou, Zhejiang; and Wuhan, Hubei. The pool of new university graduates is also smaller than is sometimes suggested. The McKinsey Global Institute in a recent report (Farrell and Grant, 2005) estimated that between 2003 and 2008, China will have 15.7 million university graduates (excluding medical graduates) of which only 1.2 million will be suitable for employment in large MNCs because the majority lack the necessary mix of skills and experience (US-China Business Council (US-CBC)).

Many MNCs have realized that sustainable growth depends on their ability to attract, retain, and motivate the best talent. Many foreign-owned firms view attracting and training their employees as a significant step in their localization strategy. The training effect of FDI has often been viewed as a positive one for domestic firms. In China, a substantial disparity exists between the wages being paid by foreign-owned firms and by local firms. Under these circumstances, it is not common for the employees trained by foreign-owned firms to leave those firms to return to Chinese companies. Therefore, many of the foreign-owned firms are able to retain the local talent they have identified and trained.

Intra-firm Innovation Networks

In his study of China's IT industry, Ernst (2008) found that China is now the largest exporter of IT goods, surpassing the US (up from tenth in 2000). *Formal corporate networks* link Chinese firms to global customers, investors, technology suppliers, and strategic partners through FDI, as well as through venture capital, private equity investment, and contract-based alliances. And *informal global social networks* link China to more developed overseas innovation systems, primarily in the US, through the international circulation of students and knowledge workers. This has led to China's integration into intra-firm global innovation networks. These global firms "outsource" some stages of innovation to specialized Chinese-based suppliers, as part of complex inter-firm networks.

3.3. STATE-OWNED ENTERPRISES IN CHINA

The economic reforms in China started with the government tolerating the growth of private domestic businesses that operated in competition with SOEs. These businesses supported the large, high-tech SOEs and became more and more competitive, driving some non-performing SOEs into bankruptcy.

The central-government-owned SOEs remain the basic pillars of China's economy. They produce almost all of the nation's crude oil, gas, and ethane, offer all the basic telecommunication services, generate 43 percent of the country's power, and manufacture 47.5 percent of the vehicles and 60 percent of high-quality steel, according to the People's Daily Report. These SOEs have evolved from bureaucratic appendages to commercial enterprises that seek to expand their strengths, minimize their weaknesses, and capitalize on market opportunities. Two recent developments have strengthened the responsiveness of Chinese firms. One is the growth of research and development (R&D) spending, which reached 1.4 percent of GDP in 2006, and the shift of R&D activity from government agencies to enterprises. The second is the growing influence of foreign firms, which elevates the risks associated with stand-pat business strategies, but also supports the efforts of domestic firms to generate a dynamic response to intense competition (Brandt and Rawski, 2008).

3.3.1. Evolution of State-owned Enterprises

On the other side of this story has been SOE reform. Developments in the private and FIE sectors over the past few decades have put tremendous pressure on the Chinese government to develop strategies to accelerate the reform of SOEs, which had become more and more of a burden to the economy. The new reform movement focused on (a) ownership change, (b) industry restructuring, and (c) improved business performance. In 1997, China piloted an ownership-reform program involving 1,000 SOEs. These companies were allowed to become shareholding companies. While the pilot scheme experienced mixed successes and failures, the State Council confirmed during the Ninth National People's Congress that the trend was established and decided to expose more companies to ownership reform.

The Chinese government is well aware of the critical role innovation has played in the development of SOEs. The starting point for SOE reform in China initially was simply a matter of survival and growth. Due to intensified competition, many SOEs came to realize that they must adopt international management standards, and catch up with or upgrade their technology. These efforts fall mainly into the categories of technological innovation and management innovation.

To promote a national reform strategy to improve the business performance of the SOEs, the State Council announced its directive in the late 1990s: "Gripping the large and letting go the small." This suggests that China will try to propel its large SOEs into competitive, large enterprises, while allowing smaller SOEs to become the targets of merger acquisitions for both foreign and domestic buyers. As a result of this initiative, three of the SOEs in this study have become listed companies on the stock market, and several of them have themselves become Chinese-owned multinational corporations that have made investments in foreign countries.

3.3.2. Types of SOEs

Over the period of economic reforms, SOEs have moved from state control to the following three categories. These categories overlap and are not mutually exclusive.

STOCKLISTED COMPANIES Many of the best-performing innovative SOEs have become listed firms on the Chinese stock markets. Unlike the financial markets in the established industrialized countries, the primary reason for creating stock markets in China was to allow state-owned enterprises (SOEs) to raise capital from Chinese households and from foreign entities by initial public offerings (IPOs) of unseasoned (never before traded) shares as a substitute for continued central government funding of such capital investment (China Stock Research). Many of these companies continue to be funded by the government and have a unique advantage over their private-owned counterparts—easier access to public resources. They thrive in large part owing to this easier access, examples being China Mobile or China National Petroleum, each being the most profitable companies in their respective domains in Asia in 2008. In 2008, 64.2 percent of SOEs (including their subsidiaries) had undertaken shareholding reforms, compared with only 30.4 percent in 2002, according to Li Rongrong, the minister in charge of the State-owned Assets Supervision and Administration Commission (SASAC). A number of large SOEs have gone public in both domestic and foreign stock markets. Of about 1,500 listed companies in China's A-share stock markets, more than 1,100 were wholly or partly state owned. Seventy-eight centrally administered SOEs were listed on stock exchanges in Hong Kong, New York, and Singapore.

LARGE INDUSTRY GROUPS As SOEs have merged or acquired assets from other SOEs, the country's state-owned economy has gradually been consolidating within critical sectors, especially in sectors that were deemed important for state security and the national economy. These critical sectors, such as oil, petrochemicals, power, national defense, telecommunications, transportation, and mining, account for about 83 percent of the total assets of centrally administered SOEs. These SOE giants have shouldered almost all the production of crude oil and natural gas, and have provided all the basic telecommunications and 55 percent of the country's power supply. Eighty-two percent of civil aviation services also have come from these SOEs. With deepening reforms, the total number of Chinese SOEs has declined; but those that have survived are growing in size. The country has 149 centrally administered SOEs, down from 196 in 2003, and the number is expected to shrink to between 80 and 100 by 2010, through merger and restructuring, according to SASAC. Although declining in numbers, the major business groups accounted for 35.91 percent of total assets, 61.54 percent of sales revenues, and 63.25 percent of profits of all SOEs in the country (*China Daily*, 2008).

CHINESE-OWNED MULTINATIONALS China has followed a manufacturing-based, export-oriented, and East Asian development strategy, allowing the country to accumulate large domestic savings. According to IMF projections, over the next five years China will reach a cumulative surplus of $3.4 trillion, which will provide even greater incentives for the national government to pursue a "go-global" investment strategy. Figures for outward foreign direct investments (OFDI) released by the OECD Investment Committee at the end of March 2008 show that Chinese companies have supplied over $90 bn of OFDI. Data from the Chinese Ministry of Commerce reveal that about 60 percent of the country's outward investments between 1979 and 2002 were directed to Asia, followed by the United States, Africa, and Latin America. According to the OECD Investment News report, published in March, 2008, China's OFDI flow and stock have surged since the end of 2000 and so stood in 2008 as the fourth and the sixth largest respectively among the emerging markets.

China encourages SOEs to invest abroad, to set up subsidiaries in other countries, and to participate in international mergers and acquisitions. To that end, China has developed consultative and legal services for overseas investment. In 2006, China's overall outbound FDI including the financial sector reached $21.2 bn, an increase of nearly 73 percent over 2005. Central government sources—presumably state-owned enterprises—have provided the majority of China's outbound FDI, providing $15.2 bn (86 percent) of the net flow of outbound non-financial FDI.

Like MNCs from the established industrialized countries, Chinese MNCs invest abroad to secure, maintain, and expand their markets. According to the OECD, a significant share of Chinese investment in the African manufacturing and construction sectors has been undertaken by small and medium-sized Chinese companies seeking to increase their market share and market size. Market-seeking is a predictable consequence of China's export-oriented policies of the last few years. Outward FDI in most cases allows a company to circumvent trade barriers and to facilitate the exportation of domestically produced products.

China's population and economic growth, its occasional natural disasters, and the explosion of its manufacturing sector have all contributed dramatically to increasing its need for natural resources, such as oil and gas, and wood. China Metallurgical Industrial Corporation's (CMIC) investment in the Channar Mine in Australia, China National Non-ferrous Metal Industrial Corporation's investment in Portland Aluminum Smelter in Australia, China International Trust and Investment Corporation's (CITIC) investment in a sawmill in Alberta, Canada and the China National Petroleum Corporation's (CNPC) equity in an oil extraction project in Canada (Pamlin) are just a few examples of Chinese resource-seeking FDI. By the end of 2003, Chinese MNCs had invested in 58 overseas oil and gas projects, and 10 important overseas mineral projects, accounting for sales revenues of $5 bn (*People's Daily China*).

Another group of Chinese MNCs invest abroad—especially in industrialized states—with the intention of acquiring "strategic assets." These are intangible assets that improve a firm's competitive advantage in the marketplace, including technological know-how, production and management systems, supply networks, and intellectual property. The focus of a strategic asset-seeking company is to acquire such intangible property to gain a competitive advantage beneficial for its long-term strategic goals. In the period 1997–2001, the United States was the second largest recipient of China's outward investments, in the amount of US$207 mn (Hong and Sun, 2004). There are many reasons Chinese companies have targeted the strategic assets of the United States and other industrialized regions. A Chinese firm might choose to merge with a foreign rival to strengthen its position against another even more powerful rivals. And Lenovo's acquisition of IBM's PC division is an example of using acquisitions to expand knowledge in the area of management expertise.

3.3.3. Innovative /Innovative Characteristics of SOEs

Many SOEs have developed local technological capability by acquiring and then using the international resources and knowledge of foreign firms.

After a quarter century of economic reform, there has been a shift toward a higher level of innovative capability in Chinese companies (Xu et al., 2003). These innovative Chinese companies have realized that in order to compete in the marketplace, it is not enough to focus on product and process innovation in a separated sequence of steps, but instead the whole organization needs to be on a continuous path of innovation. This form of innovation involves the cross-functional and cross-divisional integration of efforts within firms, and even extends to a greater integration of some activities in strategic alliances with other organizations, as well as mergers and acquisitions. All employees are drawn into the process of innovation. Innovation is reflected throughout the entire value chain, customer service, supplier relationships, management system, and organization culture. This intensity and consistency of innovation enables the enterprise to better satisfy its customers and to become more competitive in the global marketplace.

Many Chinese firms stand to learn much more from a world-class company than from other purely local organizations, teaming up with foreign firms that are positioned to make significant advances over a short period of time. Entering into IJVs may greatly enhance a local firm's position in the market, allowing it to pursue business opportunities that would have been too risky or costly otherwise. Local firms have been able to absorb management systems and technology from their partners.

The Xizi Group provides a good example. The Xizi Group was an elevator company. It founded its elevator operations in 1997, the same year in which it formed a joint venture with Otis Elevator Co. The Xizi Group contributed the production assets for the venture and began with a 70 percent share of the IJV's equity. In 2001, Otis Elevator Co. bought 50 percent of the equity from its Chinese partner, giving it an 80 percent ownership interest in the joint venture. This change in ownership was contemplated in the original IJV agreement. Xizi Group's management had been concerned that its US partner was unfamiliar with the Chinese market. Thus, the two parties agreed that the Xizi Group would maintain majority ownership for the first five years of the IJV, and resolve the ultimate ownership issue at a later date. That time came four years later, when the US partner received equity control in July 2001. In exchange for its agreement to sell its majority interest to Otis Elevator Co., the Xizi Group obtained the right to be the IJV's principal parts and components supplier. This partnership allowed the Xizi Group to have access to Otis's most up-to-date technology and first-class business management systems. Such learning processes did not end with the joint venture itself and its immediate or direct relationships; the best business practices were shared with other subsidiaries within the Xizi Group (Li et al., 2008).

In his dissertation, Mao (2006) analyzed China's electronic information industry, including four of its most innovative firms: Huawei, Lenovo, ZTE, and TCL. He found that these innovative firms all have strategic management capability. They are able to examine the external environment, and analyze their internal strengths and weaknesses to identify long-term strategic objectives. These firms have also built their technological capability so as to manage their own product/process innovation, all of them having developed their own R&D facilities. These firms have strong links with their customers, and strong marketing capabilities. They align their organizational structures with their strategic goals to implement their strategic plans. Each values human capital as well as intellectual property. SOEs must develop their capabilities and change their organizational structures in order to adapt to a competitive business environment. This evolutionary process is occurring as external conditions themselves have changed, as China has become steadily more integrated into the global economy. The VCR industry (Lu and Mu, 2011) and the automobile industry, particularly the Geely company (Chen and Wang, 2007), provide good examples of how innovation has overtaken domestic Chinese firms.

High integration into global knowledge networks can expose Chinese firms to leading-edge technology, management approaches, intellectual tools, and sources of knowledge. This integration can influence the evolution of their approach to the development of innovative capabilities. ZTE was one of the first Chinese telecom equipment providers to pursue business in overseas markets. ZTE now has about 50,000 employees and 8,000 of them are working in about 100 representative offices around the world. With more than one-third of its workforce dedicated to R&D and with 10 percent of its annual revenues channeled into this endeavor, ZTE has established 16 R&D centers and institutes across North America, Europe, and Asia.

These successful firms demonstrate their innovative capability not only in terms of technological improvement but also in their sound strategic management and intelligent modifications to their organizational structures and organizational cultures (Xu et al., 2003). They also take advantage of external resources, some collaborating with global companies to better achieve their research and development objectives (Chen, 2001). Having acquired IBM's PC division, Lenovo claims that it "strives to be a new world company that makes award-winning PCs for customers, operates as a company uninhibited by walls or organizational structures using world sourcing to harness the power of innovation across a global team." Many successful Chinese firms have not attempted to jump right into "technology leadership" strategies, or to compete head-on with global technology leaders through "radical" innovations. Instead, they appear to have focused on "incremental" and "architectural" innovations that allow them to pursue "technology diversification" strategies (Ernst, 2008).

Lu and Mu's (2011) study of the digital video player industry in China revealed how certain Chinese firms innovated by leveraging and combining international resources: having the foreign firm C-cube build an MPEG decoding chip, having Phillips build a disk drive and specialized computer, and having a Taiwanese firm build the die. Combining these components using its own software program, a new product, VCD, was created. Some Chinese firms, such as Lenovo, have very strong ties with the Chinese Academy of Sciences, a connection that helps it to quickly absorb R&D findings and potential new directions for exploration from universities and national laboratories.

China has successfully used FDI by leveraging its large market and organizationally dynamic production base to access technology. Procurement policies were used skillfully to ensure that prospective suppliers of equipment, aircraft, and computers built facilities in China. There was a complete coordination of policy on technology and on building self-reliance. With the help of Boeing, Airbus, and others, China has developed its own increasingly competitive civilian and military aerospace production within ten massive state-owned conglomerates (Venkitaramanan, 2000).

3.4. THE DESIGN OF THE STUDY

3.4.1. The Sample

The study discussed here sampled 51 international joint ventures in China through the submission of a detailed survey questionnaire. All of those surveyed were manufacturers who had operated in China for at least two years. They produce goods in industries such as food packaging, equipment fabrication, automobiles, process automation, and telecommunication. Several of the joint ventures share common parents, either on the Chinese side or the foreign side.

In addition, 12 joint ventures participated in open-ended interviews, designed to validate the survey results by eliciting greater detail about the IJV's technological capability accumulation. These interviews each took place with a general manager, deputy general manager, or a member of the IJV's board of directors. The IJVs that participated in the interview process include joint ventures at differing stages of their technological development, thus allowing a comparison of the findings based upon the stage of technological capability development.

One of the largest industry groups in South China supported this study. The group, which has since disbanded, had 572 members, of which 179 had formed joint ventures with foreign companies. Thirty-one of these IJVs (i.e. 17.3 percent) responded to this survey. Four of them were dropped from the study because they did not supply sufficient data. The industry group was comprised of companies in a variety of industries, including food, electronics, chemicals, and packaging. The conglomeration of firms was assembled by the Chinese government with a mission to implement government industrial policies and quotas. Traditionally, the Chinese economy was divided into 29 sectors, each managed by a separate ministry. For example, the Ministry of Machinery (MM) managed the machinery industry in the country, a sector that included food-processing and light-industry machinery such as bicycles, refrigerators, and some electronics (before the electronics industry exploded). The MM delegated responsibility for the management of this industry to an industry group—known as the Bureau of Light Industry—that operated at the provincial and municipal levels. As China gradually moved from a planned to a market economy, the administrative function of this bureau came to play a more important role in business management. Therefore, the bureau's name was changed in the mid-1990s to the Industry Group.

The Industry Group was disbanded in 2005 for two reasons. First, its size and the diversity of industries made it unmanageable. In addition, the Chinese government came to realize that its control over a group of profit-driven firms posed a conflict, inasmuch as the government was clearly committed to a policy of favoring SOEs. Therefore, local governments decided to manage these industries through a series of geographically dispersed administrative authorities, rather than through one "industrial" group. As the Industry Group was too unwieldy to effectively operate as one group, there need be no concern that this study suffers from reliance upon an organization that possesses one "group identity."

The survey was also distributed among the graduates of Rutgers Executive Masters in Business Administration (EMBA) program in China. Rutgers initiated an EMBA program in Beijing in 1998. The EMBA program was geared toward employees of high potential who worked at multinational corporations in China. Many of these graduates are now working in international joint ventures. The survey was sent to 100 Rutgers graduates, 27 of whom (27 percent) responded. Three of these respondents supplied insufficient data. Therefore, they were dropped from the study.

3.4.2. Sample Characteristics

China started to make efforts to attract FDI in 1979. Before 1995 there was no alternative to the joint venture mode for foreign businesses that wanted to enter the Chinese market. The sampled data seem consistent with these developments. Twenty-seven of the joint ventures are 11 years or older; only six are 5 years or younger. Among the sampled firms, 23 of them have made investment of more than US$25 mn, while 28 joint ventures have had less than US$25 mn investment.

As foreign firms could not establish wholly owned ventures prior to 1995, many of these ventures involve majority ownership by the foreign partner, but not complete ownership. In those situations, the foreign party usually retains control over key management decisions, as well as issues concerning technology transfer. This is borne out in the sampled data. More than 50 percent of these joint ventures are minority owned by the Chinese partner. Among the sample firms, in 32 of the joint ventures the Chinese partner owned less than a 50 percent share of the venture.

However, over the last 20 years, as China's economic reform has progressed, the national policy toward FDI and SOEs has changed. From the mid-1990s onwards, China began to allow foreign firms to have wholly owned ventures in China. Some of the foreign investing firms started to take more equity, and some converted from IJVs to become wholly owned foreign enterprises.

As a consequence of these changes in ownership structure, our surveyed firms can now be divided into four different types: (i) joint ventures majority owned by foreign parties, (ii) joint ventures majority owned by the Chinese partner; (iii) foreign firms that have bought out their Chinese partners, becoming wholly owned foreign subsidiaries; and (iv) enterprises absorbed into large Chinese-owned SOEs that have become stocklisted companies. Table 3.5 provides some descriptive characteristics of our sample.

3.4.3. The Survey Questionnaire

We designed a questionnaire for the purposes of this study and approached every IJV to administer the questionnaire. This led to greater reliability of the data collected. In addition, we conducted further in-depth interviews with 12 IJVs.

The questionnaire was written in English and translated into Chinese. The respondents were permitted to answer the questionnaire either in English or in Chinese. The distribution of most of the questionnaires was accomplished face-to-face; in some instances this was done by email or facsimile. Using the typology of capability levels shown in Table 3.6, we asked the respondent firms if their IJV had built capability in each of the functions at each of the capability levels listed. If the answer was yes, we also asked them how many years it took for their IJV to build such capability. In this way, we developed an understanding of the speed of capability building in each functional area in each IJV.

Table 3.5. Selected characteristics of the sample of international joint ventures

	Joint ventures			Joint ventures	
	No.	%		No.	%
Age: no of years					
0–5 years	6	12			
6–10 years	18	35			
11–15 years	11	22			
16–20 years	7	14			
21 + years	9	18			
Size: total investment (US$)			*Share of Chinese ownership*		
< 25 mn	28	55	<50% (Majority foreign-owned)	34[1]	67
25–49 mn	10	20	= 50% (50-50 joint ventures)	9	18
50–100 mn	6	12	>50% (Majority Chinese)	8[2]	16
> 100 mn	7	14			
Country of origin			*Sector of industry*		
United States	20	39	Food	3	6
Germany	4	8	Leather	5	10
Japan	7	14	Manufacture of transport equipment	7	14
Hong Kong	11	22	Electronics	9	18
Sweden	5	10	Electrical machinery	11	22
Others	4	8	General purpose machinery	13	25
			Other	3	6

Notes: 1. Of which two have become wholly foreign-owned, having bought out their Chinese partner.
2. Of which four involve large SOEs or former SOEs as the controlling Chinese partner. Across all 51 IJVs, the Chinese partner was a former SOE that is now a nationally stocklisted company in eight cases (or in 16% of the sample).

Source: Authors' elaboration.

The questions above examined the learning speed at which a particular level of technological capability was developed by the sample firms. The number of years which firms take to learn and conduct activities at one technological capability level before successfully moving to another specified level is summarized in Table 3.7. The learning speed provides indicators of the number of years taken by the sampled firms to move from one technological level to the next. From the above data, we can see that all the firms have reached basic operative capability. However, as one progresses through steadily more advanced levels of capability, so fewer and fewer firms have managed to move to the higher level of innovative capability. Some firms have become "stuck" at the various different levels of technological capability.

The data also indicate that it does not necessarily take longer on average to move up from one level to the next higher level when firms reach the more advanced stages of capability development, such as the generation of R&D innovative capability (that is, among those firms that do actually manage to move between levels in each of the phases of capability development).

Table 3.6. Innovation capability building: a typology of capability levels

Main activities Capability level	Investment functions *Decision-making and control*	Investment functions *Project preparation and implementation*	Production functions *Organization of processes and production*	*Product centered*	Supporting functions *Developing linkages*
Basic operative capabilities	Engaging primary contractor and payment estimation	Preparation of initial project outline; Construction of basic civil works	Routine operation and basic maintenance; Efficiency improvement from experience in existing tasks	Replication of product specifications and designs	Procurement of available inputs from existing suppliers; Sale of given products to existing and new customers
Basic innovative capabilities	Active monitoring and control of feasibility study, technology choice/sourcing, and project scheduling	Project feasibility study, standard equipment procurement, and simple ancillary engineering	Improving layout, scheduling, maintenance, and minor process adaptation	Minor adaptations to market needs, and incremental improvement in product quality	Searching and absorbing new information for suppliers, customers, and local institutions
Intermediate innovative capabilities	Search, evaluation, and selection of technology; Sources, tenders, negotiations, and overall project management	Detailed engineering, project scheduling, and management; Commissioning	Process improvement, licensing new technology; Introducing production organizational changes	Licensing new product technology and/or reverse engineering, incremental new product designs	Technology transfer to local suppliers to increase efficiency, quality for local supply
Advanced innovative capabilities	Developing new production systems and components; Product innovation and related R&D	Basic process design and related R&D	Innovation in processes and related R&D	Design of basic characteristics for new products; Product innovation and related R&D	Collaboration in technological development with suppliers, customers, and partners

Source: Adapted from Bell and Pavitt (1995); Lall (1992).

Table 3.7. Descriptive statistics of the sample firms

Main activities	Investment functions		Production functions		Supporting functions
Capability level	Decision-making and control	Project preparation and implementation	Organization of processes and production	Product centered	Developing linkages
Basic operative capabilities	Mean = 1.329 N = 51 Min = 0 Max = 3	Mean = 1.24 N = 51 Min = 0 Max = 3	Mean = 1.99 N = 51 Min = 0 Max = 14	Mean = 2.08 N = 51 Min = 0 Max = 14	Mean = 1.75 N = 51 Min = 0 Max = 14
Basic innovative capabilities	Mean = 1.23 N = 39 Min = 0.5 Max = 3	Mean = 1.36 N = 42 Min = 0.5 Max = 6	Mean = 2.64 N = 46 Min = 0.5 Max = 11	Mean = 2.76 N = 44 Min = 0.25 Max = 14	Mean = 2.4 N = 45 Min = 0.25 Max = 14
Intermediate innovative capabilities	Mean = 1.53 N = 39 Min = 0.5 Max = 4	Mean = 1.7 N = 40 Min = 1 Max = 8	Mean = 3.47 N = 39 Min = 0.5 Max = 10	Mean = 3.71 N = 36 Min = 0.5 Max = 10	Mean = 3.55 N = 31 Min = 1 Max = 12
Advanced innovative capabilities	Mean = 2.46 N = 13 Min = 1 Max = 7	Mean = 2.46 N = 13 Min = 1 Max = 7	Mean = 3.7 N = 20 Min = 1 Max = 9	Mean = 3.91 N = 22 Min = 1 Max = 10	Mean = 3.29 N = 29 Min = 1 Max = 8

Mean = average number of years needed to learn a particular level of technological capability

N = number of firms that have reached that level of technological capability

Min = minimum number of years taken to reach that level of technological capability

Max = maximum number of years taken for firms to research that level of technological capability

Source: Authors' elaboration.

However, a lower proportion of firms successfully made the transition to the next higher stage once they had reached more advanced capabilities. Looking at the maximum technological capability levels reached by the sample firms, more than half have reached intermediate innovative capability but have not yet moved on to an advanced capability level. The question, therefore, is whether these firms will move on to build more advanced innovative capabilities, or whether they will remain in the existing status quo or pursue other types of capability. The interviews with the managers of the sample firms indicate that some of the firms are still in the process of moving up, according to the interviewees at the time of the survey. However, two firms suggested that their foreign partners would continue to take responsibility for projects requiring a focus on research and development. In these two cases, the foreign partner regarded their China IJVs as just a production base.

This study also found that local linkages (between the IJVs and their customers and suppliers) were associated with significant knowledge flows. Twenty-nine IJVs have reached advanced innovative capability, which means that these IJVs have collaborated in technological development with their suppliers, customers, and partners. The results provide evidence that those local suppliers that have formed linkages with IJVs have been able to use these linkages to gain knowledge in innovative activities to build their own local innovative capability.

From our interviews and empirical study, it was found that exporting was an important contributory factor in explaining whether or not IJVs have been able to reach the highest levels of innovative capability. This is likely due to product quality demands and standards in high-income markets associated with global competition in those markets. However, even those IJVs that were exporting to low-income markets found that they often needed innovative capabilities to produce the cheap but effective products that were demanded in those markets.

3.5. BUILDING INNOVATION CAPABILITIES IN IJVS

In this section we will discuss our analytical findings aimed mainly at determining how firms have evolved through different "levels" of innovative capability and activity toward a more innovative type of enterprise. What factors have facilitated these learning trajectories? The common characteristic of the more locally innovative foreign-owned firms is their leveraging of their resources in the global market by maintaining strong links with their foreign headquarters. However, those successful firms do not simply "replicate" their foreign or global products in the Chinese market; instead they have modified them to accommodate local conditions.

3.5.1. Linkages between MNC HQs and the IJVs

The accumulation of technology within the international network of an IJV is a path-dependent learning process. Effective learning is reflected in an enhancement of an organization's skills and capabilities. Determining which vertical and horizontal links will exist within a global network is a critical supervisory function of MNC management. As this study confirms, alliances between IJVs and their foreign parents and affiliates have given local Chinese businesses opportunities for knowledge accumulation beyond their own internal resources. The extent of IJV linkages with foreign headquarters regulates by how much they can improve their competitive position through such linkages. Kumar and van Dissel (1996) concluded that, with effective planning and management, inter-organizational projects will facilitate access to new knowledge, and through information and technology exchanges between their staffs, the collaborating firms will experience improvement in their knowledge management capability. Knowledge absorption is a concept that subsumes topics such as knowledge recognition, knowledge source identification, knowledge acquisition, and knowledge storage. Usually, firms acquire new technology from the outside based on experience. That is, they continuously monitor changes in the external environment so as to obtain knowledge to achieve improved performance in their own internal projects.

Some researchers have concluded that knowledge recognition and knowledge creation are two important elements of knowledge acquisition, which itself is the beginning of knowledge management. Only through the formal process of knowledge acquisition can new knowledge be understood, accepted, and used by organizations (Nonaka and Takeuchi, 1995; McAdam, 2000). Cohen and Levinthal (1990) have determined that the efficiency with which an organization absorbs new knowledge from the outside, and the quality of such knowledge, will be enhanced as the organization improves its communication with outside sources. They also concluded that the capability of an organization to identify and evaluate new information rested with those employees who are interfacing with external sources, including those appointed to act as liaisons for cross-organizational projects, so-called information "gatekeepers," and knowledge "sensors." Nonaka and Takeuchi (1995) pointed out that knowledge acquisition was a social interaction that occurred primarily at the employee level.

IJV integration can be implemented in various ways that will be dictated by the knowledge or resources which each side needs. In the late 1980s and 1990s, many of the SOEs wanted to improve their management systems. Therefore, forming joint ventures with foreign companies became a potential channel for learning. The integration resulted in gains in productivity, some breakthroughs in innovation and sales revenue increases. Many of our sample firms claimed to have benefited from their relationship with foreign parents by learning and adopting western management systems. Those IJVs dispatched their personnel to foreign headquarters to learn various aspects of the parent company management system, such as total quality control or lean production, which they have now implemented as their own. Many IJVs implemented a "total quality" management system. This system permitted IJVs to improve their quality control while reducing costs. Productivity increased, but so too did quality control, resulting in the fabrication of fewer unmarketable products. These savings led to a direct reduction in unit costs. Increased product quality meant lower re-work and scrappage costs. Greater product quality also meant lower warranty costs. The net effect of implementing this total quality management system has been that a company such as Trust has reduced both its manufacturing and service costs.

Many of these IJVs have adapted the Toyota system, in which the focus is upon improving the "flow" (or smoothness) of work through the system and not upon "waste reduction" per se. Techniques to improve flow include production leveling by "pulling" production using the Kanban signaling system. Many of these workshops have implemented this visual system, which helps to monitor current inventory levels on the production line. The system helps to shorten the production cycle by improving inventory turnover. Lean manufacturing allows these IJVs to focus on getting the right parts to the right place at the right time, and in the right quantity to achieve perfect work flow while minimizing waste and maintaining flexibility.

All the interviewed firms in our sample reported that from the start, the IJVs' foreign parents made tremendous efforts to integrate the IJVs into their global networks (see Table 3.8). Senior managers of the IJV were flown to the parent's headquarters to be trained in the values and business mission of the parent. Senior managers of the parent travelled to the IJV every few months, for visits of three days or longer. During these visits, issues relating to production, finances, and human resources management were discussed. The IJV's management team gave presentations to the senior managers on the progress of each department: production, processing, purchasing, finance, and sales. The senior managers offered advice and comments on key issues. Through these exchanges, the foreign parent came to understand the operational issues of the IJV. Likewise, the IJV managers began to understand the management philosophy of the foreign parent.

Our sampling indicated that half of the IJVs were doing at least some international networking frequently. One of the sample firms reported that the IJV built strong ties with another subsidiary of the foreign parent, a company the IJV came to regard as its "sister." The sister plant transferred technology and a management system to the IJV. During the first year of the IJV, 30 of its employees (equipment operators and workshop maintenance crews) were dispatched to the sister plant for a three-month training program.

Table 3.8. Links between the IJVs and their MNC partners

A. Integrating mechanisms with MNC HQ: (number of days per year spent in various activities)	No. of days (average)
IJV top managers participating in executive development programs involving participants from headquarters	18.8
IJV top managers working at corporate headquarters	21.0
Formal training for IJV top managers at corporate headquarters	19.0
Headquarters-based managers located at the IJV for the purpose of integrating IJV top management into the organization	25.3
B. Integrating mechanisms with MNC affiliates: (frequency with which the following occur in the IJV)	No. of IJV managers reporting "very frequent"
The transfer of top managers to different international locations for the purpose of building a shared corporate philosophy	8
The seeking of advice from managers of different international locations	16
Inter-unit committees that are set up to allow managers from different international locations to engage in joint decision-making	16
Permanent teams to coordinate decisions and actions with other subsidiaries	18
Informal personal contact between managers from different international locations	19
Scheduled meetings of managers from different international locations	20
Informal communication between managers from different international locations	22
Temporary task forces to facilitate international collaboration on a specific project	25
Liaison personnel whose specific job is to coordinate the efforts of international functional areas	25

Source: The categories used in our study were adapted from O'Donnell (2000).

During this period, the operators worked side-by-side with their counterparts from the sister plant to observe how the plant operated. The training was hands-on: the operators were instructed how to run the equipment, and actually manufactured products for sale. This created an environment in which technology was freely shared across organizational and geographic borders. Because the product mix of the IJV was different from that of its sister plant, the parent introduced the IJV to other affiliated plants that could provide technological assistance with other products. Operators from the IJV were also dispatched to those plants to learn their manufacturing processes. In this way, the IJV was able to gather new information about a wide range of products from an international network of affiliates. This intra-organizational network shaped the IJV's innovation dynamics and diffusion rates.

3.5.2. Local Adaptation and Technological Capability Accumulation

From the point of view of technological accumulation, the use of technology in new environments needs adaptation. Such adaptation generates new innovation (Cantwell, 1989). As the firm is a device for collective and organizational learning through problem-solving in production—and not merely an administrator and server of markets—the major issue is not so much how the firm exploits a given competence, but rather how it establishes (geographically and by sector) a diffuse system for the creation of new competence. In order to consolidate, as well as exploit, an existing capability, it is generally necessary for a firm to extend that capability into new related fields of production and technology, and across a variety of geographic sites (Cantwell, 2001).

Because joint ventures are generally close to the local market, IJVs tend to assume responsibility for local market positioning and product adaptation to suit local conditions (see Table 3.9). The uniqueness of the local market may require the IJV to modify and adapt MNC technology to suit local conditions. Pressures for local adaptation arise from differences in consumer tastes and preferences, differences in national economic conditions and traditional practices (Ghoshal and Bartlett, 1998). Tailoring products to a large emerging market is no trivial task. Minor cultural adaptations or marginal cost reductions will not suffice (Prahalad and Lieberthal, 1998). Low-income markets in emerging economies such as China present both tremendous opportunities and unique challenges (London and Hart, 2004). These innovations are context specific, may not be technically advanced in the developed world, but may be vitally relevant to the developing countries themselves.

Table 3.9. Local adaptation activities

Local adaptation	No. of IJVs	Percentage of local adaption
% of R&D (product, process modification) incorporated into products sold by IJV that is actually performed by this IJV	36: 18: 7	<50%, 51%–99% = 100%
% of products sold by IJV that have been manufactured (to any degree) by IJV	6: 18: 27	<50%, 51%–99% = 100%
% of products sold by this IJV that have been created or substantially modified for this market	27: 15: 8	<50%, 51%–99% = 100%

Source: The categories used in our study were adapted from Harzing (2002).

Local adaptation is also a process of utilizing existing knowledge, including knowledge recently gained, to find new solutions to problems. Local adaptation is an important process by which an IJV can improve its competitive position by exploiting its accumulated knowledge more effectively and through finding new combinations (Yang, 2005).

Tetra Pak's joint venture in China is an ice cream equipment company, which reported that initially the IJV intended merely to reproduce its foreign parent's technology in the local environment. Three expatriates were brought in to carry out this mission: a general manager, a director of engineering, and a plant manager. However, very soon the managers of the IJV realized that the foreign technology was not compatible with conditions in the local marketplace. New technologies were needed through adaptation from the old. Catering to consumer tastes and preferences, and traditional practices, competitors in this local market were using less milk and more milk substitutes to produce ice cream. Thus, local ice cream equipment needed to process these substitutes into a finished product tasting as if it was made from milk. The peculiarities of this local market required the IJV to modify and adapt its parent's technology to meet these challenges. And such adaptation generated significant technological capabilities within the joint venture (Li, 2006).

The experience of this IJV teaches us that the pressure to respond to local conditions may defeat a joint venture's simple reliance upon its foreign parent's technology. As was true in the case of this IJV, incremental innovations often have to be developed. "Doing what we do, only better." Such innovation is built upon an established platform, on which a continuous stream of technological developments revolutionizes the quality of the original product. This joint venture was able to develop a complete range of new ice cream machinery, a technological capability that was subsequently upstreamed to its foreign parent. During this developmental process, the IJV enhanced the already-significant market penetration achieved previously by the Chinese partner in the domestic Chinese market, sustaining and even expanding its competitive position locally.

After five years' operation in China, the IJV was promoting its own brand name, serving not just local customers but also foreign enterprises in China. With the rapid economic development China was experiencing, the Chinese had by now become the second largest consumers of ice cream in the world. Thanks to its first-hand appreciation of this burgeoning market, as well as the generally favorable demographics of the Chinese marketplace, the foreign parent was able to foresee China's emergence as the largest market for ice cream. The second phase of the IJV's business plan kicked in: more components were added to the portfolio, and another large ice cream machinery producer in China was acquired, merging the two operations. Over the last few years, the IJV's sales growth has increased by 15–20 percent annually.

3.5.3. Linking IJV Performance with Technological Capability Accumulation

Successful firms use data to determine how to adjust their routines, thus improving performance (Argyris and Schön, 1978). Outcome measurability is critical to this process.

Outcome measurability is the degree to which the joint venture's achievements are specifiable and quantifiable. The criteria used by headquarters to evaluate subsidiary performance are likely to influence what subsidiary managers pay attention to and focus on in their operations (O'Donnell, 2000; Bjorkman et al., 2004). Implicit in this is the presence of routines that represent systematic behavioral patterns, which enable the IJV's management to assimilate a wide range of signals and assess their relevance to the organization. Performance measurements help management to select appropriate projects that have a good strategic fit. The outcome measurements advise IJV management how to monitor and manage projects through the various stages of their development. These measures also assist management to decide where and when to terminate projects, and where and when to accelerate them.

To be effective, measurements must be developed based on the priorities set by a firm's strategic plan. It is this plan that provides the guidepost to assess the effectiveness of key business initiatives and the criteria for measuring that effectiveness. Processes are then designed to collect information relevant to these measurements and reduce it to numerical form. Decision makers examine the outcomes of various measured processes, gaining useful feedback from the results to inform future management decisions.

Establishing special measurement goals allows managers to know how well their business is running, and whether its products and services conform to customer requirements. There has been an increasing realization in Chinese business of the importance of customer satisfaction and of involving customers in the quality control process. When customers are dissatisfied, they will eventually find other suppliers that will meet their needs. Poor performance from this perspective is a leading indicator of future decline. Finally, performance measurements from the MNC HQ may help IJV management to review completed projects and derive helpful lessons for future projects. The measurable goals of an IJV need to capture both the breadth of its mission and specific activities and responsibilities.

Our survey of 51 joint ventures indicates that performance measurement has been positively correlated with the accumulation of technology capability, confirming the value of this management tool (see Table 3.10). Measuring outcomes allows joint ventures to determine what remains to be accomplished in order to achieve their business objectives. Measurements provide concrete feedback for managers, helping them to see the gap between projection and

Table 3.10. Establishing performance measurement

Outcome measurability	Great extent
To what extent does each of the following statements describe the IJV?	(No. of IJVS out of 51 in total)
The objectives of this IJV are clearly stated	47
There are specific performance objectives for this IJV/performance targets are set for this IJV	48
The outcomes toward which this IJV works are specified precisely	44
This IJV's important objectives are stated numerically	45

Source: The categories used in our study were adapted from O'Donnell (2000).

reality. This capacity for vision, apparently, has helped to foster the accumulation of technological capability.

3.6. THE INFLUENCE OF FOREIGN-OWNED FIRM DEVELOPMENT ON THE CAPABILITIES OF INDIGENOUS CHINESE FIRMS

From this empirical study, we have found that all the sample IJVs have been able not only to produce increasingly efficiently or replicate products, but also to build significant levels of innovative capability. All of our sample firms have basic operative capabilities, 46 firms have reached the level of basic innovative capability, 39 firms have researched the intermediate level of innovative capability, and 20 IJVs have advanced innovative capability in production functions.

In this section, we strive to answer the question of how, if at all, the paths of learning within IJV firms have influenced, or been influenced by, the development of innovative capabilities in other firms (especially those in other firm categories) in China.

FDI can take the form of a foreign firm buying or investing in a firm in a host country. FDI allows firms to expand their business in foreign markets by participating in or exercising control over business operations in the foreign country (Hennart, 1988). The inflow of FDI can not only increase the host country's capital stock and provide increased employment opportunities for the local workforce, it can also produce a "technology spillover effect" in the host economy. This spillover effect is in part a by-product of the introduction of new technologies, challenging the innovative capacities of the local firms (Pisano, 1990).

Studies suggest that technology spillovers from FDI may be influenced by the technology gap between the domestic and foreign companies. The effect is likely to be a non-linear one, representing the balance between greater scope for learning at higher levels of a relatively modest technology gap, but a diminishing local absorptive capacity when the gap becomes too large (Cantwell, 1989; Perez, 1998). Vertical linkages between firms and personnel movements can lead to knowledge transfer. FDI can also spur local businesses to improve their own innovative capabilities independently through demonstration effects, and so to meet the heightened challenges presented by new competition. These spillover effects, when they occur, are clearly positive for the local economy (Du et al., 2008).

An empirical study by Tong and Hu (2003) supports this argument. They found that the average productivity of an industry is positively correlated with the degree of foreign presence within the industry (an indication of intra-industry spillovers) for investment originating from technologically advanced countries. This can be explained by the fact that domestic industry tends to benefit from foreign businesses with more advanced technologies. On the other hand, a higher presence of businesses with connections in Hong Kong, Macao, and Taiwan does not seem to be associated with higher productivity in domestic firms. Their study also suggested that technology spillovers may run between industries. This suggests that domestic firms may benefit significantly from an intensified foreign presence in a region in industries that closely relate to their own. These benefits may include technology transfers within buyer-seller relationships, a higher intensity of competition for markets as well as for talent, better development of suppliers and marketing networks, and so forth. Liu and Lin (2004), focusing on FDI in manufacturing within China, found positive and robust evidence of technology spillovers taking place through backward linkages to suppliers.

Similarly, Cheung and Lin (2003), in their study of FDI in all Chinese provinces during the period 1995–2000, observed positive effects of FDI on the number of domestic patent applications in China. The spillover effect was strongest for minor innovations such as external design patents, highlighting the "'demonstration effect'" of FDI. Other studies, such as those of Zhu and Lu (1998) and Hu and Jefferson (2004) support this idea of a demonstration effect, suggesting that higher FDI intensity leads to higher productivity in domestic firms, and that FDI has a positive effect on the introduction of new products in China.

Some literature examining the impact of FDI on a host country's industry has suggested that FDI stimulates a host country's technological independence (Javorcik and Spatareanu, 2003; Keller, 2002). This research suggests that FDI had a "positive" spillover effect on local economies. Other studies, however, have concluded that FDI intensified the technological dependence of the host country on multinational corporations, driving local firms to avoid competition with the MNCs (Blomstrom and Kokko, 2001; Sleuwaegen and De Backer, 2003). The Chinese case is closer to the former positive local development experience with indigenous capability building (as illustrated by some of our findings discussed earlier), but as shown by the transition from IJVs to other forms of organization, foreign-owned subsidiaries have become an integral part of the landscape of the Chinese innovation system. In other words, it is better described by the language of a steadily increasing technological interdependence rather than "independence" or "dependence." Wei et al. (2008) have argued that the diffusion of indigenous technology and local knowledge helps the productivity enhancement of multinationals, so that there can be mutual spillovers even in a late industrializing country context. This empirical study supported the contention of Cantwell (1995) that technology leaders develop international networks to exploit the territorially differentiated potential of foreign centers of excellence.

In their study of the spillover effects of FDI, Du et al. (2008) found that the higher is the absorptive capacity of an indigenous firm, the greater the spillover from FDI. This conclusion suggests that to benefit from new technology, local industry cannot simply imitate the technology, but must absorb, digest, understand, and improve the technology. In this study, it was also found that in industries with high levels of technological gap between foreign and indigenous firms, the more likely were negative spillovers from FDI. In these cases, local reliance upon imported technology to promote industrial development is likely to last longer.

3.7. WIDER OUTCOMES AND POLICY ISSUES

This section discusses what kinds of economic or other outcomes have followed from the paths of learning and innovative capability building in the sampled enterprises.

The evolution of Chinese government policy toward IJVs and foreign multinationals has become steadily more open and warmer to foreign involvement, increasingly viewing foreign-owned entities as an integral part of the Chinese business system. What is particularly significant in Chinese policy toward FDI is its focus on technology and on local market development. The Chinese have proved to be alert negotiators and expert implementers of research-related FDI projects. In the last decade or so, China has pursued the objective of offering investment incentives for foreign investors, among others, but on condition that technology of the most sophisticated kind be transferred to China.

Given economic conditions, the local institutional environment, and their target markets, many IJVs have realized that they must substantially adapt their technology for Chinese operations, and hence their efforts at local capability building. Tax incentives offered by the Chinese government encourage foreign firms to import advanced technology. Once an IJV is qualified as a "high-tech" firm, it is eligible to receive more tax benefits. These tax incentives differ by province. China has shown how the local manufacture of even sophisticated products, such as computers and aircraft, can be encouraged if procurement policies are properly coordinated with approvals for FDI (Venkitaramanan, 2000).

Starting in 2008, however, Chinese tax policy toward FDI has begun to change. Under the old policy, foreign investors were taxed at a lower rate than domestic investors. Investors in specific regions such as Pudong were eligible for special tax exemptions. All this was eliminated in the new income tax code, which mandates a neutral ownership and location of investment framework: no incentives based on the nationality of ownership or region. Incentives are instead provided for specific encouraged business activities. A limited exception to this policy allows for tax benefits for investment in the central and western regions of the country.

FDI policy has also shifted from promoting export-led growth to quality investments that support domestic-led growth. The revised policy moves toward prohibiting projects that rely on cheap Chinese raw materials, intensive energy usage, low technology, low local investment and commitment, or low local value added—such as in the areas of toys, apparel, furniture, house wares, or shoes. FDI has been encouraged in business areas such as energy and resource saving, environmental protection, transportation infrastructure, high-tech manufacturing, logistics, business outsourcing, and agricultural technology. The revised tax code, reflected in the 2007 Catalog of Foreign Investment and the 2008 Catalog of Foreign Investment in the Central and Western Regions, allows tax incentives to encourage investment in the central and western regions. The investment categories encouraged for such regions were expanded in the revised 2008 Central/Western Catalog, as an exception to the general prohibition on regional tax incentives.

Using regulatory policy, China has leveraged the attraction of its fast-growing markets to require a greater degree of technological cooperation and exchange with local enterprise. Partly as a result of this institutional and policy context, FDI has become a catalyst for significant technology upgrading and economic growth. The aircraft and automobile industries provide examples of how policy matters in transforming domestic technological innovative capability.

REFERENCES

Argyris, C., and Schön, D. (1978), *Organizational Learning: A Theory of Action Perspective*, Reading, Mass.: Addison-Wesley.

Bell, M., and Pavitt, K. (1995), "The Development of Technological Capabilities," in I. ul Haque (ed.), *Trade, Technology and International Competitiveness*, Washington, DC: The World Bank, 69–101.

Blomstrom, M., and Kokko, A. (2001), "Foreign Direct Investment and Spillovers of Technology," *International Journal of Technology Management*, 22(5–6): 435–54.

Bjorkman, I., Barner-Rasmussen, W., and Li, L. (2004), "Managing Knowledge Transfer in MNCs: The Impact of Headquarters Control Mechanisms," *Journal of International Business*, 35(5): 443–55.

Borensztein, E., Gregorio, J., and Lee, J, (1998), "How does Foreign Direct Investment Affect Economic Growth?" *Journal of International Economics*, 45: 115–35.

Brandt, L., and Rawski, T. (2008), *China's Great Economic Transformation*, Cambridge: Cambridge University Press.

Cantwell, J. A. (1989), *Technological Innovation and Multinational Corporations*, Oxford: Basil Blackwell.

—— (1995), "The Globalisation of Technology: What Remains of the Product Life Cycle Model?" *Cambridge Journal of Economics*, 19: 155–74.

—— (2001), "Innovation and Information Technology in the MNE," in A. M. Rugman and T. L. Brewer (eds.), *The Oxford Handbook of International Business*, New York: Oxford University Press, 431–56.

Chen, J. (2001), *Enterprise Technological Innovation Analysis*, Beijing: Science Press.

Chen, J. and Wang, R. (2007), "Case Study—Geely Holding Group Co., Ltd.," *Beida Business Review*, 9: 88–91.

Cheung, K., and Lin, P. (2004), "Spillover Effects of FDI on Innovation in China: Evidence from the Provincial Data," *China Economic Review*, 15: 25–44.

China Daily (2008), "Two Thirds of SOE Giants Become Shareholding Companies (Xinhua)," August 26, available at <http://www.chinadaily.com.cn/bizchina/2008-08/26/content_6972475.htm>.

China Industry Economy Statistical Yearbook (2002), Beijing: China Statistics Press.

—— (2005), Beijing: China Statistics Press.

Cohen, W., and Levinthal, D. (1990), "Absorptive Capacity: A New Perspective on Learning and Innovation," *Administrative Science Quarterly*, 35(1): 128–52.

Du, J., Li, H., and Wu, X. (2008), "Empirical Analysis on the Negative Technology Spillover Effect of Foreign Direct Investment in China," *Asian Journal of Technology Innovation*, 16(02): 33–151.

Ernst, D. (2008), "Can Chinese IT Firms Develop Innovative Capabilities within Global Knowledge Networks?" Working paper.

Farrell, D., and Grant, A. (2005), "China's Looming Talent Shortage," *The McKinsey Quarterly*, 2005(4).

Fu, X. (2008), "Foreign Direct Investment, Absorptive Capacity and Regional Innovation Capabilities in China," *Oxford Development Studies*, 36(1): 89–110.

Ghoshal, S., and Barlett, C. (1998), "Creation, Adoption, and Diffusion of Innovations by Subsidiaries of Multinational Corporations," *Journal of International Business Studies*, 19(3): 365–88.

Harzing, A. (2002), "Acquisitions versus Greenfield Investments: International Strategy and Management of Entry Modes," *Strategic Management Journal*, 23(3): 211–27.

Hennart, J. F. (1988), "A Transaction Cost Analysis of Equity Joint Venture," *Strategic Management Journal*, 9: 361–74.

Hong, E., and Sun, L. (2004), "Go Overseas via Direct Investment: Internationalization Strategy of Chinese Corporations in a Comparative Prism Access," available at <http://www.cefims.ac.uk/documents/research-28.pdf>.

Hu, A., and Jefferson, G. (2004), "Returns to Research and Development in Chinese Industry: Evidence from State-Owned Enterprises in Beijing," *China Economic Review*, 15: 86–107.

Javorcik, B. S., and Spatareanu, M. (2003), "To Share or Not To Share: Does Local Participation Matter for Spillovers from Foreign Direct Investment?" *World Bank Policy Research Working Paper*, No. 3118.

Keller, W. (2002), "Geographical Localization and International Technology Diffusion," *The American Economic Review*, 92(1): 120–42.

Klevorick, A. K., Nelson, R. S., and Winter, S. G. (1995), "Appropriating the Returns from Industrial Research and Development," *Brookings Papers on Economic Activity*, 3: 783–820.

Kumar, K., and van Dissel, H. G. (1996), "Sustainable Collaboration: Managing Conflict and Cooperation in Inter-Organizational Systems," *MIS Quarterly*, 20(3): 279–300.

Lall, S. (1992), "Technological Capabilities and Industrialization," *World Development*, 20(2): 165–86.

Li, H. (2006), "Technological Capability Accumulation in International Joint Ventures in China," unpublished PhD dissertation, Rutgers University.

—— Wu, X., and Zheng, S. (2008), Xizi Case Study and Teaching Note, 2008 Eastern Academy of Management Conference.

Liu, Z. (2001), "Foreign Direct Investment and Technology Spillover: Evidence from China," *Journal of Comparative Economics*, 30(3): 579–602.

—— and Lin, P. (2004), "Backward Linkages of Foreign Direct Investment: Evidence from China," available at <http://www.docin.com/p-98810674.html>.

London, T., and Hart, S. (2004), "Reinventing Strategies for Emerging Markets beyond the Transactional Model," *Journal of International Business*, 35(5): 351–70.

Lu, F., and Mu, L. (2011), "Learning by Innovating, Lessons from the Development of the Chinese Digital Video Player Industry," *Journal of Science and Technology Policy in China*, 2(1): 27–57.

McAdam, R. (2000), "Knowledge Management as a Catalyst for Innovation within Organizations: A Qualitative Study," *Knowledge and Process Management*, 7(4): 233–41.

Mao, W. X. (2006), "Total Innovation Management: Case Study on China's Electronic Industry," doctoral dissertation, Zhejiang University.

Nonaka, I., and Takeuchi, H. (1995), *The Knowledge-Creating Company*, New York: Oxford University Press, 33–56.

O'Donnell, S. W. (2000), "Managing Foreign Subsidiaries: Agents of Headquarters, or an Interdependent Network?" *Strategic Management Journal*, 21(5): 525–48.

OECD (2000), "Science, Technology and Industry Outlook 2000," <http://www.oecd.org/dataoecd/44/28/1894907.pdf>.

—— (2008), "OECD Investment News—Results of the Work of the OECD Investment Committee," available at <http://www.oecd.org/dataoecd/28/10/40283257.pdf>.

Perez, T. (1998), *Multinational Enterprises and Technological Spillovers*, Amsterdam: Harwood.

Pisano, G., (1990), "The R&D Boundaries of the Firm: An Empirical Analysis," *Administrative Science Quarterly*, 35(1): 153–76.

Prahalad, C. K., and Lieberthal, K. (1998), "The End of Corporate Imperialism," *Harvard Business Review*, July–August: 69–79.

Rosen, D. H. (1999), *Behind the Open Door: Foreign Enterprises in the Chinese Marketplace*, Washington, DC: Institute for International Economics.

Sleuwaegen, L., and De Backer, K. (2003), "Does Foreign Direct Investment Crowd Out Domestic Entrepreneurship?" *Review of Industrial Organization*, 22(1): 67–84.

Tong, S. Y., and Hu, A. Y. (2003), "Do Domestic Firms Benefit from Foreign Direct Investment? Initial Evidence from Chinese Manufacturing Conference on China's Economic Geography and Regional Development," Paper presented at the Conference on China's Economic Geography and Regional Development, University of Hong Kong, December 15–16.

Venkitaramanan, S. (2000), "FDI and Technology—Learning from the Chinese Example," *Financial Daily* from THE HINDU group of publications, August 28, available at <http://hindu.com/businessline/2000/08/28/stories/042820ju.htm>.

Wei, Y., and Liu, X. (2006), "Productivity Spillovers from R&D, Exports and FDI in China's Manufacturing Sector," *Journal of International Business Studies*, 37(4): 544–57.

—— —— and Wang, C. (2008), "Mutual Productivity Spillovers between Foreign and Local Firms in China," *Cambridge Journal of Economics*, 32(4): 609–31.

Xu, Q. R., Zheng, G., Yi, Z., and Wei, S. (2003), "Total Innovation Management (TIM): New Trend of the Businesses Innovation—Haier Case Study," *Science Research Management*, 2003(5): 1–7.

Yang, D. (2005), *China's Offshore Investments: A Network Approach*, Cheltenham, UK: Edward Elgar.

Zhang, T., and Gan, G. (2006), "Geographic Concentration in China's Manufacturing," *Chinese Journal of Population, Resources and Environment*, 4(1): 33–40.

Zhu, G., and Lu, D. (1998), "Evidence of Spill-Over Efficiency: Implication on Industrial Policies towards Foreign Direct Investment in China," *The Singapore Economic Review*, 43(1): 57–73.

4

India

Dinar Kale

4.1. INTRODUCTION

India presents an interesting example of a country with immense economic potential, cultural diversity, and income inequality within its population. Over the years the Indian economic policy framework has moved from a state-directed model to a market-dominated export-oriented economy. This chapter presents case studies of the Indian pharmaceutical and automobile industries. They show, within this shifting policy context, how firm-level technological capabilities have evolved. The case studies also show the key role of managerial vision, the influence of MNC firms, linkages to knowledge sources outside firms, and the entrepreneurial facility with which Indian firms have moved from imitators to innovators. In the case of pharmaceuticals, much of the innovation has been "behind the frontier," yet it has resulted in a rapidly expanding, internationalizing sector catering to customers at the "bottom of the pyramid."

This chapter is organized as follows: Section 4.2 describes key elements of the Indian industrial policy regime, tracking the transition from early protectionist policies to export-focused liberalization initiatives. Sections 4.3 and 4.4 document the evolution of policy and the development of technological capabilities in the Indian pharmaceutical and automobile industries. Section 4.5 compares the learning mechanisms used by Indian pharmaceutical and automobile firms. Section 4.6 concludes the chapter.

4.2. THE INDIAN ECONOMIC ENVIRONMENT: FROM IMPORT SUBSTITUTION TO EXPORT ORIENTATION, 1950–2008

In the post-independence era, Indian economic and industrial policy was dominated by an import-substitution ideology where state intervention and regulation played a key role in directing firm and national-level indigenous technology capability development. It was considered essential that the public sector occupied the economy's "commanding heights," and the state focused on building "temples of science" in the form of universities and higher education institutes. The Indian government adopted the import-substitution model which remained focused on indigenization. The government shaped and directed self-reliance through various policies focused on strictly regulating and restricting imports of technology to protect local technical effort by Indian firms. Forbes (1999) points out that from 1956 onwards, Indian industrial policy had two basic tenets: industrial targeting and licensing, and the imposition of foreign exchange controls over all external transactions. This resulted in the direct control of imports of capital, intermediate, and consumer goods. However, in 1990 the balance of payments crisis triggered major changes in the Indian government's industrial and economic policy orientation.

From the relatively inward-looking set of policies that was in place till the end of the 1980s, the policy regime adopted in 1991 sought to break down the walls of protection within which Indian industry had developed (Bhagwati, 1993). The liberalization of the Indian economy started in the early 1980s with the government adopting policies which substantially eased the import of industrial technology. The balance of payments crisis in 1990 gave momentum to economic liberalization and led to changes in the Indian government's industrial policy. Since 1991 there has been a shift away from import substitution and other closed economy approaches, toward industrialization with an open-economy and export promotion approach. In the 1990s, the Indian government abolished industrial licensing, removed import quotas on non-consumer goods, and took various measures to attract foreign direct investment.

Since 1990, services have contributed 54 percent of the country's GDP, while the industrial and agricultural sectors have contributed 29 percent and 17 percent respectively. According to the Economic Survey of India (2007), by 2006 the average share of imports and exports in GDP had risen to 24 percent, up from 6 percent in 1985. Inflows of foreign direct investment increased to 2 percent of GDP from less than 0.1 percent of GDP in 1990, with outflows of foreign direct investment picking up substantially at the end of 2006. There has been a massive increase in output, with the potential growth rate of the economy estimated to be around 8.5 percent per year in 2006. GDP per capita has risen on an average by 6 to 7 percent per annum from 1990. This contrasts with an annual growth rate of GDP per capita of just 1.25 percent in the three decades from 1950 to 1980. Productivity growth has been the key driver behind the jump in GDP growth, contributing nearly half of overall growth since 2003, compared with a contribution of roughly one-quarter in the 1980s and 1990s.

Moreover, with increased openness and rapid growth in exports of merchandise and IT-related services, India's share in world trade in goods and services had risen to 1.5 percent by 2005. The pharmaceutical and automobile industries in India are, in many ways, an inherited product of a microeconomic environment directed by state regulation and intervention. The different industrial policy regimes have influenced firm-level learning processes, and have shaped technological capability accumulation in the Indian pharmaceutical and automobile industries.

4.3. THE INDIAN PHARMACEUTICAL INDUSTRY, 1950–2008

The Indian pharmaceutical industry represents a successful high-technology-based industry which has witnessed self-reliant and consistent growth, aided by a sympathetic regulatory framework. The Indian pharmaceutical industry has developed sufficient capability to ensure the country is self-sufficient in addressing health-care needs. It is characterized by a low degree of concentration; a large number of firms with similar market shares; and, by international standards, relatively low-level R&D intensity, and a high level of brand proliferation. There are two types of firms in the Indian pharmaceutical industry; those in the formal and informal sectors.

Total industry exports rose from Rs.7,848 million in 1990–1 to Rs.68,520 million in 1999–2000. The growth of exports has been quite rapid since the mid-1990s (Figure 4.1). The industry grew rapidly in the 1990s, with an

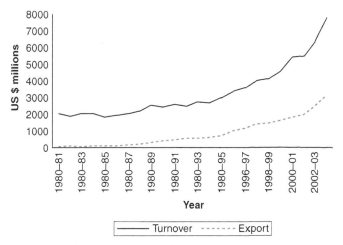

Fig. 4.1. Turnover and export growth in the Indian pharmaceutical industry

Source: Author, using data from Kale et al. (2008).

average growth rate of about 15 percent for bulk drugs and 20 percent for formulations (Kale et al., 2008).

The export performance of the Indian pharmaceutical industry is particularly significant as it reflects a shift in focus from the domestic toward the global market. The increasing share of formulation drugs in exports suggests an upgrading of technological capabilities, specifically the transformation of manufacturing facilities and process technologies to meet more demanding international standards. Prior to 1970, the industry was relatively small and was modest in terms of its production capabilities. Then, from 1970 to 1990, the output of the industry grew remarkably and from 1990 it grew faster still.

Until 1970, the Indian pharmaceutical industry was regulated through a strict patent regime which complied with British law. Unlike other sectors, the Indian government encouraged foreign and Indian firms to invest in this sector. However, due to the failure of these policies to meet health-care requirements, the government made strategic industrial and regulatory policy changes in the 1970s to infuse life into the industry. The weakening of the Patent Act in 1970 and the 1978 Drug Policy provided incentives to Indian firms but a strict regime for foreign MNCs. Another key piece of legislation was the Drug Price Control Order of 1979, which empowered government to fix the sale price of 347 indigenous manufactured drugs, making them more accessible to the Indian population. After 1990, the Indian government liberalized the economy and opened the pharmaceutical sector to foreign MNCs. Following on from that, in 2005 the government adopted a TRIPS (Trade Related Intellectual Property Rights)-compliant patent regime.

Table 4.1 shows that by 2007 the top three domestic firms, in terms of operating revenues, were Ranbaxy Laboratories, Cipla Ltd, and Dr Reddy's Laboratories (DRL). The only Indian subsidiary of a multinational firm with operating revenues sufficient to place it within the top ten Indian firms is seventh-ranked GlaxoSmithKline Ltd (GSKIndia), a subsidiary of the United Kingdom-based GlaxoSmithKline (GSK). Ranbaxy laboratory, with a turnover of Rs.41.98 billion, is the largest Indian firm, closely followed by DRL with Rs.41.62 turnover, which is the latest entrant into the top ten. Cipla and Glaxo have roots in the pre-independence era and are now respectively third and seventh largest with turnovers of Rs.38 and 18 billion respectively. All the Indian firms in the top ten are privately owned businesses (with family ownership) and more than 50 percent of their turnover comes from overseas markets.

Since 1970, foreign MNCs have played second fiddle to the country's entrepreneurial generic drug makers. During this period neither the Indian market nor domestically available production capabilities attracted new foreign investors. As a result, at least in the Indian domestic market, foreign MNCs entering India more recently have been playing "catch-up" with incumbent firms.

Glaxo India, a subsidiary of a British firm, has been in existence for over 75 years and has grown over the years to employ nearly 4,000 staff. It manufactures in its own facilities, and locally subcontracts approximately 30 percent of its production. In general, the R&D budgets of domestic firms are substantially smaller than those of the established foreign multinationals. Ranbaxy, for example, had R&D expenditures of 7 percent of sales in 2005 and Dr Reddy's Laboratories' expenditures were 10 percent, as compared to an average R&D expenditure of 15 percent for the top 15 global pharmaceutical companies in 2005. The following section details the evolution of capabilities in the Indian pharmaceutical sector, based on studies by Kale (2005), Kale and Little (2007), and Kale et al. (2008).

The Evolution of Capabilities in the Indian Pharmaceutical Industry: From Imitation to Innovation

The Indian pharmaceutical industry has come a long way. From importing bulk drugs it has moved into exporting formulations to the highly regulated markets of the developed world. This has involved different learning processes and stages which are captured by the "capability creation model" (Figure 4.2). This model reveals that the industry has moved from basic R&D capabilities to advanced-level R&D capabilities by undertaking different types of activities.

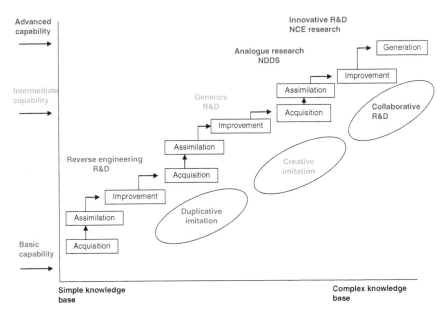

Fig. 4.2. Pharmaceutical capability creation model
Source: Derived from Kale (2005).

These have involved R&D processes such as duplicative imitation, creative imitation, and collaborative R&D.

Before 1970, foreign firms accounted for a large share of Indian pharmaceutical production. Most Indian firms' initial forays into the pharmaceutical business involved marketing and distribution of imported pharmaceuticals. The Indian population was largely dependent on imports from foreign firms based in the UK, France, and Germany. The cost of these medicines was largely out of reach for the majority of the population. After independence, the government focused on pharmaceuticals as a priority area and both private and public investments were sought under the industry policy resolution. Several foreign multinational firms invested in India throughout the 1950s and 1960s. Some multinational companies only set up marketing and distribution facilities, importing bulk drugs from their manufacturing facilities. When the Indian government increased pressure on the import of finished products, foreign MNCs set up formulation units and restricted imports to bulk drugs.

The Indian government set up research institutes such as the Central Drug Research Institutes and the National Chemical Laboratory. This was done under the umbrella of CSIR (Council for Scientific and Industry Research) laboratories. Investments were made in public sector enterprises to establish a domestically owned pharmaceutical industry. The first priority for the government was to become independent of imports as India was importing almost 90 percent of its bulk drugs requirement. Therefore, in 1954, the Indian government set up a public sector pharmaceutical firm, Hindustan Antibiotics Ltd (HAL), for the production of penicillin and sulfa drugs and, in 1961, with Russian cooperation, the Indian government set up another pharmaceutical firm, Indian Drugs and Pharmaceuticals Ltd (IDPL). The public sector units, along with the research institutes and MNC firms who started manufacturing in India, developed the knowledge base required for the industry and emerged as the main source of industrial entrepreneurs a decade later.

Case Studies from the Private Sector, 1947–1970

Cipla

In 1935 Dr K. A. Hamied set up Cipla or "The Chemical, Industrial and Pharmaceutical Laboratories Ltd." On August 17, 1935, Cipla was registered as a public limited company with an authorized capital of Rs.600,000. In 1944, Cipla decided to construct a modern pharmaceutical works and laboratory. With severe import restrictions hampering production, the company decided to start manufacturing the basic chemicals required for pharmaceuticals. In 1951, Cipla entered into an agreement with a Swiss firm for manufacturing foromycene. In 1952, the company set up its first research division for attaining self-sufficiency in technological development and, by 1960, started operations at a second plant at Vikhroli, Mumbai, producing fine chemicals. In 1961, the Vikhroli factory started manufacturing diosgenin. This heralded the manufacture of several steroids and hormones derived from diosgenin. In 1960, Dr Yusuf Hamied, the founder's son and current CEO, returned with a doctorate in chemistry from Cambridge and joined Cipla as an officer in charge of research and development.

GSK

Glaxo India was incorporated in 1924 under the name of H. J. Foster & Co. Ltd as an Agency House for distributing the well-known Baby Food, Glaxo, of the then UK company, Joseph Nathan & Co. Two years later, the company became a wholly owned subsidiary of Joseph Nathan & Co. In 1950, the company changed its name to Glaxo Laboratories (I) Ltd and by 1956 established a manufacturing base for production of vaccines at Worli, Mumbai. By the 1960s, manufacturing units were further extended at Aligarth and Thane for production of infant food and vitamin A, steroids, and other drugs from basic stages. In 1968, 25 percent of the company was sold to Indian shareholders and by the beginning of 1971, the company had established an R&D lab in Mumbai.

Ranbaxy

Ranbaxy Laboratories Ltd was established in 1961 and listed on the Bombay Stock Exchange in 1973. The company traces its roots to 1962, when Bhai Mohan Singh's family entered into a collaborative agreement with the Italian pharmaceutical firm Lepetit SpA for the manufacture of the typhoid drug "Chloramphenicol" in India. In 1967, a change in Lepetit's strategy prompted the family to buy them out. Ranbaxy started as a manufacturer of active pharmaceutical ingredients and soon began looking at international markets to secure these ingredients. In 1977, Ranbaxy established a subsidiary in Nigeria through a joint venture, and in 1984 it expanded operations to Malaysia.

The Post-1970 Era: Duplicative Imitation and the Emergence of Basic Technological Capabilities

To encourage the growth of the domestic industry and reduce dependence on foreign pharmaceutical firms, the Indian government took forward three key policy initiatives in the 1970s. The first such initiative was the Drug Price Control Order to control the prices of drugs. The second was the adoption of a weak patent act, the Indian Patent Act of 1970. The third initiative was the elaborate use of industrial licensing to build up capabilities through the adoption of the Drug Policy of 1978. The Foreign Exchange Related Act (FERA) also influenced the working of foreign MNCs in India as these firms had to reduce their foreign holdings to 40 percent.

The 1970 patent law changed the industry structure and market by reducing entry barriers for entrepreneurs to operate in this science-based industry. This law legalized reverse-engineering R&D and paved the way for Indian firms to build basic capabilities in pharmaceutical R&D. Gradually, Indian pharmaceutical firms moved into the area of manufacturing formulations and followed with backward integration into production of bulk drugs. Indian pharmaceutical firms focused on adapting technology to firm and country specificity and efforts in these directions fostered the development of a knowledge base. These firms used reverse engineering or duplicative imitation as the main mechanism for knowledge acquisition, and built a basic capability in process R&D. Managers working in public sector units, research institutes, and other Indian firms sensed the opportunities that emerged after 1970, and started creating their own firms on the basis of skills acquired through reverse engineering. Indian pharmaceutical firms started developing drugs by copying or using known processes to manufacture products at lower cost. Indian firms and research institutes simply traced back the knowledge embodied in the patent and reverse engineered the process, albeit with some minor modifications. Reverse-engineering R&D helped Indian firms to develop basic capabilities in pharmaceutical product development and management.

In this "reverse-engineering era," the focus of Indian pharmaceutical firms was on the number of products a firm could reverse engineer and the time required for imitative process development. Indian firms competed in a fiercely competitive domestic market and profits were directly related to the efficiency of production processes used by firms. Indian firms put intensive in-house effort into developing cheap processes, resulting in rapid acquisition and assimilation of reverse-engineering expertise across all firms. Kim and Nelson (2000) point out that a reverse-engineering strategy also involves activities that sense potential needs in a market, activities that locate knowledge or products which would meet market needs, and activities that would infuse these two elements into a new project. In this sense, Indian pharmaceutical firms built the organizational capabilities required to operate scale-intensive manufacturing facilities, and created strong marketing and distribution networks domestically.

By the end of the 1980s, Indian firms were manufacturing practically every new molecule which was commercially viable without access to process details from the innovator company. As Table 4.1 shows, the second half of the 1980s saw a remarkable increase in the output of the industry in terms of bulk drugs and formulation production performance. This period also saw Indian pharmaceutical firms consolidate their position in the domestic market.

Table 4.1. Growth in Indian pharmaceutical industry during the 1980s

	Year	Bulk drugs (Rs. million)	Formulations (Rs. million)	Total
1	1980–1	2,400	12,000	14,400
2	1981–2	2,890	14,340	17,230
3	1982–3	3,450	16,600	20,050
4	1983–4	3,550	17,600	21,150
5	1984–5	3,770	18,270	22,040
6	1985–6	4,160	19,450	23,610
7	1986–7	4,580	21,400	25,980
8	1987–8	4,800	23,500	28,300
9	1988–9	5,500	31,500	37,000
10	1989–90	6,400	34,200	40,600

Source: Elaborated using data from OPPI (2001).

One of the indicators of Indian firms' superior imitative capabilities is the shortening of the time lag between the introduction of a drug in the global market by the inventor, and the marketing of the same drug in the Indian market. Over the years, Indian firms have been able to progressively shorten the lag between the introduction of a drug by its inventor and its introduction in the Indian market (Keayla, 1996).

The weakening of the patent act and the drug price control order of the 1970s forced foreign MNC pharmaceutical firms to reduce their operations in India, thus providing a space for Indian domestic firms to expand in the local market.

GSK

In 1971, Glaxo built its R&D laboratory at Thane while relocating the SmithKline & French plant from Mumbai to Bangalore. In response to the Foreign Investment Act, the parent Glaxo group reduced its equity stake from 75 percent to 40 percent in 1983. Glaxo set up a plant for the production of bulk drugs at Mysore. During this period, Glaxo diversified into the food sector through its joint ventures with Vegepro Foods and Feeds Ltd and Hindustan Foods Ltd.

Cipla

Cipla opted for an aggressive product development (reverse-engineering) strategy that catapulted it into the top league. In many therapeutic categories, such as anti-asthmatics, Cipla offers the widest range of possible products. Focusing on process research, Cipla has made substantial progress in new drug delivery systems (NDDS) and chiral synthesis. Cipla has already developed its first chirally resolved molecule, salbutamol, which is an anti-asthma drug. Two of Cipla's anti-asthmatic devices, namely Rotahaler and Zerostat spacer, are patented internationally.

Ranbaxy

Ranbaxy laboratory's initial forays into R&D activities began in the late 1970s. Until 1979, there was no research to speak of, and the R&D division employed only eight people. The initial effort in R&D was focused on formulating bulk drugs into dosage forms, and on developing cheap processes to synthesize bulk drugs. In the 1980s, Ranbaxy began focusing on developing novel production processes to tap generic markets in advanced countries. In 1985, Ranbaxy found a novel way to manufacture the anti-ulcerant Ranitidine, the world's best-selling drug, and the generic version of Glaxo's Zantac.

 However, the real breakthrough in process R&D came with the development of an innovative and novel process for Cefaclor. The molecule was owned by Eli Lilly through a patent the firm had obtained in 1979. This antibiotic was one of the best-selling drugs in the 1980s. Ranbaxy started work on developing a new seven-stage process for the production of Cefaclor in 1988. Ranbaxy invested a lot of resources to develop a new process for synthesizing Cefaclor despite internal doubts about committing R&D resources to a product that was difficult to manufacture. The number of steps involved in the synthesis of the product, and its potential for hazardousness and associated costs, made the product too expensive for the Indian market. Another problem stemmed from the fact that Eli Lilly had filed more than 70 patents for process improvements to protect the drug from generic competition. But after spending three years and nearly Rs.20 million, Ranbaxy emerged as the only other manufacturer of Cefaclor. Not only did the firm produce the product successfully, but it also managed to obtain high yields from its process. Subsequently, in 1992, Ranbaxy started a joint venture with Eli Lilly for the manufacture and supply of Cefaclor. The development of a non-patent-infringing process for the antibiotic in 1992 gave Ranbaxy international recognition and huge profits. This success proved important for the future progress of innovative R&D in Ranbaxy.

DRL

Dr Reddy's Laboratories (DRL), founded by Dr Anji Reddy in 1984, has grown into a fully integrated pharmaceutical company with an annual turnover of Rs. 20,081million (US$500 million) in 2003. Dr Anji Reddy began his career with the Indian Drugs and Pharmaceuticals Ltd (IDPL), a public sector company, after completing his doctoral research at National Chemical Laboratories

India. At IDPL, Dr Reddy gained hands-on experience in the manufacturing and implementation of new technologies in bulk drugs. After working for six years, he set up two bulk drug companies called Uniloyds and Standard Organics in partnerships with two other colleagues.

However, he decided to go it alone and set up a new company, DRL, in 1984. Dr Reddy's competence was his focus on organic synthesis and, under his leadership, DRL successfully commercialized a variety of new technologies. After a few years, Dr Reddy developed a group of scientists with core skills in process research, which enabled DRL to develop processes for a number of molecules in a short time span. DRL started as a bulk drug company and thanks to the efforts of Dr Reddy, it moved into the formulations business. In 1986, it started operations on branded formulations and within a year launched Norilet, DRL's first recognized brand in India. But big success came with the launching of Omez, Omezaprozole, which DRL managed to launch at a 50 percent lower price compared with other brands prevalent in the Indian market at that time. DRL successfully reverse engineered many popular patented drugs to expand its therapeutic presence, and within a year of its inception, DRL became the first Indian company to export bulk drugs or advanced pharmaceutical ingredients to Europe.

Post-liberalization, Creative Imitation, and the Development of Intermediate Technological Capabilities

After the liberalization of the pharmaceutical market in the mid-1990s, some Indian pharmaceutical firms moved toward export markets, and specifically highly regulated generic markets in advanced countries. Indian pharmaceutical firms adopted the strategy of "creative imitation" to manufacture products by developing non-infringement processes which could be converted into a patent creating value for the firm in a market. In the post-1990 era, Indian firms started developing processes which contained some patentable novel elements. Creative imitation allowed Indian pharmaceutical firms to develop the regulatory capability required to access global markets, build organizational structures able to manage original research, and gain entry into the generic markets of advanced countries.

Indian pharmaceutical firms initially exported formulation products to the least developed or developing countries, but after 1990 they started exporting formulation products to generics markets in advanced countries (Table 4.2). An important event in the expansion of a generic market in the US was the enactment of the Waxman-Hatch Act in 1984. This abolished the requirement for fresh clinical trials of generic drugs and replaced them with simpler and less expensive "bioequivalence" and "bio-availability tests."

Table 4.2. Share of bulk drugs and formulations in total exports

No.	Years	Bulk drugs (%)	Formulations (%)
1	1990–1	47	53
2	1991–2	44	56
3	1992–3	70	30
4	1993–4	71	29
5	1994–5	66	34
6	1995–6	64	36
7	1996–7	59	41
8	1997–8	57	43
9	1998–9	52	48
10	1999–2000	55	45

Source: Elaborated using data from OPPI (2001).

Table 4.3. Foreign acquisitions by Indian pharmaceutical companies

No.	Year	Indian firm (acquirer)	Name of the firm acquired	Country
1	1995	Ranbaxy	Ohm Labs	USA
2	1997	Sun Pharmaceuticals Ltd	Caraco	USA
3	1998	Wockhardt	Wallis	UK
4	2000	Ranbaxy	Basics	Germany
5	2000	Ranbaxy	Veratide	Germany
6	2002	Ranbaxy	Signature	USA
7	2002	Unichem	Niche Generics	UK
8	2002	Dr Reddy's Laboratories	BMS	UK
9	2002	Dr Reddy's Laboratories	Meridian	UK
10	2003	Wockhardt	CP Pharma	UK
11	2003	Zydus Cadila	Alpharma	France
12	2004	Ranbaxy	REG Aventis	France
13	2004	Glenmark	Lab Killinger	Brazil
14	2004	Dr Reddy's Laboratories	Trigenesis	US
15	2004	Jubilant Organosys	PSI group	Belgium

Source: Author, based on annual reports (1995–2003).

Indian pharmaceutical companies have adopted various strategies to enter the US generic market. Many Indian pharmaceutical firms have set up their marketing infrastructure in the US. Some firms have acquired US-based firms to set up an operation (see Table 4.3), while other firms are forming alliances with generic firms operating in the US for the supply of advanced pharmaceutical ingredients or formulation generic products.

Since 1990, Indian pharmaceutical firms have invested heavily in improving production facilities and have adopted good manufacturing practices and now, most leading companies have their manufacturing facilities approved by the US Food and Drugs Administration (FDA) and the UK's Medicine and

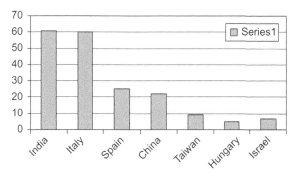

Fig. 4.3. US FDA-approved plant outside US
Source: Author using data from the US FDA.

Healthcare Products Regulatory Agency (MHRA). By 2003, India had the highest number of FDA-approved plants outside the US. India's 61 such plants are just ahead of Italy's 60 plants (Figure 4.3).

Indian pharmaceutical firms have filed patents for indigenously developed novel and non-infringing processes with the regulatory authorities in Europe and the US. Filing patents in different regions helped these firms to acquire the minimum regulatory expertise. This proved to be an effective mechanism for gathering the knowledge required for the successful filing of patents in the US and Europe. It was further strengthened by the successful filing of patent applications through the generics Abbreviated New Drug Application modality (ANDA) in the US. By 2000, Indian pharmaceutical firms had firmly established generics R&D capabilities and associated regulatory capabilities (Table 4.4). There has been a spate of Drug Master File (DMF) submissions to regulators since 2000 and now even small firms are getting into the value-added ANDA segment. In 2003, Indian pharmaceutical firms filed 73 ANDA applications with US FDA, constituting 20 percent of the total. At the end of 2003, Indian firms had a total of 106 ANDAs approved by the FDA, with 108 more on file, but not yet approved. In 2003, Indian firms submitted 119 DMFs, almost 30 percent of total DMF submissions to the US FDA.

Exposure to global markets, realization of future regulatory changes, and creative orientation to imitative research all facilitated the development of a "research tradition" in these firms. Nelson and Pack (1999), reflecting on imitative learning, suggest that "an imitator working with an extremely sparse set of clues about the product might well adopt the more prestigious title of 'innovator', since most of the problem is really being solved independently." This upward movement of Indian firms represents the intermediate capability stage as the products resulting from generic R&D require input of original knowledge and can give leverage to firms in global markets.

Table 4.4. Share of Indian firms in ANDA approvals and DMF submissions to USFDA

Year	ANDA			DMF		
	Total	ANDA by Indian firms	Share of Indian approvals	Total	DMF by Indian firms	Share of Indian submissions
1997	572	10	1.7	371	31	9.7
1998	484	9	1.9	944	38	4.0
1999	380	8	2.1	390	44	11.3
2000	583	21	3.6	355	37	10.4
2001	436	18	4.1	344	59	17.2
2002	753	32	4.2	368	79	21.5
2003	627	56	8.9	426	119	28.2

Source: Adapted from US FDA (2003).

In the case of Indian pharmaceutical firms, creative imitation in the form of generics R&D accelerated their movement toward the acquisition of advanced-level capabilities further up the value chain in pharmaceutical R&D. Creative imitation in the form of generics R&D has increased Indian pharmaceutical firms' awareness of opportunities in new drug delivery systems research. Managerial experience in generics R&D has given Indian firms some understanding of the complexities involved in innovative research and the organizational infrastructure associated with it. Through their generic business, these firms have built information channels with scientific communities in economically advanced countries.

GSK

In 1993, Glaxo Group raised its equity from 40 percent to 51 percent and consolidated domestic operations by selling its investment in Hindustan Foods Ltd and Dempo Dairy Industries Ltd. By the end of the 1990s, Glaxo had also sold its interests in the Agrivet Farm Care (AFC) business. In 1999, Glaxo India completed 75 years of operations in India. In 1995, Glaxo set up a state-of-the-art Pharmacy Research & Development Centre inaugurated at Thane to cater to unmet medical needs and to exploit local commercial opportunities. In 1998, Glaxo acquired Biddle Sawyer to gain entry into three significant segments, oncology, gynecology, and osteoporosis. Also, 95 percent of Biddle Sawyer's portfolio was out of the Drug Price Control Order, which effectively meant higher margins, and it had a licensing agreement with the Japanese pharmaceutical firm, Takeda, for 12 brands (Hindu, 2002). However, in 2002, GSK shut down the company after it found that the plant did not comply with international good manufacturing practices norms. In 2001, Glaxo India became GlaxoSmithKline Beecham following international acquisition and sold one of its manufacturing plants to Glenmark, another Indian company. In 2002, the company entered into an in-licensing alliance with Eisai Pharmaceuticals, Japan and launched gastrointestinal products.

Cipla

Cipla has been looking for ways to grow through tie-ups and alliances with other generic firms like Watson and Ivax. The big breakthrough for Cipla came in 2001 when the company offered to provide key AIDS drugs required for one year for one person at $350 to NGOs, and at $600 to governments, and at $1,200 to retail distributors. Cipla realized that AIDS was going to be a major disease in advanced and developing countries and therefore offered a cheaper product on the basis of its superior skills and cheap raw materials. Cipla collaborated with the Indian Institute of Chemical Technology (IICT, Hyderabad) and started producing and marketing the simplest drug, Zidovudine (or AZT) in 1991 and then proceeded to develop generic versions of Stavudine and Lamivudine (Guennif, 2004). AIDS cocktails were selling at $10,000–$15,000 (cost per patient per year) in the USA and Europe and were beyond the purchasing capacities of developing countries' people and governments. The foreign MNCs threatened to fight Cipla, but due to public pressure, these firms cut the price of their own drugs—by up to 90 percent. Cipla had a strong belief in its process R&D skills and started exporting products all over the world.

Ranbaxy

Ranbaxy was listed on the Luxembourg Stock Exchange in 1994 and raised money to establish a global presence in generic drugs manufacturing through a combination of overseas investments and foreign acquisitions. After the listing, Ranbaxy invested close to $100 million over a four-year period globally and created physical infrastructure in different parts of world. Ranbaxy entered the US in 1995 by acquiring an FDA-approved manufacturer, Ohm Laboratories. In 1996, it started a joint venture with another US-based firm, Schein Pharmaceuticals, to market Ranitidine in the US. In 1998 Ranbaxy established a 100 percent-owned subsidiary in the US and started marketing products under its brand name. Within just four years of starting its US operations, Ranbaxy touched the US$100 million mark for sales in the US. From the beginning of 1995, Ranbaxy stepped up its R&D expenditures from 2 percent of sales to 5 percent, and started establishing state-of-the-art multi-disciplinary R&D facilities at Gurgaon (near New Delhi), India. The company's new strategic intent was to ascend the research value chain and, accordingly, it began to establish capabilities in the areas of discovery research, delivery systems, and clinical research.

In 1999, Ranbaxy registered its first success in innovative R&D with the development of a once-a-day dosage for the Ciprofloxacin molecule. This improvement in dose administration promised greater patient compliance compared with the multiple dosages required by the patent holder, Bayer and, hence, was a major step forward. A big milestone for the company was recorded in 1992, when it reached a marketing agreement with Eli Lilly & Co. Ranbaxy started work on developing a new seven-stage process for the production of Cefaclor in 1988, and after three years and spending nearly $2 million, Ranbaxy emerged with a non-infringing process for the manufacturer of Cefaclor and also managed to obtain higher yields from its process as compared with Eli Lilly's original production process. This breakthrough led the companies to set up a joint venture in India to produce and market Lilly's branded pharmaceuticals for the domestic market, while Lilly agreed to begin marketing Ranbaxy's generic medications in the US. Ranbaxy, thereby, gained access to the world's single largest drugs market, namely the US generic market.

DRL

DRL strengthened its Indian operation by acquiring American Remedies Ltd in 1999 and merging Cheminor Drug Ltd (CDL) with DRL in April 2000. This acquisition and merger made DRL the third largest pharmaceutical company in India, after Ranbaxy and Glaxo (I) Ltd. With India's shift from a weak patent regime to the post-2005 strong patent regime, the broad strategy of DRL was to develop new molecules for licensing through innovative R&D and to target advanced markets for specialty generics products. DRL began its major international operations by entering Russia through a joint venture with Biomed in 1992, and in 2002 DRL converted this joint venture into a 100 percent-owned subsidiary. DRL started targeting the US generic market and began to build state-of-the-art manufacturing facilities in 1994. Within three years, DRL filed its first ANDA for Ranitidine 75 mg tablets, and improving on that, in 1999 it submitted an application for Omeprazole. But the big achievement of DRL's generic foray came in 2001. In that year, DRL became the first Indian company to launch a generic drug, Fluoxentine, with 180-day market exclusivity in US. As a result of market exclusivity, DRL's international sales of Fluoxentine 40 mg, a generic version of Eli Lilly's Prozac, increased massively. The generic turnover touched $23.2 million for the third quarter of 2001, with Fluoxentine contributing 87 percent of these sales.

In January 2003, DRL launched Ibuprofen 400, 600, and 800 mg tablets in the US under its own brand name. Ibuprofen became the first generic product to be marketed under the DRL brand name and thus represented a significant step in DRL's efforts to build a strong and sustainable US generic business. Direct marketing of Ibuprofen was the first step in building DRL's fully fledged commercial organization in the US market. In 2002, DRL started its European operation by acquiring two pharmaceutical firms in UK. The acquisition of BMS Laboratories and its wholly owned subsidiary, Meridian UK, allowed DRL to expand geographically and gave the company an opportunity to enter the European market. During this period, DRL aggressively pursued the Paragraph IV route of patent challenge, which is a high-risk, high-return strategy where firms apply for patent-challenging validation of existing patents and in doing so, they take on the original patent holder.

The Post-TRIPS Environment: Collaborative R&D and the Development of Advanced Technological Capabilities

The move from intermediate R&D capabilities to advanced R&D capabilities is very challenging due to the difference in the knowledge base and organizational capabilities. The advanced level of technological capabilities in the case of pharmaceutical R&D involves new chemical entity research, either by using research strategies, such as analogue research, or new drug delivery systems. Analogue research involves working on predetermined targets for specific diseases to develop molecules that alter the target's mechanism in the diseased person, while rational or structure-based drug design involves the determination of a disease-causing protein's three-dimensional structure. Once the structure is known, novel chemical entities are designed to "lock in" to the protein, with the aim of reversing or arresting a disease's progression.

The main focus in drug delivery system research is on improving the effectiveness of an existing drug, in terms of dosage, length of treatment, and biodegradability. Many Indian pharmaceutical firms with a proven track record in process R&D see new drug delivery systems as a risk-free strategy. The drug delivery improvements do not impinge on the product patents and the cost of stage I and II trials for an improved drug cost almost 10 percent of a new drug. An improved version of an existing drug also assures good market success.

From 1995, large Indian firms started investing heavily in new drug discovery research and new drug delivery system research as a response to the emerging post-TRIPs scenario. In terms of new chemical entity research, Indian pharmaceutical firms do not compete with multinational giants like Pfizer or Glaxo; instead their strategy is to leverage technical skills. These firms have filed patents for innovative products by using analogue research as their main strategy (Table 4.5). Indian pharmaceutical firms are working with already-validated or known targets, where the structural activity of the compound is well-known and they try to find a compound that possesses better efficacy or fewer side effects.

Table 4.5. Indian pharmaceutical firms' new chemical entity pipeline

No.	Companies	Molecules in clinical trials
1	Ranbaxy	6
2	DRL	4
3	NPIL	1
4	Lupin	2
5	Dabur	2
6	Wockhardt	1
7	Torrent	2
8	Glenmark	1
9	Sun Pharma	2
10	Orchid	1

Source: Author, based on annual reports, 2003.

Initially, Indian firms faced major constraints such as lack of financial and infrastructural resources, an insular knowledge-base and lack of scientists trained in innovative R&D. To meet the financial cost, Indian pharmaceutical firms started investing the revenue generated from generic businesses into innovative R&D. The alternative strategy to cover these financial costs was to partner with foreign MNC pharmaceutical firms through licensing of molecules or drug delivery system technology. These licensing agreements usually involve milestone payments and limited marketing rights. The low cost of research in India has also helped Indian pharmaceutical firms to overcome financial constraints associated with new drug discovery. The cost of drug discovery and development in India could be 10 percent of the cost involved in the development of a new molecule in advanced countries. The other major constraint faced by Indian pharmaceutical firms was the gaps in knowledge concerning new chemical entity research, especially in the various disciplinary areas involved in drug discovery. Indian pharmaceutical firms filled these gaps by hiring Indian scientists experienced in drug discovery R&D, and by adopting a strategy of collaborative research with Indian and overseas research institutes. In the post-1995 era, R&D scientists became the focus as Indian firms hired scientists from India as well as overseas universities, companies, and research institutes.

The new drug discovery research requires knowledge about various disciplinary areas and effective knowledge transfer mechanisms to facilitate the flow of knowledge. Indian pharmaceutical firms employed a collaborative R&D approach to tap disciplinary knowledge bases in research institutes. Indian research institutes have built the strong supporting infrastructure required in drug discovery R&D, comprising the analytical instruments and facilities for research still lacking in most firms in the industry. For example, the National Chemical Laboratory has a combinatorial chemistry machine while the Central Drug Research Institute owns a high throughput screening machine. Indian pharmaceutical firms collaborate with Indian research institutes to use these supportive infrastructural facilities.

Recognizing the imperative to take proactive measures to give a necessary fillip to R&D, the government set up various schemes to encourage collaboration between research institutes and industry. In 1995, under the Department of Science and Technology, the Indian government launched a program called the New Millennium Leadership Technology Initiative to bring industry and academia together. The Indian government also took major initiatives to increase interactions between industry and public R&D institutions in areas of innovative pharmaceutical R&D. In 2000, the Indian government created a Pharmaceutical Research and Development Support Fund with an initial allocation of Rs.1500 million as a planned fund for promotion of R&D in the industry. In the post-TRIPs era, many initiatives were launched as a response to the changing needs of the industry and knowledge generation. The research institutes redefined their role for a post-TRIPS scenario by investing in the development of expertise in drug discovery research, generics research, and the building of different relationships for each expertise.

Thus, Indian pharmaceutical firms are developing advanced pharmaceutical R&D capabilities by adopting collaborative research strategies.

Cipla

Unlike other Indian firms, Cipla has focused on its core strengths and did not invest in new chemical entity research. The major focus of its R&D is still on the development of patent-free processes for known molecules. With this strategy, Cipla has exported raw materials, intermediates, prescription drugs, over the counter products, and veterinary products from its Indian operations rather than establishing manufacturing plants overseas. Cipla, with its core strengths in process R&D and manufacturing, has emerged as a key player in the service sector. The company offers technology for products and processes and earned revenues of about Rs.2,200 million during the year 2008–9. The company's innovative strategy involves establishing partnerships with patent holder firms to develop improved versions by using chiral chemistry. Consequently, Cipla is aiming for continuous innovation, and complements this by achieving operational and marketing excellence. The company has consistently been able to produce modern drugs for the domestic market far more cheaply than foreign MNCs can manage. This strategy has been effective in a price-sensitive market.

Ranbaxy

In the post-TRIPS era, Ranbaxy continued with its internationalization strategy by consolidating its US operations, and expanding European operations through acquisition. Within just four years of starting its US operations,

Ranbaxy touched the US$100 million mark for sales in the US. After entering the UK market in 1995, Ranbaxy swiftly expanded into Central and Eastern Europe. A manufacturing plant in Ireland provides the backbone of Ranbaxy's European business. In 2004, the company led further expansion in the European market, by acquiring the fifth largest generics company in France. In 2006, Ranbaxy acquired two generic companies, namely, Terapia in Romania and Ethimed in Belgium, and followed that by buying the large unbranded generic product portfolio of Allen SpA in Italy.

In June 2008, Malvinder Singh, CEO and owner of Ranbaxy, and his brother Shivinder sold their entire 35 percent stake to Daiichi for Rs.100 billion. Subsequently, Daiichi Sankyo invested another Rs.100 billion to raise its stake to about 64 percent, taking complete control of the company. Although Ranbaxy was highly profitable, its promoters felt that the company could not compete on a global scale with its existing resources. For example, in 2007 legal and professional fees cost the company Rs.1.5 billion and net profits were Rs.6 billion. These costs were rising and Ranbaxy needed more investments to emerge as a competitor at a global level. The family could have chosen to merge with a bigger company, but then it would have become a junior partner. It chose instead to withdraw its entire holding.

Daiichi Sankyo is mainly present in the Japanese and the US markets—both mature markets which give good profits—but have modest growth prospects. Its profit margin in 2007–8 was an enviable 11 percent. It rewarded its shareholders handsomely; its payout ratio was 51 percent. In Ranbaxy, it met a company with great potential but unequal to its immediate challenges. It is a good combination. Daiichi Sankyo retained Malvinder Singh as chairman and managing director of Ranbaxy, so that he could continue to lead the company. However, by mid-2009, Malvinder Singh had resigned from the company.

DRL

DRL received two severe setbacks in the 1990s. The first of these was the rejection of an out-licensed molecule by the company Novo Nordisk in 1998. DRL had out-licensed Ragaglitazar, an insulin sensitizer molecule to Novo Nordisk. However, in 1998, this molecule showed adverse side effects in clinical trials. Subsequently, Novo abandoned research on the molecule in 2002, and returned another, Balaglitazone (with a prospective use for diabetes), in 2004, without putting it through trials.

The second setback occurred in March 2004, when DRL lost its filing for the specialty chemical, amlodipine maleate (AmVaz), a variation of Pfizer's amlodipine besylate (Norvasc), in a higher court after a lower court had ruled in its favor. A favorable ruling would have brought in an estimated $200 million in sales for DRL, but that was not to be. These twin shocks affected DRL's sales and profits; its net profit crashed from Rs.3.40 billion in

2003 to Rs.2.5 billion in 2004. However, this forced the company to rethink its aggressive generic market strategies. In the post-2005 period, DRL has adopted strategies aimed at the consolidation of its domestic market through cooperation rather than by competition with foreign MNCs in generic markets, while continuing its own internationalization through acquisitions and investments in innovative R&D.

As a cooperation strategy, in 2006, DRL signed an agreement with Merck to distribute and sell the generic versions of the latter's Proscar and Zocor after their patents expired in the US market. DRL was able to distribute and sell generic versions of Proscar and Zocor with 180-day exclusivity after the patents expired for each product. Taking this strategy further, in 2009, DRL and GSK entered into a partnership to develop and market generics and formulations in emerging markets. Under the terms of the agreement, DRL provided GSK access to its diverse portfolio and future pipeline of more than 100 branded pharmaceuticals. Under the ten-year collaboration, both companies will market drugs in fast-growing therapeutic segments such as cardiovascular, diabetes, oncology, and gastroenterology and pain management. This was a new direction for both firms and is aimed at reaching large markets in middle- and low-income economies. The products will be manufactured by Dr Reddy's and will be licensed and supplied to GSK in various emerging markets such as Africa, the Middle East, Latin America, and Asia Pacific excluding India. Revenues will be reported by GSK and will be shared with Dr Reddy's as per agreed terms. In certain markets, products will be co-marketed by DRL and GSK.

To reduce drug discovery risks further, DRL has developed a strategy of collaborative research. The company formed an agreement with the UK-based Argenta Discovery for the development and commercialization of a novel approach to the treatment of chronic obstructive pulmonary disease. Both companies have agreed to fund the joint collaboration up to proof-of-concept. Based on an out-licensing strategy, DRL has out-licensed Balaglitazone to the Danish-based company, Rheoscience.

The Indian pharmaceutical industry has also been an aggressive investor in overseas markets and spent $1 billion on such investment in 2005. From 2000 onwards, Indian firms have acquired 26 firms in Europe and the USA and six in developing countries. Table 4.6 shows the international expansion and performance of the top Indian pharmaceutical firms. Ranbaxy, DRL, and Wockhardt have earned more than 60 percent of their revenues from international markets and have a manufacturing presence in advanced markets such as those of the US and Europe. In the past, joint ventures and subsidiaries were the major modes of entry by Indian firms into these markets, but after 2000 acquisition has emerged as the main mode of overseas expansion, especially in the European market.

Table 4.6. Top Indian firms and international expansion

Name of the firm	Year established	No. of overseas manufacturing plants	No. of overseas acquisitions from 1990	Turnover (2005) US$ million	% from overseas (2005)
Ranbaxy	1962	9	11	1,340	80
DRL	1984	2	4	546	66
Wockhardt	1959	3	4	324	67
NPIL	1988	5	3	313	30
Sun	1983	4	3	292	40

Source: Adapted from Kale (2005).

4.4. THE INDIAN AUTOMOBILE INDUSTRY

The Indian automotive industry is worth around US$34 billion and contributed around 5 percent of India's GDP in 2007. In that year, it produced over 1.5 million vehicles and employed approximately 13 million people (KPMG, 2007). It ranked 11th in car production and 13th in commercial vehicle production globally.

India's auto industry has experienced significant transformation in the last five decades and, specifically, after 2000. Table 4.7 shows that in 2007–8 the passenger vehicle segment registered a cumulative growth of 12 percent (SIAM, 2007). Figure 4.4 plots the growth of the Indian passenger car industry from 1999–2000. The rapid growth in this sector has been mainly driven by the substantial increase in the purchasing power of the Indian middle class, availability of financial options, competitive pricing as well as a reduction in government tariffs that have helped lower the price of vehicles. The Indian passenger market is skewed toward mini and compact vehicles; these

Table 4.7. Automobile domestic sales

Category	No. of vehicles						
	2002–3	2003–4	2004–5	2005–6	2006–7	2007–8	2008–9
Passenger vehicles	707,198	902,096	1,061,572	1,143,076	1,379,979	1,549,882	1,551,880
Commercial vehicles	190,682	260,114	318,430	351,041	467,765	490,494	384,122
Three-wheelers	231,529	284,078	307,862	359,920	403,910	364,781	349,719
Two-wheelers	4,812,126	5,364,249	6,209,765	7,052,391	7,872,334	7,249,278	7,437,670
Grand total	5,941,535	6,810,537	7,897,629	8,906,428	10,123,988	9,654,435	9,723,391

Source: Elaborated on the basis of data provided by SIAM (2009).

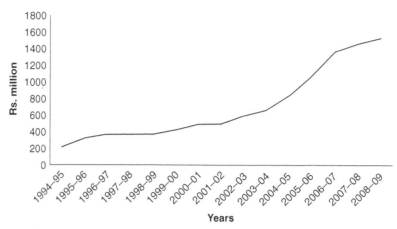

Fig. 4.4. Turnover of passenger car manufacturers in India
Source: Author, using data from SIAM (2010).

segments account for almost 80 percent of car sales in the country (Sagar and Chandra, 2004).

From 2000 exports were becoming an important component in the growth of Indian auto firms. Exports have grown at a compound annual growth rate of 30 percent per annum. Figure 4.5 shows that in 2007 exports had reached 198,000 units and had grown by 19 percent (SIAM, 2007). In the year 2007, 71 percent of Indian car exports comprised compact cars; these were exported to South America, Africa, Europe, Latin America, and the Middle East. However, compared to the global industry at large, the Indian industry still remains small: in 2007, it accounted for 3.15 percent of world vehicle production (OICA, 2007).

The passenger car sector is dominated by three or four players, accounting for 85 percent of total annual sales (SIAM, 2007). Figure 4.6 shows the market shares of leading players in the Indian automobile industry for 2007. The industry leader is Maruti Udyog Ltd (MUL) with 46 percent market share, followed by Tata Motors, Hyundai Motors, and Mahindra & Mahindra. In the last two decades, these firms have emerged as India's leading automobile manufacturers and innovators in the passenger car segment. By 2008 Maruti had two manufacturing facilities located in Gurgaon and Manesar, south of New Delhi. Maruti's Gurgaon facility has an installed capacity of 350,000 units per annum. The Manesar facilities, launched in February 2007, comprise a vehicle assembly plant with a capacity of 100,000 units per year and a diesel engine plant with an annual capacity of 100,000 engines and transmissions. The Manesar and Gurgaon facilities have a combined capability to produce over 700,000 units annually.

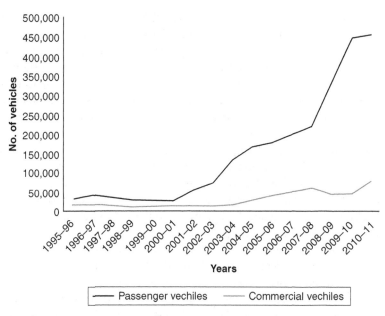

Fig. 4.5. Passenger car export trends
Source: Elaborated using data from SIAM (2011).

Market Shares

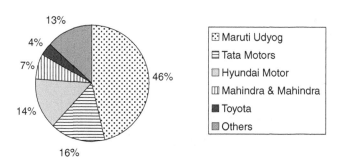

Fig. 4.6. Market shares of key players in passenger vehicle market
Source: Elaborated using data from SIAM (2011).

Telco (Tata Engineering and Locomotive Company), renamed as Tata Motors in 2002, is India's largest automobile company, with revenues of $8.8 billion and 23,000 employees (Tata Motors, 2007–8). It belongs to the business conglomerate Tata Group, and was ranked as the world's fourth largest truck manufacturer, the second largest bus manufacturer, and the 21st largest car manufacturer in 2007 (OICA, 2007). Tata Motors was listed on the New York Stock Exchange (NYSE) in 2004 and the manufacturing base in India has spread across Jamshedpur (Jharkhand), Pune (Maharashtra), Lucknow (Uttar Pradesh), and Pantnagar (Uttarakhand). The company is setting up two new plants: at Dharwad (Karnataka) and Sanand (Gujarat). Tata Motor's journey from construction equipment manufacturing to producing the world's cheapest car is quite remarkable. In the last five decades, Tata Motors has emerged as a car manufacturer with the most comprehensive research, design, and development capabilities in the country.

Hyundai Motor Indian Company—a wholly owned subsidiary of Hyundai—began commercial production in 1998 and after a few years emerged as the second largest and fastest-growing car manufacturer in India (Sagar and Chandra, 2004). Figure 4.7 charts the capability creation model for the Indian automobile sector. Saripalle (2006) points out that India's auto sector has evolved through three different policy regimes which may be characterized as an era of protectionism (1950–83), deregulation (1983–93), and liberalization (post-1993). In the deregulation and liberalization era, foreign direct investment was allowed in two waves: the first was in 1983 (restricted FDI) and the second in 1993 (mature FDI). All these policy changes had a significant impact on the development of firm-level capabilities, the domestic market, and industrial structure.

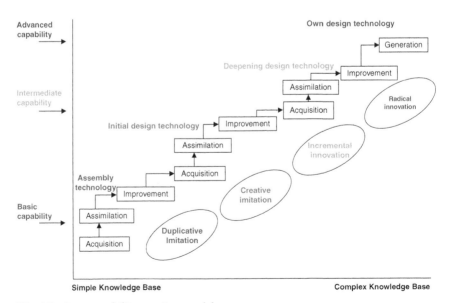

Fig. 4.7. Auto capability creation model
Source: Author, building on Kale and Little (2007).

The Evolution of Capabilities in the Indian Automobile Industry: From ISI to Liberalization

The protection and licensing regime, 1950 to 1984

Soon after Independence in 1949, the Indian government banned the import of completely built vehicles, and from 1953, the government adopted a policy that allowed only those firms that had a local manufacturing program to operate. The existing players were thus protected from any foreign or domestic competition. The industry was tightly regulated by government "red tape" and the market was supplied by two manufacturers: Hindustan Motors (HM) and Premier Automobiles Ltd (PAL). Government also imposed price controls and, as a result, within a few years the numbers of car manufactures was reduced from 12 to five. The era of protectionism was marked by restriction on the entry of foreign companies and the imposition of steep tariffs against imports. The HM-manufactured Ambassador car was based on the 1950s Morris Oxford. PAL, in collaboration with Fiat, produced the Fiat 1100, branded as the Padmini. HM and PAL were licensed to make just 50,000 cars between them. In the 1960s the Indian government refused permission for HM and PAL to upgrade their models through foreign collaborations (D'Costa, 1995).

Tata Motors Ltd, formerly known as Telco, was set up to manufacture locomotives and other engineering products in 1945. Telco manufactured its first commercial vehicle in 1954 in collaboration with Daimler-Benz AG, and the first vehicle rolled off the production line within six months of the contract. In 1959, Telco established an R&D center at Jamshedpur, and by 1961 started exports of Tata Mercedes-Benz trucks to Sri Lanka. By the time collaboration ended in 1969, the import content was reduced significantly (Venugopal, 2001). To develop design and development capability, in 1966 Telco established its Engineering Research Center (ERC) at Pune to provide impetus for automobile R&D; the first of its kind in India. ERC built a strong team of 800 qualified designers and engineers and undertook design and development of vehicles as well as machine tools, dies, fixtures, and other capital equipment. In 1975, Telco acquired Investa Machine Tools & Engineering in Pune and soon commissioned an alloy foundry at Pune to meet its press tools and casting requirements. In 1979, Telco established a large complex in the western part of the country to augment its production facility in Pune.

From the beginning, Telco put an emphasis on training its employees. In the Pune complex, the first building was a training center (Venugopal, 2001). It worked with local institutes and developed courses for workmen, supervisors, and engineers. By the late 1970s, Telco widened its product range to cover heavy commercial vehicles and progressively introduced a number of new models of its own design. The industry witnessed a compound annual growth rate of 3.5 percent in the 1959–80 period. Due to the protectionist environment, firms were mainly insulated from competition and had an assured market (Saripalle, 2006).

Deregulation: 1980 to 1990

From 1970 the Indian government gradually added the automotive industry to the list of core industries which were prioritized for promotion. The government started treating the industry's needs favorably and set up policies to promote competition, efficiency, and modernization. With that vision in mind, the early 1980s witnessed the beginning of the deregulation of the Indian auto industry: the government allowed entry of domestic manufactures in the passenger car segment; permitted increased foreign participation and overseas collaborations; and, finally, reduced the impact of production licenses on the scope of manufacturing operations.

In 1975, as matter of general industrial policy, the government permitted automatic capacity expansion of 25 percent every five years while removing price controls. In 1981, the Indian government announced a new policy of allowing "broad-banding" of licenses. This was a specific policy measure that permitted a vehicle manufacturer to produce different kinds of vehicles instead of just one as decreed by the industrial licenses. In the past, it was mandatory for an automobile manufacturing company to obtain a license from the Indian government for each type of vehicle it proposed to manufac-ture. With the "broad-banding" policy, the Indian government encouraged production of a range of related products and the pursuit of economies of scale. The government also introduced a more liberal import regime. In 1986, importers of capital equipment were allotted a near 50 percent increase in their foreign exchange quotas; previously imports were restricted to reduce the outflow of scarce foreign exchange.

The First Wave of FDI

FDI in the auto sector was first allowed in 1983 when Suzuki was invited in as a joint venture partner. In 1971, Sanjay Gandhi, son of Indira Gandhi, established Maruti Ltd with the mission of developing indigenously designed, affordable, cost-effective, low maintenance, and fuel-efficient cars. However, despite government support, Maruti failed to develop the indigenously pro-duced "peoples' car," and, subsequently, in 1980, the government of India took over the company. In 1983, Maruti formed a joint venture with the Suzuki Motor Corporation of Japan. Initially, the Indian government was in favor of a joint venture with Volkswagen and the VW Golf was the chosen car. However, the government felt that the Golf was an expensive car for the Indian market, and decided to go to Europe and Japan to search for partners. The Indian government wanted an overseas partner to bring in a 40 percent equity stake and had talks with Nissan, Mitsubishi, Daihatsu, and Suzuki. Only Suzuki was willing to take up a 26 percent equity share with an option to raise it to 40 percent. Thus, the government chose Suzuki as a partner and the 550 cc Fronte model as the "people's" car.

Subsequently, India allowed four Japanese firms—Toyota, Mitsubishi, Mazda, and Nissan—to enter the Indian market for light commercial vehicles (LCVs) through joint ventures with Indian companies. In the 1980s, these four firms collaborated with private Indian firms, and some shared equity with state-level governments. Indian firms such as Telco, Mahindra & Mahindra, Hindustan Motors, Premier automobiles, and DCM entered into joint ventures with international players like Mercedes, Ford, General Motors, and Peugeot for the assembly of medium-sized cars from knocked-down kits. Table 4.8 lists the major joint ventures in the Indian automobile sector. Foreign partners now hold all, or much, of the equity in most of these cases, even though most of them initially formed joint ventures involving an equal share of equity (Mukherjee and Sastry, 1996). The inability of Indian partners to contribute toward capacity expansion allowed foreign partners to increase their stake or to take total control by buying out their Indian partners (Sagar and Chandra, 2004).

Japanese participation in the automobile industry brought significant changes to the structure of the passenger car market, including that of utility vehicles (D'Costa, 1995). An established producer, Standard Motor, left the passenger car segment altogether and domestic players in the commercial vehicle segment started developing passenger cars, albeit on a limited scale.

The Birth of Maruti Udyog Ltd (MUL)

The establishment of Maruti Udyog Ltd (MUL) in 1981 marked a new phase for the automobile industry in India. Within a decade, production of passenger cars increased fivefold and MUL went on to capture more than 50 percent of the domestic market. The Indian government established MUL with the objective of modernizing the Indian automobile industry and producing indigenously developed cars for the needs of a growing population. A joint venture agreement was signed with the Suzuki Motor Company in 1983 by which Suzuki acquired 26 percent of the equity and agreed to provide its latest technology as well as Japanese management practices.

MUL created history by going into production in a record 13 months, rolling out its first vehicle, the Maruti 800, in 1984. This was the first domestically

Table 4.8. Entry of MNC firms in India and different modes

No.	Foreign company	Indian partner	Manufacturer name	Foreign equity	Year of incorporation
1	Fiat	Premier Auto Ltd	Premier Auto Ltd		
2	Daimler-Benz AG	Telco (Tata Motors)			1954
3	Suzuki Motor Company (Japan)	Government of India	Maruti Udyog Ltd		1982
4	Toyota	DCM	DCM Toyota India Ltd		1985
5	Mazda	Swaraj	Swaraj Mazda India Ltd		1985
6	Isuzu	Hindustan Motors		0%	1986
7	Hino	Ashok-Leyland			1985
8	Nissan	Premier Auto Ltd			1986
9	Peugeot, France	Premier Auto Ltd	Premier Auto Ltd	68.3	1994
10	Ford Motor company (USA)	Mahindra & Mahindra	Ford India Ltd		1995
11	Mitsubishi Motors, Japan	C.K. Birla Group	Hindustan Motors		2002
12	Toyota Motor Corporation, Japan	Kirloskar Motors Ltd	Toyota Kirloskar Motors Ltd		
13	Daimler-Benz AG	Tata Motors	Mercedes-Benz India Ltd		2004
14	Fiat Auto SpA (Italy)	Tata Motors	Fiat India Ltd	50	2007
15	Renault (France)	Mahindra & Mahindra			2005

Source: Author's own compilation from various secondary data sources.

produced car in the country with completely modern technology. In the beginning, the Maruti 800 model had 97 percent import content, and only tires and batteries were sourced locally. The government set up a 93 percent local content target to be hit within five years, and so the company started to encourage local start-ups. The company attracted entrepreneurs by offering them land at its complexes and supplied electricity from its own power station. In addition, Suzuki engineers helped the new manufacturers with automation and management practices such as just-in-time manufacturing. Up until 1990, MUL dominated the Indian market with the Maruti 800 becoming the car of choice, with a 62 percent market share. Before MUL arrived, the Indian auto sector had been offering just two models for decades; this figure climbed to eight after MUL's entry.

The Entry of Telco (Tata Motors) into the Passenger Car Sector

Gradually, established players such as Telco entered the commercial passenger car segment, capitalizing on their engineering capabilities, interchangeable parts, sufficient volumes, and economies of scale (D'Costa, 1998). Under the Indian government's "broad-banding" license policy, Telco entered the light commercial vehicle market, and, in 1985, introduced the Tata 407. Telco followed it with two further models in 1987: the Tata 608 and 709. In 1985, Telco applied to the Indian government for permission to produce the Honda Accord passenger car in collaboration with Honda. Permission was refused under FERA by the Indian government. Consequently, Telco began design and development work on a "pick-up" that could carry both goods and passengers. This was the "Tatamobile"—a utility vehicle launched in 1988. This was based on the Tatamobile designer parameters and was technically known as the Tata 207 platform, but with new modifications. Telco introduced two new models: the Tata Sierra, a two-door personal transport, and the Tata Estate, a four-door vehicle. The ERC successfully carried out the design and development work for Telco's commercial vehicles and played a key role in the design and development of the Tata Sierra and Tata Estate in the 1980s.

Benefiting from a now liberalized import regime in 1992, Telco obtained know-how from AVL Austria for the development of a fuel-injected petrol engine to provide a petrol option on 207 platform vehicles. In the same year, it imported know-how for the design and body styling of a five-door version of the Tata Sierra which was then under development. When these machines were imported, engineers and workers were sent to the foreign manufacturer's facilities for training. Tata Motors performed large parts of its manufacturing activities in-house. It installed facilities to manufacture engines, gearboxes and transmission mechanisms, body panels, castings and forgings, and important component sub-assemblies. Telco established a machine tools division and started manufacturing its requirements for machine tools and die fixtures in-house. In 1994, the machine tools division built four basic robots for spot-welding and arc welding, with technology imported from the Nachi-Fujikashi Corporation of Japan. The division also started manufacturing CNC (computerized numerically controlled) machines for use in its vehicle manufacturing operations.

Deregulation of the auto industry segment allowed the entry of a new player (MUL), increased competition, severe restructuring pressures on existing players, and an increase in market concentration. It had a positive impact on the performance of the auto industry as reflected in a compound annual growth rate of 18.6 percent from 1980 to 1990. Even after industry deregulation, due to an obsession with self-reliance, the production of passenger cars throughout the 1980s and early 1990s remained tightly regulated through licensing.

From 1993 Onwards: The Liberalization
of the Indian Auto Sector

The economic liberalization drive begun in 1991 started a significant phase in the development of the Indian automobile industry. Licensing was abolished in 1991, and the weighted average tariff was lowered from 87 percent to 20 percent in 1997. In 2001, the Indian government removed auto import quotas and permitted 100 percent foreign ownership of firms in the sector. The government reduced excise duties to 24 percent on passenger cars and focused on developing supportive infrastructure. In this period, Mahindra & Mahindra made a transition from being a "tractor and jeep maker" to becoming a modern passenger car maker. In 2002, Mahindra & Mahindra launched the Scorpio as a sports utility vehicle (SUV); a product of in-house design and development effort. In 1989, Suzuki increased its equity stake to 40 percent and three years later to 50 percent. In addition, Suzuki paid a control premium of Rs.10 billion to the Indian government for complete management control. In the post-2000 period, Maruti has slowly started moving toward building its own design and development capability and has carried out a minor in-house facelift of its best-selling model, the Zen. Currently, Maruti is working with its now parent company, Suzuki, to develop an Asian car, and is planning to set up an R&D center with an investment of US$200 million.

During this period, another Indian firm, Tata Motors, made rapid strides toward developing an advanced level of technological capability, by launching the first indigenously developed Indian car, the "Tata Indica." Venugopal (2001) explains in detail the efforts of Tata Motors to develop the "Tata Indica." In 1993, Ratan Tata, Chairman of Telco, mooted the idea of making a small car indigenously without licensing or financial or technological collaborations with a foreign car manufacturer. Ratan Tata is himself passionate about cars and his ambition was fueled when the Indian government turned down Telco's proposal for a joint venture with Honda to manufacture the Honda Accord. In 1994, Ratan Tata formally announced that Telco was committed to making a car that would be built indigenously and would be affordable for common people. Tata budgeted US$500 million for the Indica project and raised finance using various financial instruments such as global depository receipts (GDRs) and Yankee Bonds. The proceeds were maintained abroad in foreign currency and withdrawals were timed to meet foreign currency needs (Venugopal, 2001).

Tata Motors set up a design team at the ERC in mid-1994, and, by 1995, the team came up with two basic models. However, Ratan Tata brought in the Italian car designing institute Institute of Development in Automotive Engineering (IDEA) for further design development. A team of designers from Tata Motors, led by the program manager, interacted with the IDEA team for the entire duration of the project. Some designers and engineers were seconded to IDEA. Tata was assisted by Le Moteur Moderne of France in configuring gasoline engines. Tata Motor entered into a joint venture agreement with Cummins Engine Co. Inc. to manufacture high horsepower and emission-friendly diesel engines in 2003. Cummins joint venture helped Telco to develop diesel engines to conform to strict emission norms and helped the company to introduce a diesel version of cars and trucks.

Tata Motors decided to perform key activities in-house, such as engine and transmission manufacturing, welding and painting of body panels, and car assembly. All other activities were outsourced. Tata Motors involved major suppliers in the design process, making them early partners. The smaller vendors were grouped into two tiers: Tiers 1 and 2. The Tier 2 vendors supplied parts to Tier 1 vendors, who put together the sub-assemblies and supplied them to Tata Motors. In 1997, Telco invested in Tata Autocomp Systems Ltd (TACO), a company promoted by Tata Industries, to set up a series of joint ventures with internationally acclaimed component manufacturers. Subsequently, TACO formed a joint venture with leading auto component manufacturers, which became key suppliers to Tata Motors.

Tata Motors imported several major items of equipment from foreign suppliers, such as high-speed machining centers from Germany and the USA, and gear-cutting machines from Germany and Italy. In 1995, Telco purchased the Australian plant of Nissan for US$20 million. This plant, which subsequently closed down, was producing the Nissan Bluebird. The Nissan plant, together with 21 robots, were shipped to Telco's machine tool division and installed at a factory in Pune. Three presses for forming body panels of the Indica were commissioned. Of these, one was bought new from Germany. The other two presses were bought as used equipment from Mercedes-Benz and modified to suit Indica (Venugopal, 2001). In January 1999, Tata Motors launched the indigenously developed Tata Indica, a modern hatchback with a diesel engine.

In 2008, Tata Motors launched the Tata Nano, the world's cheapest car, priced at US$2,500. The Tata Nano was a product of the Tata's own R&D and involved innovative designs to keep the cost down. Tata Motors brought in suppliers such as Bosch, a German maker of appliances and motors, and Delphi, a world leader in automotive parts. This was done in the early stage design, challenging these companies to become full partners in the Nano's innovation through developing lower-cost components. Looking downstream at the manufacturing and distribution chain, Tata plans to build the Nano as a kit, shipping parts to local businesses for assembly.

The Second Wave of FDI

The second wave of FDI played a crucial role in changing industry structure and brought dynamism and intensive competition to the Indian auto industry.

The auto sector was subject to further significant market opening from 1993, though it still remained heavily regulated. Foreign MNCs were required to make specified capital investments and meet export obligations. Nevertheless, a high volume of FDI was encouraged with the sector's liberalization. Additionally, government policies such as import barriers and local content requirements contributed to the influx of FDI. High tariffs forced original equipment manufacturers (OEMs) to set up plants in India because they could not access the market through exports. Local content requirements of up to 70 percent forced OEMs and their suppliers to make significant capital investments. These changes led to an influx of globally competitive automakers into the Indian passenger car market. Specifically, 12 foreign MNCs—including Ford, General Motors, Hyundai, Daewoo, Honda, Toyota, Fiat, and Mercedes-Benz—entered the market. Many of these foreign MNCs entered the Indian market through a 100 percent-owned subsidiary such as Hyundai, while firms such Daimler-Benz established partnerships with local firms (Table 4.8). In 2004, Tata Motors signed a joint venture agreement with Daimler-Benz to manufacture Mercedes-Benz passenger cars in India. Mercedes held 51 percent of the equity in the joint venture, and a plant was set up in the Pune complex at a cost of US$106 million. The Mercedes-Benz India Ltd (MBIL) plant assembled completely knocked-down kits imported from abroad and concentrated on producing a luxury car in relatively small numbers.

Previously, there were only four car assemblers in the country, with MUL holding 62 percent of total market share (Gulyani, 2001). The entry of global players made the Indian auto industry more efficient and domestic markets very competitive. The increased competition led to restructuring, resulting in cost cutting, enhanced quality, and improvements in responsiveness to demand. As a result, from 2001–7 car sales have grown at an impressive compound annual growth rate of 15.5 percent. Of total sales, roughly 10 percent were accounted for by exports. The export of Indian cars has grown at a compound annual growth rate of 30 percent since 2001, and 71 percent of Indian car exports comprise compact cars. Hyundai Motor India has emerged as the leading exporter, with a 68 percent share in total exports. Currently, there are more than 30 international-quality models in the market, some of which are now being exported back to the home markets of foreign-owned MNCs.

Outward FDI from the Indian Auto Sector

Indian firms with global aspirations, such as Tata Motors and Mahindra & Mahindra, are acquiring firms overseas, establishing new subsidiaries, and forming new partnerships in foreign countries. Tata Motors has been at the forefront of overseas acquisition in the Indian auto industry. In 2004, it bought Daewoo's truck manufacturing unit, now known as Tata Daewoo Commercial Vehicle, in South Korea. In 2007, Tata Daewoo Commercial Vehicle Co. Ltd launched the heavy duty truck, Novus, in Korea and this proved to be an important source of learning for Tata Motors' heavy commercial business segment. To augment its presence in Europe, in 2005 Tata Motors acquired a 21 percent stake in Hispano Carrocera SA, a Spanish bus manufacturing company. Tata Motors has also established assembly plants in Malaysia, Kenya, Bangladesh, Spain, Ukraine, and Russia. In 2006, Tata Motors acquired a stake in Marco Polo, Brazil, to manufacture and assemble fully built buses and coaches. In 2008, Tata Motors completed the acquisition of Jaguar Land Rover for $2.3 billion. Mahindra & Mahindra has also opened subsidiaries in Australia, South Africa, Italy, and Uruguay to assemble knocked-down units and to supply auto components. In 2005, Mahindra & Mahindra acquired a leading auto component manufacturer, the Stokes Group of the UK.

4.5. A COMPARATIVE ANALYSIS OF THE INDIAN AUTOMOBILE AND PHARMACEUTICAL INDUSTRIES, AND THE IMPACT OF POLICY ON FIRM-LEVEL PROCESSES OF TECHNOLOGICAL LEARNING

In tandem with other industries, India's pharmaceutical and automobile industries have undergone significant transformation over the last five decades. This period has seen the expansion of both industries, the emergence of local R&D capabilities, and a reconfiguration of capabilities in existing firms.

The Influence of Government Policy on the Development of Technological Capabilities

Over the last five decades there has been substantial development of technological capabilities in both the Indian pharmaceutical and automobile industries. In the case of the auto industry, the establishment of Maruti Udyog Ltd—and its subsequent acquisition by Suzuki Motor—paved the way for the emergence of a modern Indian industry. In the case of the Indian pharmaceutical industry, a weakening of patent law had a similar effect and infused life into the industry. Saripalle (2006) suggests that protectionist policies *did* encourage the acquisition of basic production capabilities; however, these did not equip the firm with the coordination capabilities necessary for survival in a competitive environment.

For example, government pursued a policy of indigenization until 1993, and this has created a chain of world-class auto component suppliers, as well as having developed the firm-level coordination capabilities required to manage them. In the case of the Indian auto industry, government policies and the need to reduce costs provided an impetus for indigenization. Sagar and Chandra (2004) credit the process of indigenization as a key factor responsible for the enhancement of technological capabilities. Indigenization requires modifying designs to suit local needs, sourcing components from local suppliers and validating all components and subsystems according to Indian standards. This requires collaborative effort between local suppliers and parent company engineers. This led to a gradual movement of Indian firms toward the development of technological capabilities. MUL had an aggressive plan for indigenization from its inception, and by 1990, it had achieved 95 percent local content. Tata Motors' Indica model embodied roughly 95 percent local content for both the petrol and diesel versions (KPMG, 2007). Indian firms are already drawing on local engineering design capabilities that have allowed Tata Motors and Mahindra & Mahindra to develop entirely new vehicle platforms locally. The lead designers of the Tata Nano and the Scorpio are the products of Indian engineering institutes and those who have worked in Indian companies.

The Key Role of Foreign Partners and the Impact of Foreign Direct Investment

The McKinsey Report (2003) shows that the entry of foreign MNCs has resulted in increased productivity, higher output, better and cheaper products, and (most probably) higher wages. The analysis of the auto industry suggests that sector performance has improved steadily since 1993. Labor productivity has grown at an annual rate of 20 percent. The production facilities of foreign MNCs in India are 38 percent as productive as US plants on average. Auto industry output has grown at over 15 percent per year, up from 13 percent in 1983–93, and from less than 1 percent in the decade prior to 1983. Significantly, the components industry has benefited from spillover effects, more than tripling its size during the period as new car sales boomed and OEMs outsourced more of their cost base. Competition was also provided by international components firms, which entered the sector to serve foreign-owned assemblers, resulting in increased quality and reliability.

The impact of inward FDI on increased productivity and competitiveness has ensured that benefits accrue to consumers and employees. Firms, on the other hand, have been forced to reduce their margins with the increased competition. In the 1980s, Maruti-Suzuki used to enjoy profit margins of 10–12 percent, significantly higher than the global average of 5 percent. However, with the influx of new inward FDI, Maruti-Suzuki's profit margin declined to 3–4 percent, while European and US firms selling larger cars have been losing money. Some local assemblers went out of business because of the competition; others entered into joint ventures with foreign firms to keep afloat. A few local assemblers that developed products customized to local needs have managed to remain in business.

FDI also contributed to improving auto-sector productivity in upstream activities. Supplier productivity increased as foreign firms co-located suppliers (i.e. put them in a common area) and required home-country suppliers to invest in India. This led to the creation of a reliable auto-component supplier industry, which encouraged more foreign MNCs to enter the Indian market. Overall, the impact of FDI on the auto industry was highly positive.

However, McKinsey (2003) suggests that foreign MNCs' full productivity potential has not been realized because of other factors external to the industry, such as local content requirements (which forced firms to set up subscale-component manufacturing plants), high import tariffs (which compelled MNCs to establish subscale operations in larger car segments even as high domestic taxation suppressed demand), and poor infrastructure (which led to production inefficiencies and larger inventories).

In contrast to its policies toward other sectors, the Indian government did not discourage foreign firms from competing in the Indian pharmaceutical market (Smith, 2000). In other sectors, self-reliance was pursued at high cost, but pharmaceutical policies emphasized national health. Due to lack of a local alternative to foreign MNCs' technology, the government did not discourage their presence in the country. Thus, until 1970, the Indian pharmaceutical industry consisted almost entirely of foreign MNCs, most of which maintained minimal physical operations in India. Some of these firms, such as Hoechst Marion Russell, have had a stronger presence, with the company establishing an R&D center in India. The Hoechst Research Center has been in existence from 1972, and from its inception, it has focused on new drug discovery research and herbal research. However, in 1998, the Indian firm Nicholas Piramal India Ltd acquired the center to start its own drug discovery R&D.

Inward FDI for the Indian pharmaceutical sector did not have the same impact on production and R&D efficiency as it did in the automobile sector due to the fact that in the auto industry the regulatory environment was more open, the domestic market was more competitive, and indigenous firms had superior imitative capabilities. Due to the strengthening of the intellectual property regime in the pharmaceutical sector, Indian pharmaceutical firms have been able to start to collaborate with foreign MNCs in innovative R&D as well as in service areas such as contract manufacturing and custom synthesis.

Linkages to External Knowledge Sources Outside the Firm and Diaspora Connections

Indian pharmaceutical firms have extensively hired Indian scientists working overseas in the laboratories of foreign MNCs to help them develop innovative R&D capabilities. Firms have also targeted returning postgraduates and post-doctoral students trained in areas of medicinal chemistry and biology from overseas universities. These firms were mainly attempting to fill knowledge gaps by hiring Indian scientists who specialized in medicinal chemistry and biology. Currently, around 20 percent of the scientists working on innovative research projects have either trained at overseas universities or have experience of working abroad in MNC laboratories (Kale, 2005).

Indian automobile firms are also attracting Indian engineers based overseas, working in MNCs. Tata Motors and Mahindra & Mahindra are attracting these engineers to return to work in India. Tata Motors brought V. Sumantran from General Motors to lead the Tata Indica project. V. Sumantran had 15 years' experience of work with General Motors before joining Tata Motors. Dr Pawan Goenka, who led the design team for Mahindra & Mahindra, had a PhD from Cornell University and spent 14 years with General Motors' research center in Michigan before returning to India.

Inter-sectoral Firm Learning

The leading Indian firms in the pharmaceutical and auto industries are part of family-owned business groups. In the 1980s, many Indian businesses invested in unrelated activities as a means of protecting their income from government protection policies and a stringent tax regime. Khanna and Palepu (1997) suggest that the profitability of group-affiliated firms exceeds that of other companies; however, the relation is non-linear. Beyond a certain level, diversification is associated with higher profits. They argue that these groups make up for missing institutions such as underdeveloped financial markets, the imperfections of labor markets, limited enforcement of contracts, inadequate rule of law, and other institutional deficiencies. Business groups fill these gaps by building institutions for the benefit of group members.

In emerging markets, firms find it difficult to attract investment in new ventures owing to the limited availability of information and the absence of safeguards. In this case, diversified firms can point to their track record to attract investment. For example, historically, Tata companies have come together to finance their new ventures. In 1982, the Tata Group created Tata Industries, a venture capital vehicle funded with a special pool of investment money earmarked for member companies. Indian groups are creating value by developing managers and spreading the cost of professional development throughout the group. Such groups have internal management development programs, often with dedicated facilities and which are geared toward developing the skills of experienced managers, and in some cases, for all levels of employees. Tata Administrative Services, an in-house training program with a national reputation for excellence, was established in 1956 and has aimed at creating a cadre of general managers for the Tata Group.

Khanna and Palepu (1997) further suggest that such groups can provide much-needed flexibility for labor markets in general. Governments in emerging markets usually have strict labor laws, making it difficult for companies to adjust or lay off their workforces. Examples in India suggest that Indian business groups develop extensive internal labor markets of their own. When one company in a group faces declining prospects, its employees can be transferred to other group companies that are on the rise—even to companies in otherwise undesirable locations. The faster-growing companies benefit by receiving a ready source of reliable employees and groups are able to put new talent to good use. By allocating talent to where it is most needed, conglomerates have a head start in beginning new activities. In the case of the Tata Group, group companies are encouraged to facilitate the mobility of talented employees to other companies if that is to the benefit of both. Cross-company teams of "stars" are assembled to resolve difficult problems any individual company is having.

Despite the elimination of capacity licensing, Indian law still requires that companies get permission for a range of decisions such as businesses closures, changes to commodity prices, and decisions to import raw materials. The law establishes subjective criteria for many of these decisions, so Indian bureaucrats have a great deal of discretion in how they apply these rules. Diversified groups can add value by acting as intermediaries when their individual companies or foreign partners need to deal with the regulatory bureaucracy. Experience and connections give conglomerates an advantage. The larger the company, the easier it is to carry the cost of maintaining government relationships (Khanna and Palepu, 1997). Tata today enjoys strong market shares in many sectors of the Indian economy, having advantages in learning as well as through access to capital, owing to the diversified nature of the group.

Analysis of Indian pharmaceutical human resources (HR) and R&D practices shows the influence of Indian IT firms' efforts to attract and retain top-level talent. Indian pharmaceutical firms are now employing similar practices to retain and absorb overseas scientists (Kale et al., 2008). For example, when DRL started redesigning HR processes, it discovered that there were no good models in the pharmaceutical industry, but it found inspiring revolutionary HR systems developed by Indian IT companies. Thus, it hired its HR President and HR Vice-President from two leading Indian software companies. In 2002, DRL hired G. Rajkumar, general manager (learning and development) from

Infosys, a leading Indian software firm, to run education of technical staff in intellectual property and project management skills.

Pharmaceutical firms launched new initiatives, such as performance-linked pay, attractive stock options schemes, performance management systems, and leadership development programs, and benchmarked them against IT firms. Thus, inter-organizational learning through the observation of other sectors' leading firms had a significant role to play in guiding certain aspects of technological learning in Indian pharmaceutical firms. In contrast, the Indian auto industry is yet to show evidence of inter-sectoral influences on firm learning strategies.

Firm Sizes and Managerial Vision

The Indian auto industry is dominated mainly by diversified and large business groups, such as the Tata Group and Mahindra & Mahindra, whereas the Indian pharmaceutical industry shows clear evidence of entrepreneurship and the key role of small firms. For example, the Indian auto market is dominated by three or four firms with strong market shares, while the Indian pharmaceutical industry represents a fragmented picture, characterized by a large number of firms each of which has a similar market share. In the case of the Indian pharmaceutical industry, the 1970 Patent Act reduced entry barriers and enabled entrepreneurial scientists to work in public sector companies. Pharmaceutical product distributors then started manufacturing units producing bulk drugs. For example, Dr Anji Reddy, founder of DRL, was working as a scientist with the Indian public sector company, Indian Drug and Pharmaceutical Ltd. However, in the case of the automobile industry, the government protection regime increased entry barriers and deterred entrepreneurial activity.

Anji Reddy's vision is to take DRL into the top ten of global pharmaceutical companies and he believes that this can be done through original molecule research. He explains that the most competitive purely generics company still ranks no higher than 26th in the world pecking order. There is no way that a purely generic company can become one of the top ten pharmaceuticals company in the world without its own independent drug discovery. This belief has shaped Dr Anji Reddy's vision. DRL received severe setbacks in the 1990s, with Novo Nordisk returning an out-licensed molecule and DRL losing a patent battle with Pfizer. However, based on Anji Reddy's vision, DRL continued to invest in R&D expenditure at around 10 percent of sales.

Similarly, motivation for Cipla's strong defense of weak patent laws and focus on cheap drugs lies at the heart of the vision of Dr Hamied, CEO and son of the company's founder. Dr Hamied's vision has been influenced by a mix of motivations—profit, social conscience, and nationalism—and by birthright. His father, a follower of Mahatma Gandhi's brand of Indian nationalism, had financial support from his family to study chemistry in England. Instead, he changed course and went to Germany, then the world's leader in chemicals. On a Berlin lake, he met a Lithuanian Jewish socialist, Mr Hamied's mother. They fled Germany as it shifted into Nazi hands, and the Chemical, Industrial and Pharmaceutical Laboratories, later known as Cipla, was founded in 1935. The company still keeps a sort of shrine to the day in 1939 that Gandhi visited, writing in the guest book, "I was delighted to visit this Indian enterprise" (McNeil Jr, 2000). This background shaped Dr Hamied's vision and informed the company's strategies after Independence.

Kale et al. (2008) also show that "firm-specific managerial vision" played an important role in shaping firm-level technological learning in the Indian pharmaceutical industry. They further point out that, in the case of Ranbaxy, Parminder Singh's vision that Ranbaxy could be a big player in the US generic market was both audacious and unforeseen. In the late 1980s, the relationship between the owner of Ranbaxy, Bhai Mohan Singh, and his son, Dr Parminder Singh, soured over differences with respect to Ranbaxy's growth strategy. As a result, Dr Singh took total control of the company in 1992, ousting his father, and challenged Ranbaxy's top management team with his dream of transforming Ranbaxy into "an international, research-based pharmaceutical company." He consistently questioned imitative R&D mindsets among the company's scientists.

Anji Reddy's ambition to show that Indian firms could overturn patents and win, guided DRL's forays. Similarly, in the case of the Indian automobile industry, the ambition and vision of Ratan Tata to develop the first "Indian car" and then the "people's car" were the driving forces behind the development of the Tata Indica and Tata Nano. In the case of Mahindra & Mahindra, the ambition of Anand Mahindra to transform a tractor manufacturing company into a passenger car firm fueled the design and development effort for the Scorpio.

The Internationalization Motives of Indian Pharmaceutical and Auto Firms

An analysis of Indian pharmaceutical firms' internationalization strategies suggests that acquisition is the preferred route for Indian firms' international expansion. Benefits are created through synergies formed by the product pipeline of Indian firms and assets provided by overseas firms. Indian firms have a large pipeline of products, cheap manufacturing facilities, and an ambition to enter the advanced markets of Europe and the US. However, Indian firms lack distribution networks, regulatory capabilities, and high-end technological capabilities. Thus, the overseas expansion of Indian firms is related to the need to improve global competitiveness, to acquire assets (including research and contract manufacturing firms in order to further boost their outsourcing capabilities), to move up the value chain, and to improve their product offerings and consolidate their existing market shares.

In the post-liberalization era, the leading Indian auto manufacturers are in the process of transforming themselves from local players into global companies. Increasingly, foreign sales are made through directly owned or joint venture-based foreign operations rather than through exports from Indian manufacturing facilities. Indian companies have bought capacity or made alliances with other automakers in East Asia, South America, Africa, and Europe. For the top five Indian automakers, revenue from overseas markets is close to an average of 9 percent. However, compared to the Indian pharmaceutical industry, the overseas expansion of the auto industry is still at a nascent stage. For example, in 2005–6 Ranbaxy earned 80 percent of its revenues from overseas markets, compared to an equivalent figure of 10 percent for Tata Motors. The main challenge for Indian automakers is to establish a reputation for world-class technology, which requires substantial and long-term investments.

4.6. CONCLUSIONS

Case-study evidence on the Indian pharmaceutical and auto industries suggests that in emerging market economies government policies—specifically protectionist policies in the early stages of development—have played an important role in the rise of basic technological capabilities. However, Saripalle (2006) shows that, in the case of the Indian auto industry, firms established before 1985 experienced their highest growth rates in the protection phase before 1991. Conversely, firms established after 1985 have exhibited their highest growth rates in the deregulation period. This clearly indicates the limitation of government policies in influencing the technological development of an industry in an internationally competitive environment. Firm-level learning in companies such as Tata Motors or Mahindra & Mahindra is influenced by managerial vision and operates through collaboration and competing with foreign MNC firms in domestic markets. Similarly, in the case of the Indian pharmaceutical industry, the weakening of the Patent Act and the adoption of the Drug Policy of 1978 reduced entry barriers and allowed the growth of basic technological capabilities. Technological learning was also critically assimilated through international business connections. These took the form of opportunities to export to the US and European generic markets, outward FDI, and the utilization of diaspora connections to fill knowledge gaps.

Analysis of firms operating in the Indian pharmaceutical and automobile sectors shows that the transformation of technological capabilities requires a deliberate effort by firms to invest in different mechanisms of learning. Rigid ideas about sequences and stages may be misleading, especially at the firm level. This research shows that the learning processes which underlie accumulation and development of knowledge require technical as well as organizational knowledge and management capabilities. The important aspect of this learning involves unlearning the competencies which might have been useful in an earlier era but are not relevant in new environments. The learning-by-doing aspect (the link to production experience) remains necessary but not sufficient to ensure the development of innovative capabilities. Thus, our studies of the Indian pharmaceutical and automobile industries suggest that the move from basic to intermediate and then to advanced-level capabilities is neither linear nor automatic. This finding supports observations made by researchers like Bell and Pavitt (1993) and Forbes and Wield (2002).

REFERENCES

Bell, M., and Pavitt, K. (1993), "Technological Accumulation and Industrial Growth: Contrasts between Developed and Developing Countries," *Industrial and Corporate Change*, 2(2): 157–210.

Bhagwati, J. (1993), *India in Transition: Freeing the Economy*, Oxford: Clarendon Press.

D'Costa, A. P. (1995), "The Restructuring of the Indian Automobile Industry: Indian State and Japanese Capital," *World Development*, 23(3): 485–502.

—— (1998), "An Alternative Model of Development? Co-operation and Flexible Industrial Practices in India," *Journal of International Development*, 10: 301–21.

Economic Survey of India (2007), available at <http://indiabudget.nic.in/es2007-08/esmain.html>.

Forbes, N. (1999), "Technology and Indian industry: What is Liberalisation Changing?" *Technovation*, 19: 403–12.

—— and Wield, D. (2002), *From Followers to Leaders: Managing Technology and Innovation*, London: Routledge.

Guennif, S. (2004), *AIDS in India: Public Health Related Aspects of Industrial Policy and Intellectual Property Rights in a Developing Country*, CSH Occasional Paper 8, Centre de Sciences Humaines, New Delhi, India: Rajdhani Art Press.

Gulyani, S. (2001), *Innovating with Infrastructure: The Automobile Industry in India*. New York: Palgrave.

Hindu Business Line (2002), "Glaxo Closes Biddle Sawyer Operations," available at <http://www.thehindubusinessline.com/2002/07/02/stories/2002070202440100.html>.

Kale, D. (2005), "Re-developing Knowledge Creation Capability: Innovating in the Indian Pharmaceutical Industry under TRIPS Regime," unpublished PhD thesis, The Open University, UK.

—— Athreye, S., and Ramani, S. (2008), "Experimentation with Strategy and the Evolution of Dynamic Capability in the Indian Pharmaceutical Sector," UNU MERIT Working Paper, 2008-041.

Kale, D. and Little, S. E. (2007), "From Imitation to Innovation: The Evolution of R&D Capabilities and Learning Processes in the Indian Pharmaceutical Industry," *Technology Analysis and Strategic Management*, 19: 589–611.

—— Wield, D., and Chataway, J. (2008), "Diffusion of Knowledge through Migration of Scientific Labour in India," *Science and Public Policy*, 35(6): 417–31.

Keayla, B. K. (1996), "New Patent Regime: Implications for Domestic Industry, Research and Development and Consumers," National Working Group on Patent Laws (Centre for Study on GATT Laws), New Delhi.

Khanna, T., and Palepu, K. (1997), "Why Focused Strategies may be Wrong for Emerging Markets," *Harvard Business Review*, 75(4): 41–50.

Kim, L., and Nelson, R. R. (2000), "Introduction: Technology and Industrialisation in Newly Industrialising Countries," in L. Kim and R. R. Nelson (eds.), *Technology, Learning and Innovation: Experiences of Newly Industrialising Economies*, Cambridge: Cambridge University Press.

KPMG (2007), *India Automotive Study 2007: Domestic Growth and Global Aspirations*, Mumbai, India: KPMG.

McKinsey (2003), *New Horizons: Multinational Company Investment in New Economies*, San Francisco, USA: McKinsey.

McNeil Jr, D. (2000), "Selling Cheap 'Generic' Drugs, India's Copycats Irk Industry," available at <http://www.nytimes.com/2000/12/01/world/selling-cheap-generic-drugs-india-s-copycats-irk-industry.html?pagewanted=all&src=pm>.

Mukherjee, A., and Sastry, T. (1996), "Recent Developments and Future Prospects in the Indian Automotive Industry," available at <http://dspace.mit.edu/bitstream/handle/1721.1/1633/Sastry3.pdf>.

Nelson, R. R., and Pack, H. (1999), "The Asian Miracle and Modern Growth Theory," *Economic Journal*, 109(457): 416–37.

OICA (2007), <http://oica.net/wp-content/uploads/world-ranking-2007.pdf>.

OPPI (2001), *OPPI Pharmaceutical Compendium*, Mumbai: Organisation of Pharmaceutical Producers of India.

Sagar, A. D., and Chandra, P. (2004), "Technological Change in the Indian Passenger Car Industry," BCSIA Discussion Paper 2004–05, Energy Technology Innovation Project, Kennedy School of Government, Harvard University.

Saripalle, M. (2006), "Learning across Policy Regimes: The Impact of Protection vis-à-vis Competition in the Indian Automotive Industry," MPRA Paper 10 1701, <http://mpra.ub.uni-muenchen.de/1701/>.

SIAM (2007–11), Society for Indian Automobile Manufacturers, <http://www.siamindia.com/>.

Smith, E. S. (2000), "Opening Up to the World: India's Pharmaceutical Companies Prepare for 2005," Asia Pacific Research Center, available at <http://APARC.stanford.edu>.

Tata Motors (2007–8), Annual Report, available at <http://www.tatamotors.com/investors/financials/annual-reports.php>.

US FDA (2003), Drug Approvals and Databases, <http://www.fda.gov/Drugs/InformationOnDrugs/ucm135778.html>.

Venugopal, R. (2001), "Telco's Small Car," *Asian Case Research Journal*, 5(1): 49–69.

5

Malaysia[1]

Rajah Rasiah

5.1. INTRODUCTION

Faced with a small domestic market, rising unemployment, and an uncertain political future following independence from Britain in 1957 and a failed import-substitution regime over the period 1958–71, the government opened free trade zones from 1972 to attract export-oriented light and labor-intensive firms to Malaysia. Electronics and garments became the leading foreign direct investors in Malaysia under this export-oriented regime.

The electronics industry has become Malaysia's chief manufactured export earner since 1974 and a leading contributor to manufacturing value added and employment since 1980, though its shares have fallen since 1995. Garments accounted for Malaysia's second largest manufacturing export until the 1980s. A combination of rising costs, the emergence of new low-wage producers (especially China and Vietnam), and the withdrawal of the Multi-Fiber Arrangement (MFA) quotas in 2004 have slowed down value-added growth in the industry. Lacking domestic markets, garment firms in Malaysia have increasingly acquired and developed technological capabilities to coordinate better export operations. Instead of closing down operations, competition has driven informal modes of learning and innovation to sustain electronics and garment exports. Although some of the foreign flagship electronics firms are engaged in path-creating knowledge activities globally—e.g. Intel and AMD—their operations in Malaysia are largely confined to limited activities in assembly and test operations. Both industries lack the presence of formal corporate R&D because most of the electronics and garment firms in Malaysia are not at the technology frontier.

[1] I am grateful to Jan Fagerberg, Edmund Amann, Martin Bell, and John Cantwell for their constructive comments.

Although both industries are export-oriented and light, electronics and garments provide sufficient contextual contrast to establish differences in learning and innovation drivers and patterns. Whereas electronics is a technology-creating industry, garments is a technology-using industry. Yet, upgrading in both industries in Malaysia is driven by different instruments in value chains and embedding institutions. Whereas shortening product cycles, the miniaturization process, and enabler properties continue to drive high-end electronics operations in locations shaping the technology frontier, cut-throat competition and the labor-intensive nature of garment manufacturing continues to drive operations to low-cost sites endowed with good infrastructure, large supplies of trainable labor, and security. Hence, while electronics continues to expand in the United States, Europe, Japan, Korea, Taiwan, Singapore, and Malaysia, garment manufacturing is dominated by China, India, and Turkey, with strong growth in Vietnam, Bangladesh, and Cambodia. In addition to the motives of firms (see Cantwell and Mudambi, 2005), global regulatory developments and national and provincial policies have been critical in the choice of location, acquisition, and upgrading in both industries. Given its classification as strategic and its capacity to drive increasing returns, the electronics industry has enjoyed considerable government support in Malaysia. Garment manufacturing began to receive similar support following the financial crisis of 1997–8 that threatened to raise unemployment rates.

Taking account of the theoretical background provided by Chapter 2, this chapter will examine the processes of technological upgrading over time. The choice of these two industries from Malaysia provides sufficient contextual differences. Garment firms connect with the embedding innovation system significantly differently from electronics firms. The electronics industry is a platform where new technologies drive performance, while the absorption and adaptation of technologies from other firms drive performance in garment firms (see Best, 2001; Hobday, 1995; Rasiah, 1994). Hence, a comparison of learning and innovation activities in these two sets of industries will provide an interesting context within which to explain their economic relevance to the Malaysian economy. This comparison enables us to answer the four critical questions outlined in the introductory chapter.

5.2. ELECTRIC-ELECTRONICS AND TEXTILE-GARMENTS

This section provides the national context for the two industries by discussing their contribution to Malaysia's manufacturing sector, and changes in their ownership structure. The electric-electronics and textile-garment industries of

Malaysia were begun by Japanese foreign capital in 1965 and 1957 respectively, seeking to supply the domestic market with final consumer goods (see Rasiah, 1988, 1993). By 1968, the share of foreign equity in the fixed assets of the two industries had fallen to 52 and 70 percent respectively as local firms began to participate in production and the small domestic market became saturated (Hoffmann and Tan, 1980; Jomo, 1990). Whereas the initial wave of export-oriented electric-electronics and textile-garment firms from the developed countries were driven by a search for low wages but safe and secure tax havens (see Sciberras, 1977), the Malaysian government attracted these firms to tax-free export-processing zones in the country to create employment opportunities (Lim, 1978).

The contribution of the electric-electronics industry in manufacturing employment and value added rose in the period 1972–9 and in 1985–97, before showing a trend fall in 2000–5 (see Figures 5.1 and 5.2). The contribution of the textile-garment industry to manufacturing employment and value added also rose in 1972–9 before showing a trend fall, with a slight increase in 1990. Electric-electronics exports in manufacturing exports rose over the period 1972–2000 before falling in 2007, while those of the textile-garment industry reached their peak in 1985 before declining (see Figure 5.3).

The focus on dexterity skills and low wages in the 1970s and the early 1980s attracted strong female labor force participation in electronics and garment manufacturing. These export-oriented industries accelerated rural-urban migration so that poverty levels in the country fell as employment opportunities grew in export-processing zones and disguised unemployment fell in both rural and urban areas. For example, the most important province for the two export-oriented industries, Penang, experienced a fall in the incidence of poverty from 53.0 percent in 1970 to 0.3 percent in 2006, when the corresponding rates at national level were 52.0 percent in 1970 and 6.0 percent (Rasiah and Vinanchiarachi, 2012). The unemployment rate in the province fell from 11.1 percent in 1970 to 2.5 percent in 2006, while national rates were 8.1 percent in 1970 and 3.1 percent in 2006.

Both industries emerged following the relocation from abroad of multinational corporations, initiated by Japanese capital. However, whereas Hong Kong and Taiwanese firms became important in the manufacture of garments, American firms initiated and continued to dominate semiconductor manufacturing in Malaysia. The first wave of industrialization in Malaysia was associated with light garment and electronics manufacturing. Both industries were attracted by import-substitution incentives: Johor Textiles started in Johor Bharu in 1957 and Matsushita electric started in Shah Alam in 1965 respectively (see Rasiah, 1988, 1993). National Semiconductor was the first semiconductor producer to open operations in Malaysia in 1972. The small domestic market

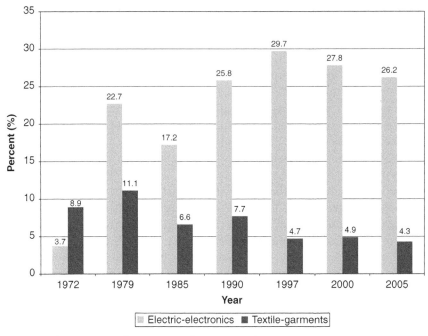

Fig. 5.1. Share in manufacturing employment, Malaysia, 1972–2005
Source: Author, based on DOSM (1985–2007).

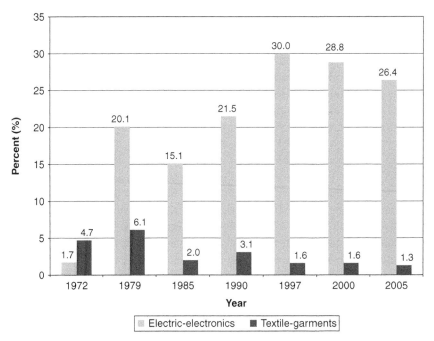

Fig. 5.2. Share in manufacturing value added, Malaysia, 1972–2005
Source: Author, based on DOSM (1985–2007).

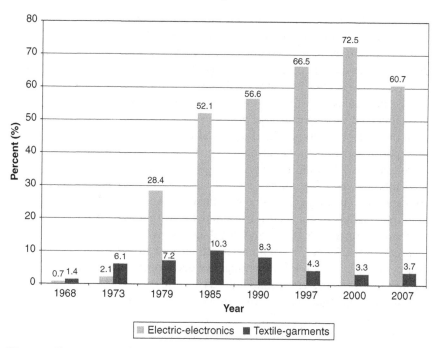

Fig. 5.3. Share in manufacturing exports, Malaysia, 1968–2007
Source: Author, based on DOSM (1985–2007).

made it difficult for import substitution to generate sufficient jobs to tackle poverty and unemployment in the country. Hence, export-oriented industrialization became the prime driver of manufacturing growth in Malaysia from 1972. Earlier export-oriented initiatives following the Investment Incentives Act (IIA) of 1968 and the launching of the New Economic Policy in 1971 (Malaysia, 1972) did not prove successful until the Free Trade Zones (FTZ) were opened in 1971. Tariff and tax-free locations, and profit repatriation guarantees offered by the government made the FTZs successful. Employment in the electric-electronics and textile-garment industries grew on average by 44.6 and 12.6 percent per annum in 1971–9.

Until 1979 foreign ownership in the two industries rose as the Malaysian government opened export-processing zones, before falling in the subsequent period of 1979–85 as the focus of government policy shifted toward local heavy industries (see Figure 5.4; Jomo, 1990). The new Mahathir administration initiated an aggressive inward-oriented policy in the early 1980s to support national participation in manufacturing. The shift in government policy toward national capital and a decline in foreign investment in 1981–5 drove a slowdown in employment growth in the two industries: annual average growth in employment and value added in electric-electronics fell to

5.2 and 11.4 percent per annum and in textiles and garments to 2.0 and 9.6 percent per annum in the period 1979–85 (Rasiah, 2008: Tables 7 and 8). The national economy faced a contraction in GDP in 1985, which accompanied falling commodity prices, rising debt servicing (as the yen appreciated), and a cyclical downturn in the electronics industry.[2]

The mid-1980s slowdown drove the government to take counter-cyclical measures that included reviving generous incentives for export-oriented foreign firms, depreciation of the ringgit, and further liberalization of ownership in export-oriented manufacturing. The government enacted the Promotion of Investment Act in 1986 to help revive growth in export-oriented industries. FDI inflows were also boosted strongly by relocations from Japan, Taiwan, South Korea, and Singapore, following the Plaza Accord of 1985 that triggered the appreciation of their currencies and the withdrawal of the generalized systems of preferences (GSP) from the Asian newly industrialized countries in February 1988. Hence, foreign ownership in the two industries rose again in the period 1985–90, boosting annual average employment and value-added growth in the electric-electronics industry by 21.6 and 21.1 percent per annum and in the textile-garment industry by 12.4 and 20.7 percent respectively (see Rasiah, 2008: Tables 7 and 8).

Foreign ownership in both industries rose slightly in the 1990–3 period as the Malaysian economy faced a tightening labor market following rapid expansion (see Figure 5.4). However, from 1993 foreign ownership in the electric-electronics industry fell gradually, while it increased in the textile-garment industry. Whereas local firms focusing on contract manufacturing and consumer electronics using largely foreign labor from Indonesia and Bangladesh have started substituting production in the electronics industry, closures increased among local textile and garment firms. Garment firms have increasingly relocated their labor-intensive operations to locations enjoying preferential access to major markets, while upgrading into higher value-added activities in Malaysia. Hence, employment and value added in the electric-electronics industry grew by 14.6 and 21.3 percent per annum, while for textile-garments growth was at the slower rates of 1.6 and 8.6 percent per annum respectively in 1990–7 (Rasiah, 2008: Table 8).

Foreign ownership has continued to fall in the electric-electronics industry because of serious labor shortages in Malaysia and the emergence of more attractive manufacturing sites for labor-intensive operations in China, Vietnam, and Philippines (see Figure 5.4). Employment and value added in the electric-electronics industry grew by only 5.4 and 2.1 percent respectively per annum and in the textile and garment industry by -0.1 and -4.8 percent respectively per annum in 2000–5. Both industries also faced an absolute contraction in real

---

[2] Caused by the removal of tax holidays following the expiry of incentives in the period 1981–5 (see Rasiah, 1995).

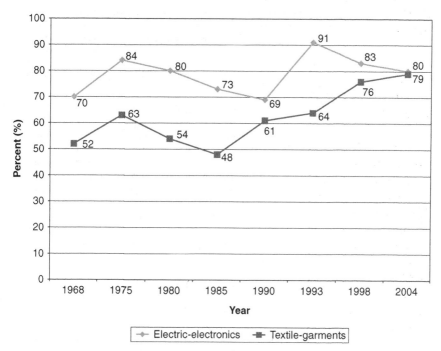

Fig. 5.4. Foreign ownership share, selected industries, Malaysia, 1968–2004
Source: Author, based on DOSM (1985–2007).

labor productivity. Labor productivity in the electric-electronics and textile-garment industries recorded -4.5 and -5.3 percent growth in 2000–5. A combination of slow upgrading and the lack of human capital has been documented as the prime reason for this contraction (Malaysia, 2006).

The slowdown in the garment and electronics industries in Malaysia from 1990 and 2000 respectively is also obvious from the decline in global market shares of exports (see Table 5.1). Malaysia's share in global exports of electronics rose from 2.7 percent in 1990 to 5.4 percent in 2000, before falling to 4.7 percent in 2006. Export shares of its competitors—Korea, Singapore, and Taiwan—also rose from 1990 to 2000 before falling in 2006. China's share of exports of electronics items in the global export market rose sharply from 4.5 percent in 1990 to 19.8 percent in 2006. The fall recorded by Korea, Malaysia, and Taiwan is largely a consequence of the relocation of labor-intensive manufacturing operations to China and other countries in Southeast Asia. However, whereas local firms accounted for much of the relocation from Korea and Taiwan as they retained the higher value-added stages in their own home countries, transnational firms relocated operations from Malaysia following the emergence of low-cost sites and a tightening labor market.

Table 5.1. Share of important exporters, electronics and garments, 1990–2006

	Share of world exports (%)			Share of sector in national exports (%)	
	1990	2000	2006	2000	2006
Electronics, Office & Telecom Equipment					
Brazil	0.2	0.2	0.3	4.3	2.9
Canada	1.9	2.1	1.0	7.5	3.8
China	1.0	4.5	19.8	17.5	29.7
European Union (25)	NA	29.2	28.8	11.6	9.2
Hong Kong, China	4.3	5.2	8.6	24.7	38.6
Indonesia	0.0	0.8	0.4	11.1	6.0
Japan	22.5	11.2	6.9	22.6	15.3
South Korea	4.8	6.1	5.8	34.1	25.7
Malaysia	2.7	5.4	4.7	53.3	42.2
Mexico	1.5	3.5	3.2	20.5	18.6
Philippines	0.6	2.6	1.8	63.2	55.4
Singapore	6.4	7.6	8.1	53.6	43.4
Taiwan	4.7	6.0	4.4	39.0	30.3
Thailand	1.2	1.9	2.0	27.0	22.5
United States	17.3	15.9	9.4	19.6	13.2
Vietnam	NA	0.1	0.1	4.5	3.6
Garments					
Bangladesh	0.6	2.1	2.6	75.8	76.6
Cambodia	0.0	0.5	0.9	69.8	70.4
China	8.9	18.2	30.6	14.5	9.8
European Union (25)	NA	26.9	26.8	2.2	1.8
Hong Kong, China	14.2	12.2	9.1	11.9	8.8
India	2.3	3.1	3.3	13.7	8.3
Indonesia	1.5	2.4	1.8	7.2	5.5
South Korea	7.3	2.5	0.7	2.9	0.7
Malaysia	1.2	1.1	0.9	2.3	1.8
Mexico	0.5	4.4	2.0	5.2	2.5
Morocco	0.7	1.2	1.0	32.3	25.5
Pakistan	0.9	1.1	1.3	23.8	23.1
Philippines	1.6	1.3	0.8	6.4	5.5
Romania	0.3	1.2	1.4	22.5	13.7
Sri Lanka	0.6	1.4	1.0	51.8	44.2
Thailand	2.6	1.9	1.4	5.4	3.3
Tunisia	1.0	1.1	1.0	38.1	27.6
Turkey	3.1	3.3	3.8	23.5	13.9
United States	2.4	4.4	1.6	1.1	0.5
Vietnam	NA	0.9	1.7	12.6	14.9

Source: Author elaboration from WTO, *International Trade Statistics* (2007).

Korean and Taiwanese firms at the frontier in semiconductor manufacturing that preside over high value-added operations include Samsung, Hynix, and LG Electronics, and Taiwan Semiconductor Manufacturing Corporation (TSMC), United Microelectronics Company (UMC), Vanguard and Winbond (see Mathews and Cho, 2000; Amsden and Chu, 2003).

Malaysia's share in global exports of garments fell from 1.2 percent in 1990 to 1.1 percent in 2000 and 0.9 percent in 2006 (see Table 5.1), while China's grew from 8.9 percent in 1990 to 30.6 percent in 2006. Vietnam's share grew from 0.9 percent in 2000 to 1.7 percent in 2007. Export shares from the least developed countries (LDCs) of Bangladesh and Cambodia also expanded over this period. Export shares from South Korea, Hong Kong, and Taiwan had started falling earlier because of rising production costs, appreciation of their currencies following the Plaza Accord of 1985, and the withdrawal of the generalized system of preferences from February 1988. Whereas local firms from Hong Kong, Korea, and Taiwan have relocated operations to mainland China, Southeast Asia (in the 1980s) and the LDCs, from the 1990s local firms in Malaysia have faced a shakeout with the remaining firms upgrading to remain competitive.

The contribution of electric-electronics and textile-garments to the Malaysian economy fell over the period 2000–6 (see Table 5.1). The share of electric-electronics and textile-garments in overall exports fell from 53.2 and 2.3 percent in 2000 to 42.2 and 1.8 percent in 2006 (see Table 5.1). Despite the slowdown, the industries have remained important to the Malaysian economy, with significant contributions to employment and exports.

Given their importance in the national economy this chapter seeks to examine the nature of technological upgrading that has taken place in electronics and garment firms in Malaysia and their relationship with firms from other industries and research institutions.

5.3. METHODOLOGY AND DATA

This chapter draws on the technological capability framework. Lall (1992) provided the first typology of technological capabilities by taxonomies and trajectories, which was later followed by Bell and Pavitt (1995), Ariffin (2000), Ariffin and Bell (1999), Ariffin and Figueiredo (2004), Figueiredo (2002, 2003), and Rasiah (1994, 2003, 2007).

Measurement and Specification of Technology Variables

The assessment uses different types of technological capabilities and economic performance outcomes (see Table 5.2), as well as incidence of participation at different levels of trajectories (see Table 5.3). The key variables to be examined are set out in Table 5.2, while Table 5.2a sets out a glossary of additional acronyms employed in the analysis.

Table 5.2. Variables, proxies, and measurement formulas

Variable	Proxies	Specification	Estimation*
HR	TE	Training expenditure/payroll (%)	Normalized
	SI	Skilled workers/workforce (%)	
Process technology	PTE	Process technology expenditure/sale (%)	
R&D	RDE	R&D expenditure/sale (%)	Normalized
	RDP	R&D personnel/workforce(%)	
Labor productivity	VA/L	Value added/employment in Malaysian ringgit	
Export intensity	X/Y	Export/output (%)	

Note: Using the formula $(X_i - X_{mn})/(X_{mx} - X_{mn})$ where X_{mn} and X_{mx} refer to minimum and maximum observations, the scores for the two proxies are then added and divided by 2.
Source: Author.

Table 5.2a. Glossary of additional acronyms

Acronym	Meaning
JIT	Just in time
	Materials requirement planning
MRPI	Materials resources planning
MRPII	Integrated materials resources planning
MST	Minimum stock turnaround
OBM	Original brand manufacturer
ODM	Original design manufacturer
OEM	Original equipment manufacturer
QCC	Quality control circle
QS	Quality system
SGA	Small group activities
SPC	Statistical process control
SQC	Statistical quality control
TPM	Total preventive maintenance
TQC	Total quality control
TQM	Total quality management

Source: Author.

Estimation of Economic Outcomes

The impact of technological capabilities on economic performance relies on elasticity estimations between capabilities and performance. In addition to examining annual average growth rates of labor productivity and changes in the export intensity of output, the chapter also examines the productivity-technology and the export-technology elasticities over the period 2000–7.

Whereas labor productivity and export-intensity growth are estimated using the usual annual average growth rate formulas, elasticities were estimated by dividing the two separately by each of the technological capabilities.

Table 5.3. Taxonomy and trajectory of firms

Degree of complexity	HR	Process	Product
Simple activities (1)	On the job and in-house training	Dated machinery with simple inventory control techniques	Assembly or processing of component, CKD and CBU using foreign technology
Minor improvements (2)	In-house training and performance rewards	Advanced machinery, layouts, and problem-solving	Precision engineering
Major improvements (3)	Extensive focus on training and retraining; staff with training responsibility	Cutting-edge inventory control techniques, SPC, TQM, TPM	Cutting-edge quality control systems (QCC and TQC) with original equipment manufacturing (OEM) capability
Engineering (4)	Engineers engaged in adaptation activities; separate training department	Process adaptation: layouts, equipment, and techniques	Product adaptation
Early R&D (5)	Engineers engaged in product development activities; separate specialized training activities	Process development: layouts, machinery and equipment, materials and processes	Product development capability. Some firms take on original design manufacturing (ODM) capability
Mature R&D (6)	Specialized R&D scientists and engineers wholly engaged in new product research	Process R&D to devise new layouts, machinery and equipment prototypes, materials and processes	New product development capability, with some taking on original brand manufacturing (OBM) capability

Note: CKD—completely knocked-down parts; CBU—completely built-up units.
Source: Author, developed from Lall (1992), Rasiah (1994, 2007), Figueiredo (2002, 2003).

Data

Two sets of data are used in the chapter. The first, covering 103 electronics and 56 garment firms, was drawn from a structured sampling process chosen on the basis of ownership and size that was supplied by the Department of Statistics, Malaysia (see Table 5.4).[3] From this list, firms with operations starting in 1974 and earlier were approached for time-series assessment. Because semiconductor and woven garments-dominated firms have such a long history of operations, the smaller sample was confined to this narrow

[3] The survey was assisted by Khazanah (the federal government's investment company) and undertaken by Pemm Consult, a private survey company located in Subang.

Table 5.4. Breakdown of sampled data, 2007

	Electronics	Garments
Survey		
Mailed	165	89
Responses	103	56
Percent (%)	62.4	62.9
Interview		
Approached	20	25
Responses	12	14
Percent (%)	60.0	56.0

Source: Author, compiled in 2008 from Khazanah survey (see note 3).

range of industries. Because of the need to differentiate the capability development of foreign and local firms, local firms that started operations in the 1980s were added to both sets of industries. Overall, 12 semiconductor and 14 woven garment firms responded to the more detailed study (see Table 5.4). All ten of the foreign semiconductor firms in the sample were in operation by 1974, while the two local firms started operations in the 1980s.

The data collected from the sample of firms is shown in Table 5.3. Levels 4–6 shown in Table 5.3 refer to innovation activities that require extensive use of engineers.

5.4. TECHNOLOGICAL CAPABILITIES

This section examines how firms have evolved through different "levels" of technological capability and activity toward a more innovative type of enterprise, and what factors have facilitated and constrained these learning trajectories in the electronics and garment industries in Malaysia. There has been considerable technological upgrading in the firms. However, while the nature of garment manufacturing and markets suggests that its long-term contraction is unavoidable (see Rasiah, 2009), a quickening of learning and innovation can arrest the slowdown experienced by the electronics industry.

Electronics and Garments

Firms in both industries reported increased absorption of cutting-edge technologies by 2007. All electronics and garment firms in the sample reported having International Standards Organization (ISO) 9000 series certification in

2007 (see Figures 5.5 and 5.6). The incidence was less for the ISO 14000 series, which takes account of environmental issues: 57 (55.3 percent) electronics and 29 (51.8 percent) garment firms. The incidence of participation among electronics firms in statistical quality control (SQC), total preventive maintenance (TPM), total quality management (TQM), quality control circles (QCCs), materials requirement planning (MRP), materials resource planning (MRPI), and integrated materials resource planning (MRPII), just-in-time

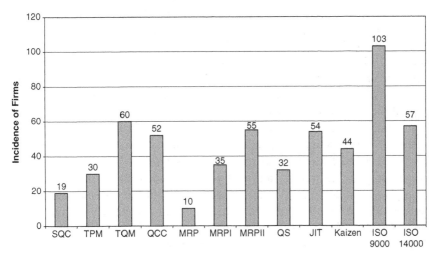

Fig. 5.5. Process techniques, electronics firms, 2007

Source: Plotted from author's survey conducted in 2008.
For list of acronyms, see Table 5.2a.

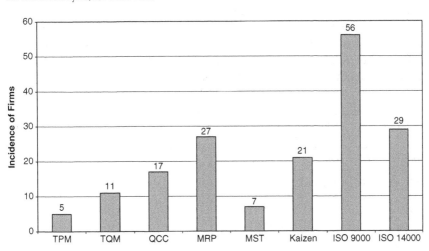

Fig. 5.6. Process techniques, garment firms, 2007

Source: Plotted from author's survey conducted in 2008.
For list of acronyms, see Table 5.2a.

(JIT), and kaizen (continuous improvement) in the electronics sample were 19 (18.4 percent), 30 (29.1 percent), 60 (58.3 percent), 52 (50.5 percent), 10 (9.7 percent), 35 (34.0 percent), 55 (53.4 percent), 54 (52.4 percent), and 44 (42.7 percent) in 2007 (see Figure 5.5). The incidence of participation among garment firms in TPM, TQM, QCC, MRP, minimum stock turnaround (MST), and kaizen were 5 (8.9 percent), 11 (19.6 percent), 17 (30.4 percent), 27 (48.2 percent), 7 (12.5 percent), and 21 (37.5 percent). No garment firm reported participation in SQC, MRPI, and MRPII. The greater focus on quick deliveries and low defects explains why the incidence of participation in cutting-edge technologies is higher in electronics than in garment firms.

The descriptive statistics of the key variables are shown in Appendices 5.1 and 5.2. Firms in both industries show a significant increase in human resource (HR) practices, process technology (PT), and R&D intensity over the period 2000–7 (see Table 5.5). However, not only are intensities higher, the rate of increase is also higher in the electronics firms than in garment firms. The human resource proxies of training expenditure in sales (TE) and skills intensity (SI) for semiconductor firms rose from 1.6 and 75.6 percent respectively in 2000 to 2.3 and 81.7 percent respectively in 2007. The commensurate scores for garments were 1.3 and 49.3 percent respectively in 2000 and 1.2 and 51.3 percent in 2007. Process technology expenditure in sales for electronics and garment firms rose from 3.4 and 1.3 percent respectively in 2000 to 5.6 and 1.6 percent in 2007. R&D expenditure in sales (RDE) and R&D personnel (RDP) in workforce for electronics firms rose from 1.1 and 8.3 percent respectively in 2000 to 2.0 and 9.8 percent respectively in 2007. The commensurate changes recorded in the garment industries were 0.4 and 0.9 percent respectively in 2000 to 0.5 and 1.0 percent in 2007. The stronger and higher increase in capabilities in electronics firms compared to garment firms is explained by both the higher technological change faced in the value chain as well as greater support given to them by the government through the provision of R&D incentives and grants. Classified as strategic, electronics firms have enjoyed special grants from the Malaysian government since 2005.

Table 5.5. Technological capabilities, electronics and garment firms, 2000–2007

Variable	Electronics				Garments			
	N	2000	N	2007	N	2000	N	2007
PTE	86	3.7(10.27)*	97	5.6(12.71)*	51	1.5(4.11)*	56	1.6(4.55)*
RDE	86	1.1(6.17)*	95	2.0(6.55)*	51	0.4(3.97)*	56	0.5(4.03)*
RDP	86	8.3(7.42)*	100	9.8(9.41)*	51	0.9(5.53)*	56	1.0(5.05)*
TE	85	1.6(9.37)*	100	2.3(9.11)*	51	1.3(7.16)*	56	1.2(7.37)*
SI	81	75.6(57.2)*	100	81.7(60.9)*	51	49.3(33.3)*	56	53.6(35.7)*

Note: One-tail "t" test results in parentheses; * significant at 1 percent.
See Tables 5.2 and 5.2a for construction and meaning of variables.
Source: Author's survey conducted in 2008.

The higher technological intensities among electronics firms compared with garment firms are also reflected in the incidence of participation in knowledge-intensive activities (see Table 5.6). It was only in lower knowledge intensity levels that garment firms showed a higher incidence of participation compared with electronics firms. Local firms assembling low value-added items such as consumer electronics appliances and printed circuit boards located in Senawang and Johor have largely remained at levels 1–4 of knowledge intensity operations. Garment firms enjoyed 88 percent incidence of participation in level 2 product technology activities compared with 71 percent among electronics firms. Garment firms showed 84 percent incidence of participation in level 3 HR and PT activities and 73 percent in level 3 product technology activities, compared with 83 percent incidence in level 3 of HR and PT and 64 percent in level 3 product technology activities among electronics firms. Garment firms also enjoyed a marginally higher incidence of participation in level 4 HR and PT activities than electronics firms: 68 percent against 67 percent. In addition to having a much higher incidence of participation in level 4 product technology activities (55 percent against 38 percent), electronics firms enjoyed a higher incidence of participation in level 5–6 knowledge intensities than garment firms in all three technological capabilities. Only electronics firms located outside Penang and the Kelang Valley and engaged in low value-added activities in printed circuit board (PCB), monitor, and consumer electronics assembly lacked participation in levels 4, 5, and 6 activities. However, only one electronics firm among both sets of industries reported participation in level 6 activities.

Foreign firms dominated ownership of electronics and garment firms engaged in levels 4, 5, and 6 of knowledge-intensive activities. In electronics, the breakdown of firms' participation in levels 4 and 5 HR and PT activities was 58 foreign and 11 local firms, and 30 foreign and 4 local firms respectively (see Table 5.6). In product technology activities, 59 foreign and 5 local firms were engaged in level 4

Table 5.6. Knowledge depth, electronics and garment firms, 2007

	Electronics			Garments		
	HR	PT	Product technology	HR	PT	Product technology
1	103(100)	103(100)	103(100)	56(100)	56(100)	56(100)
2	103(100)	103(100)	73(71)	56(100)	56(100)	49(88)
3	85(83)	85(83)	66(64)	47(84)	47(84)	41(73)
4	69(67)	69(67)	57(55)	38(68)	38(68)	21(38)
5	35(34)	35(34)	11(11)	17(30)	17(30)	5(9)
6	1(1)	1(1)	1(1)	0(0)	0(0)	0(0)

See Tables 5.2 and 5.2a for construction and meaning of variables.
Source: Author's survey conducted in 2008.
Note: Figures in parentheses refer to percentages of total.

activities, while 10 foreign firms and 1 local firm were engaged in level 5 activities. One foreign firm reported participation in level 6 HR, PT, and product technology activities.

Foreign firms also dominated knowledge-intensive activities among garment firms. In HR and PT activities, 35 foreign and 3 local firms participated in level 4 activities (see Table 5.6). The commensurate figures for level 5 activities were 16 and 1. In product technology activity, 19 foreign and 2 local firms participated in level 4 activities, while 5 foreign firms and 1 local firm engaged in level 5 activities. None of the firms was involved in level 6 knowledge-intensive activities. Two inferences can be made from these results. First, the lack of preferential support for latecomer national firms has meant that these firms have not been able to out-compete foreign firms endowed with superior assets from their foreign plants. Second, the higher incidence of participation in knowledge-intensive activities by foreign firms offers national firms spillover opportunities. Rasiah (1994, 1995) showed evidence of strong backward and forward spillovers appropriated by national firms from the operations of foreign semiconductor and textile firms.

Semiconductors and Woven Garments

To analyze the learning and acquisition of technological capabilities in the two industries, a more focused sample of semiconductor and woven garment firms is examined to provide a more informed analysis. Semiconductor and woven garment firms have been the longest operating electronics and textile and garment firms respectively in the sample, having begun manufacturing in 1972. Technological change in these firms has been extensive, with particular surges in absorption during moments of crisis caused by the entry of latecomer competitors and overproduction and changes in trade governance instruments—e.g. the provision of the generalized system of preferences (GSP) as well as the Multi-Fiber Arrangement (MFA) involving textile-garments. Government policy responded to these opportunities and obstacles.

The sample of semiconductor firms comprises 8 American firms, 1 Japanese firm, 1 German firm, and 2 local firms. All foreign firms had begun production by 1974, while both local firms in the sample opened operations in the 1980s. Semiconductor firms showed a high intensity of use of cutting-edge process technology by 1990.

The acquisition of JIT capability among semiconductor firms increased from 1 (10 percent) in 1980 to 9 (75 percent) in 1990 and all 12 (100 percent) in 2000 and 2007 (see Table 5.7). The ISO 9000 series, which certifies the use of manufacturing procedures as defined in the manual or advertisements of firms was first acquired by 7 (58.3 percent) firms in 1990 and subsequently by all 12 (100 percent) in 2000 and 2007. All semiconductor firms in the sample had acquired the ISO 14000 series in 2000 and 2007, which entails certification of environmental practices at a manufacturing site. Small group activities (SGA), directed at informal ways of generating ideas and innovations to raise productivity, was reported by the Japanese firm in 1980, and spread to 9 (75 percent) firms in 1990 and 2000, and 10 (83.3 percent) firms in 2007. TPM was reported by 9 (75 percent) firms in 1990, 10 (83.3 percent) firms in 2000, and 11 (91.7 percent) firms in 2007. The use of MRP was reported in 1980 by 3 firms and by 2 firms in 1990. There were 2, 3, and 2 firms using MRPI in 1990, 2000, and 2007. The most sophisticated inventory planning and control technique, i.e. MRPII was reported by 7 (58.3 percent) firms in 1990, 9 (75 percent) firms in 2000, and 10 (83.3 percent) firms in 2007.

The use of cutting-edge process technologies was less intense in the 14 woven garment firms. None of the firms reported the use of cutting-edge process control techniques in 1974 (see Table 5.8). Two firms used MRP techniques in 1980. There were 7 (50.0 percent), 2 (14.3 percent), 2 (14.3 percent), and 4 (28.6 percent) firms reporting ISO 9000 certification and use of SGA, TPM, and MRP in 1990. Three firms reported use of minimum stock turnaround (MST) inventory control technique in 2000 and 2007. All 14 firms reported enjoying ISO certification in 2000 and 2007. The number of firms enjoying ISO 14000 certification was also high in 2000 (9) and 2007 (10). Three (21.4 percent) firms reported the use of SGA and TPM activities in 2000 and 2007, while the use of MRP rose from 6 (42.9 percent) firms in 2000 to 7 (50.0 percent) firms in 2007.

Because of shortening product cycles and volatile fluctuations in demand, delivery times are much shorter in semiconductor firms. Semiconductor firms are also associated with very low defect rates. The mean delivery times fell from 9 (rounded) days in 1974 to 5 (rounded) days in 1980 and 1 day thereafter. Flights accounted for the main portion of delivery times as

Table 5.7. Utilization of process technology, semiconductor firms, 1974–2007

	1974	1980	1990	2000	2007
JIT	0	1	9	12	12
ISO 9000	0	0	7	12	12
ISO 14000	0	0	0	12	12
SGA	0	1	9	9	10
TPM	0	0	9	10	11
MRP	0	3	2	0	0
MRPI	0	0	2	3	2
MRPII	0	0	7	9	10
Delivery times (days)	9	5	1	1	1
Rejects (%)	5.731	0.997	0.015	0.000	0.000

Note: Figures refer to number of firms.
See Table 5.2a for list of terms and their meanings.

Source: Author survey (2008).

Table 5.8. Utilization of process technology, woven garment firms, 1974–2007

	1974	1980	1990	2000	2007
MST	0	0	0	3	3
ISO9000	0	0	7	14	14
ISO14000	0	0	0	9	10
SGA	0	0	2	3	3
TPM	0	0	2	3	3
MRP	0	2	4	6	7
Delivery times (days)	120	89	77	52	39
Rejects (%)	11.95	6.73	2.37	1.59	0.85

Note: Figures refer to number of firms.
See Table 5.2a for list of terms and their meanings.
Source: Author survey (2008).

throughput times fell sharply in the period 1990–2007. Reject rates fell from 5.7 percent of output in 1974 to 1.0 percent in 1980. From 1990 onwards, reject rates have approached parts per million levels.

With longer product cycles and low margins, garment firms use shipping and trucks as their prime transport mode. Nevertheless, rising fabric costs and the withdrawal of MFA quotas has driven efficiency improvements and the hiring of low-wage foreign labor in garment firms in Malaysia. The mean delivery times for woven garment firms fell from 120 days in 1974 to 89 days in 1980, 77 days in 1990, 52 days in 2000, and 39 days in 2007.[4] The mean defect rates for woven garment firms were 12.0 percent in 1974, 6.7 percent in 1980, 2.4 percent in 1990, 1.6 percent in 2000, and 0.9 percent in 2007.

Table 5.9 shows changes in the level of knowledge intensities for semiconductor and woven garment firms over the period 1974–2007. In 1974, all the foreign firms from both sets of sub-industries reported only having levels 1–3 of knowledge intensity. Foreign subsidiaries in Malaysia simply imported machinery and equipment, and used designs and production technology from their parent plants to export whatever was produced. Productivity was low in the 1970s as firms used labor-intensive technology, requiring high levels of dexterity, routinization, diligence, and supervision to meet targets and standards. For example, each bonding machine in semiconductor firms was manually operated by a female worker who was supported by a material handler and a quality control inspector under strict supervision (see Rasiah, 1988). A skilled worker is required to inspect incoming fabric, cut, make, and trim (CMT) shirts and pants in woven garment firms (Rasiah, 1993). Such routinized specialization left workers confined to execution tasks.

---

[4] All figures rounded.

Delivery times were much longer in woven garment firms compared with semiconductor firms. On average it took 120 days for orders to arrive from woven garment firms compared to 9 days in semiconductor firms. The managements of these firms reported that local orders were too small for them to take the trouble of going through customs procedures in Malaysia to sell anything in the domestic market (see also Rasiah, 1988, 1993).[5] Work was highly labor-intensive, with unskilled and semi-skilled females accounting for all direct tasks.

Dramatic changes in firm-level technological capabilities took place in the 1980s. Intense competition in product markets, with its consequent impact on sharply falling prices, drove firms to introduce firm-level technological changes. These included layout reorganizations, adaptation to machinery, and rewarding innovations—to reduce production costs and improve customer delivery. Semiconductor firms began restructuring their process layout, organizational structure, and acquired cutting-edge process techniques such as JIT, MRP, MRPI, and MRPII, TPM, QCCs, SGA, SQC, and TQM from 1984.

The introduction of kaizen-type changes led to continuous modifications of machinery and equipment and layouts in these firms. Among the firm-level innovations that evolved in these firms was the introduction of sticky tape to simplify and quicken the extraction of good dies from fabricated wafers for the die-attachment process, shipping tubes to connect each set of processes, laser marking, coordination of durability and functional tests, and the adaptation of electron beam-induced current (EBIC) that multiplied magnification capabilities to facilitate failure laboratory analysis. A number of these process innovations—which were all achieved only in foreign semiconductor firms—led to patent take-up in the United States (see Rasiah, 1996). Process layouts and organization structures were constantly restructured to lower overhead costs, absorb clean-room technologies, and facilitate more effective supply-demand coordination. Tele-monitoring of the production process by the major buyers also made its way into all the foreign and local semiconductor firms in the 1980s. The principles of user-producer relations involving large buyers and producers became very important (see Lundvall, 1988, 1992).

The 1980s were also characterized by the massive introduction of automation in semiconductor assembly and test operations. Increasing demand for precision engineering arising from intense miniaturization drove significant absorption of auto-controlled systems in semiconductor firms. The semiconductor firms themselves drove considerable adaptations to absorb automation. Whereas four employees (machine operator, material handler, quality

---

[5] Although local import-substituting woven garment firms existed in 1974, they were driven out of business by the 1990s.

inspector, and the supervisor) coordinated one die-bonding machine in semi-conductor firms in 1974, by 1990 one worker—using automated machinery—handled all these processes without the need for supervisors. The technically skilled worker trained in statistical process control and using TPM, JIT, and QCC and SGA principles had become a knowledge-intensive worker by 1990.

Coinciding with the introduction of JIT and MRPII techniques, the key drivers of such changes, such as Intel, National Semiconductor (which changed its name to Fairchild in 1990), AMD, and Texas Instruments, sought proximate suppliers to achieve continuous improvements in productivity. Whereas National Semiconductor started its own machine tool firm called Micro Machining, and set up Dynacraft to manufacture lead frames, Texas Instruments started an automation plant in Singapore to supply these services. Intel began an elaborate program to develop prototypes of machinery and equipment in-house and to outsource them to fostered local suppliers from 1984. Plastic injection-molding firms were also developed in this way. Indeed, Eng Technology, Prodelcon, Metfab, Rapid Synergy, Polytool, and LKT Engineering evolved as Intel's fostered firms. Intel also launched its own suppliers—e.g. Samatech, Shinca, Shintel, Globetronics, and Unico—which were all eventually sold to local buyers. AMD sought preferred suppliers such as Polytool, but did not invest extensively in jointly developing prototypes.

Similar developments by Motorola at Wong Engineering and its own offshoot BCM, and the synergies that these developments provided to stimulate the opening of independent suppliers such as Atlan and Cirrus, drove the emergence of 45 firms in 1989 that expanded to 155 firms in 1993 and 455 firms in 2001 (see Rasiah, 2002: 110). Rasiah (1994, 2002) also reported five tiers of supplier activity supported by semiconductor firms in Penang. In the interest of their own self-expansion plans, flagship semiconductor firms such as Intel drove the co-evolution of the machine tool and plastics injection firms (see Rasiah, 1994). Accounts of the development of local firms have been reported by Lai and Narayanan (1999, 2000) and Ariffin (2000). However, as the transnationals began relocating assembly activities to China, the Philippines, and Vietnam, the demand for such supplier services began to fall from the mid-1990s. Local firms such as Eng Technology and LKT Engineering relocated operations to function as global service providers to foreign firms. However, the fall in demand arising from the relocation of manufacturing activities by transnationals from Malaysia has discouraged supplier activity from the late 1990s.

The rising demand for human capital to support in-house operations, as well as upgrading in supplier firms to support horizontal integration and reintegration (see Best, 2001; Best and Rasiah, 2003), pushed semiconductor firms to use networking links to influence the setting up of training centers in Malaysia. The Penang Skills Development Center (PSDC) was set up in 1989 through just such an informal alliance of multinationals, state officials, and supplier firms. The Penang state government leased the premises of the former Penang Development Corporation (PDC) to the center at only 1 ringgit a year, recognizing that it was subsidizing a public good. This center is widely regarded as an outstanding training center that has consistently upgraded its training facilities to meet cutting-edge skills demand. Less successful training centers were also started in the Kelang Valley and Johor to meet the growing demand for knowledge workers in the electronics industry.

The sources of knowledge acquisition by semiconductor firms ranged from learning-by-doing (including through the absorption of QCCs, SGA, and kaizen activities), engineering and business journals, consultants (e.g. Schonberger was hired by Intel to implement JIT in 1984), specialized training, buyers and suppliers. The deepening achieved by the pool of personnel in Malaysia led to all 10 foreign subsidiaries expanding into level 4 HR and PT activity and seven firms expanding into level 4 product technology activity by 1990 (see Table 5.9). Three foreign firms also participated in level 5 HR and PT activities with considerable take-up of process patents in the United States. The two local firms in the sample were not engaged in level 4–5 activities in 1990. None of the firms, however, was engaged in level 6 knowledge-intensive activities in 1990.

Rapid restructuring in woven garment firms started only in the period 1990–3 as the scramble for workers intensified in key manufacturing locations such as Penang and North Western Johor, combined with rising fabric costs (initially caused by export taxes introduced by exporting governments to stimulate downstream activities) (see Rasiah, 1993). Hence, by 1990, woven garment firms had only evolved to participate in level 4 HR and PT activities (see Table 5.9). All firms—both foreign and local—had already achieved level 2 activities. Five foreign and two local firms were engaged in level 3 HR and PT activities. One local firm, which ventured into manufacturing using its own brands, was engaged in level 3 product technology activity in 1990. The sole advanced firm engaged in level 4 HR and PT activity is a Hong Kong firm with its headquarters in Jersey Island.

The government launched the Second Industrial Master Plan (IMP2) in 1996, targeting clustering as the driver of industrial widening and deepening (Malaysia, 1996). The lack of human capital, however, threatened to drive foreign firms out of Malaysia in the 1990s as the labor market tightened, and China, Vietnam, and Philippines became attractive sites for labor-intensive operations. Meanwhile brighter and technically qualified Malaysians emigrated to Singapore, the United States, and Australia. Fearing the impact on employment, the government, provided generous tax holidays and grants in 2005 to liberalize imports of human capital from abroad to keep the knowledge-intensive semiconductor firms in Penang and Johor.

As a consequence, key flagship firms managed to gain a critical mass of engineers and scientists to upgrade strongly into designing activities—reworking as well as designing functionally to coordinate the coupling of integrated circuits for a wider range of uses. Intel, AMD, and Osram started their own design centers in Malaysia. Also, following the launching of the Third Industrial Master Plan (IMP3) in 2006, the government extended the provisions for movement of skilled foreign labor to Penang and Johor in 2005—from its original confinement to the Multimedia Super Corridor (MSC) in 1997. The government also provided capital upfront to stimulate further participation in designing activities and wafer fabrication activities. Although most electronics firms were still confined to level 4 knowledge-intensive activities by 2007, 9 semiconductor firms had ventured into level 5 HR and PT activities, while 7, all of them foreign firms, were engaged in level 5 R&D activities (see Table 5.9). The two national firms still specialized in subcontracting manufacturing, with one in assembly and test and the other in wafer fabrication. Both national firms were engaged in level 4 HR and PT activities and level 3 RD activities.[6]

Forced to innovate because of high labor turnover in the 1990s, as the labor market tightened and following the withdrawal of the MFA in 2004, those woven garment firms that remained in operation in Malaysia experienced massive restructuring. Firms began introducing auto-scan (to inspect incoming fabric), computer-aided design and computer-aided manufacturing (Cad-Cam), semi-automated stitching of zippers and sleeves to reduce defects, speed up production, and reduce reliance on dexterous workers. Pen Apparel introduced wrinkle-free treatment technologies to adapt woven garments to meet changes in customer demand.

In addition, Pen Apparel, South Island Garment, Eastern Garments, and Soutex integrated processes from the purchase of woven fabric, CMT, packaging, and the shipment of cartons of woven garments to the big buyers such as Walmart and Marks and Spencer. Some garment firms in Malaysia have diversified into other activities in the garment value chain. One national firm in the sample managed to expand into the sale of its own brand names to Asia and Africa, while two foreign firms extended their designing activities from Hong Kong to Malaysia. By 2007 four foreign firms and one national firm managed to participate in level 5 HR, PT, and RD activities (see Table 5.9).

Government policy instruments assisted in the upgrading that took place in woven garment firms in two major ways. First, the government's introduction

---

[6] There is one local semiconductor firm (Silterra) in Malaysia engaged in wafer fabrication and designing activities, but it is not in the sample because it only started operations in 2000.

Table 5.9. Knowledge intensity, semiconductor and woven garment firms, 1974–2007

1974	Semiconductor			Woven garments		
KD	HR	PT	Product	HR	PT	Product
1	10	10	10	10	10	10
2	10	10	8	7	7	3
3	3	4	2	3	3	0
1990	Semiconductor			Woven garments		
KD	HR	PT	Product	HR	PT	Product
1	12	12	12	14	14	14
2	12	12	12	14	14	14
3	12	12	12	7	7	0
4	10	10	7	1	1	0
5	3	3	0	0	0	0
2007	Semiconductor			Woven garments		
KD	HR	PT	Product	HR	PT	Product
1	12	12	12	14	14	14
2	12	12	12	14	14	14
3	12	12	12	13	13	11
4	12	12	10	10	10	7
5	9	9	7	5	5	5
6	0	0	0	0	0	0

Source: Author's survey. Please see Table 5.2a for a list and description of the variables.

of incentives for participation in training activities and the Human Resource Development Act of 1992 eventually drove several woven garment firms to come together to set up the Malaysian Textile Manufacturers Association (MTMA) to support training and designing operations. Whereas semiconductor firms needed to train their workers regularly because of the knowledge-intensive nature of the work, similar developments in garment firms only took place in the 1990s and only in a few firms. The Human Resource Development Fund (HRDF)[7] was initially little used by garment firms, but training expenditure began to rise once the managements of firms chose to upgrade from the late 1990s. The shift to higher value-added activities has driven demand for training since the late 1990s, though a number of firms still retained low value-added activities by hiring low-wage foreign workers. Led by former managing directors with tacit knowledge of the industry, the MTMA has been playing an important role in support of upgrading in the firms that managed to remain

---

[7] The government had introduced the double-deduction tax incentive (DDTI) in 1988 to stimulate training in the manufacturing sector. This incentive was retained for firms with employment of 50 and less once the HRDF was introduced in 1992 (Malaysia, 1996).

Table 5.10. Labor productivity and export intensity, 2000–2007

	Electronics			Garments		
	2000	2007	2000–2007[1]	2000	2007	2000–2007[1]
VA/L(MYR)	78493.0*	87618.5*	1.8*	9715.2**	9989.7*	2.2*
	(2.8)	(3.7)	(7.5)*	(2.3)	(2.6)	(123.9)
(X/Y)%	60.1*	71.3*	2.9*	69.7*	72.8*	1.0***
	(15.33)	(14.97)	(2.6)	(15.5)	(17.7)	(1.8)
N	81	99	81	51	56	51

Note: [1] Average annual percentage change computed using firms that existed in 2000 and 2007; *, **, and *** refer to statistical significance at 1, 5, and 10 percent respectively.
VA = value added; L = labor input; MYR = Malaysia; X/Y = exports divided by total sales
Source: Author, computed from Khazanah survey (see note 3).

Table 5.11. Labor productivity elasticities, 2000–2007

	Electronics	T	Garments	T
TE	0.27	2.07**	0.71	2.01**
SI	1.03	0.72	0.32	1.15
PTE	0.23	1.82***	0.43	2.03**
RDE	0.14	2.26**	0.11	1.99**
RDP	0.64	4.17*	0.25	2.67*
N	81		51	

Note: *, **, and *** refer to statistical significance at 1 percent, 5 percent, and 10 percent respectively. Only firms in existence in 2000 and 2007 were used for the computations.
TE = training expenditure/sales; SI = skills intensity; PTE = process technology spending/sales; N = number of firms; RDE = R&D spending/sales; RDP = number of R&D personnel/total workforce
Source: Computed from author's 2008 survey using SPSS 10 package.

after the MFA shakeout in 2004. Provisions in the IMP3 for driving the co-evolution of support industries such as machinery and equipment, materials, and environment-friendly chemicals have yet to translate into results. Also, the lack of R&D scientists and engineers has restricted further upgrading in a number of electronics firms and the transition of garment firms upstream to materials.

Overall, it can be seen that considerable technological upgrading has taken place in the electronics and garment firms in Malaysia. While competition—especially from the emergence of new sites—has been the prime driver, government incentives and grants have also helped firms make this transition. However, participation in the knowledge-intensive levels of 5 and 6 remained low in 2007.

Despite low average growth rates in labor productivity, the relationship between technological capabilities and labor productivity and export intensity

Table 5.12. Export-intensity elasticities, 2000–2007

	Electronics	T	Garments	T
TE	0.38	3.96*	1.79	4.01*
SI	1.47	5.23*	0.82	4.37*
PTE	0.32	3.22*	1.07	3.02*
RDE	0.20	3.51*	0.29	2.77*
RDP	0.92	3.89*	0.64	2.96*
N	81		51	

Note: *, refers to statistical significance at 1 percent.
TE = training expenditure/sales; SI = skills intensity; PTE = process technology spending/sales; N = number of firms; RDE = R&D spending/sales; RDP = number of R&D personnel/total workforce

Source: Computed from author's 2008 survey using the SPSS 10 package.

over the period 2000–7 was strong (see Tables 5.11 and 5.12). Apart from skills intensity, all other technological capability variables were correlated positively with labor productivity (see Table 5.11). A 1 percent rise in TE, SI, PTE, RDE, and RDP respectively will raise labor productivity in the electronics industry by 0.3, 1.0, 0.2, 0.1, and 0.6 percent respectively. A 1 percent rise in TE, SI, PTE, RDE, and RDP will raise labor productivity in the garment industry by 0.7, 0.3, 0.4, 0.1, and 0.3 percent respectively. The statistically significant results show that labor productivity can be raised most in the electronics industry by increasing skills intensity and R&D personnel participation in the workforce. Labor productivity in the garment industry can be raised most by increasing training expenditure and process technology expenditure.

All the technological capability variables were correlated positively with export intensity (see Table 5.12). A 1 percent increase in TE, SI, PTE, RDE, and RDP will raise X/Y (exports as a share of total sales) in the electronics industry by 0.4, 1.5, 0.3, 0.2, and 0.9 percent respectively. A 1 percent increase in TE, SI, PTE, RDE, and RDP will raise X/Y in the garment industry by 1.8, 0.8, 1.1, 0.3, and 0.6 percent respectively. The results show that the export intensity of electronics firms can be increased most by raising skills intensity and R&D personnel intensity in the workforce. The export intensity of garment firms can be increased most by raising training expenditure, process technology expenditure.

Although labor productivity and export intensity grew slowly in 2000–7, the evidence shows that technological capabilities were positively correlated with labor productivity and export intensity. Skills and R&D personnel intensity in the workforce showed the strongest influence on labor productivity and export intensity in electronics firms. Training and process technology expenditure showed the strongest influence on labor productivity and export intensity in garment firms.

5.5. CONCLUSIONS

This chapter examined the development of technological capabilities, their drivers, and the impact on the economic performance variables of labor productivity and export intensity in electronics and garment firms. The technological capabilities of all firms improved significantly over the 2000–7 period. Firms in the more focused semiconductor and woven garment industries also progressed significantly, participating in higher levels of knowledge intensities over the period 1974–2007. However, the incidence of firms' participation in the levels 5–6 knowledge-intensity category was very low.

The low participation of firms at the frontier levels of technology may explain why the electric-electronics and the textile-garment industries have been plagued by a slowdown in labor productivity growth, with garment manufacturing recording an absolute contraction over the period 2000–5. Malaysia's share in global electronics and garment exports has also declined in this period. Although the mean average growth rates of firms in both industries showed positive labor productivity and export-intensity growth over the period 2000–7, these rates have been low, thereby requiring technological upgrading. The statistical results show that labor productivity and export intensity in electronics firms can be raised most by increasing skills and R&D personnel in workforce intensities. Increasing training and process technology expenditure will help raise labor productivity and export intensity most in garment firms.

Whereas the absolute contraction in garment manufacturing appears unavoidable, following the termination of MFA quotas and the emergence of China, upgrading in the electronics industry must be speeded up for the industry to sustain its contribution to the national economy. High value-added activities such as designing and R&D operations must expand in the industry so that firms can compete with more competitive firms abroad. Whereas lead firms in the electronics industry have moved to the frontier of the technology in the competitor countries of Korea and Taiwan, most firms in Malaysia are still not engaged in designing and R&D activities (levels 5 and 6 knowledge-intensive activities). Despite significant strides in firms' acquisition of technological capabilities and participation in knowledge-intensive activities, Malaysia's electronics firms need further deepening (see Best, 2001). Government policy should emphasize the upgrading of human capital, including R&D personnel, to speed up the movement of firms to the technology frontier.

Appendix Table 5.A1. Descriptive statistics of technological and export intensities, electronics firms, Malaysia

Year: 2000

	Size	RDE	RDP	X/Y	PTE	SI	TE	VA/L
Mean	751.6	1.1	8.3	0.6	3.7	73.4	1.6	78,493.0
Median	149.0	0.5	4.7	0.7	3.0	72.7	1.0	38,454.5
Maximum	6,000.0	10.0	50.0	1.0	20.0	100.0	10.0	757,601.2
Minimum	10.0	0.0	0.0	0.0	0.0	35.0	0.0	1,223.15
Std. dev.	1,200.6	1.5	10.1	0.3	3.2	0.2	1.7	11,9564.4
Skewness	2.2	3.4	1.8	−0.3	2.0	−0.8	1.9	3.5
Kurtosis	7.9	16.8	6.7	2.1	10.1	3.3	7.9	18.1
Jarque-Bera	156.9	848.4	96.4	3.8	237.6	8.9	134.6	936.1
Probability	0.0	0.0	0.0	0.2	0.0	0.0	0.0	0.0
Sum	63,889.0	91.0	716.9	53.4	320.5	5,334.1	138.3	6,357,934.0
Sum sq. dev.	121,000,000.0	197.6	8,633.0	5.9	844.8	1,5679.3	255.6	1,140,000,000,000
N	85	86	86	86	86	81	85	81

Note: TE = Training expenditure/sales; SI = skills intensity; PTE = process technology spending/sales; N = number of firms; RDE = R&D spending/sales; RDP = number of R&D personnel/total workforce; X/Y = exports/total sales; VA = value added; L = labor input.

Source: Author Computed from UNU-MERIT (2007) Survey.

(continued)

Appendix Table 5.A1. Continued

Year: 2007

	Size	RDE	RDP	PTE	X/Y	SI	TE	VA/L
Mean	775.8	2.0	9.8	5.6	0.7	81.7	2.3	87,618.5
Median	242.5	0.9	6.3	5.0	0.7	80.0	1.0	47,235.8
Maximum	6,437.0	15.0	57.1	20.0	1.0	100.0	10.0	45,6015.7
Minimum	7.0	0.0	0.0	0.0	0.0	35.0	0.0	744.4
Std. dev.	1,217.2	2.8	10.4	4.3	0.2	13.4	2.5	81,499.8
Skewness	2.6	2.2	1.5	0.8	-0.7	-0.6	1.3	2.1
Kurtosis	9.9	8.0	6.2	3.5	3.2	3.5	3.8	7.5
Jarque-Bera	308.3	177.8	81.0	11.3	9.4	7.7	31.6	154.8
Probability	0.0	0.0	0.0	0.0	0.0	0.0	0.0	0.0
Sum	77,577.0	191.3	983.1	542.6	70.3	8,173.2	231.5	7,109,644.0
Sum sq. dev.	147,000,000.0	757.6	10,742.2	1803.8	5.5	17,850.7	630.2	651,000,000,000.0
N	100	95	100	97	100	100	100	99

Note: TE = training expenditure/sales; SI = skills intensity; PTE = process technology spending/sales; N = number of firms; RDE = R&D spending/sales; RDP = number of R&D personnel/total workforce; X/Y = exports/total sales; VA = value added; L = labor input.

Source: Author, computed from UNU-MERIT (2007) survey.

Appendix Table 5.A2. Descriptive statistics of technological and export intensities, garment firms, Malaysia

Year: 2000

	Size	PTE	RDE	RDP	TE	X/Y	SI	VA/L
Mean	391	1.5	0.4	0.9	1.3	0.7	49.3	9,715.2
Median	250	1.3	0.4	1.0	1.3	0.9	47.5	1,895.0
Maximum	3,000	2.3	3.3	1.6	2.2	1.0	77.0	218,519.0
Minimum	18	0.8	0.0	0.0	0.4	0.0	30.0	960.0
Std. dev.	476.5	0.4	0.5	0.6	0.5	0.3	9.5	30,350.4
Skewness	3.6	0.3	4.3	-0.5	0.2	-1.1	0.7	6.6
Kurtosis	18.9	1.8	27.1	1.5	1.9	2.9	3.6	45.7
Jarque-Bera	642.8	3.8	1,391.0	6.7	3.0	9.5	5.0	4,242.1
Probability	0.0	0.1	0.0	0.0	0.2	0.0	0.1	0.0
Sum	19,950	75.6	19.4	45.3	65.8	37.6	2513.5	495,474.1
Sum sq. dev.	11,354,663	9.818459	11.72457	18.59037	14.816	5.188565	4540.1	46,100,000,000
N	51	51	51	51	51	51	51	51

Note: TE = training expenditure/sales; SI = skills intensity; PTE = process technology spending/sales; N = number of firms; RDE = R&D spending/sales; RDP = number of R&D personnel/total workforce; X/Y = exports/total sales; VA = value added; L = labor input.

Source: Author, computed from UNU-MERIT (2007) survey.

(*continued*)

Appendix Table 5.A2. Continued

Year: 2007

	Size	PTE	RDE	RDP	TE	X/Y	SI	VA/L
Mean	382	1.6	0.5	1.0	1.2	0.7	53.6	9,989.671
Median	255	1.6	0.5	1.2	1.1	0.8	51.9	3500
Maximum	2,500	2.7	1.0	2.0	2.4	1.0	77.5	216,333.8
Minimum	30	1.0	0.0	0.0	0.4	0.0	35.7	969.6
Std. dev.	399	0.5	0.3	0.7	0.4	0.3	11.9	28,680.99
Skewness	3	0.6	-0.1	-0.4	0.4	-0.9	0.3	6.821306
Kurtosis	15	2.4	1.8	1.7	2.5	2.5	2.0	49.60169
Jarque-Bera	444	4.6	3.5	4.9	2.2	7.8	3.3	5,501.624
Probability	0	0.1	0.2	0.1	0.3	0.0	0.2	0
Sum	21,383	92.1	27.3	57.6	65.0	39.3	3003.9	559,421.6
Sum sq. dev.	8,755,080	13.0	6.1	25.3	11.0	5.3	7,838.8	4.52E + 10
N	56	56	56	56	56	55	56	56

Note: TE = training expenditure/sales; SI = skills intensity; PTE = process technology spending/sales; N = number of firms; RDE = R&D spending/sales; RDP = number of R&D personnel/total workforce; X/Y = exports/total sales; VA = value added; L = labor input.

Source: Author, computed from UNU-MERIT (2007) survey.

REFERENCES

Amsden, A., and Chu, W.W. (2003), *Beyond Late Development: Taiwan's Upgrading Policies*, Cambridge, Mass.: MIT Press.

Ariffin N. (2000), "The Internationalization of Innovative Capabilities: The Malaysian Electronics Industry," doctoral thesis submitted to Science Policy Research Unit (SPRU), Sussex University, UK.

—— and Bell M. (1999), "Firms, Politics and Political Economy: Patterns of Subsidiary-Parent Linkages and Technological Capability Building in Electronics TNCs in Malaysia," in K. S. Jomo, G. Felker, and R. Rasiah (eds.), *Industrial Technology Development in Malaysia: Industry and Firm Studies*, London: Routledge.

—— and Figueiredo P. N. (2004), "Internationalisation of Innovative Capabilities: Counter-Evidence from Electronics Industries in Malaysia and Brazil," *Oxford Development Studies*, 32(4): 559–83.

Bell, M., and Pavitt, K. (1995), "The Development of Technological Capabilities," in I. ul Haque (ed.), *Trade, Technology and International Competitiveness*, Washington DC: World Bank.

Best, M. (2001), *The New Competitive Advantage*, Oxford: Oxford University Press.

—— and Rasiah, R. (2003), *Malaysian Electronics at the Crossroads*, Vienna: UNIDO.

Cantwell, J., and Mudambi, R. (2005), "MNE Competence-Creating Subsidiary Mandates," *Strategic Management Journal*, 26(12): 1109–28.

Figueiredo, P. N. (2002), "Learning Processes Features and Technological Capability Accumulation: Explaining Inter-firm Differences," *Technovation*, 22: 685–98.

—— (2003), "Learning, Capability Accumulation and Firms Differences: Evidence from Latecomer Steel," *Industrial and Corporate Change*, 12(3): 607–43.

Hobday, M. (1995), *Innovation in East Asia*, Cheltenham, UK: Edward Elgar.

Hoffmann, L., and Tan, S.E. (1980), *Industrial Growth, Employment and Foreign Investment in Peninsular Malaysia*, Kuala Lumpur: Oxford University Press.

Jomo, K. S. (1990), *Growth and Structural Change in the Malaysian Economy*, Basingstoke: Macmillan.

Lai, Y. W., and Narayanan, S. (1999), "Technology Utilisation Level and Choice: The Electrical and Electronics Sector in Penang, Malaysia," in K. S. Jomo, G. Felker, and R. Rasiah (eds.), *Industrial Technology Development in Malaysia: Firm and Industry Studies*, London: Routledge, 107–24.

—— —— (2000), "Technological Maturity and Development without Research: The Challenge for Malaysian Manufacturing," *Development and Change*, 31(2): 435–58.

Lall, S. (1992), "Technological Capabilities and Industrialisation," *World Development*, 20(2): 165–86.

Lim, Y. L. Y. C. (1978), "Multinational Firms and Manufacturing for Export in Less-Developed Countries: The Case of the Electronics Industry in Malaysia and Singapore," doctoral thesis, University of Michigan, Ann Arbor.

Lundvall, B. A. (1988), "Innovation as an Interactive Process: From User-Producer Interaction to the National Innovation Systems," in G. Dosi, C. Freeman, R. Nelson, G. Silverberg, and L. Soete (eds.), *Technology and Economic Theory*, London: Pinter Publishers.

Lundvall, B. A. (1992), *National Systems of Innovation: Towards a Theory of Innovation and Interactive*, London: Pinter Publishers.

Malaysia (1985–2007), *Industrial Surveys*, various issues, Putra Jaya, Malaysia: Department of Statistics, Malaysia (DOSM).

Mathews, J., and Cho, D. S. (2000), *Tiger Technology: The Creation of a Semiconductor Industry in East Asia*, Cambridge: Cambridge University Press.

Rasiah, R. (1988), "The Semiconductor Industry in Penang: Implications for the New International Division of Labour Theories," *Journal of Contemporary Asia*, 18(1): 44–65.

—— (1993), "Competition and Governance: Work in Malaysia's Textile and Garment Industries," *Journal of Contemporary Asia*, 23(1): 3–24.

—— (1994), "Flexible Production Systems and Local Machine Tool Subcontracting: Electronics Component Transnationals," *Cambridge Journal of Economics*, 18(3): 279–98.

—— (1995), *Foreign Capital and Industrialization in Malaysia*, Basingstoke: Macmillan.

—— (1996), "Institutions and Innovations: Moving Towards the Technology Frontier in the Electronics Industry in Malaysia," *Journal of Industry Studies*, 3(2): 79–102.

—— (2002), "Government-Business Coordination and Small Enterprise Performance in the Machine Tools Sector in Malaysia," *Small Business Economics*, 18(1–3): 177–95.

—— (2003), "How Important is Process and Product Technology Capability in Malaysia and Thailand's FDI-Driven Electronics Industry," *Journal of Asian Economics*, 14(5): 785–811.

—— (2007), "The Systemic Quad: Technological Capabilities and Economic Performance of Computer and Component Firms in Penang and Johor, Malaysia," *International Journal of Technological Learning and Development*, 1(2): 179–203.

—— (2008), "Ownership, Institutions and Technological Intensities: Automotive and Electronics Firms in East and Southeast Asia," in J. Eatwell and P. Arestis (eds.), *Issues in Finance and Industry: Essays in Honour of Ajit Singh*, Basingstoke: Palgrave Macmillan.

—— (2009), "Malaysia's Textile and Garment Manufacturing at the Crossroads," *Journal of Contemporary Asia*, 39(4): 530–42.

—— and Vinanchiarachi, J. (2012), "Drivers of Technological Upgrading and Economic Synergies: Evidence from Four Dynamic Clusters in Latin America and Asia," mimeo, Kuala Lumpur.

Sciberras, E. (1977), *Multinational Electronics Component Companies and National Economic Policies*, Connecticut: JAI Press.

UNU-MERIT (2007), "Firm-Level Data Collected from Manufacturing Firms in Southeast Asia," fieldwork sponsored by UNU-MERIT, Maastricht.

6

South Korea and Taiwan

Keun Lee and John A. Mathews

6.1. INTRODUCTION

As indicated in earlier chapters, we are concerned here with the firm-level aspects of technological and economic catch-up. But, of course, the founding of firms requires entrepreneurial vision, a sense of daring and courage in the risking of resources (often including personal resources), and the acquisition of sound intelligence as to the state of play with regard to technology, markets, and competitive rivalry. Gaining market entry is the most important issue to be tackled by challenger firms and constitutes the most important aspect of their strategizing.

The central concern of this chapter is what makes firms innovative (or able to move from imitation to innovation, to adapt Kim's (1997) phrase). This question is important because there are a relatively large number of cases of short-lived catch-up based on cheap wage-based manufacturing for exports. In other words, a critical issue is not just growth but sustained growth; this requires innovative capabilities to some degree (Lee and Mathews, 2010). We see the process of becoming an innovative firm as a process of capability building (Teece, 2000; Lall, 2000) and one which calls for supportive institutional arrangements. As noted by Mathews (2002a), one of the important characteristics of latecomer firms is that along the dimension of strategic intent, the firm is focused on catch-up as its primary goal, and catch-up in this context means primarily convergence in terms of technical capabilities. However, learning and building capabilities are not easily accomplished because technological knowledge is difficult to locate, price, and evaluate. Additionally, its transfer cannot be wholly embodied in equipment or instructions, patents, designs, or blueprints (Lall 2000: 15). Part of the catch-up strategy concerns evaluating and implementing means of accessing such knowledge, while another aspect is concerned with putting the knowledge to good use.

This chapter examines the cases of firms in Korea and Taiwan which went through their high-growth catch-up phase over the last five decades. While there are certain commonalities in the two countries' experiences, their institutional arrangements, particularly those supporting firm-level innovation, are different (Mahmood and Singh, 2003; Choung and Hwang, 2000). Whereas the Korean economy has been led by big conglomerates, the Taiwanese economy has in general featured a large number of small and medium-sized enterprises (SMEs) in each new stage of upgrading, i.e. fresh entrants to the new industry being entered. In this sense, it is interesting to identify the factors that are common to the catch-up experience of firms from these two countries. This is the issue that we address in this chapter.

While some authors, such as Hobday (2000) and Teece (2000), emphasize commonalties between Korea and Taiwan in terms of OEM (original equipment manufacturing) based outward-oriented growth, we instead pay attention to the limitations imposed by such growth strategies, taking into account the strictures outlined by Huang and Chu (2010). We emphasize the continuous change and restructuring of firms in Korea and Taiwan. Our central proposition is that a successful catch-up experience at the firm level requires continuous upgrading in the same industry, as well as successive entries (another kind of upgrading) into new and promising industries, to be repeated over and over again.

We start with an overview of the catching-up process in Korea and Taiwan, highlighting why upgrading and successive episodes of industry entry are critical. The following sections illustrate how firms in Korea and Taiwan achieved successful catch-up by driving upgrading in the same industries and at the same time engineering successive waves of new entry into new and higher value-added industries. We show how crises and industry cycles offered these latecomers windows of opportunity for catch-up. Industry cycles, especially downturns, tend to make access to foreign knowledge and resources easier and cheaper than would otherwise be the case. This issue of entry timing will then be further linked to the issue of entry modes. Case materials will be largely drawn from automobile and electronics industries in Korea and Taiwan, including very recent examples, such as solar photovoltaic (PV) cells in Taiwan.

We emphasize that catching-up processes (or what we have also called "fast-follower strategies," as in Mathews et al., 2011) can be a key means of diffusing technologies available today. They are used both within advanced countries (as one firm fast-follows another) and in the developing countries as they seek to converge on the developed world. In the latter case, for example, these strategies are found in the practices of some Chinese firms. These firms have learnt from the prior experiences of Korea and Taiwan and are now applying these experiences in the new conditions of the 21st century. One of the most important sectors where catch-up strategies operate today is the energy sector, where renewable energies are being developed at a prodigious rate, and countries that build such renewable energy sectors, through fast-followership or catch-up, are emerging as the leaders of tomorrow. This certainly applies to some firms in China, but also to Korea and Taiwan, which, in their different ways, are building new low-carbon technology economies. Thus, the significance of catch-up strategies, both for continuing development in a global setting, and for efforts to decarbonize industrial systems, could hardly be over-emphasized.

6.2. INTRODUCING KOREA AND TAIWAN

Both Korea and Taiwan passed through a period of Japanese occupation and achieved independence after World War II. Immediately after the war their level of income was very low when compared with neighboring countries. But this situation changed rapidly as these economies pursued catch-up strategies appropriate for the situation that prevailed in the global economy at that time.

The starting point was very low. In 1960, per capita incomes in both Korea and Taiwan were around US$150 (in current terms), lower than most comparable countries such as the Philippines ($257), Malaysia ($300), Chile ($554), Brazil ($208), and South Africa ($422), but closer to the level of Nigeria ($103) (Lee and Kim, 2009). However, by the early 1980s, Korea and Taiwan had reached the level of middle-income countries like Chile or Argentina, reduced the gap with Brazil substantially, and even surpassed some previously richer countries like the Philippines. The stories are basically the same regardless of the per capita GDP measured in current or constant dollars. Then, in the next two decades and by the 2000s, Korea and Taiwan reached the level of high-income countries with per capita GDPs higher than US$10,000. In the year 2000, the per capita incomes of comparable countries like Brazil, Argentina, Malaysia, and South Africa were by then only one-third or one-fourth of those of Korea or Taiwan. There is a major issue to be explained here.

If we look at the number of US patents as an indicator of technological capabilities, we see that patent growth rates by Korea and Taiwan are higher than the average for the representative advanced economies. During 1975–99, only Korea and Taiwan exhibited more rapid accumulation of patents than the top developed economies (Park and Lee, 2006); while the average annual growth rate of the US patents registered by the six developed economies (G7 excluding USA) was 3.25 percent per annum during the 1975–95 period, that of Korea was 31.8 percent and that of Taiwan 23.1 percent. Owing to the rapid increase in the rate of patenting, Korea and Taiwan increased substantially their share in total US patents. Among those US patents attributable to non-US inventors, Taiwan's share increased from 0.17 percent in 1975 to 0.75 percent in 1985 and 3.73 percent in 1995; Korea's share also increased from a mere 0.04 percent in 1975 to 0.21 percent in 1985 and 3.49 percent in 1995 (Park and Lee, 2006). By the year 2001, Taiwan had reached the enviable position of having the world's third highest per capita patenting rate at the United States Patent and Trademark Office (USPTO), ahead of every other country except the US and Japan (Hu and Mathews, 2005). Thus there is a prima-facie case that these countries utilized innovation, and in particular an improvement in their national innovative capacity, as measured by patenting rates, to drive their catch-up. As noted already in Chapter 3, China has been following a similar trajectory, in rapidly ramping up its innovative capacity as measured by patenting rates at the USPTO (Hu and Mathews 2008), and in terms of patenting within China.

What were the historical origins of the innovative firms in these two economies that underpinned these achievements? What were the origins of "innovative" *Chaebols* in Korea? *Chaebol* firms were not particularly innovative in their early years but became so during the 1990s as they invested heavily in R&D, as verified in Choo et al. (2009). However, their later innovative capacity continues to be influenced by their origins. After liberation from Japanese colonial rule and the Korean War, the Korean economy in the 1950s was very poor in every respect. There was no interest among MNCs in realizing investments in Korea. Given the lack of FDI and meager domestic financial resources, the modernizing government, led by the former President Park Chung-Hee, decided to promote a selected number of private companies by arranging preferential access to local loans and foreign exchange. These companies were also to be given protection in local markets in the form of import restrictions and asymmetric tariffs (high for consumer goods and low for capital goods). In addition, restrictive policies were implemented toward FDI, such as a 50 percent cap on foreign equity holdings, a measure which was enforced until the late 1980s. The rents guaranteed by these policies served as a critical financial resource for new product development, while pressure to become competitive by doing more R&D came from firms' exposure to world market competition. This competitive pressure was reinforced by the government through the award of privileged access to loans based on export performance. As Jung and Lee (2010) argue, such a unique combination of local protection (rents) and discipline from export competition was the key to Korean success.

Some of the Korean *Chaebols* engaged in foreign joint ventures (JVs) from the beginning. This proved to be an effective institutional vehicle for learning and securing access to foreign knowledge. Several electronics affiliates of Samsung, for example, started as joint ventures with Japanese companies (Lee and He, 2009). Subsequently, Samsung bought out its Japanese partners. The role of foreign firms and FDI was more pronounced in the case of Taiwan. As noted in Amsden and Chu (2003), foreign participation was quite high, even in the 1960s. However, the share of domestic ownership gradually increased throughout the following decades such that local Taiwanese firms eventually emerged as leaders in their industry.

Despite the shared achievements of Korea and Taiwan, these countries took somewhat different paths toward catching up (Lee, 2005; Mathews and Cho, 2000; Lee and Mathews, 2010). The *Korean path* is led by a few large firms which are nationally owned and independent from foreign-owned MNCs in terms of financing, production, and marketing. During the 1970s in the earliest stages of catch-up, these firms were supported by government research institutes (GRIs) in gaining free or cheap access to technology, but soon they consolidated their own in-house R&D capacity and emerged as technological leaders. However, they still sometimes needed government help in the form of public participation in R&D consortia in large-scale and high-risk projects. These firms were independent and not integrated into foreign MNCs or their global production networks in the sense that their equity shares were not owned by the MNCs. However, they relied on a diverse range of firms in the mature industrialized countries. These provided knowledge in the form of embodied technology, licensing, co-development, and horizontal collaborations. On the other hand, the *Chaebol* were also independent of one another, without much collaboration or exchange of knowledge between them. In contrast, each *Chaebol*, behaving like a "flagship firm," maintained its own network of subcontracting or collaborating firms. One way of expressing this is to remark that in Korea there was operating not just one "national system of innovation" but in fact three such national systems—each in turn operated by Samsung, Hyundai, and LG!

In contrast, the *Taiwanese path* was initially led by a large number of small and medium-sized enterprises (SMEs) which were more or less integrated with foreign MNCs in terms of finance, production, and marketing. During the very early stages of this path, these firms started out as OEM (original equipment manufacturing) contractors for the MNCs and became closely integrated with the *global production networks* (GPNs). This helped them to access new knowledge and to upgrade to higher tiers in their respective GPNs (Ernst, 2002; Ernst and Kim, 2002). Some firms proved highly successful, becoming large-scale enterprises operating OBM (original brand manufacturing) and subsequently ODM (original design manufacturing). However, large firms, such as Acer, continued to participate in a good deal of subcontracting with foreign MNCs. The R&D activities of these firms were more pronounced in sectors that allowed an easy appropriation of returns and gains in market share at the expense of incumbent enterprises from the established industrialized countries. On the other hand, in sectors requiring greater capital intensity and higher risk, they were supported by the GRIs such as the Industrial Technology Research Institute (ITRI), which provided sources of new knowledge or even gave rise to spin-off firms. On the other hand, these Taiwanese firms engaged in intense collaboration and knowledge exchange.

Business networks in Taiwan, as typically observed in electronics, were geo-graphically agglomerated, sometimes involving local subcontracting (Amsden and Chu, 2003; Mathews, 2002c). The benefits of this network density to the local assemblers were low transactions costs and high global visibility for new orders.

6.3. WHY ARE SUCCESSIVE UPGRADING AND ENTRY STRATEGIES NEEDED?

The Korean and Taiwanese cases reveal that upgrading in the same industry and successive entry into promising new industries occurred over the course of industrial development. Our proposition is that unless these two kinds of upgrading are pursued, the chances for successful catch-up are slim. There are two issues involved here: one from the perspective of the latecomer and the other from that of the front-runner, or incumbent firm.

First, from the latecomer perspective, we note that while the current success with the OEM strategy tends to make wage rates rise accordingly, new cheaper labor sites in "next-tier down" countries can emerge to replace a country's position in the global value chains. This condition forces firms to move up to higher value-added activities in the same industries. Second, we note that the innovators in the "front-runner" countries tend to generate new higher value-added industries. As innovations arise, established industries mature and may degrade into lower value-added activities, forcing firms to enter newly emerging industries and higher valued-added activities.

The need for these two kinds of upgrading stems partly from typical inter-national industrial life cycles such that new industries have tended to be created by the developed world, and partly from the fact that it always used to be the case that latecomer countries and firms tended to inherit these industries after they had become mature and their products standardized (Suarez and Utter-back, 1995). Given this life cycle, an important attribute of successful catch-up has been to permit entry at an earlier (higher value-added) stage of cycles as time goes on; however, this is possible only with enhanced absorptive capabil-ities. Otherwise, a company may be doomed to remain stuck in lower-wage activities or lower-wage industries, with few chances for long-term success.

Successive Upgrading and Entry into New Industries

Examples of upgrading in the same industries are numerous in East Asia. For example, semiconductor firms in Korea and Taiwan started from integrated

Table 6.1. Taiwan Tatung's successive entries since the 1960s

Product	Introduction dates
Black & white TVs	1964
Color TVs	1969
B&W TV picture tubes	1980
VCRs	1982
High resolution color TV tubes	1982
PCs	Mid-1980s
Hard disk drives	Mid-1980s
TV chips/ASICs	Late 1980s
Sun workstation clones	1989
14 inch color monitors	1991

Source: Adaptation from Khan (2002).

circuits (IC) packaging or testing (low value-added activities), then moved to IC fabrication and eventually to IC design (highest valued-added) (Mathews 2006; Mathews and Cho 2000).There are many cases of successive entry into higher value-added activities found in Taiwan and Korea. For instance, as shown in Table 6.1, the Tatung company in Taiwan has made successive entries since the 1960s into new activities, starting with black and white TVs in 1964, color TVs in 1969, VCRs and PCs in the mid-1980s, hard disk drives in the mid-1980s, TV Chips/ASICs (application-specific integrated circuits) in the late 1980s, and workstation clones in 1989 (Khan 2002).

The Samsung group in Korea is well known for having made successive entries into new industries over the 60 years of its history. As shown in Figure 6.1 below, Samsung started with involvement in light manufacturing industries, such as textiles, but then entered consumer electronics, then semiconductors, then telecommunications equipment, and then flat panel displays. Through this process, the state played an important role in providing institutional support by means such as joint R&D consortia and technology transfer arrangements, as well as tax and credit concessions for newer industries.

In Taiwan, successive entries were made by firms in radios, then TVs, telephones, watches, fans, calculators, notebook PCs, and cellular phones. These were all produced by the same companies or by those connected with them. The same holds in the case of Korean firms, like Samsung or LG, as they have become increasingly diversified through entry into a variety of consumer goods production. By contrast, in the semiconductor industry and then particularly in the flat panel display industry (to be discussed below), many newly created Taiwanese firms entered the industry. The same observation can be applied to the most recent industry associated with this development: solar cells. Although such dynamic changes could occur without state intervention, it is often the case that coordination by state agencies can expedite processes of dynamic change.

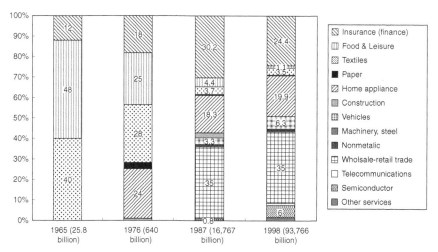

Fig. 6.1. Changes in Samsung Group's sales composition

Source: Author elaboration based on data in Chang (2003), Figure 3.3.

6.4. THE CRISIS OF OEM AND UPGRADING TO ODM/
OBM IN A GIVEN INDUSTRY

Dilemmas and the Crisis of the "Standard
Development" (OEM) Model

Given that innovation can be defined as a product or process new to the firm rather than to the world or marketplace (Hobday, 2000: 131), latecomer firms from Asia faced at least two important competence disadvantages; notably their dislocation from the major international sources of innovation, and their distance from advanced markets and the user-producer links essential to innovation. However, OEM has been one of the chief institutional mechanisms used to overcome these barriers to entry and to enable technological learning to occur. OEM is a specific form of subcontracting where finished products are made to the precise specification of a particular buyer who then markets the products under their own brand name, through their own distribution channels. In Taiwan and Korea, OEM accounted for a significant share of electronics exports during the 1970s, 1980s, and even the 1990s (Hobday, 2000: 133). These beginnings have shaped the options available to OEM fast-followers as they face the conditions of the 21st century (Huang and Chu, 2010).

While latecomer firms readily achieve an early stage of development through producing products designed by others (the OEM model), they face uncertain long-term prospects as potential technology suppliers refuse to sell designs or licenses or switch production orders to other lower-wage sites or countries (Lee, 2005). The fundamental reason for the unfolding of an "OEM crisis" has to do with the difficulty of learning how to design. In the Korean case, there were products to imitate, but no designs were forthcoming from incumbent producers since they were reluctant to transfer design technology to potential rivals. In Taiwan, the crisis was such that foreign vendors switched their OEM orders to firms in other lower-wage economies like Malaysia. The Taiwanese firms then realized that they had to upgrade their design capability if they were to keep their customers. Specifically, they had to design an "imitative" product by themselves and to start to sell this under their own brand name.

Design capability is not easily acquired simply by continuing as a subcontractor or through networking with local producers. The case of Acer in Taiwan shows how difficult it is to move out of the OEM phase, and to move into OBM (Khan, 2002; Hobday, 2000; Mathews, 2002b). Acer was the most representative high-tech start-up to emerge in Taiwan in the late 1970s and the early 1980s. Initially, Acer relied on product innovation and OEM, with experience gained by individuals who had worked overseas in the USA. The firm started with just 11 engineers in 1976 and achieved total sales of 1.4 billion US dollars in 1993. ACER led the Taiwanese computer industry in the 1980s with a 60 percent market share in Taiwan. Since then, it has begun to distribute directly to customers abroad in order to challenge other brand leaders and move beyond OEM. But, it had to retreat from OBM back to OEM or ODM after heavy losses between 1990 and 1993. After that, Acer was constrained to maintain an ODM strategy, with a large percentage of its sales made to IBM and others. Only very recently, has it been reported to be trying to return to an OBM-based strategy.

Overcoming the Crisis: The Korean Story[1]

Hyundai Motors

The main business of the Hyundai group was building and construction, and it entered the automobile industry as a completely new initiative in the early 1970s by establishing a joint venture with the Japanese car maker, Mitsubishi. The Japanese company provided engines and other key components, and Hyundai at first simply assembled them. Hyundai was a licensed producer but not an OEM producer, as it used its own brand in the export and local market. However, when Hyundai wanted to develop its own engines,

---

[1] These cases of crisis overcoming in Korea and Taiwan are from Lee (2005); Hyundai (Lee and Lim, 2001) and Samsung (Kim, 1997).

Mitsubishi refused to assist Hyundai in designing and producing engines, for fear of creating a rival.

Hyundai therefore decided to concentrate R&D expenditure on engine development. The company was able to gain access to the external knowledge of specialized R&D firms like Ricardo Co. in England. Since the business of the Ricardo Company was not to produce and sell the cars but to sell the underlying technology, their attitude toward latecomers, like Hyundai, was different from that of car assemblers. The process was not easy, and involved a co-development by the two entities in which a new engine emerged. More than 1,000 prototypes were produced until they finally succeeded after seven years.

Hyundai's development of its own engines, fuel-injection system, and other parts was basically the fruit of its own initiatives and was achieved without help from the government, which basically provided only domestic market protection. Hyundai's technological development also involved skipping a generation in engine design since the new engines incorporated fuel-injection systems rather than the carburetor-based technology, then the industry standard.

Samsung's Memory Business

In the 1970s, several Korean firms started the fabrication of memory chips through wafer processing. This was accomplished as part of subcontracting relationships with foreign firms. There was no systematic government help in this endeavor save for some minor assistance from a government research institute (GRI) called KIET (Korea Institute for Electronics Technology; now known as ETRI). The period from the late 1970s to the early 1980s represented a period of high-level technology absorption. All foreign companies present in Korea sold their shares to domestic firms, including *Chaebols* like Samsung. Through its own initiative and without government help, Samsung first started to produce 64K DRAM chips in the early 1980s. At that time, the government's position was said to favor Korean firms entering the industry by producing technically obsolete K chips—but it was the decision of private firms to skip this stage and enter directly into 64K DRAM production.

How was this possible? Access to the external knowledge base partly holds the key to this question. At the time that Korean firms including Samsung were considering production of 16K DRAM, it was a period of transition in the DRAM sector as the industry standard moved from 16K to 64K. Samsung was able to buy 64K DRAM design technology from what was then a small US-based venture company, Micron Technology Inc. (located outside Silicon Valley and therefore not subject to industry pressure against "leakage"), and manufacturing technology from the Japan-based Sharp. Thus, such stage-skipping catching up was made possible by access to the external knowledge base in the form of licensing, and finding firms like Micron that were cash-strapped and willing to trade technology for revenue flow.

However, to move up from the 64K to the 256K DRAM, Samsung found that it was not easy or cheap to buy the design of memory chips (Kim, 1997). Thus, they decided to develop their own design technology for 256K DRAMs and beyond. In this process, the role of overseas R&D listening posts in Silicon Valley and returning designers was critical. Samsung's 256K DRAM chip, designed by its Silicon Valley team, turned out to be better than its Japanese counterpart. After Samsung's independent development of the 256K chip, some foreign companies offered to sell Samsung their 1M DRAM designs, but Samsung refused to purchase them since it thought it could develop these on its own.

At this time, government industrial policy tended to lag behind the progress made by private initiatives. Only in 1986 did the government initiate the formation of a semiconductor R&D consortium with the participation of Samsung, LG, and Hyundai to develop successive generation memory chips, starting with 4M chips and ending with 256M chips. Development of 256M chips by the Korean firms was a world-first event. In this sense, the Korean firms now became "path-leaders," their technological capability having reached the final stage of new product concepts and their design through reverse engineering. In sum, the case of DRAM chips can be considered an example of a stage-skipping catch-up process that relied upon access to the external knowledge base through licensing and overseas R&D listening posts and that took advantage of mass production and the investment capabilities of conglomerate firms.

The Taiwanese Story

Private Learning Effort: Electronic Calculators in Taiwan

In the case of Taiwan, a characteristic set of institutional innovations has tended to be followed as firms entered one sector after another. Starting with the era of the electronic calculator, which reached its peak in the mid-1980s, a point was reached from which a trend away from OEM toward ODM began and which later paved the way to notebook and cell-phone manufacture (Amsden and Chu, 2003: 28–32). Since the early 1980s, the Taiwanese manufacturers had mastered the skill of design integration, which enabled them to be the first to market (if not lowest in cost). This enabled them to win the most profitable original design contract from foreign prime contractors. It is important to note that despite collaborative relations with foreign vendors, acquisition of design capability required active learning effort on the part of the Taiwanese. Taiwanese engineers travelled extensively to study LSI (large-scale integration) applications, and eventually, by combining what they saw and what they learned from Japanese suppliers, they became adept at integrating into a small space a large number of parts and components. The latter were sourced globally at the lowest prices. Thus, catch-up in this sector involved a clear focus on the transfer of technology and experimenting with adaptations and improvements.

Public-Private Joint R&D Consortia: Laptop PCs in Taiwan

While the above is an example of the acquisition of detailed design capability, the acquisition of more fundamental design capability—or the basic design platform—was possible with the help of a government research institute such as the ITRI (Industrial Technology Research Institute). A notable example here is the public-private R&D consortium that was assembled to develop laptop PCs and which ran for a year and a half from 1990 to 1991 (Mathews, 2002a). This consortium, which had a capital base of less than US$2 million, developed a "common machine architecture" for a prototype. This could easily translate into a series of standardized components that was produced by manufacturers through mass production. The consortium represented a watershed after some previous failures, indicating the potential of R&D consortia to help establish new "fast-follower" industries.

6.5. INDUSTRY CYCLES AND SUCCESSIVE ENTRIES TO NEW INDUSTRIES

Industry Cycles as a Window of Opportunity for Latecomers

While business cycles have long been the subject of research, industry cycles and their link to strategic choices made by firms, especially the latecomers, seem to be less studied. In what follows, let us start by introducing the arguments made in Mathews (2005) on the role of industry cycles as a window of opportunity for latecomers. In a sense, industry cycles can be seen as similar to the concept of leapfrogging. Here, the emergence of a new techno-economic paradigm opens up a window of opportunity for latecomers who can save on the costs of investing in older vintages of capital by jumping directly to the latest generation of technology (Perez and Soete, 1988; Lee and Lim, 2001). Park and Lee (2006) observe that Korean and Taiwanese firms boasted more successful catch-up in shorter technological cycle sectors, where leapfrogging behavior was facilitated. This is because, where such short cycles apply, technologies change quickly and thus the latecomer does not have to master the old technologies.

Industry cycles are observable in many sectors, most notably in semiconductors, but also in such diverse sectors as shipbuilding, chemicals, oil rig operations, and many more (Mathews, 2005). All such industries are characterized by large investments, and it is the mismatches that occur between investment and production dynamics on the one hand, and market demand dynamics on the other, that appear to drive the cyclical behavior. In such industries, both incumbents and challengers must make strategic choices in terms of timing and capacity; if they fail to do so, they will be quickly eliminated. Industry cycles play a vital economic role in that they create opportunities for the challengers or the late entrants to stir up and renew the industry. While upturns create opportunities to harvest profits, and expand production, markets, and employment, it is the downturns that play a cleansing role, forcing weaker players into bankruptcy. This releases resources that can be picked up by stronger incumbents or by challenger firms looking to enter the industry.

Downturns and crises can also serve to stimulate new kinds of firms, as the situation in Korea after the 1997 crisis indicates. While the Korean economy experienced difficulties in the wake of the 1997 financial crisis, it quickly recovered. Remarkably, the economy recorded 9 percent real growth in 1999, and the stock price index rose much beyond the pre-crisis level. But, the recovery that occurred was not simply due to the revival of the *Chaebols*, but was also triggered by the rapid emergence of small and medium-sized high-tech and new-tech firms (Lee and Kim, 2000). Of course, the rise of small and medium-sized firms was assisted by the break-up of former *Chaebols*. This led to the release of financial and human resources which have contributed to the birth of many start-ups and spin-offs.

The surge in new business creation was helped by the growth of the KOSDAQ stock market, modeled on NASDAQ in the USA. Only two years after its establishment, KOSDAQ stimulated the emergence of hundreds of small and medium-sized venture companies and start-ups. Many ambitious youngsters joined KOSDAQ-listed firms from universities and many established professionals left the giant *Chaebols* to join the new firms. Having financed their investment from equity rather than through the banking systems, these new and flexible firms have proven much better in terms of debt structure. At the peak of the KOSDAQ market, the capitalization of its listed firms came close to that of the KSE (Korean Stock Exchange) firms. Lee and Kim (2000) compare the productive efficiency of venture firms (typically IT or high-tech companies) and their non-venture KOSDAQ-listed counterparts. The comparison also included *Chaebols* and non-*Chaebol* firms listed on the regular Korea Stock Exchange. This study, using panel data covering the 1996–9 period, found that the average level of productive efficiency of venture firms was the highest.

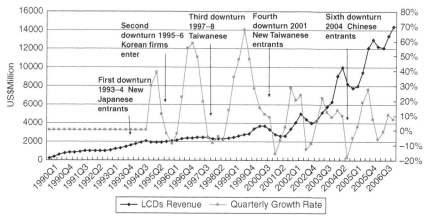

Fig. 6.2. Growth of the flat panel display industry and its cyclical dynamics, 1990–2006

Source: Author elaboration based on data in Mathews (2005).

The TFT-LCD Industry

The flat panel display industry is a creation of the last two decades—although its basic innovations go back to the 1970s and 1980s in both the US and Japan. Despite the industry's youth, it has already experienced several distinct upturns and downturns, and, in 2008, was entering its sixth downturn (Figure 6.2). The thin film transistor-liquid crystal display (TFT-LCD) current trajectory began in 1991 when the industry innovators—Sharp, NEC, IBM Japan, and Toshiba (which joined forces in the unique US-Japanese JV, Integrated Display Technologies, Inc.)—first perfected mass production for the new panels. At that time, they were the undisputed leaders. The competitive dynamics of the trajectory played out in terms of the quest for commercially acceptable yields, and in terms of finding new applications. The first such "killer application" was displays for laptop PCs, and the race was soon on to produce larger and larger screens as well as better resolution.

The very large investments involved in rushing to meet this new application led to a supply-demand imbalance, and the new industry tipped into its first downturn in 1993–4. This created a space for new Japanese entrants—and firms such as Matsushita and Hitachi, and new entrants like Hosiden, all entered at this time. They were able to make use of new "Generation-2" equipment, being promoted by new players such as AKT—a joint venture between the Japanese firm Komatsu and Applied Materials of the US. The new entrants were able to achieve productivity gains from the use of the new equipment. All these players then enjoyed profits as the industry moved into upswing again, from 1994–5.

Korean Firms' Entries in Downturns

Growth during this second upswing, with so many new entrants, became over-heated, exceeding 40 percent per annum for the first time, and again excess capacity tipped the industry into a second downturn in 1995–6. This time the new entrants came not from Japan, but from Korea—led by Samsung and LG. These firms had managed to acquire the technology without licensing it from the Japanese incumbents, something quite unexpected. A little-noticed feature of the first downturn had been that Samsung opened an R&D lab in Japan, to take advantage of unemployed Japanese engineers. Samsung basically acquired the technological capability to build panels during this first downturn, combining this new knowledge with its existing mastery of semiconductor (and in particular DRAM) fabrication, to build Generation-2 pilot fabrication lines. Samsung and LG entered the industry through aggressive counter-cyclical investment in 1995–6, utilizing the newest Generation-3 fabrication equipment, at the time that the incumbents were being forced to pull back on their investments. It requires a particular kind of courage, or daring, to engage in counter-cyclical investment. The firm poured investment funds into an industry at the very time when prices and production were falling, and other firms were cutting back on investment.

Taiwan Firms' Entries in Downturns

Opportunity for the Taiwanese firms came in the immediate wake of the 1997 Asian financial crisis. At this time, Korean firms were forced to suspend all investment, and Japanese firms, feeling the effects of the crisis through their exposure in Southeast Asia, also cut back, creating a new downturn. This time the players that were ready were Taiwanese firms. Already there had been several efforts by Taiwanese firms such as Acer Display Technology and UMC's spin-off Unipac to enter TFT-LCD production, but their efforts had been abortive. There had been sustained efforts by the government-owned Industrial Technology Research Institute (ITRI) to build capabilities in TFT-LCD, as an anticipated successor to the country's great success in semiconductors (Mathews, 1997). So there was what might be called sufficient "absorptive capacity" in Taiwan for an all-out assault on the TFT-LCD sector. What was lacking was the opportunity, and access to the very latest technology. This changed in 1997–8 with the third downturn, and a new willingness on the part of Japanese firms to license technology to Taiwanese partners—partly as a way for the Japanese to fend off the Korean challenge. So, during this downturn, no fewer than five Taiwanese new entrants plunged in, utilizing new equipment generations (3.5G and 4G).

The massive investments made by these Taiwan new entrants swung the industry into a short-lived upturn in 1999–2000, when once again all firms

enjoyed profits. Samsung was again driving this upswing with its new investments in 4G substrate lines, allowing it to cut extra panels for a wider variety of
applications—from laptop screens to ever larger desktop monitors and new
applications in cell phones, PDAs (personal digital assistants), and digital still
cameras. This directly challenged Japanese incumbents, such as Sony and Seiko-
Epson, in these fields. Growth was spectacular in 1999, increasing by more than
100 percent to $13.8 billion, and was healthy again in 2000, growing by 25 percent
to $17.4 billion. But it was followed by another downturn—the fourth—which
was equally spectacular. Prices for panels peaked in the final quarter of 1999, and
then they fell continuously through 2000 and into the third quarter of 2001—in
some cases falling to half their previous levels. Revenues contracted (despite
continued growth in unit sales) by 13 percent, to $15 billion. Profits plunged
again—particularly for the new Taiwanese entrants—and this time, there were
some consolidations. Japanese firms were feeling the pinch, and some combined
forces, such as Toshiba and Hitachi which formed a JV, and in Taiwan the
leaders, Acer Display and Unipac, combined forces, to create AU Optronics,
which thus became the world No. 3 in terms of revenues.

This fourth downturn created more space for new entrants, and the opportunity
was seized by new Taiwanese firms such as Quanta Display (an affiliate of PC
maker Quanta), Innolux (an affiliate of the electronic giant HonHai), and Toppoly
(an affiliate of PC maker Compal)—which was the first Taiwanese firm to focus on
a variant of TFT-LCD technology, namely low-temperature polysilicon (LTPS).
But this time the Koreans, led by Samsung, were also engaging in counter-cyclical
investment, to build capacity in next-generation 5G lines, driven by competitive
rivalry with the new Taiwanese entrants. All these new entry initiatives were
possible because patent protection for the technologies had expired.

Subsequent downturns experienced in the industry have created opportunities for entry by new firms, this time from China. Thus in the fifth downturn,
in 2005, the Chinese firm BOE-Hydis (a joint venture between Hydis and
Beijing OptoElectronics) succeeded in breaking into the industry—ahead of
the expectations of industry participants. Thus, as the industry approaches
two decades since the first mass production displays appeared in 1990, it
continues to exhibit strongly cyclical properties that make life very difficult
for the incumbent firms of Japan, Korea, Taiwan, and now China, while
creating opportunities for new players.

The Global Financial Crisis since the 2009 as an Another Opportunity for Catch-Up

Stories from the downturn that started in 2008 also indicate that downturns
occur when some market shake-up happens due to different strategies for
investment. One example is the story of LG Display, which was established in

1995 and grew quickly to become the No. 2 in global LCD panel markets. Company observers suggest that its growth was driven by aggressive investment during a downturn (Jin, 2009). During the current downturn, in contrast to its Japanese rivals, LG Display invested 3.1 trillion Won in its eighth-generation LCD plant in Paju area, and this 8G production facility started production in March 2009. With the LCD sector recovering faster than expected, driven by robust demand for TVs in China and elsewhere, the new plant helped the company cope with surging orders, which have created a panel shortage. Thus, LG Display was expecting to return to profit by the second quarter of 2009, after posting massive losses in the previous two quarters.

In automobiles, Hyundai Motors seems to be reaping benefits from the collapse of its American competitors, and is using this downturn as an opportunity to increase market shares by aggressive marketing schemes. Although global recession has been taking its toll on every car maker, including Hyundai, Hyundai is significantly increasing its market share in the American market, with its combined share with Kia climbing as high as 7.6 percent during the first five months of 2009, 2 percentage points up from the previous year (Choi, 2009). Its market share in European markets has also increased. In China, Hyundai's January to May sales jumped more than 60 percent compared to the same period the previous year. While it was helped by the troubles of GM and Ford, it was also assisted by the fact that Hyundai has a relatively strong, small and compact car line-up, with such vehicles accounting for about 55 percent of its overseas sales.

Solar PV Industry

A third "pillar" of Taiwan's high-tech sector is now the solar photovoltaic (PV) industry, which is rapidly emerging as a new sector, attracting new entrants such as E-Ton, Gintech, and Motech. The solar cell industry has emerged globally in the last decade as a major source of growth and industrial prosperity, as it contributes an ever-growing proportion of clean power to an energy-hungry world. In this setting, Taiwan has emerged in the last five years as a major solar cell producer. From a small share of global production of just 4 percent in 2005, the country's output has risen to over 10 percent of global supply in 2007 and nearly 12 percent in 2008. Its leading firm, Motech, one of the early leaders, was one of the world's top ten solar cell producers, and has been expanding its activities all along the photovoltaic value chain, from polysilicon production and ingot and wafer fabrication at the source end, to modules and solar photovoltaic (PV) systems at the customer end. The value of production reached over NT$100 billion in 2008 (equivalent to US$3.5 billion). This made Motech an attractive target for the established TFT-LCD player AU Optronics (AUO), when it acquired Motech in 2010.

The solar PV industry in Taiwan is another exemplary case of catch-up, this time with leading Taiwanese firms focusing on the emergent dominant technology of crystalline silicon, just as they did with flat panel displays in TFT-LCD. As firms acquire a foothold in the industry, they expand as rapidly as possible along the value chain—as E-Ton is doing in Taiwan in PV systems. Interestingly, the Korean *Chaebol* have not yet made a move into solar PVs but are keeping the sector under close review, building up patent portfolios to be utilized as and when Samsung, LG, et al. make a move (particularly in the emerging PV field of thin-film solar PV, utilizing production technology very similar to that used in the TFT-LCD sector). The other interesting feature of the solar PV industry in Taiwan is that leading players from the semiconductor sector (such as TSMC) and from the TFT-LCD sector (such as AUO) have announced their intention of entering the PV sector, bringing with them their considerable technological experience, capabilities, and brand names—as AUO has in fact done through its linkage with Motech (Mathews et al., 2011).

From the Timing of Entry to the Modes of Entry

While the above cases of TFT-LCD and solar PV noted a common feature of late entrants, namely taking advantage of the opportunity in a downturn, another important issue is the mode of entry. Already from the examples above, we note a difference between Korea and Taiwan in utilizing downturns as a window of opportunity. The Korean *Chaebols* were more independent, not relying upon formal transfer from the incumbent firms, but rather hiring or scouting engineers who used to work for the leading firms. In comparison, the Taiwanese firms seem to be more interdependent with the forerunners, openly receiving technology transfer from Japanese firms. This difference centers on the mode of gaining access to foreign knowledge.

It is worth noting that Korea and Taiwan followed different patterns in their modes of access to the foreign knowledge needed for late entry. This implies that while entry mode is a matter of choice over strategy from the point of view of the incumbent, it is, from the latecomer point of view, more a matter of choosing the right method of gaining access to foreign knowledge. While the examples above have already shown the availability of diverse access modes, the modes sometimes can take the form of mergers and acquisitions (M&As).

LG Electronics provides an interesting instance of this approach, with its acquisition of the American company, Zenith, to absorb source technology needed in order to enter the digital TV industry. Korean firms were far behind Japanese firms in the consumer goods industry during the analog era. Recognizing this disadvantage, the strategy of Korean firms in the 1990s was to redirect their investment away from analog technology toward investment in emerging digital technologies. However, Korean firms lacked core source technologies in this emerging field, which were all initiated by US, European, or Japanese firms. While Samsung set up R&D labs in the USA, LG took an alternative approach, acquiring US firms. Its target was Zenith, which had developed the original technology in digital broadcasting (Lee et al., 2005).

As early as 1990, LG had a minor share of 15 percent in Zenith. In 1996, LG's share was increased to more than 50 percent and finally to 100 percent in 2000. For digital TV, except for the digital signal receiving and retrieval element, the existing technology of analog TV, especially monitor technology, could be used. Thus, the entry strategy by the Korean firms was to combine what they had with the outside source technology owned by foreign firms. With its share in Zenith, LG was able to get some help and use the technology without fear of patent violation. Owing to its acquisition of Zenith, LG now receives US$5 as royalty payment for every digital TV set produced globally. Of course such a strategy is feasible only after a latecomer becomes an incumbent.

Channels of access to foreign knowledge evolve over the course of catch-up (as discussed for example in Lee, 2005). First, in the earliest stage, the primary channel of learning is technical guidance from foreign OEM buyers or learning by working in FDI firms. The key technology is embodied in imported machinery and equipment. It basically comprises learning-by-doing with no capacity or even intention for planned technological development. In the next stage, when the latecomer firms recognize the need for more systemic learning and planned technological development, such firms tend to resort to technological licensing and actively seek learning or transfer from any FDI partners. Licensing had been the main form of acquisition of foreign technology in Korea during the 1970s and the 1980s. In Taiwan, in the TV monitor industry in the 1980s, which emerged after the television industry of the 1970s, the main channels were licensing or joint ventures (Amsden and Chu, 2003). In this stage, the critical factor for effective learning would be the absorptive capacity of latecomer firms, which also depended on the education system and other elements of the national innovation system of the country.

In the next stage, the latecomer firms establish a certain degree of in-house R&D capacity, with a clear idea of what should be done and how, and the way in which resources are to be allocated. With licensing or learning from foreign partners revealing its limits, the latecomer firms often rely on public-private R&D consortia, research of the existing literature, overseas R&D listening posts, co-development contracts with foreign R&D or technology specialist firms, and/or international mergers and acquisitions. In the 1990s, the main channel of access was the government laboratory in the case of the notebook industry in Taiwan. It was also the case that, from the early 1990s, a small number of Korean firms began to establish overseas R&D outposts, mainly to obtain easier and faster access to foreign technologies that were hard to acquire through imports or licenses. These overseas listening posts also served as a window on recent trends in technological development. The final stage can be characterized as a horizontal collaboration or alliance based on complementary assets. Some Korean firms, such as Samsung, have reached this stage, and are now engaged with leading firms such as Intel, Sony, Toshiba, and Microsoft in diverse modes of alliances, as are Taiwanese firms such as TSMC in semiconductors and AUO in flat panel displays and solar PV.

6.6. CONCLUDING REMARKS

This chapter has sought to analyze certain aspects of catch-up in South Korean and Taiwanese industrial enterprises. We were also concerned as to how innovative firms might be generated to provide a solid basis for national-level catch-up; that is, catch-up that is sustained and not simply a short-lived phenomenon. The proposition that we have defended is that successful catch-up requires continuous upgrading in the same industry, as well as successive entry (another kind of upgrading) into new and promising industries over the course of industrial development.

In upgrading in the same industry, the common dilemma was how to acquire design capability for product differentiation and product innovation; design capability is not easily acquired simply through a network of domestic producers or by continuing with international subcontracting. The Korean solution included cross-subsidizing a huge amount of R&D among affiliates, as well as promoting R&D consortia with support from government research institutes (GRIs). The Taiwanese solution was more reliant on the GRIs themselves. These developed parts and components, the technology for which was transferred to private firms.

In fashioning successive entries, Korean firms were more independent, not relying upon formal transfer from the incumbent firms, but rather hiring or scouting engineers who used to work for the leading firms. In comparison, the Taiwanese firms were more interdependent with sector pioneers, relying upon explicit technology transfer from Japan or from domestic GRIs, and building their absorptive capacity through participation in global production networks.

In sum, the latecomer firms have utilized diverse channels of knowledge access and learning. These have included modalities such as OEM, licensing, JVs, co-development with foreign specialized R&D firms, transfers of individual scientists or engineers, reverse brain drains, overseas R&D centers, strategic alliances, and international M&As. All these constitute effective channels of knowledge transfer around which firms are able to strategize.

The experience of Korea and Taiwan has revealed several interesting patterns, which will be tested as firms seek to extend the catch-up and fast-follower strategies in the 21st century. First, upgrading often involves a radical break with the past, backed up by massive and decisive investment, sometimes in the form of public-private collaborations or group-level inter-firm sharing of risks. While quite different capabilities are needed for each step, a common capability of rapid absorption of technology is needed for all catch-up efforts. Second, while new industries in the developed world tend to be created by new firms, entries into new industries in the Korea and Taiwan have tended to be realized by established firms or groups of networked firms (as in Taiwan). Such firms or networks would have had to accumulate certain absorptive and execution capacities. Third, industry cycles, whether in the case of downturns or technological paradigm shifts, often serve as a window of opportunity for latecomers. There can be little doubt that catch-up and fast-followership represent strategies of extraordinary efficacy in bringing firms, and the countries that house them, to participate effectively in the global 21st century economy.

REFERENCES

Amsden, A. H., and Chu, W-w. (2003), *Beyond Late Development: Taiwan's Upgrading Policies*, Cambridge, Mass.: MIT Press.

Chang, S. J. (2003), *Financial Crisis and Transformation of Korean Business Groups: The Rise and Fall of Chaebol*, Cambridge: Cambridge University Press.

Choi, H.-s. (2009), "Improved Quality Powers Hyundai Success," *Korea Herald*, June 29.

Choo, K., Lee, K., Ryu, K., and Yoon, J. (2009), "Performance Change of the Business Groups in Korea over Two Decades: Investment Inefficiency and Technological Capabilities," *Economic Development and Cultural Change*, 57(2): 359–86.

Choung, J.-Y., and Hwang, H.-R. (2000), "National Systems of Innovation—Institutional Linkages and Performance in the Case of Korea and Taiwan," *Scientometrics*, 48(3): 413–26.

Ernst, D. (2002), "Global Production Networks and the Changing Geography of Innovation Systems: Implications for Developing Countries," *Economics of Innovation and New Technology*, 11(6): 497–523.

——and Kim, L. (2002), "Global Production Networks, Knowledge Diffusion, and Local Capability Formation," *Research Policy*, 31: 1417–29.

Hobday, M. (2000), "East versus Southeast Asian Innovation Systems: Comparing OEM- and TNC-Led Growth in Electronics," in L. Kim and R. Nelson (eds.), *Technology, Learning and Innovation*, Cambridge: Cambridge University Press.

Hu, M.-C., and Mathews, J. A. (2005), "National Innovative Capacity in East Asia," *Research Policy*, 34(9): 1322–49.

————(2008), "National Innovative Capacity of China," *Research Policy*, 37(9): 1465–79.

Huang, Y., and Chu, W. (2010), "Enhancement of Product Development Capabilities of OEM Suppliers: Inter- and Intra-organisational Learning," *Journal of Business & Industrial Marketing*, 25(2): 147–58.

Jin, H.-J. (2009), "Big Bets Pay Off for LG Display," *Korea Herald*, June 29.

Jung, M., and Lee, K. (2010), "Sectoral Systems of Innovation and Productivity Catch Up: Determinants of TFP Gap between the Korean Firms and the Japanese Firms," *Industrial and Corporate Change*, 19(4): 1037–69.

Khan, H. (2002), "Innovation and Growth: A Schumpeterian Model of Innovation Applied to Taiwan," *Oxford Development Studies*, 30(3): 289–306.

Kim, L. (1997), *Imitation to Innovation: The Dynamics of Korea's Technological Learning*, Boston, Mass.: Harvard Business School Press.

Lall, S. (2000), "Technological Change and Industrialization in the Asian Newly Industrializing Economies," in L. Kim and R. Nelson (eds.), *Technology, Learning and Innovation*, Cambridge: Cambridge University Press.

Lee, K. (2005), "Making a Technological Catch-up: Opportunities and Barriers," *Asian Journal of Technology Innovation*, 13(2): 97–131.

—— and He, X. (2009), "Project Execution and Vertical Integration Capability of a Business Group: Samsung Created in Korea, Replicated in China," *Asian Business and Management*, 15(3): 271–87.

—— and Kim, B. Y. (2009), "Both Institutions and Policies Matter but Differently at Different Income Groups of Countries: Determinants of Long Run Economic Growth Revisited," *World Development*, 37(3): 533–49.

—— and Kim, S. (2000), "Characteristics and Efficiency of the Venture Companies in Korea: Comparison with Chaebols and Other Traditional Firms," *Seoul Journal of Economics*, 13(3): 335–60.

—— and Lim, C. (2001), "Technological Regimes, Catching-Up and Leapfrogging: Findings from the Korean Industries," *Research Policy*, 30(3): 459–83.

—— —— and Song, W. (2005), "Emerging Digital Technology as a Window of Opportunity and Technological Leapfrogging: Catch-Up in Digital TV by the Korean Firms," *International Journal of Technology Management*, 29(1–2): 40–63.

—— and Mathews, J. (2010), "From Washington Consensus to BeST Consensus for World Development," *Asian-Pacific Economic Literature*, 24(1): 86–103.

Mahmood, I. P., and Singh, J. (2003), "Technological Dynamism in Asia," *Research Policy*, 32(6): 1031–54.

Mathews, J. A. (1997), "A Silicon Valley of the East: Creating Taiwan's Semiconductor Industry," *California Management Review*, 39(4): 26–54.

—— (2002a), "Competitive Advantages of the Latecomer Firm: A Resource-Based Account of Industrial Catch-Up Strategies," *Asia Pacific Journal of Management*, 19(4): 467–88.

—— (2002b), *Dragon Multinational: A New Model of Global Growth*, New York: Oxford University Press.

—— (2002c), "The Origins and Dynamics of Taiwan's R&D Consortia," *Research Policy*, 31(4): 633–51.

—— (2005), "Strategy and the Crystal Cycle," *California Management Review*, 47(2): 6–31.

—— (2006), "Catch-up Strategies and the Latecomer Effect in Industrial Development," *New Political Economy*, 11(3): 313–36.

—— and Cho, D. S. (2000), *Tiger Technology: The Creation of a Semiconductor Industry in East Asia*, Cambridge: Cambridge University Press.

——Hu, M.-C., and Wu, C.-Y. (2011), "Fast-Follower Industrial Dynamics: The Case of Taiwan's Emergent Solar Photovoltaic Industry," *Industry and Innovation*, 18(2): 177–202.

Park, K., and Lee, K. (2006), "Linking Technological Regimes and Technological Catch-Up: Analysis of Korea and Taiwan Using the US Patent Data," *Industrial and Corporate Change*, 15(4): 715–53.

Perez, C., and Soete, L. (1988), "Catching-Up in Technology: Entry Barriers and Windows of Opportunity," in G. Dosi, C. Freeman, R. Nelson, G. Silverberg, and L. Soete (eds.), *Technical Change and Economic Theory*, London: Pinter Publishers. London.

Suarez, F. F., and Utterback, J. M. (1995), "Dominant Designs and the Survival of Firms," *Strategic Management Journal*, 16(6): 415–30.

Teece, D. (2000), "Firm Capabilities and Economic Development," in L. Kim and R. Nelson (eds.), *Technology, Learning and Innovation*, Cambridge: Cambridge University Press.

Part IIB

Innovative Firms in Emerging Markets Country Experiences (Latin America)

7

Brazil

Edmund Amann and Paulo N. Figueiredo

7.1. INTRODUCTION

Motivated by the analytical frameworks elaborated in Chapter 1, this chapter will examine evidence of catching-up and overtaking processes in Brazilian firms. The analysis of these phenomena will be carried out under two distinct policy regimes; one related to the predominance of import-substitution industrialization (ISI) policy and the other to the open and outward-looking regime, characterized by the period after 1990. In analyzing catching-up and overtaking processes, the key concern of this chapter will be to determine the ways in which firms' acquisition of technological capabilities evolved in response to the transformation in the policy environment. Thus, our critical focus centers on the influence that policy liberalization has exerted on firms' technological behavior.

In what follows, the bulk of our discussion (in Sections 7.4 and 7.5) will be centered on the experiences of firms operating on the technological frontier or on those who lag just behind it. While it would probably be fair to say that the sample overall is characterized by a relatively innovative collection of firms, there is sufficient variation in the sample to reasonably mirror the marked variation in the population as a whole.[1] The firms featured in our sample operate in two distinct types of sector: natural resource processing and assembled products. In the case of the former, our discussion will center on the steel industry and the forestry, pulp, and paper complex. For the latter, our focus will be placed on the aerospace sector.

Our decision to focus on firms in these sectors reflects the fact that they especially benefited from huge government support in the ISI period. This applied regardless of whether the enterprises concerned were in the public or private sector. Following the structural reforms of the early 1990s, such

---

[1] See Section 7.3 for evidence regarding the overall population.

government support has scaled down dramatically, forcing firms in these sectors to compete and innovate globally on the basis of their own resources. Our choice of sectors therefore provides a useful means of understanding how firm-level innovation fares under contrasting policy regimes.

The second reason for our choice of sectors reflects a deliberate attempt to combine types of approaches to industrial capability building in developing countries. The first relates to a traditional preoccupation with the high-tech content of manufacturing activities in product-based industries geared toward the export market (see e.g. Lall, 1990, 2003; Cimoli and Katz, 2003). The second refers to sectors (in the natural resource-processing industries) which have been historically overlooked, largely as a result of the assumption that, in some sense, they are technologically less dynamic. In examining experiences from both kinds of sector in this chapter, we hope to observe common processes and challenges as far as innovative capability building is concerned. In so doing, we challenge traditional assumptions concerning the inherent technological dynamism of these sectors.

The third reason for our choice of sectors relates to the simple fact that they account for a substantial proportion of industrial GDP and a large chunk of Brazilian exports. Our examination of innovative capability, as a set of knowledge-related assets, and learning, as an input in innovation, is consistent with the framework elaborated in Chapter 1.

The structure of this chapter is as follows. In Section 7.2 we provide a brief overview of the evolution of the industrial policy environment in Brazil over the past 70 years. Next, Section 7.3 provides a brief, industry-wide overview of processes of capabilities building, catching up, and overtaking. Sections 7.4 and 7.5 contain the bulk of the discussion. Section 7.4 examines the experiences of the firms in the natural resource-based product-processing industries (specifically steel and the forestry, pulp, and paper complex) from the 1930s through to the present. Section 7.5 then analyzes the experiences of Embraer, a firm in the aerospace sector, from the 1940s through to the present. Finally, Section 7.6 draws together our main findings, comparing the experiences of firms within and between our chosen sectors and the wider industrial economy.

7.2. CHANGES IN THE POLICY ENVIRONMENT IN BRAZIL: A BRIEF OVERVIEW

The origins of industrial policy in Brazil can be traced back to the *Estado Novo* of President Getúlio Vargas. In the early 1940s, the Vargas administration experimented with what has become known as "informal ISI," establishing basic industries (notably steel) and encouraging reduced dependence on imports. By the 1950s, this process had broadened and formalized, with the elevation of tariff and non-tariff protection and the prioritization of consumer durables industries, the most celebrated case being that of automobiles. The period saw a significant influx of foreign direct investment and it was primarily through associated transfers that technologies necessary for the industrialization process were acquired (Amann and Baer, 1999). Despite this, the Brazilian state did begin to take the first steps toward a policy explicitly designed to build up indigenous technological capabilities. Thus, in 1951, the National Research Council (CNPq) was established (Meyer-Stamer, 1997).

The period from the 1960s to the early 1980s saw the deepening of ISI, a process which accelerated after the launch of the 1974 Second National Development Plan. This period saw the rapid growth of capital-intensive process industries such as steel and pulp and paper. It also witnessed an intensification of tariff and non-tariff barriers, the establishment of state-owned enterprises (SOEs) in strategic sectors and heavy investment in transport, energy, and communication infrastructure (Baer, 2008). The military government in power during this time sought not only to suppress imports but also to build up, as never before, indigenous technological capabilities across a range of sectors.

By the early 1980s it had become clear that Brazil's development model was in severe difficulties. Although ISI had been very effective at building up new industrial sectors and diversifying the economic base, it had not proven compatible with overcoming the external constraint. Thanks to the effects of protection, many Brazilian industrial products were not competitive on global export markets. As a result, Brazil had found itself saddled with a growing current account deficit and external debt obligations. The eruption of the debt crisis in 1982–3 forced the authorities to critically examine the ISI model. The initial result of this was the so-called "New Industrial Policy" in 1985–8 which involved limited trade liberalization through tariff reform.

The timid trade and industrial policy reforms of the late 1980s were dramatically eclipsed by the initiatives taken by the Collor government in the early 1990s. The Collor administration (the first directly elected since the 1960s) set out to dismantle the structures of ISI, rapidly putting into place a rolling four-year program of tariff cuts and progressive abandonment of non-tariff measures. By the mid-1990s nominal average tariff levels had been reduced by half, while the vast majority of import prohibitions had been abandoned (Amann, 2000). The Collor government, and its successor, also stepped up the privatization program, with the result that many SOEs in the process industries (notably petrochemicals and steel) left public ownership. SOEs in the transport energy and telecommunications sector were also sold off in the 1990s, as was Embraer (the focus of one of the case studies).

The major break in strategy represented by these developments was, perhaps surprisingly, reflected much less strongly in the technology policy arena (Amann, 2002). With the exception of the Information and Communications Technology (ICT) market reserve initiative (abandoned in 1990), the essential architecture of technology policy remained intact, though with reduced funding. In the present decade, the Lula and Rousseff administrations have proven reluctant to deepen the trade policy reforms instituted in the 1990s. At the same time, mainly thanks to the exhaustion of suitable opportunities, the government has been slow to engage in further privatizations. Nonetheless, the Lula administration has remained broadly committed to integrating Brazil into the global economy. In this context, the emphasis placed by the Cardoso administration on building up enterprise competitiveness has been maintained.

The most important policy development of the Lula administration was been the launch of the Industrial, Technological, and Foreign Trade Policy Initiative (PITCE) in March 2004. The PITCE incorporates three conventional elements and one genuine innovation. Regarding the former, the PITCE has built on previous practice by expanding the number of special innovation-related credit lines operated by the Brazilian National Economic and Social Development Bank (BNDES) (Sennes, 2008). In addition, the patent office has benefited from a program of modernization, while FINEP's (Financiadora de Estudos e Projectos (Research and Projects Financing)) budget has been increased sevenfold. The genuinely innovative component to the package has been the creation of ABDI (the Brazilian Industrial Development Agency). The objective of ABDI has been to provide a focal point for the coordination of the government's efforts to boost innovation in the private sector. In this connection, the government has aimed to further improve links between public and private sector entities. To this end, the government secured passage of the Innovation Law in 2004. The law provides a legal framework for the signing of public-private partnerships to boost innovation among enterprises.

7.3. INNOVATIVE CAPABILITIES AND POLICY LIBERALIZATION: THE BROADER CONTEXT

Starting in the next section, our three case studies—steel, pulp and paper, and aircraft—will demonstrate the complexities and firm specificities of both the capability accumulation process and its linkages with variations in the policy environment. In order to place these findings into context, however, it is worth first examining the experience of firms in a broader range of sectors. This will be accomplished using a range of evidence, some drawn from individual case studies and some derived from surveys, including the PINTEC (Pesquisa de Inovação Tecnológica) survey.

Evidence from steel, pulp and paper, aircraft, and the automotive sector in the next section clearly reveals the technological dynamism that characterizes some firms. Some enterprises, it will be revealed, have reached the frontier, or are, at least, moving toward it. This presents a very hopeful picture. But how representative is it? In the first place, it is important to recognize that enterprises displaying world-leading innovative capabilities such as Embraer and Aracruz are not isolated examples. Leite (2005) and Amann (2008) discuss the evolution of Petrobrás and its emergence as a world-leading exponent in the field of deep-water exploration and production. Further examples of world-leading innovative capabilities are not hard to find in Brazil and, once again, the achievements which have been realized are strongly linked to the accumulation of capabilities under a supportive public sector and their subsequent deployment and enhancement in a more open economic environment. Two of the most obvious examples in this area are the biotechnology and software sectors. In the case of the former, Brazilian Agricultural Research Corporation (Embrapa), a long-established, well-funded public sector research enterprise has become a leading-edge developer of new crop strains and a pioneer in the emerging area of biofuels. Working alongside private sector partners, a new biotech cluster has emerged. In the case of software, Brazil has developed world-leading capabilities in banking and enterprise management software, thanks partly to the now-defunct "Market Reserve" policy and, from the 1990s on, the Softex 2000 program.

In the case of other capital goods sub-sectors, where the frontier was moving less rapidly (e.g. mechanical equipment and shipbuilding), efforts tended to be centered on the development of in-house capabilities, with quite a heavy emphasis on process, rather than product, innovation. Nonetheless, there is still evidence of attempts to rise through the hierarchy of innovation and to approach more closely the frontier. The experience here corresponds with the findings of Ariffin and Figueiredo (2006) who examined the impacts of globalization on the consumer electronics industry in the industrial pole of Manaus. The authors find, contrary to the expectations of some, that this transnational corporation (TNC)-dominated industry had taken real steps to build up local innovative capabilities, especially as these concerned the production process (product development largely occurs outside Brazil).

Still, it would be a mistake to suppose that these findings would be typical of all enterprises and all sectors. In particular, all of the evidence reviewed so far relates to the experience of large enterprises, be they subsidiaries of TNCs, privatized firms, domestic private concerns, or SOEs. What of the remainder of the industrial economy? In order to arrive at any conclusion here, one would ideally deploy the results of a comprehensive national technological capabilities survey in which would be documented movement between capability levels for all firms. Unfortunately, no such survey exists and so, accordingly, it is necessary to draw tentative inferences from the key survey data which are available. The first such data to be considered derive from the Brazilian statistical office (IBGE—Instituto Brasileiro de Geografia e Estatística) PINTEC survey.

As immediately become apparent from Tables 7.1–7.3, innovative activity, particularly that which could be described as "new to the world," is not a common feature of all enterprises. Of the 16,345 firms declaring that they had undertaken product innovations in 2005, only 203 assessed the product to be genuinely novel in global terms (Table 7.2). Such activity would likely be associated with frontier-defining advanced innovative capabilities, though an exact correspondence here is improbable. A similar pattern may be observed in Table 7.3, where only an extremely small proportion of firms declared their process innovation activity to be new to the sector in global terms. Much more common, as the tables reveal, is innovative activity associated with upgrading existing products or processes or developing products or processes which already exist either domestically or internationally. In this sense, the data would tend to suggest that the frontier-defining characteristics of enterprises such as Klabin or Embraer are the exception rather than the rule.

The data in all three tables reveal yet another interesting trend: the sectoral concentration of innovative activity, especially of the more ambitious, "new to the world" variety. As is readily apparent, such activity is quite heavily concentrated in just a few sectors, especially chemicals, machinery and equipment, and software.

Drawing on the Paep/Seade database, Costa and Queiroz (2002) offer an illuminating inter-sectoral comparison of firm capabilities based on whether enterprises were domestically or foreign owned. Table 7.4 summarizes the authors' findings with regard to the "systematic effort index." This offers a rough proxy measure of deeper and more complex technological capabilities (ibid. 1440).

Examining the data in Table 7.4, it becomes clear that taken as a whole the Brazilian industrial sector demonstrates "a slightly modest accumulation of improvement and generation capabilities" (ibid. 1440). At the same time, such higher scores as are observable are associated with "lower-tech" industries and not necessarily "higher-tech" ones such as drugs. This finding contrasts with the evidence Costa and Queiroz uncover for operational capability where higher scores are associated with the technological intensity of the sector concerned. Another interesting finding to emerge from the data is that "foreign affiliates appear to perform better than domestic firms in locally accumulating more complex capabilities" (ibid. 1440). Overall, however, the survey material is suggestive of a relatively modest accumulation of more advanced capabilities across the board.

Drawing together the various strands of the evidence which has so far been presented, it becomes clear that the Brazilian industrial sector is characterized by significant inter-firm and inter-sectoral differences with regard to

Table 7.1. Prevalence of innovation type by sector, 2001–2003 and 2003–2005

	Firms							
	2001–2003				2003–2005			
		Which implemented…				Which implemented…		
Sector	Total number of firms	Product or process innovation	Incomplete or abandoned projects	Only strategic or organizational innovation	Total number of firms	Product or process innovation	Incomplete or abandoned projects	Only strategic or organizational innovation
Total	**84,262**	**28,036**	**2,315**	**30,972**	**95,301**	**32,796**	**2,200**	**34,403**
Extractive industries	**1,888**	**415**	**25**	**568**	**1,849**	**427**	**78**	**578**
Manufacturing industry	**82,374**	**27,621**	**2,290**	**30,404**	**89,205**	**29,951**	**1,977**	**33,359**
Food and drink	10,606	3,563	304	3,343	11,588	3,771	321	3,831
Textiles	3,173	1,111	42	1,281	4,154	1,382	69	1,713
Wood products	5,102	1,609	105	1,439	5,089	1,440	36	1,627
Cellulose, pulp, and paper	1,593	490	60	658	1,784	565	33	697
Chemical products	3,509	1,529	123	1,058	3,801	1,900	100	1,031
Non-metallic mineral products	6,685	1,331	134	2,237	6,643	1,558	129	2,581
Basic metallurgical products	1,399	473	90	478	1,470	676	33	398
Machinery and equipment	5,411	2,354	186	1,554	5,799	2,282	224	2,105
Electrical equipment	1,705	699	50	631	1,892	865	94	532
Electronics and communications equipment	614	348	16	148	644	367	14	142

(Continued)

Table 7.1. Continued

	Firms							
	2001–2003				2003–2005			
	Which implemented…				Which implemented…			
Sector	Total number of firms	Product or process innovation	Incomplete or abandoned projects	Only strategic or organizational innovation	Total number of firms	Product or process innovation	Incomplete or abandoned projects	Only strategic or organizational innovation
Motor vehicles	1,947	772	74	572	2,214	819	14	713
Furniture	6,707	2,264	162	3,080	7,087	2,304	79	3,004
Recycling	312	43	—	42	470	106	16	39
Services	—	—	—	—	**4,246**	**2,418**	**144**	**466**
Telecommunications	—	—	—	—	393	180	5	149
Information technology and software	—	—	—	—	3,811	2,197	137	318
Research and development	—	—	—	—	42	41	1	-

Source: Elaborated from IBGE/PINTEC data.

Table 7.2. Degree of novelty of product innovation by sector, 2005

Sector	Degree of novelty for process or product for innovating enterprise — Product								
	New for enterprise but already exists on domestic market			New for enterprise but already exists on world market			New for world market		
	Total	Upgrading of existing product	Completely new for the enterprise	Total	Upgrading of existing product	Completely new for the enterprise	Total	Upgrading of existing product	Completely new for the enterprise
Total	**16,345**	**8,386**	**7,959**	**3,122**	**2,626**	**496**	**203**	**159**	**44**
Extractive industries	**102**	**46**	**56**	**15**	**8**	**7**	**1**	**1**	**—**
Manufacturing	**14,774**	**7,583**	**7,191**	**2,719**	**2,323**	**396**	**174**	**150**	**24**
Industry									
Food and drink	2,086	934	1,152	302	274	28	10	9	1
Textiles	677	357	319	134	129	5	4	4	—
Wood products	787	169	618	50	49	1	1	1	—
Cellulose, pulp, and paper	230	114	116	33	29	4	2	2	—
Chemical products	1,186	754	432	319	233	86	27	17	10
Non-metallic mineral products	613	368	245	57	40	18	3	2	1
Basic metallurgical products	302	114	188	60	57	3	2	2	—
Machinery and equipment	1,207	807	401	484	435	50	36	33	3
Electrical equipment	170	126	44	112	104	8	2	2	—
	319	204	115	96	74	22	14	13	1

(Continued)

Table 7.2. Continued

Sector	Degree of novelty for process or product for innovating enterprise								
	Product								
	New for enterprise but already exists on domestic market			New for enterprise but already exists on world market			New for world market		
	Total	Upgrading of existing product	Completely new for the enterprise	Total	Upgrading of existing product	Completely new for the enterprise	Total	Upgrading of existing product	Completely new for the enterprise
Electronics and communications equipment									
Motor vehicles	1,318	747	571	109	99	10	4	4	—
Furniture	924	544	381	47	42	5	3	3	—
Recycling	73	20	54	—	—	—	—	—	—
Services	1,470	757	713	388	295	93	28	8	20
Telecommunications	133	81	52	18	9	9	7	3	4
Information technology and software	1,330	672	659	348	280	69	10	4	7
Research and development	6	4	2	22	6	16	11	2	9

Source: Elaborated from IBGE/PINTEC data.

Table 7.3. Degree of novelty of process innovation by sector, 2005

	Degree of novelty for process or product for innovating enterprise								
	Process								
Sector	New for enterprise but already exists in sector in Brazil			New for the enterprise but already exists in sector worldwide			New for the sector in global terms		
	Total	Upgrading of existing process	Completely new for the enterprise	Total	Upgrading of existing process	Completely new for the enterprise	Total	Upgrading of existing process	Completely new for the enterprise
Total	**24,658**	**17,706**	**6,952**	**1,504**	**1,184**	**320**	**115**	**88**	**27**
Extractive industries	397	292	105	13	10	4	3	2	1
Manufacturing	**22,683**	**16,132**	**6,551**	**1,308**	**1,049**	**259**	**100**	**82**	**18**
Industry									
Food and drink	2,835	2,029	806	147	132	16	6	6	—
Textiles	997	639	358	119	117	2	1	—	1
Wood products	1,329	640	688	23	17	6	1	1	—
Cellulose, pulp, and paper	502	310	192	18	17	1	3	2	1
Chemical products	1,084	731	353	224	166	59	11	8	3
Non-metallic mineral products	1,294	1,104	190	85	79	6	2	—	2
Basic metallurgical products	552	432	121	34	25	9	4	2	2
Machinery and equipment	1,208	887	321	94	84	10	47	41	7
Electrical equipment	216	164	52	25	16	9	1	1	—
	622	465	157	72	61	11	8	8	—

(Continued)

Table 7.3. Continued

Sector	Degree of novelty for process or product for innovating enterprise								
	Process								
	New for enterprise but already exists in sector in Brazil			New for the enterprise but already exists in sector worldwide			New for the sector in global terms		
	Total	Upgrading of existing process	Completely new for the enterprise	Total	Upgrading of existing process	Completely new for the enterprise	Total	Upgrading of existing process	Completely new for the enterprise
Electronics and communications equipment									
Motor vehicles	1,778	1,271	508	63	59	4	1	1	—
Furniture	1,354	1,034	320	22	22	—	—	—	—
Recycling	106	58	49	—	—	—	—	—	—
Services	**1,578**	**1,282**	296	**183**	**126**	58	**12**	4	8
Telecommunications	130	114	17	14	12	2	4	1	3
Information technology and software	1,439	1,163	275	150	107	43	1	—	1
Research and development	9	5	4	20	7	13	7	3	4

Source: Elaborated from IBGE/PINTEC data.

Table 7.4. Improvement and generation capabilities: the systematic effect index (range 0–100)

Manufacturing sector	Domestic	Foreign
Clothing	18	53
Leather products	9	0
Pulp and paper	14	7
Chemicals	11	11
Drugs	3	10
Rubber and plastic products	18	28
Non-metallic mineral products	16	19
Basic metals	9	95
Fabricated metal products	13	30
Mechanical machinery	9	10
Electrical machinery and components	29	23
Electronic and telecommunications equipment	6	15
Medical precision and optical instruments	15	22
Motor vehicles	12	32
Total	6	20

Source: Adapted from Costa and Queiroz (2002: 1439).

innovative capability and closeness to the frontier. While there are examples of world-leading capability across a range of sectors, by the same token it has to be recognized that such examples need to be set beside a greater number of cases where enterprises have accumulated little or no innovative capability. To obtain more detailed insight into the factors driving the accumulation of innovative capability, the discussion now turns to the consideration of the case studies.

7.4. CAPABILITY BUILDING IN NATURAL RESOURCE-PROCESSING INDUSTRIES

7.4.1. Capability Accumulation for Moving Close to the Innovation Frontier: Evidence from Brazil's Steel Industry

This section provides evidence surrounding the accumulation of technological capability that permits latecomer firms to catch up with early innovators in industrialized countries. The evidence derives from the steel industry in Brazil. Building on classical studies of direction and rates of technological capability accumulation in developing countries (e.g. Dahlman and Fonseca, 1978; Maxwell, 1981; Bell et al., 1982), Figueiredo (1999, 2001, 2003) elaborated on the taxonomy of levels of capabilities as presented in Chapter 2 in order to examine the capability accumulation paths in two large steel firms in Brazil (USIMINAS and CSN) over their lifetime of 40–50 years.

Following their start-up and initial absorption phase, both CSN and USI-MINAS went through an expansion process from the 1960s to the 1980s as state-owned firms. From the early 1990s, these firms began to operate within a new set of economic conditions in Brazil. These were marked by the privatization of the whole steel industry, combined with a set of actions to deregulate and open up the economy to foreign competition. In parallel, new government policies sought to stimulate the development of industrial technological capability. In contrast to CSN, USIMINAS entered the 1990s holding the best position in Brazil's steel industry as far as techno-economic performance was concerned (see Figueiredo, 2002, 2003). In 1990 CSN faced the deepest financial crisis in its history. This was combined with a succession of strikes that had started during the 1980s. In 1990 the federal government not only denied financial help to CSN; it also threatened to close it down. The new corporate leadership that took over in March 1990 engaged in CSN's recovery: for the first time in CSN's history, systematic in-house efforts on technological capability accumulation were made throughout the firm.

7.4.1.1. *Differences between the Two Companies in Terms of Capability Accumulation*

Start-up of CSN and USIMINAS during the ISI period

Both USIMINAS and CSN started as state-owned flat steel companies with inadequate technological capabilities. However, their technological capabilities were accumulated in different ways. During the start-up and initial absorption phase, USIMINAS accumulated basic and advanced levels of production-based capability for process and production organization and product-centered activities. In addition, USIMINAS moved into the accumulation of basic and intermediate capability levels for process and production organization. In contrast, CSN passed through this phase without having completed the accumulation of basic production-based capability for these two functions. In addition, CSN did not move into the accumulation of levels of innovative capability. More specifically, the differences are as follows.

PROCESS AND PRODUCTION ORGANIZATION CAPABILITY ACCUMULATION Even before the plant start-up, USIMINAS began to build organizational units to support its operational activities. However, the building of such units was absent in CSN in the start-up and initial absorption phase. Constrained by financial difficulties and pushed by leadership to break even, USIMINAS engaged in intense efforts to absorb and even "stretch" plant capacity, leading to the accumulation of its own "capacity-stretching" capability. In contrast, the evidence indicates that CSN passed through that phase with little engagement in process quality improvement, operating the plant inefficiently, and at low capacity utilization rates compared with USIMINAS. While USI-MINAS accumulated basic and advanced levels of production-based capability and moved into the accumulation of intermediate innovation capability level for process and production organization activities, CSN failed to accumulate either level of capability during the start-up and initial absorption phase.

PRODUCT-CENTERED CAPABILITY ACCUMULATION USIMINAS rapidly accumulated basic and advanced levels of capability for product-centered activities, with consistent product quality and diversification strategies. In parallel, the company moved into the accumulation of intermediate innovative levels of that capability by engaging in innovative product activities on an independent basis. In contrast, CSN put no effort into efficient routine product manufacture or product improvement activities. As a result, the company failed to accumulate basic production-based capability and basic innovation product-centered capability during the start-up and initial absorption phase.

In relation to learning mechanisms linked to start-up and initial absorption phase activities during the ISI period, although similar external knowledge acquisition mechanisms were present in both firms, they differed in terms of the variety of learning mechanisms they used (see Table 7.5): 31 mechanisms were present in USIMINAS, but only 12 in CSN. For example, USIMINAS sought to hire expertise from different backgrounds, particularly highly experienced steel engineers and managers to head operational units and steel experts to head top management positions. In contrast, CSN limited its intake to local and newly graduated engineers and technicians and only a few experienced engineers. Overseas training in USIMINAS involved a mix of short- and long-term courses, routine plant operations, innovative projects (e.g. research techniques for product development), technical visits, and observation. These activities covered a relatively large number of individuals.

In contrast, in CSN, these activities were limited to a group of engineers who were trained in routine plant operations. In the mid-1960s an ambitious learning mechanism was created in USIMINAS to scan the latest codified knowledge on steel technology and bring it into the firm (channeling of external codified knowledge). As one manager put it: "In 1966 we were in the middle of nowhere with an ambitious goal of becoming an internationally competitive steel firm. Bringing new knowledge into the firm, quickly and effectively, was crucial to meet that goal."[2] It was found that the technical

---

[2] In order to implement this learning process in USIMINAS, the technical information center (TIC) was structured. Far from a being a conventional library, TIC started as a group of 12 individuals recruited under criteria that included knowledge of foreign languages and aptitudes to search and disseminate knowledge. For more than 25 years TIC was led by the same metallurgical engineer who reported directly to the firm's president. By the late 1990s, it had become an indispensable learning process that stimulated and supported innovative activities in USIMINAS.

information center (TIC) also worked as a knowledge socialization process. This learning mechanism, based on "channeling of external codified knowledge," also had a second "face": a knowledge-sharing mechanism. This was implemented through the TIC by converting published technical papers into short texts that were written in a "journalistic way." These were widely distributed throughout the firm in order to reach employees at the lowest level in the plant. This contributed to (i) homogenizing the "language" used across the firm; and (ii) triggering group discussions and teamwork to carry out innovative activities, thereby "refreshing" their mindsets. However, a learning mechanism such as TIC was absent in CSN up to the late 1990s.

With respect to internal learning mechanisms (Table 7.5), 27 mechanisms were found in USIMINAS and only three in CSN. Although both firms were involved in project design and plant installation, USIMINAS had taken the lead in different project-engineering activities, avoiding full delegation to the Japanese suppliers. The involvement of CSN's employees with the American suppliers, however, was limited. In addition, during the 1940s and early 1950s CSN was delegating critical engineering activities to consultants rather than seeking to perform them independently. In contrast, USIMINAS engaged in systematic improvements in existing facilities through "capacity-stretching" efforts and deliberate manipulation of key production process parameters across different operational units. These practices were absent in CSN. As a result, individuals in CSN had a smaller variety of learning mechanisms with which to increase their understanding of the principles involved in the technology compared with USIMINAS's.

Expansion of USIMINAS and CSN during the ISI period

The evidence outlined above indicates that both USIMINAS and CSN engaged in the development of innovative technological capabilities over the conventional expansion phase. However, the manner and rate at which those capabilities were accumulated in the two companies were different. By the late 1980s, USIMINAS had accumulated intermediate and advanced capability for process and production organization within less than 30 years of plant start-up. In contrast, CSN, after more than 40 years, had accumulated capability in-between only basic and intermediate levels of innovation capability. In other words, CSN followed a slow and inconsistent accumulation path as opposed to that of USIMINAS. In particular, the differences are as follows.

PROCESS AND PRODUCTION ORGANIZATION CAPABILITY Within less than 30 years, USIMINAS was able to accumulate intermediate to advanced levels of innovative capability. In contrast, CSN, after about 43 years, had not moved beyond basic innovation capability for process and production organization.

Table 7.5. Overall assessment of key features of learning mechanisms in USIMINAS and CSN

Key features		Start-up and initial absorption during the ISI period		Expansion phase during the ISI period		Post-ISI period	
		USI (1956–1972)	CSN (1938–1953)	USI (1973–1989)	CSN (1954–1989)	USI (early 2000s)	CSN (early 2000s)
Overall variety	External learning mechanisms	31	12	42	23	46	34
	Internal learning mechanisms	27	3	39	4	45	27
	Totals	58	15	81	27	91	61
Intensity		the majority continuous	the majority intermittent	all continuous	the majority intermittent	all continuous	initially, the majority intermittent; later, the majority continuous
Functioning		the majority good	none good	the majority good	the majority poor	the majority excellent	the majority moderate/good

Source: Adapted and expanded from Figueiredo (2003).

In USIMINAS, the accumulation path was marked by continuous process improvements and permanent upgrading of organizational units. In contrast, in CSN, it was marked by scarce and intermittent process improvement efforts. Although CSN had built up organizational units that were similar to USIMINAS's, they barely engaged in continuous process and production organization improvements. By the late 1980s, USIMINAS had integrated its production, planning, and control (PPC) and process control systems, drawing on its own capabilities. At that time, CSN still had not accumulated the basic capability to develop its own automated systems. In addition, USIMINAS responded to the energy crises by engaging in additional process improvements. In contrast, although CSN might have had some concern about the effects of those crises on its performance, the concrete responses produced, in terms of innovative efforts on process improvements, were limited.

PRODUCT-CENTERED CAPABILITY USIMINAS engaged vigorously and continuously in the accumulation of capabilities to design and develop its own steels. On most occasions, it was pushed by top management's explicit corporate goals. In contrast, CSN engaged only intermittently in those types of activity. This may reflect the top management's inconsistency as far as the development of in-house innovative product capability was concerned. When USIMINAS had developed its "second-generation" steels drawing on its own capabilities, CSN was still engaging in the early stages of product development activities, which were preceded by some earlier intermittent projects. Thus, USIMINAS was able to accumulate, within less than 30 years, advanced innovation capability for products, while CSN took nearly 45 years to accumulate product capability at basic to intermediate levels only. In addition, USIMINAS could draw on its own basic routine process and product capabilities to have its new steels efficiently manufactured. In contrast, CSN's new steels were poorly manufactured, reflecting the incomplete accumulation of basic production-based capability for process and product capability.

In relation to external learning mechanisms associated with expansion activities during the ISI period, USIMINAS used 42 external knowledge-acquisition mechanisms, whereas CSN used 23 (Table 7.5). Although similar learning mechanisms were present in both firms, in USIMINAS most of them contained a wider number of mechanisms than those in CSN. For instance, while CSN only hired newly graduated or military engineers, USIMINAS sought to pull in more "project champions" from Nippon Steel, steel experts, and PhD engineers. In other words, USIMINAS pulled in more diverse and robust expertise than CSN. Additionally, USIMINAS engaged in a wider variety of mechanisms than CSN, for example, different types of overseas training, use of technical assistance, and interaction with suppliers and users.

In relation to internal knowledge acquisition, Table 7.5 shows that 39 learning mechanisms were present in USIMINAS and four in CSN. Both firms were engaged in routine plant operations. However, in USIMINAS, individuals were engaged in continuous equipment improvements, process and production organization, and a number of operators, technicians, and engineers had been trained overseas. In contrast, in CSN, the engagement of individuals in continuous improvement across the plant was limited. Their routine operations activities were also not supported by continuous training. In other words, USIMINAS's innovative pattern of "learning-by-doing" with "learning-before-doing" was absent in CSN. This suggests that in USIMINAS operational employees were in a better position to learn more about the principles underlying the technology than CSN's. This contributed to the strengthening of the existing routine operations capability in USIMINAS (basic and advanced). In contrast, it contributed to the incomplete accumulation of this type of capability in CSN.

Capability building during the post-ISI period: from the early 1990s

Although USIMINAS did not move into the accumulation of new levels of innovative capabilities, it was able to sustain, deepen, and routinize its intermediate to advanced capability levels for process and production organization within approximately 35 years. In contrast, after 50 years, CSN accumulated intermediate level of capability for products and for process and production organization. In parallel, over 50 years, CSN eventually completed the accumulation of basic and advanced levels of production-based capability for process and production organization and products.

PROCESS AND PRODUCTION ORGANIZATION CAPABILITY In response to the new conditions in Brazil in the early 1990s, USIMINAS engaged in a company-wide reorganization, involving, in particular: the creation of a technical division within each operational unit; greater integration between the operational units themselves, and between them and the production support units (research center, automation unit); and a review of the role of the metallurgical department to guarantee effective integration. In addition, USIMINAS had its quality system upgraded through the PAQ (Progama de Avanço de Qualidade—Quality Advance Program) implementation, leading to new certifications (e.g. ISO 9000 and QS 9000). The company also engaged in continuous improvement and routinization of its integrated automated process control and production, planning, and control (PPC) systems. These activities suggest a deepening of the intermediate level of innovation capability and advanced production-based capability for process and production organization. In response to its operational and financial crisis, the threat of closure, and the new set of conditions in Brazil in the early 1990s, CSN engaged vigorously, from 1990 to 1995, in a review of its routine production practices. The review involved the introduction of new tools to improve process and production organization (e.g. total quality management—TQM). Those efforts, however, were negatively affected from 1996 by: (i) the company being organized into "business units," resulting in the implementation of new tools in a non-integrated way; (ii) a reduction in top management's support for the TQM program. In contrast, USIMINAS was able to strengthen integration in the plant, achieving coordination across units to deliver products on a just-in-time (JIT) basis.

In contrast to USIMINAS, CSN did not have any organizational unit engaged in such integration and support for the operations units (e.g. the USIMINAS Metallurgical Dept). In addition, the Process Development Superintendency was closed down in CSN, preventing this unit from providing technical support for process improvement to the operational units. During the 1990s, USIMINAS was able to develop new automated systems in-house for PPC and process control. They contributed to increasing the integration between those two systems through the Automation Unit. It should be remembered that this type of integration has positive implications for operational performance. By the 1990s CSN had not developed any integrated automated systems for PPC and process control. Although in the 1990s the Information Technology Superintendency existed in CSN, this unit did not engage in continuous and significant systems development in the way the Automation Unit in USIMINAS had been doing since the 1970s. In addition, the evidence suggests that both USIMINAS and CSN reduced their process activities in their research centers, as described later in this chapter. However, while CSN made a dramatic reduction, USIMINAS kept the strategic activities of process research, permitting continuous support to the production units. In sum, within 35 years USIMINAS had sustained and routinized intermediate to advanced innovative capability for process and production organization. Slower than USIMINAS, it had taken CSN nearly 50 years to accumulate basic to intermediate capability for process and production organization.

PRODUCT-CENTERED CAPABILITY ACCUMULATION   In response to the opening up of Brazil's economy, new demands from users, and the world trend toward greater interaction with the automotive industry, USIMINAS engaged in continuous efforts, particularly in upgrading its existing quality system to meet international product quality standards; adding value to its products by upgrading their chemical and mechanical properties; interacting with users in product design, development, and application activities; and increasing market share through a consistent product strategy. Like USIMINAS, CSN sought to respond to these new conditions. However, it engaged in activities associated with capability for products at lower levels than USIMINAS. For example, CSN had built a basic product quality control system, while USIMINAS already had its system routinized. CSN had to re-engage in product development activities at basic to intermediate levels. In contrast, by the late 1990s USIMINAS was deepening innovative product activities at the advanced level. While USIMINAS had improved integration between the research center and the operations units for product development, CSN still had difficulties in improving this type of integration. Additionally, USIMINAS consistently pursued increased market share in the domestic automotive industry. In contrast, CSN entered the 1990s with a similar goal, but, from 1996, its product strategy became inconsistent. In sum, by the mid-1990s, within 35 years, USIMINAS had deepened and routinized its advanced innovation capability for products. Again, CSN had taken much longer to accumulate this type of intermediate to advanced innovation capability level.

In terms of external learning mechanisms during the post-ISI period, specifically during the 1990s, Table 7.5 shows that 46 external knowledge-acquisition mechanisms were present in USIMINAS and 34 in CSN. The increase in the variety of learning mechanisms in CSN suggests an improvement in its knowledge-acquisition processes in the 1990s in comparison to the 1970s–1980s period. However, this improvement was not enough to achieve the standard attained by USIMINAS. While in USIMINAS most learning processes had a diverse content of mechanisms, in CSN key learning processes were still absent (e.g. routinized overseas training before new technical activities). Additionally, it was not until the 1990s that shopfloor operators were included in overseas training in CSN, while in USIMINAS this had been in use since the 1960s.

Concerning internal learning, Table 7.5 shows that 45 learning mechanisms were present in USIMINAS and 27 in CSN. In USIMINAS the process of operating the plant following international efficiency standards had become routinized by the 1990s. This activity was influenced by training processes, with the implementation of the fourth version of USIMINAS's quality system that had started in the 1960s. This contributed to the deepening and sustaining of its routine capability (advanced) for process and production organization, product and equipment-related activities. In CSN in the 1990s, for the first time in its existence, concern about efficient operation spread across the plant through the implementation of the technology absorption group (TAG) and later the TQM training process—both of which were strongly supported by top management.[3] As a result, the way employees engaged in routine plant operations contributed to completing the accumulation of operational capabilities (basic and advanced) in CSN.

These two firms were able to accumulate innovation capabilities in a different manner and at different speeds. USIMINAS accumulated innovation capabilities that permitted it to approach a technological position close to the international frontier; however, the company did not reach the level attained by POSCO of South Korea. CSN, in turn, took more time than USIMINAS to

---

[3] TAG was an informal organizational arrangement created in late 1989 as a response to the financial crisis in CSN. Through this arrangement, top management sought to engage a large number of operators, technicians, and engineers in systematic improvements in process and production organization, products, and equipment-related activities.

accumulate innovation capabilities and to move toward the innovation frontier. However, CSN did not reach the same innovation level that had been
attained by USIMINAS.

7.4.2. Overtaking Incumbents to Achieve World-Leading Innovative Capability Building: Brazil's Forestry, Pulp, and Paper Industries

The study reported here examines a catch-up mode in which firms sought to
drive away from their existing technological trajectory at an *early stage* in the
development of their innovation capability in the natural resources-processing
industries. This involved a qualitative departure from the trajectory already
mapped out by earlier innovators, so opening up qualitatively different segments of the international technological frontier. Such a process is slightly
different from Lim and Lee's (2001) notion of a *path-creating catch-up mode*,
in which this only occurs *after* considerable trajectory-following innovation
has already taken place. The engagement of firms in this new trajectory
involved a combination of firm and government efforts across discontinuous
policy contexts. However, there was a high degree of *variability* in the "depths"
and speed of firms' innovation capability-building paths: from world-leading
to followers and laggards, as indicated in Table 7.6 below.

For the Brazilian firms examined here, use began to be made of pulp from
eucalyptus trees, something that firms in North American and Scandinavian
countries were not doing. Relatively early in the game, therefore, Brazilian
firms could not simply copy what the recognized industry leaders were doing.
They had to develop technologies suitable for their own distinctive operations.
Using different raw materials and developing effective ways to accomplish this
were innovations in any meaningful sense of the term.

The genesis of all these developments can be traced to the early 1920s.
During this period, Brazil experienced a growing demand for paper and a
progressively severe scarcity of pulp. Despite the rapid growth rates of the
paper industry in Brazil, by the late 1930s the participation of local raw
materials in the local paper industry was as low as 3 percent. From the early
1940s, the import restrictions imposed by external factors like World War II
and the Korean War stimulated industrial leaders to begin a campaign for
Brazil's self-sufficiency in pulp "to free the country from cyclic instability that
threatened growth of local pulp and paper industries and industrial development."[4] This prompted the Getulio Vargas government (1930–45) to implement measures that marked the beginning of protectionism and the ISI policy.

---

[4] Declaration issued by industrial leaders at that time. Found in archival records.

These events also triggered individual and organizational initiatives to search for new raw materials.

Drawing on the findings of previous experiments, by 1946 the firm Melhoramentos had achieved consistently positive results (paper surface and opacity) from using eucalyptus pulp to make tissue paper. Based on such results, the firm's top management decided to substitute the imported "aspen" pulp (*Populus sp*) with eucalyptus. The feasibility of eucalyptus as a raw material for pulp and paper production had been proved in the laboratory and some small-scale production had been achieved. However, Brazil lacked the technology (knowledge) to transform eucalyptus (e.g. *Eucalyptus saligna*) into an innovative, sustainable, and competitive raw material for large-scale pulp and paper production. Firms and government had to organize themselves to engage in this kind of innovation.

7.4.2.1. *Organizing for Innovation during the Initial Formal ISI Policy Context (1950s–1960s)*

This period was marked by two kinds of institutional and organizational effort. These were vital to build the knowledge bases that permitted firms to engage in a qualitative discontinuity of technological trajectory during the subsequent period. On the one hand, there was the formation of the institutional frameworks that took up the tasks of designing the policies that sought to stimulate forestry and pulp and paper firms' technological development in Brazil. These also involved the building of government-led research facilities and research-funding arrangements that were crucial to complementing firms' innovation capabilities. As firms lacked proper research capabilities, they built up a kind of collective external R&D arrangement that was implemented on the basis of an interaction between private and government facilities. On the other hand, there were intra-firm efforts to build up their own innovation capability base. These intra-firm capability-building efforts were crucial to absorb the knowledge generated through the interaction with the external R&D arrangements located in Brazil, but also abroad. In turn, as firms engaged in more sophisticated technological activities, they demanded specific inputs from government-owned education and research facilities.

In 1952, the National Economic Development Bank (BNDE) was created and became a key institution supporting investments in Brazil's infrastructure, industrial expansion, and firm-level technological efforts, especially in pulp and paper.[5] From the mid-1960s, BNDE conditioned its funding for the pulp

---

[5] BNDE was created in 1952 but it was not until 1956 that its structure was complete. It was created to develop project analyses and implement policies to support industrialization in Brazil by providing long-term funding to industry. It became the first institution in Brazil dedicated to long-term funding of infrastructure and industrial development.

Table 7.6. Number of sampled pulp and paper mills that have reached particular levels of capability for specific technical functions (by the end of fieldwork—December 2006)

Levels of technological capabilities	Forestry	Pulp	Paper
⬆️□	4 [57 percent]	4 [44 percent]	4 [36 percent]
(6) Innovation frontier	Alpha, Theta, Sigma-A, Delta	Alpha, Delta, Sigma-A, Sigma-B	Delta, Kappa, Sigma-A, Sigma-B
⬆️□ (5) Advanced innovation	6 [86 percent] Alpha, Theta, Sigma-A, Delta, Beta Kappa	6 [67 percent] Alpha, Delta, Sigma-A, Sigma-B, Gamma Kappa	9 [82 percent] Delta, Kappa, Sigma-A Sigma-B, Gamma, Zeta-B, Lambda, Epsilon, Zeta-A
⬆️□ (4) Intermediate innovation	7 [100 percent] Alpha, Theta, Sigma-A, Delta, Beta, Kappa, Zeta-A	8 [89 percent] Alpha, Delta, Sigma-A, Sigma-B, Gamma, Kappa, Beta, Theta	10 [91 percent] Delta, Kappa, Sigma-A, Sigma-B, Gamma, Zeta-B, Lambda, Epsilon, Zeta-A, Iota
⬆️□ (3) Basic innovation	7 [100 percent] Alpha, Theta, Sigma-A, Delta, Beta, Kappa, Zeta-A	9 [100 percent] Alpha, Delta, Sigma-A, Sigma-B, Gamma, Kappa, Beta, Theta, Zeta-A	11 [100 percent] Delta, Kappa, Sigma-A, Sigma-B, Gamma, Zeta-B, Lambda, Epsilon, Zeta-A, Iota, Theta

Production-based capabilities: capabilities to use existing technologies and production system

⬆️□ (2) Advanced innovation	All [100 percent]	All [100 percent]	All [100 percent]
⬆️□ (1) Basic operations	All [100 percent]	All [100 percent]	All [100 percent]

Note: For mills Zeta-A, Sigma-A, Gamma, and Epsilon (see source to Table 7.1), the capabilities they had accumulated under previous ownership were considered as "entry" capabilities in the period covered by our study.

Source: Derived from Figueiredo's empirical study.

and paper industries on the basis of them sourcing their own supply of wood from planted forests. This, in turn, was in line with the Forestry Law, an explicit policy of the Brazilian federal government, in 1966, to stimulate reforestation activities. This also sought to stimulate the diffusion of eucalyptus. Such incentives involved a reduction of 50 percent in the income tax of individuals and firms.[6] The Brazilian Institute for Forestry Development (known as IBDF) was created in 1967 to implement such a policy.[7]

Such measures influenced the scope of firms' activities (upstream integration) and, consequently, their engagement in systematic reforestation efforts (e.g. Kappa, Theta-Forestry, and Delta). These projects led to an increased demand for high-quality seeds and for qualified human resources in silviculture activities. However, there were significant hurdles: until the mid to early 1960s the science of silviculture was incipient in Brazil. Also firms also did not have the research capabilities in forestry associated with sustainable and feasible large-scale pulp and paper based on eucalyptus. In order to overcome these obstacles a series of initiatives were taken, as illustrated briefly below.

From the mid-1950s, the firm Kappa engaged in systematic experiments on the use of eucalyptus for large-scale pulp and paper production.[8] Although some foreign laboratories were already producing eucalyptus pulp, the existing scientific literature still classified such raw material as improper for printing and office paper manufacturing. The son of the firm's owner engaged in a research project to challenge such findings. Despite the innovative efforts made, firms had very few (if any) capabilities to carry out the necessary more sophisticated activities based on systematic R&D. Additionally, Brazil lacked qualified human resources in forestry innovation. This triggered a demand for specialized professionals to undertake forestry research.

Responding to firms' demands, in the early 1960s the College of Agriculture of the University of São Paulo (Esalq) began to offer degree courses in forestry (from undergraduate level to PhDs).[9] It enlarged its postgraduate programs with the support of government agencies for the provision of studentships and laboratories for pilot production of pulp and paper.[10] This can be considered a kind of indirect industrial policy. Inspired by the model of the Forestry School

---

[6] This was formalized under Federal Law 5106 of September 1966.

[7] This policy was formally implemented from 1967 to 1987. Between 1967 and 1986 reforestation projects associated with this policy covered 6.2 million hectares, of which 52 percent were based on eucalyptus. From 1967 to 1987 eucalyptus reforestation projects increased by 14.1 percent annually on average, while pine-based projects increased by 13.8 percent.

[8] This firm started up in 1941 on the initiative of an entrepreneur and immigrant, Mr Leon Feffer. His older son was given the task of searching for a solution to the raw material problem.

[9] This school originally started up in 1901. In 1934 it was integrated into the University of São Paulo.

[10] National providers of scholarships included the National Council for Scientific and Technological Development (CNPq) and the Brazilian postgraduate agency (Capes). Funding for the building of laboratories came from the State of São Paulo Research Foundation (Fapesp).

of North Carolina University, Esalq began to structure its research activities to meet the industry's demands.[11]

During the early 1960s some companies began to request studies and experiments from Esalq to help speed up their forestry development activities. In October 1967, a meeting involving 13 firms, Esalq, and the IBDF generated the guidelines for a research program on forestry improvement. In December 1967, a meeting involving 18 firms led to the creation of the Forestry Science and Research Institute (known as IPEF). Its initial focus was to carry out research into raw material of high quality and competitive cost for Brazil's pulp and paper industries. The associated firms defined the research guidelines for IPEF in order to meet their own needs. The main research goal focused on increasing eucalyptus productivity (which in 1968 was around 24m³/ha/year). This was pursued via a search for new species to provide seeds.

By the late 1960s the emergence of Aracruz (Alpha), on the initiative of 12 entrepreneurs, represented a decisive thrust in the push into the commercial success of the new technological trajectory. Aracruz began its eucalyptus plantation program in the south-eastern state of Espírito Santo in 1967. Initially, Aracruz considered *Eucalyptus grandis*, *E. Saligna*, *E. urophylla*, and *E. Alba* as the most suitable species. Aracruz's forestry business was built up on the basis of eucalyptus plantations using seeds produced by Fepasa (the railroad company in Rio Claro, São Paulo state), where the forestry scientist Mr Navarro had carried out the earliest experiments in the 1920s. However, there were problems of uncontrolled hybridization and high variability in growth rates, stem forms, and wood properties indicating inadequate sources of seeds. Consequently, the *E. Saligna* faced susceptibility to trunk rot, whereas the *E. Alba* showed variations in physical or biochemical characteristics (phenotypical). Their average productivity was no higher than 22 to 26 m³/ha/year. These problems prompted Aracruz to move from vegetative propagation, based on seeds, into tree improvement and clonal programs.[12] To tackle these problems in a more systematic manner, Aracruz had to set up, as early as 1968, its forestry research center.

7.4.2.2. Achieving a Qualitative Discontinuity in Technological Trajectory during the ISI Policy Context (1970s–1980s)

While the 1970s in Brazil were marked by macroeconomic growth, the 1980s were blighted by a mix of recession, hyperinflation, and a sequence of failed macroeconomic stabilization plans. Indeed, while in the 1960s and 1970s the Brazilian economy experienced huge investments in infrastructure and in basic industries, during the 1980s such investments were severely reduced.

---

[11] In addition to Esalq, there also were two other universities that had been offering forestry studies: the Federal Universities of Viçosa (UFV) and Paraná (UFPR).

[12] See also Campinhos (1999) and Evans and Turnbull (2004).

This was accompanied by general industrial stagnation. During the 1970s, under the National Development Plan (1975–9), Brazil achieved self-sufficiency in pulp and paper. Despite the economic stagnation of the 1980s, pulp and paper production grew by 3.5 percent annually on average and paper and paper exports grew by 17.2 percent annually on average.

The 1970–80 period in Brazil was marked by innovations based on clonal forestry such as macro- and micro-cuttings, tissue culture, and clonal deployment.[13] Firms like Aracruz took the lead in introducing new vegetative propagation techniques. In parallel, firms continued to improve their process and production organization activities and process efficiency at the level of mills.

From the early 1970s on, Aracruz began to perfect its own genetic improvement program based on clonal forestry to increase productivity in its eucalyptus pulpwood plantations. By combining strategies of sexual and asexual propagation, Aracruz's research indicated that gains in volume production and wood quality could be achieved using hybrid clones (e.g. *E. grandis* x *E. urophylla*).[14] In 1979 Aracruz decided to gradually replace its plantations derived from seeds with clonal plantations. Cloning enabled Aracruz to use the results of its selection and breeding program. Aracruz initially selected 5,000 trees from a 36,000 ha plantation, of which 150 clones were identified as potentially suitable. Only 31 of the very best were used in the plantation program. By 1979, Aracruz first commercial clonal plantation with 1,000 ha had been established; by 1989 it had evolved to 15,000 ha. By 1987 Aracruz's annual production of cuttings was 16.8 million. As a result of this cloning strategy, Aracruz's eucalyptus productivity went up to 45 m^3/ha/year.[15]

Aracruz pioneered the introduction of the rooting stem-cutting on an industrial scale. The company was able to propagate clones that were resistant to the feared fungus that caused canker in eucalyptus plantations. In 1984, nearly 17 years after having started its research activities, Aracruz achieved international recognition by being awarded the Marcus Wallenberg Prize (Sweden).[16] Consequently, the mass production of clonally propagated

[13] Clonal plantations offer a number of advantages compared to those developed with seedlings: (i) cloning enables genetic gains from selection and breeding to be captured quickly; (ii) it is a cost-effective way of using hybrids (e.g. *Eucalyptus urophyllax* x *E. grandis*); (iii) it permits easier use of desirable characteristics such as pulp yields and disease resistance; (iv) it produces a uniform material for processing in the production process. However, such benefits are only fully obtained if there is integrated planning and implementation of plantation strategies, including tree breeding, clonal testing, operational propagation, and clonal deployment. See Evans and Turnbull (2004).

[14] Sexual propagation involves the exchange of genetic material between two parent trees, while in asexual reproduction, the new plants are genetically exact copies or clones of a single parent tree.

[15] See also Ikemori (1990); Evans and Turnbull (2004).

[16] Established in 1980 in Sweden, under the Marcus Wallenberg Foundation, this is a highly respected prize that seeks to encourage and stimulate path-breaking scientific achievements

planting stock soon diffused to other firms in Brazil (by the late 1980s, Delta's production of cuttings had reached10 million/year).

However, the rooting stem-cutting technology presented its own drawbacks such as an accelerated maturation process causing rapid loss of rooting predisposition and alterations of root system architecture causing root deformation (De Assis, 2001).[17] This prompted the company to upgrade its forestry R&D center, to strengthen links with local universities, and to begin to build partnerships with cutting-edge international research institutes. The organizational arrangement involving IPEF and firms proved decisive for progress in Brazil's forestry between 1969 and the 1975. However, in the late 1970s the quantity of seeds produced was not sufficient to meet the ever-growing demand.

Additionally, the industry put pressure on the government to improve the regulation of imported seeds and suspicious reforestation projects that benefited from the federal incentives. As a result, in 1977 the whole institutional framework relating to the pulp and paper industry was restructured. An interorganizational arrangement was created to control for the quality of seeds and to issue certifications of planted areas. The newly created Brazilian Agricultural Research Corporation (Embrapa)[18] took on responsibility for the National Program of Forestry Research, incorporating previously separate programs. In 1984 Embrapa created the Working Group for Forestry Genetic Improvement whose objectives were to issue guidelines for the use of genetic material, to create procedures for experiments, and to organize scientific and technical meetings. In the 1980s there was a division of labor between Embrapa and IPEF in terms of research activities: while Embrapa took over the genetic improvement programs, IPEF dedicated itself to the new research needs relating to forestry handling and exploitation as firms' plantations reached the stage of cuttings.

By the late 1980s, 20 years after the first systematic forestry research activities had begun, Brazil had consolidated its position as a major exporter of pulp and paper derived from innovative eucalyptus forestry. At the same time, industrial policy based on the ISI regime was weakened. In 1987 the government ended the fiscal incentive for the plantation of forests, which had begun in 1966, and played a major role in stimulating forestry development in Brazil. Some firms realized that, because of their specific forestry characteristics and research needs, they could no longer draw on the collective R&D

which contribute significantly to broadening knowledge and to technical development within the fields of importance to forestry and pulp and paper industries.

[17] This is why new technologies, including rooting of micro- or mini-cuttings, have improved rooting potential, rooting speed, and root system quality, have reduced costs, and have shown their potential to substitute for root stem cuttings (see De Assis, 2001; Evans and Turnbull, 2004).

[18] Embrapa was created in April 1973.

arrangements around IPEF and Embrapa, but needed to strengthen their own research capabilities. But not all firms did so. Conversely, in 1983 a firm such as Aracruz had already taken the initiative of building its own R&D center dedicated to pulp and paper activities. This added to the forestry research unit that had been built in the late 1960s. In the late 1980s, the creation of the firm Votorantim Celulose e Papel (VCP) (Sigma-A and Sigma-B here), with support from BNDES, represented another major thrust to expand research activities in forestry and pulp and paper in Brazil.

7.4.2.3. Innovation Capability Building in the Market-Led Policy Context of the 1990s

For the pulp and paper industries, the shocks induced by trade liberalization and macroeconomic stabilization in the 1990s were worsened by a global fall in paper prices. Large paper firms, like Delta, almost collapsed and had to radically re-focus their scope. Additionally, the strategic collaboration between government and the forestry and pulp and paper industries, which had marked the industrial policy process during the 1950s–1980s period, was replaced by a kind of "principal-agent" type of policy. In this type of fruitless policy-making, industry is kept at arm's length and governments issues directives (see Rodrik, 2004).

Despite the discontinuity in the institutional framework in the early 1990s, firms like Alpha, Delta, Sigma-A, Sigma-B, Kappa, and Theta (forestry) showed resilience by intensifying their efforts in innovation capability building. First, greater attention was given to innovation capability building in pulp and paper-making processes and products. These were based on the introduction of changes in chemical and equipment-related processes in order to incorporate innovations that had been implemented earlier upstream in the forestry segment. These, in turn, impacted the firms' innovative (and competitive) performance. For instance, because of the progress that firms such as Alpha, Delta, Sigma-A, and Sigma-B had made in genetic improvements in the upstream forestry segment, the wood that was used in their production processes required fewer chemicals for pulping and bleaching (e.g. wood with a reduced lignin content) and, consequently, fewer liquid effluents. It is estimated that there is an economic gain of around US$1 million annually from each percentage point of lignin reduction in wood, in the first phase of the pulp-making process alone, for a mill producing 300,000 tonnes per year (de Assis, 2001).

Second, from the early 1990s pulp and paper firms realized that in order to secure competitive positions on the world market, they had to respond proactively to growing pressures from regulators and society relating to environmental concerns (see Dalcomuni, 1997). Consequently, intense efforts were made by most of firms in the case study to accumulate environmentally related innovative capabilities. By 1992 the firm Alpha had adopted elementally chlorine-free (ECF) and totally chlorine-free (TCF) processes. This was implemented at the same time as leading firms in Canada and Scandinavia. However, Alpha went further, creating a variant in the TCF process, with a much lower level of absorbable organic halogens (AOX). This process became known as Alpha chlorine-free (ACF) and was patented in 1997. One year later, the firms Sigma-A and Sigma-B also created their own versions of the TCF process. By 1995, 10 of the 13 firms researched here had already changed their processes to TCF.

Third, firms concomitantly intensified their efforts on forestry R&D capability accumulation. For instance, new techniques for cloning eucalyptus were developed such as mini- and micro-cutting. Compared to stem-cuttings (macro-cuttings), the rooting of micro- or mini-cuttings improves rooting potential, rooting speed, root system quality, and reduces costs. These technologies are very similar in concept and operational procedures. The main difference is in the origin of the initial propagules. Micro-cuttings use the apices obtained from micro-propagated plantlets, whereas the mini-cutting is based on the rooting of auxiliary sprouts from rooted stem-cuttings (see Evans and Turnbull, 2004).

In the early 1990s the development of micro-cutting technology for eucalyptus contributed significantly to the progress in systems for large-scale production of vegetative propagules *ex vitro*. Originally, the system was based on mini-hedges established through rooted mini-cuttings, grown in small containers. The idea of hydroponics, an operational indoor system based on drip-fertigated sand beds, was introduced in Brazil through projects led by researchers like E. Higashi and colleagues. Later, researchers in the firm Alpha (see Campinhos et al., 2000) used the same concept in a highly efficient intermittent flooding system, where containers of the mini-stumps became immersed in a nutritive solution for fertigation. These systems began to produce annually about 25,000 propagules of *E. grandis* x *E. urophylla* hybrids compared with 120 propagules m^{-2} for conventional clone banks or hedges.

7.4.2.4. Innovation Capability Building under the "New Industrial Policy" of the Early 2000s

During the 2000–7 period, especially from 2003, the Lula administration sought to re-establish the role of government policy in Brazil's economic development. This was achieved through the design and implementation in 2004 of the Industrial, Technological and Foreign Trade Policy. However, such "industrial policy" was conceived in a conventional manner: it involved the selection of four sectors (micro-electronics, software, pharmaceutical, and capital goods) to receive special funding and related support. The problem is that government bureaucrats do not have enough knowledge to take an *ex-*

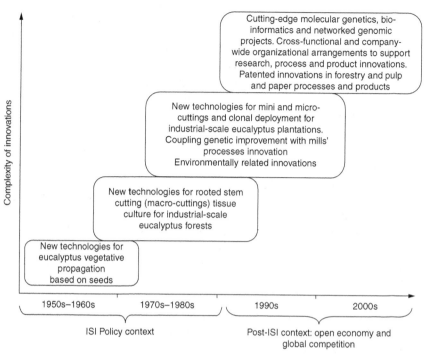

Fig. 7.1. Evolution of the pulp and paper case-study firms' successful innovative performance

Source: Derived from Paulo Figueiredo's empirical work.

ante stand on the industrial activities that should be promoted (Rodrik, 2004). The policy also contradicted Brazil's large industrial diversification as it overlooked other important sectors.

In 2007 a new industrial policy, the Productive Development Plan, began to be designed on the basis of the selection of 24 industrial sectors and a number of specific goals. For the pulp and paper sector, the goal was to keep its position among the world's five largest producers and increase R&D investments to 2 percent of sales. However, again, the principle was based on a "principal-agent" and "picking-winners" type of policy. Nonetheless, during the early 2000s leading firms sought to deepen and expand their genomic research capabilities in order to keep up their internationally innovative performance. The new direction in capability accumulation—along the eucalyptus-based technological trajectory—was reflected in the firms' innovative performance by the early 2000s. This involved different kinds of innovation *cumulatively implemented* by some of the firms in terms of new technologies, new processes and products, starting in the upstream forestry segment and moving, cumulatively and additively, into the pulp and paper areas, across different policy regimes (see Figure 7.1).

For instance, from 2001–4 the firms Sigma-A, Sigma-B, Kappa, and two other firms jointly undertook the large-scale ForEST research project (Eucalyptus Genome Sequencing Project Consortium), funded by the State of São Paulo Research Foundation. Drawing on DNA micro-arrays and bio-informatics, this project identified about 15,000 genes via the sequencing of approximately 100,000 ESTs (expressed sequence tags). It led to the development of a technology that permitted the identification of the genes involved in wood genetic control. This, in turn, led to new improvements in the chemical properties of the pulp and paper-making processes of those firms involved in the project (see also Grattapaglia, 2004).

Another large-scale research, the Genolyptus Project—Brazilian Network of Eucalyptus Genomics Research—was implemented from 2002 to 2008. The initiative involved 13 firms in the forestry, pulp and paper industries (among them Alpha, Kappa, Beta, Gamma, Delta, Theta, Sigma-A, and Sigma-B) and seven universities, under the coordination of Embrapa. This group managed to persuade the Brazilian Ministry of Science and Technology to fund the project. One of the novelties of this project is the intensity, refinement, and comprehensiveness of efforts directed at field experiments to generate the structure of phenotypes needed to study the functions of genes. Additionally, by adopting a multidisciplinary approach, this multiple knowledge-based project involves researchers from genetics, biochemistry, molecular biology, breeding, statistics, phytopathology, wood technology, as well as industrial process engineers (see Grattapaglia, 2004).

Based on a pre-competitive design, this project has been advancing molecular breeding in eucalyptus. It is based on building a suite of genomics, field, and information resources to discover, sequence, map, validate, and understand the underlying variation of genes and genomic regions of economic importance in eucalyptus, with a focus on wood and disease resistance and its implications for the pulp and paper industries in Brazil. By doing this, Brazil became one of the few countries to undertake cutting-edge eucalyptus genomic research based on a nationwide biotechnology network.

During the 2000s, the firms with higher capability levels began to pay greater attention to the organizational dimension of capabilities to support innovations, especially to link their advances achieved in forestry with innovative activities in pulp and paper-making processes. Specifically, such efforts aimed at integrating the design of the biology of trees with the requirements of production processes and end-users. Organizationally, such efforts involved reconfigurations of existing R&D and non-R&D arrangements (e.g. in Alpha, Kappa, Delta, Sigma-A, Sigma B) and the creation of cross-functional, company-wide, and inter-disciplinary committees and dedicated teams to tackle innovative projects. As a researcher from one of the firms described:

During the 1980s and early 1990s our research focus was on wood itself. Now [2000s] our research seeks to find genetic materials that add new value to our pulp and paper products and ensure financial return to the company. At the moment we undertake a project based on eight different genetic materials with implications for wood density and innovations in processes phases like pulping, bleaching, and physical-mechanical properties of the bleached pulp. By the time we finish this project, we will be able to match the features of wood production with the needs of specific paper markets like printing or tissue.

In 2002 the firms Sigma-A and Sigma-B reorganized their R&D units into the Center for Pulp Technological Development to integrate activities that had been operating separately: research, quality, and technical assistance. Interviews suggested that by combining these different knowledge bases, the company sought to speed up product development projects to improve performance. For instance, in 2005 this unit designed software based on a complex set of equations, to calculate the economic value of a clone, allowing the firm to choose the best clone for specific sites. In 2002, the firm Delta reconfigured its research center based on a review of routines and procedures, documentation, and analysis processes. Drawing on its biotechnology capabilities, in 2005, this firm co-developed with Sadia, a large Brazilian exporter of chilled and frozen food, a "water-barrier package" that increased the safety of packed frozen food. From 2003 up to the fieldwork in 2007, Delta had been ranked as the first and second most innovative supplier of Tetra-Pak worldwide. By 2004, Alpha had obtained nearly 30 patents and by the time of the fieldwork, had 17 patents under analysis and was strengthening its intellectual property system.

7.4.2.5. *The Experience of the Natural Resource-Processing Sectors in Long-Term Perspective*

Scrutiny of the paths of capability building over the lifetime of these firms in the steel and pulp and paper industries in Brazil reflects the variability in the manner and speed of capability accumulation. For instance, of the two scrutinized steel firms, USIMINAS was able to approach international innovation levels more rapidly, while CSN did so much later. Neither firm, however, moved far enough to reach the innovation frontier level, not even USIMINAS. In contrast, among the pulp and paper firms, only four of them were able to reach world-leading innovation levels, while others were able to approach the innovation frontier level. Some of them, however, did not move beyond the basic to intermediate capability levels. In general terms, the highly successful pulp and paper firms took more time than the steel firms to accumulate innovation capabilities. However, the former were able to accumulate world-leading innovation capability levels. Table 7.7 summarizes the

	ISI policy context (1950s–1980s)			Post-ISI policy context: open economy and global competition (1990s–2000s)		
Innovation capability levels	Plus nothing else	Plus firms' 'proactive' innovation capability-building strategies	Plus other government-originated direct influences on firms followed by firms' responses	Plus nothing else	Plus firms' innovation capability-building strategies	Plus other government-originated direct influences on firms followed by firms' responses
Innovation frontier						Alpha Delta Kappa Theta (forestry)
Advanced innovation			Alpha Delta Kappa	Gamma Zeta-B Lambda		USIMINAS
Intermediate innovation		Theta (pulp) Iota Beta Gama Lambda Zeta-B Epsilon	USIMINAS	Iota Theta (paper) Beta		CSN
Basic innovation		Theta (paper) Zeta-A	CSN			

Fig. 7.2. Summarized relationship between industrial policy and innovation capability building in natural resources and process-intensive firms in Brazil

Source: Derived from Figueiredo's empirical work.

different rates of capability accumulation in the steel and pulp and paper firms.

Indeed, individual firms' responses differed across the two samples (pulp and paper), across mills of the same sector, and across specific technical functions within mills in terms of the direction and speed and timing of capability development. This, in turn, seems to reflect the specific learning strategies of each firm. However, these were not linear paths of capabilities accumulation. There were qualitative discontinuities in these transitions, not only technically, but in terms of the organizational composition of capabilities for diverse activities.

In the case of the forestry and pulp and paper industries, early in the process of capability building, Brazilian firms were constrained by several factors as they sought to break with the existing technological trajectory. This led to a kind of catch-up path that was slightly different from what is normally referred to in the related literature (e.g. Lim and Lee, 2001). However, not all firms achieved this type of technological catch-up successfully and some failed to gain a "new" technological trajectory. Firms' paths were marked by variability in terms of the extent and speed of innovation capability building. While a few cases were able to attain a world-leading capability level, others moved toward the innovation frontier and some remained far behind it. Moving beyond common generalizations that suggest a twofold and simplistic distinction between ISI versus open and global competition based on "ISI

Table 7.7. Differences in the rates of technological capability accumulation between USIMINAS (1962–1997) and CSN (1946–early 2000s) (approximate number of years needed to attain each level and type of capability)

	Steelmaking firms				Forestry, pulp and paper firms		
	Capabilities for process and production organization		Capabilities for product-centered activities		Forestry	Pulp	Paper
	USIMINAS	CSN	USIMINAS	CSN			
Total: [(A + B + C + D) + E]	35	35	35	50	*57*	*57*	*55*
(E) World-leading (innovation frontier)	Not attained	Not attained	Not attained	Not attained	4	3	3
Sub-total: (A + B + C + D)	35	50	35	50	*53*	*54*	*52*
(D) Advanced innovation	5	Not attained	10	Not attained	5	4	7
(C) Intermediate innovation	5	5	10	5	4	5	8
(B) Basic innovation	15	5	5	5	4	5	10
(A) Production-based (basic and advanced)	10	40	10	40	40	40	27

Source: Derived and expanded from Figueiredo (2002, 2003) and Figueiredo et al. (2008).

versus non-ISI," the findings here suggest that there was much going on in these two broad periods, as summarized in Figure 7.2 above.

The findings here do not support the view that the ISI policy context constrained the depth of innovative capability building at the "intermediate" (incremental) level of innovation, thus setting up a long-lasting discontinuity in the deepening of innovation capability in Brazil. Indeed, the end of the ISI policy regime may have been destructive for some sectors in Brazil (e.g. automotive, micro-electronics), thus imposing a discontinuity on the accumulation of innovative capability during the main phases of the ISI context, a view advocated in Reinhardt and Peres (2000), Ocampo (2001), and Cimoli and Katz (2003). Neither do the findings here support the "inherent discontinuity."

Indeed, firms that were able to cross micro-level and macro-level discontinuities successfully did not rely solely on the ISI policy regimes, nor on the external R&D arrangements that emerged during the 1960s and 1970s. Instead they engaged in deliberate and consistent building of their knowledge bases and innovation capability to engage in innovation activities.

7.5. ASSEMBLED-PRODUCTS CASE-STUDY

7.5.1. Privatization, the Transition from ISI, and the Accumulation of Technological Capabilities in the Brazilian Aerospace Sector: The Case of Embraer

7.5.1.1. Introduction

The aerospace industry represents an iconic "high-technology" sector and, as such, has been the scene of rapid movement in the technological frontier over the last half century. The capital costs and technological complexities involved in participating in the sector have meant that, for the most part, it has remained the preserve of a handful of the established industrial economies with much of the world's production being concentrated in Europe and North America. The emergence of Brazil as a major player in the global aerospace industry represents a notable exception to this trend.

The purpose of what follows is to shed some light on Embraer's accumulation of technological capabilities and the interplay between this and the policy environment. Our concern will be to examine the processes by which Embraer, in certain areas of activity, has now attained world-leading capabilities, moving from behind the international technological frontier to the frontier itself. The analysis will gauge the extent to which this process can be characterized as a sequential progression from basic, to intermediate, to advanced and, finally, to world-leading capabilities. Additionally, the discussion considers the role of privatization, the transition from ISI, internationalization, and inter-firm linkages for the path of Embraer's capabilities accumulation.

7.5.1.2. The Accumulation of Technological Capabilities in the ISI Period (1969–c.1990)

The development of Embraer's technological capabilities has followed an unusual path, the determination of which has been affected by deliberate policy initiatives, variations in market demand, and changes in the nature of supplier relationships. The roots of Embraer's capabilities can be traced to the Instituto de Pesquisa e Desenvolvimento (IPD), an agency which sprang from the Aeronautics Technological Center (CTA) and Instituto Tecnológico de Aeronáutica—Aeronautical Technological Institute (ITA) in the 1950s. The formation of the IPD reflected a long-held national desire to gain competence in aircraft design and construction. Whereas the policy-makers' original vision had been to gain a full range of capabilities (basic, intermediate, and advanced) across the whole range of aircraft technologies (Cassiolato et al., 2002), the financial, practical, and technical difficulties of this approach soon determined a more circumscribed strategy.

Thus, the emphasis of the IPD centered on the design of airframes, with the result that critical, high value-added sub-systems (especially engines, hydraulic systems, and avionics) would remain the province of specialized (mainly US) suppliers such as Collins and Pratt and Witney (Silva, 1999). Consequently, it is important to recognize that the Embraer's strategy was, from the very start, biased toward airframe and systems integration specialization. In this respect, its approach held (and continues to hold) much in common with its peers in the industry such as Bombardier, Airbus, and Boeing. However, as Frischtak (1994) points out, Embraer's trajectory was unusual compared with its emerging counterparts. This is because Embraer's capabilities were not acquired as part of a more conventional process of progression from maintenance activity to assembly of imported components to manufacturing under license. Instead, the capability to design and manufacture airframes was established from the very beginning thanks to the efforts of the IPD.

The IPD's first major project involved the design and development of a robust twin-propeller short-range transport, the Bandeirante. This program, initiated in the 1960s, was aimed at meeting Brazil's particular air transportation need for a rugged aircraft, capable of transporting personnel and cargo, operating from short airstrips with high reliability and low maintenance costs. The Brazilian Air Force (the FAB) were key customers, but the aircraft was also designed to serve civilian makers both at home and overseas. As indicated previously, the focus of the design and manufacturing efforts centered on the airframe and it was here that technological capabilities needed to be accumulated.

While, by the standards of the time, the Bandeirante was behind the frontier—being neither pressurized nor jet propelled—in terms of the airframe design, the task that the IPD and the CTA had set themselves was exceptionally ambitious. Whereas many emerging enterprises might have established basic design capabilities (such as minor adaptations of existing designs) as a precursor to gaining intermediate capabilities (typically through the licensing of new technologies and/or reverse engineering) and then advanced capabilities (product innovation and related R&D), the Bandeirante team proceeded directly to designing and testing an entire airframe while also acting as systems integrators so as to facilitate the inclusion of avionic, hydraulic, and engine systems (Silva, 1999). Thus, from the very start the objective was to develop and deploy advanced capabilities. This atypical trajectory (reminiscent in many respects of pioneer rather than modern aerospace manufacturers) could only have succeeded provided a pre-existing R&D infrastructure was in place. As we have seen, the creation of the IPD and the CTA in the 1950s ensured that this was the case.

While advanced capabilities were attained by the late 1960s in terms of product design, Silva (1999) points out that the same could not be said for process technologies. Fabrication of prototypes (the first flew in 1968) was achieved through traditional craft methods and the facility for serial production had not been established. The challenge of transition to full-scale aircraft manufacturer would fall not to the IPD but, rather, to a specially created enterprise, Embraer. The initial presence of a fully realized product design capability in contrast with the absence of a manufacturing capability represents another atypical feature of this case.

The creation of Embraer as a state-owned industrial enterprise in 1969 represented an attempt to capitalize on Brazil's hard-won airframe design capabilities through the commercialization and serial production of IPD's designs. As might be expected, the launch of Embraer required substantial financial support from the state (Hira and De Oliveira, 2007) and involved the transfer of key personnel from the IPD and the CTA (Silva, 1999). Like these institutes, Embraer was located in São José dos Campos in São Paulo state. In contrast to the capabilities accumulation strategy of the IPD, that of Embraer would place relatively more emphasis on the establishment of relationships with foreign suppliers and technology licensors.

As indicated previously, Embraer's first challenge lay in putting the CPD-developed Bandeirante into full-scale production. As Silva (1999) points out, the difficulties involved in acquiring and implementing the relevant process technologies were very significant. Some idea of the scale of these problems is given by the fact that five years separated the first successful flight of the Bandeirante in 1968 and its entry into production in 1973. The delay experienced here is perhaps not surprising when one considers the fact that the IPD, Embraer's predecessor, never prioritized operational capabilities, its mission being to master airframe design and the basic principles of systems integration. At the same time, Embraer, unlike its European and North American counterparts, had no track record in serial aircraft production. Given the enormous learning opportunity presented to the latter through mass serial production (not least through World War II), Embraer had much distance to make up. The problem was only exacerbated by the fact that Brazil had only recently entered into mass production of technologically complex goods and, as a consequence, there was little domestic outside experience on which to draw. It can be argued that the emergence of Embraer as a corporate rather than research-only entity was a way of addressing this operational capabilities gap.

Faced with the pressure to put the Bandeirante into production, Embraer sought to draw on the experience of foreign producers, signing an agreement with Italy's Aeromacchi (Frischtak, 1994). The Italian enterprise had already associated itself with Embraer following an agreement the latter signed to produce a jet fighter, the Xavante, under license. As a result of the licensing agreement and resulting personnel transfers from Italy, Embraer was able to absorb "critical production knowledge in tooling, parts manufacture, tracing technology, assembly of planes, organization of procurement of materials, quality control, technical documentation and organization of assembly lines" (Ramamurti, 1987: 185). Further basic operational capability in process technologies was acquired through two further agreements signed with Northrop and Piper, both of the US. The Northrop agreement involved Embraer producing vertical fins, rudders, wings, and belly pylons for F5 aircraft ordered by the FAB. Through these arrangements, Embraer acquired further capabilities in chemical milling, metal to metal and honeycomb bonding, and, of great importance later on, composite materials (Frischtak, 1994).

The Piper agreement was less ambitious in scope initially since it involved Embraer assembling light aircraft kits imported from the USA. As time went by, Embraer was able to refine and upgrade the process technologies which had been transferred, allowing improvements in production rates, product quality, and flexibility in the face of fluctuations in market demand. Frischtak (1994) provides a detailed case study of these processes in operation in the case of the Brasília twin-prop pressurized transport aircraft. The case study (based on estimation of learning curves) establishes how incremental learning-by-doing, in conjunction with deliberate innovation efforts, pushed Embraer to the industry frontier of productivity in fuselage production by the 1980s. Thus, in the operational sphere, Embraer had, prior to privatization, attained advanced capabilities and the productivity performance figures to match. Unlike its early product designs, however, attainment of these capabilities had relied critically on technology transfer and subcontracting agreements with foreign enterprises.

Just as Embraer deliberately set out to acquire operational capabilities in the 1970s and 1980s, this was also true in the case of innovative capabilities relating to product design. The challenge here was to move on from the behind-the-frontier technologies embodied in the non-pressurized Bandeirante to the close-to-frontier technologies represented by later types such as the pressurized turboprop EMB 120 Brasília and the AMX fighter jet. As with the Bandeirante, in its product innovation and design efforts Embraer confined itself to the airframe, leaving propulsion and avionics systems to outside, US suppliers. This allowed the new aircraft to incorporate elements of the then emerging (and now commonplace) fly-by-wire systems. The key innovative challenge facing Embraer was to manage the transition from the design of non-pressurized to pressurized cabins. This ultimately successful, though long drawn-out effort (Silva, 1999) represented the attainment of advanced product innovation capabilities in an area of aerospace at, rather than behind, the frontier. Adding to Embraer's difficulties during the development phase of the 120 (the first half of the 1980s) was the financial and fiscal crisis afflicting Brazil. Rather than rely on state aid, the 120 program was realized using funds borrowed from commercial banks (Frischtak, 1994). The experience gained in engaging in private sector-funded advanced product innovation activity was to prove valuable in the post-privatization period.

The AMX sub-sonic fighter jet project also represented an attempt to enter the production of products closer to (if not actually on) the technological frontier. Despite Embraer's considerable experience, by the early 1980s (when design and development began), the technological discontinuities between passenger transports and fighter jets meant that a traditional in-house design approach was simply not feasible. For this reason Embraer entered partnership with two Italian enterprises, Aeritalia, and long-time collaborator Aeromacchi. The AMX project (which has seen some 200 aircraft built) enabled Embraer to gain capability in fast jet design, critical aerodynamic performance, and integration of weapons systems. The experience gained in jet design with the AMX was put to use in the late 1980s with the launch of a project to create a family of regional passenger jets. This project would become the centerpiece of Embraer's emergence from crisis in the early 1990s as a successful privatized company.

7.5.1.3. *Privatization, Internationalization, and the Accumulation of Technological Capabilities (1990–2008)*

By the beginning of the 1990s Embraer had become a significant producer of light, turboprop and piston transport aircraft and had gained limited military sub-sonic jet production experience. In reaching this point, as has already been indicated, Embraer had accumulated advanced innovative capabilities in the design of products which, while successful in sales terms, could not be described as advancing the frontier of innovation. After a difficult start, in terms of achieving advanced operational capabilities (those relating to the manufacturing process), Embraer had succeeded, realizing world-class productivity and quality levels, having earlier achieved basic operational capabilities through its experience in partnership with Piper (as an assembler of knock-down kits) and Aeromacchi (as a joint-venture partner on the Bandeirante and AMX projects).

Still, Embraer's product range could not be described as cutting-edge or frontier-advancing, focusing as it did on sub-sonic (rather than supersonic) strike fighters, propeller-driven training aircraft, and turboprop driven transports. The difficulty with this position is that it left Embraer as a niche player, alongside such enterprises as Saab-Fairchild, Beechcraft, and Dornier rather than such serious volume producers such as Boeing and Airbus (in the civilian sector) and Lockheed-Martin, Northrop ,and Mc Donnell-Douglas (later to be incorporated into Boeing) in the military. In order to increase volumes, and to become a major international player—at least in the civilian market—it would be necessary to move away from dependence on turboprops and into the production of capable, reliable passenger jets (Silva, 1999). This would involve not only operating on the product design and manufacturing frontier but, indeed, advancing it.

The need to take such an ambitious step—to acquire world-leading innovative capabilities—was motivated by a number of policy and environmental factors. In the first place, given the fiscal exhaustion of the Brazilian state by the early 1990s, public sector support for R&D and aircraft production could no longer be counted on. The continuation of national technological capabilities in aircraft design and production under these circumstances could only be guaranteed provided it was underpinned by strong commercial sales. By the early 1990s it had become clear that success in this regard could well mean a movement to jet production since, in the context of prospective global air transport deregulation, the market for fast and reliable small to medium-sized passenger jets appeared promising, and more generous official export finance facilities were beginning to emerge. At the same time, there appeared to be growing market resistance to the sort of turboprop-driven passenger transports in which Embraer—with the Bandeirante and Brasilia—had specialized. For Embraer, the impetus to move toward passenger jet production and to operate on the frontier was further intensified by the loss of a major contract to supply 711 prop-driven training aircraft to the military in the early 1990s (Cassiolato et al., 2002). The loss of this contract led, in the short run, to Embraer cutting its workforce by half. This unpromising set of circumstances provided the background to Embraer's privatization in 1994.

The privatization of Embraer marked a new chapter in the enterprise's strategy of technological capability accumulation. Whereas in the past this had focused on gaining the necessary capabilities to design and produce products approaching, but not actually on the technological frontier, the new strategy focused heavily on an all-out push to design and produce aircraft that were at the leading edge of what was technically possible. In doing so, it was hoped (correctly, as it turned out) that Embraer could be catapulted from its long-held position as a niche player into a mainstream producer, to eventually rank alongside Boeing and Airbus. The centerpiece of this new strategy were the ERJ 135/140/145 and the 170/90 programs. These aircraft were designed with a view to offering large-jet style speed and comfort, with a range of up to about 2000 nm, and yet with the ability to land on short runways. As such, these aircraft, with their efficient new engines, could offer a cost-effective replacement for earlier turboprops and, on more lightly trafficked routes, narrow-bodied jet aircraft such as the Boeing 737 and the Airbus 318/319 family.

Work on developing these aircraft could be traced back to the late 1980s, but progress accelerated following privatization in 1994. The movement into passenger jet production presented special challenges in terms of airframe fabrication, incorporation of glass cockpit avionic systems, successful choice and integration of power plant. In meeting these challenges, the fundamental point to note is that basic, intermediate, and advanced design and production capabilities already existed from earlier programs. In particular, with the EMB-120 Brasília program, Embraer had gained experience in designing and then serially producing pressurized fuselages, a critical component of passenger jet aircraft. Of equal significance, from its inception, Embraer had deliberately set out to accumulate capability as a systems integrator. In the Bandeirante and Brasília programs, Embraer had successfully sourced and integrated critical systems from outside suppliers, reserving for itself a design and fabrication role which centered on the airframe. This approach, however, represented only the starting point of the design and manufacturing philosophy underpinning the ERJ 135/140/145 and 170/90 programs.

Given that the range, cost, and complexity of technologies in these programs were much greater than in their predecessors, Embraer's ability to originate as high a proportion of the design and manufacturing activity itself has been consequently more limited. Another factor constraining the enterprise here has been the much more restricted access to public funds and credit during the early phase of jet airliner development in the immediate postprivatization period (Cassiolato et al., 2002). Additionally, given Brazil's import liberalization drive of the early 1990s, it suddenly became far more cost effective to import critical component parts and assemblies (Amann, 2000). Accordingly, Embraer's entry into the passenger jet market has seen the emphasis placed yet more intensely on systems integration and the forging of links with foreign subcontractors. In contrast to previous interactions with suppliers (which generally provided off-the-shelf finished systems which Embraer incorporated into its aircraft), the ERJ 135/140/145 and 170/90 programs have seen deliberate collaboration in R&D activity between Embraer and some of its suppliers. Such collaborative activity is typical of world-leading capability of the type routinely exemplified by Airbus and Boeing. It is important to be aware, however, that the level of collaboration with suppliers regarding the design and development of systems is not uniform, either across the suppliers themselves or the systems they supply. Cassiolato et al. (2002) describes a three-tier system of suppliers for the ERJ 135/140/145 and 170/90 programs.

The first tier is composed of risk-sharing partners. These partners are predominantly foreign enterprises (e.g. Gamesa of Spain, Hamilton Sundstrand of the US) who not only provide sub-systems but share in the R&D cost of developing them and actively collaborate with Embraer in the process. While foreign-owned, many of these enterprises (e.g. Rolls Royce) have established local subsidiaries in Brazil in order to better facilitate research collaboration with and product supply to Embraer. Bernardes (2003) describes the emergence of "knowledge networks" from this process of collaboration as world-leading innovations are carried out on the frontier. As a result of this, at the frontier of collaborative R&D, new capabilities have been built and Embraer has moved from simply being a systems integrator to a fully fledged coordinator of international R&D activity (Figueiredo et al., 2008). In the case of the ERJ 135/140/145 family, these risk-sharing partners were responsible for the development and manufacture of major components of the airframe such as the wings (Gamesa of Spain) and the center fuselage (Sonaca of Belgium). The development and manufacture of sections of the airframe by outside partners represented a break in the established practice by Embraer, which in the case of earlier passenger transports had retained this capability in-house.

The second-tier suppliers, by contrast with the first, are not party to a risk-sharing agreement with Embraer, but rather supply technologically complex sub-systems and components such as the avionics systems (Honeywell of the US) or engines (Rolls Royce of the UK). While there is user-producer interaction here, the mode of participation of suppliers in the project corresponds to the "traditional" Embraer strategy of working alongside established suppliers to incorporate their pre-designed systems (albeit sometimes appropriately modified) into the new aircraft. As with the first tier of suppliers, the second tier is predominantly comprised of foreign enterprises. In the third tier of predominantly local and domestically owned suppliers (grouped around São José dos Campos), by contrast, Embraer provides the detailed designs which are then produced by the subcontractors. The items produced here have lower technological content than those produced by first- and second-tier suppliers. As with the second tier of suppliers, this mode of subcontracting has a long pedigree with Embraer. However, as might be expected, the scope for learning through user-producer interaction is somewhat more limited here.

The sense that Embraer is increasingly focusing on its role as a systems integrator and lead participant in international collaborative R&D efforts is accentuated when one compares the ERJ 135/140/145 programs on the one hand and the later 170/90 programs on the other.

Compared with the ERJ 145 (developed in the early 1990s), the ERJ 170/90 (developed in the late 1990s and early 2000s) has made much greater use of risk-sharing partnerships, with entire sections of the airframe (and not just engines, avionics, air conditioning) produced and designed by foreign enterprises (these include Kawasaki, Honeywell, and GE). As a result, according to Bernardes (2003), Embraer has just a 45 percent share in the design of the ERJ 170/90. The only example of a major sub-system running counter to this outsourced production/design trend is the wing, where Embraer in the 170/90 (unlike the ERJ 145) has internalized design and production.

Whatever concerns one might have from a "national capabilities" perspective about Embraer's current technological trajectory, there is no doubt that its emphasis on international research collaboration, risk-sharing partnerships, and systems integration has allowed Embraer to push the frontier, developing aircraft that are genuinely at the cutting edge of performance, reliability, and efficiency. As a result, Embraer has moved from behind the frontier (as a producer of turbo-props) to a world-leading producer of cutting-edge regional jet transports. In fact, Embraer now leads the field in this area, eclipsing sales of its nearest rival Bombardier and encroaching, with the 170/90 range, on territory once thought the inviolable preserve of Airbus and Boeing. As has been seen, Embraer's decision to decentralize design and production was motivated by its own post-privatization resource constraints and the steep technological and financial challenges involved in moving to the frontier. While this decision might be viewed as a contingent response to adverse external pressures, Embraer's risk-partnership approach is increasingly common across the global aerospace sector. Perhaps the most prominent example here is Boeing's new 787, where the design and manufacture of major sections (including fuselage sections) have been allocated to foreign partner enterprises.

7.6. CONCLUSIONS

As indicated at the beginning of this chapter, our central concern has been to evaluate the degree to which the abandonment of ISI and the movement toward greater openness may have impacted the process of capability accumulation. A summary of our key findings is presented in Table 7.8. Our case studies provided some evidence to suggest that the heightened competitive pressure brought about by the opening of the Brazilian market has prompted firms to progress up the hierarchy of capabilities, approaching or indeed reaching the global frontier. Such a positive outcome was observable in the case of the pulp and paper sector where enterprises such as Aracruz and Klabin achieved world leadership, putting themselves in the position to define the frontier itself. In the case of steel, the termination of ISI proved a stimulus to the innovative efforts of both USIMINAS and CSN, the latter, it has to be said, building on a less successful legacy of capabilities accumulation than the former. Perhaps the most celebrated example of progression to the frontier is embodied in the case of Embraer. Here, market opening and a partial withdrawal of state support obliged the firm to intensify its export competitiveness. As a result, it developed a new family of regional jets, moving from behind the frontier to actually defining it through the deployment of advanced innovative capabilities.

Table 7.8. Main changes in industrial policy regimes in Brazil

	Periods	Key features of policy regime		Some sectoral implications
Protectionist and inward-looking policy regime	*Early 1940s:* informal	Implementation of an "import-substitution policy" under the first Vargas government, especially for basic industries. This was a response to constraints derived from the world financial crash and WWII. Main measures sought to minimize heavy dependence on imported production inputs and raw materials.		Motivation to create the first steel company (CSN). Stimulation for pulp and paper firms to look for new and local sources of raw material and emergence of local capital goods for pulp and paper. Establishment of the Aeronautics Technological Centre (CTA).
	Late 1950s: formal set-up of ISI	Introduction of a protectionist regime on the basis of *ad valorem* tariffs. Federal government had discretionary power to control the level of imports and activated the *Lei do Similar Nacional* (the Law of Similars), under which a product could only be imported if it could be proved that a similar product was not produced in Brazil. The Kubistschek government formally intensified the ISI policy and state-led industrialization, but combined it with attracting FDI, through the "Targets Plan."		The National Development Bank (BNDE), created in 1952, became a major funder of investments in the emerging sectors.
	1960s–early 1980s: intensification and reconfiguration of the ISI policy	Expansion of non-tariffs barriers based on: (i) a list of 1,300 products that were not permitted to be imported (the so-called "C Annex"); (ii) all firms were required to submit their annual plan for imports in advance to the federal government; (iii) access to fiscal subsidies and subsidized credit was conditional on the domestic content of an investment project. Imports were made under special regimes granted to exporters (drawback) or were non-competitive capital and intermediate goods. Incentives for exports were expanded in parallel with state-funded industrial expansion projects.	→	Significant expansion of installed capacity in basic industries (e.g. steel and pulp and paper). Creation of state-owned companies like USIMINAS (1963), Embraer (1969), and the emergence of private company Aracruz Forests (1967), leading to the start-up of Aracruz's first fiberline in 1978.
	1985–1988: The "New Industrial Policy"	New policies sought (formally) to reduce redundancy in the tariff structure, to lower manufacturing tariffs from 90 to 43%, and to reduce the number of special regimes. However, as shown in Kume (1989) and Hay (2001), in practice, such measures had little impact: (i) tariffs plus taxes continued to lead to redundant protection in virtually all sectors; non-tariff barriers and the "the	→	Increase in investment projects (expansions) funded by BNDE and substantial growth observed in pulp and paper industries.

(Continued)

Table 7.8. Continued

Periods	Key features of policy regime	Some sectoral implications
	Law of Similars" remained in place. Indeed, such reforms were not as radical as formally announced, particularly due to the strong opposition from local producer interest groups (see Kume, 1989). During this period, the limitations of the ISI policy were recognized and preliminary steps were taken toward greater economic openness.	The policy of "minimum national content of product components" was replaced by the "basic (or minimum) production process policy."
Outward-looking policy regime	*Early 1990s:* consolidation of the trade liberalization policy followed by macroeconomic stabilization from the mid-1990s	Reforms introduced by the Collor administration from March 1990 represented a *major break* with the protectionist regime of the past (Hay, 2001). Such reforms covered three areas: (i) the C Annex (the list of 1,300 products with prohibition on import) was eliminated; (ii) all relevant non-tariff barriers were removed; (iii) introduction of a four-year tariff reduction program to bring all tariffs into the range of 0 to 40%. Reductions were carried out as scheduled until October 1992, when the federal government decided to advance the timetable by six months. In 1994 the "Real Plan" was introduced in order to achieve macroeconomic stabilization. This policy has to date proved successful in taming inflation and stabilizing the Brazilian economy.	Privatization of the steel industry (from 1993), followed by Embraer in 1994. New entrants and consolidation in the forestry, pulp and paper industry. Intensification of exports. Strong concern with export performance. All firms were forced to obtain the ISO 9000 certification.

Sources: Elaborated on the basis of Kume (1989), Moreira and Correa (1998), Hay (2001), and Armijo (2005).

An interesting feature of some of our case studies is the prevalence of privatization, which, in the 1990s, went hand in hand with the dismantling of trade barriers. In the steel and aircraft sectors, privatization could be viewed as *the* high profile policy event of the last two decades. Counter to some pessimistic expectations, the advent of privatization did not prove an obstacle to capabilities accumulation. Indeed, the evidence presented suggests that, if anything, the reverse has been true with Embraer and USIMINAS (though not CSN) aggressively closing the gap with the frontier. However, as should be evident, for the most part, firms featured in our case studies progressed toward the frontier regardless of whether they were privatized or not. This conclusion points to a broader question: can any systematic relationship be observed between firm types (and movement between firm types) and patterns of capabilities accumulation? The answer here appears to be a qualified "no." Our case studies examined firms that remained in domestic private sector hands, were transformed from SOEs to privatized enterprises, and those which operated as subsidiaries of transnational corporations. For the most part, firms made efforts to progress toward the frontier regardless of their status or (in regard to privatization) changes in their status. Rather than firm type being a governing factor in enterprise capability accumulation, variables such as the internal technological logic of individual sectors, and the desire to confront external competition, appear to be of more significance.

Another very important issue concerns the linkage between explicit state industrial and technology policy and patterns of capability accumulation. The evidence presented in the case studies suggested that such policies have been, in particular instances, of significant importance. Perhaps the most clear example of this can be found in the case of Embraer, where a network of public laboratories, targeted R&D support, and, latterly, generous official export finance packages have played a critical role in the development of what are now world-leading capabilities. The pulp and paper sector, too, has been the beneficiary of targeted support, not least through the Brazilian government's Quality and Productivity Program. This initiative has also impacted the steel sector.

An interesting feature characterizing recent patterns of capabilities accumulation in some of the enterprises featured in the previous section was their deepening relationship with outside suppliers and customers. In the case of the pulp and paper sector, enterprises seeking to accelerate progress to the frontier outsourced some engineering tasks to foreign suppliers as they sought to upgrade the production process. Embraer, in the aircraft sector, has taken matters a step further by increasingly subcontracting the design and manufacture of sub-systems to third parties. As discussed, this has placed Embraer ever more in the central role of systems integrator and project manager. At the same time, Embraer has sought to match its products ever more closely to market demand by working alongside customers right from the inception of the design phase. From the perspective of the technological dependence literature, such developments may appear to be retrograde steps. However, as argued, they merely mirror developing practice among world-leading TNCs, which, to an increasing degree, are willing to outsource aspects of their innovation tasks where suitable cost-effective competencies exist.

The past two decades have seen a fundamental reorientation in the Brazilian economy. Having dispensed with the ISI model, Brazil has become more open to trade and capital flows. At the same time, the state has progressively withdrawn as a direct producer of goods and services. This more liberal economic environment has posed severe challenges for the Brazilian industrial sector. The need to achieve competitiveness on global markets has, in many instances, acted as a spur to capabilities accumulation. In some cases—notably aircraft and pulp and paper—attempts by firms to respond to the new policy environment have resulted in the development of world-leading innovative capabilities. Even in the cases of enterprises not yet on the frontier, evidence was presented to suggest that they were fast moving up the hierarchy of capabilities, positioning themselves ever closer to the cutting edge.

Although these positive developments can be viewed as a reaction to greater economic openness, they cannot be fully understood without reference to a well-established legacy of government policy. From the ISI period right up to the present day, a complex web of industrial and technology policies has exercised a critical—and positive—impact on the trajectories of capabilities accumulation. However, as the previous section demonstrated, large swathes of the industrial sector remain effectively technologically inert. The challenge for policy-makers—and researchers—in the future will be to understand the determinants of this inertia and how to address it with appropriate policy instruments.

REFERENCES

Amann, E. (2000), *Economic Liberalization and Industrial Performance in Brazil*, Oxford: Oxford University Press.

—— (2002), "Globalisation, Industrial Efficiency and Technological Sovereignty: Evidence from Brazil," *Quarterly Review of Economics and Finance*, 42(4): 874–88.

—— (2008), "Technology, Public Policy and the Emergence of Brazilian Multinationals," Brookings Institution paper.

—— and Baer, W. (1999), "From Technology Absorption to Technology Production: Industrial Strategy and Technological Capability in Brazil's Development Process," *Economia Aplicada*, 3(1), January–March: 109–38.

Ariffin, N., and Figueiredo, P. N. (2006), "Globalisation of Innovative Capabilities: Evidence from Local and Foreign Firms in the Electronics Industry in Malaysia and Brazil," *Science, Technology and Society*, 11(1): 191–227.

Armijo, L. E. (2005), "Mass Democracy: The Real Reason that Brazil Ended Inflation?" *World Development*, 33(12): 2013–27.

Baer, W. (2008), *The Brazilian Economy*, Boulder, Colo.: Lynne Rienner.

Bell, M., Scott-Kemmis, D., and Satyarakwit, W. (1982), "Limited Learning in Infant Industry: A Case Study," in F. Stewart and J. James (eds.), *The Economics of New Technology in Developing Countries*, London: Frances Pinter.

Bernardes, R. (2003), "Passive Innovation System and Local Learning: A Case Study of Embraer in Brazil," paper presented at the International Conference on Strategic Systems of Innovation for Development in the Third Millennium, November.

Campinhos, E. (1999), "Sustainable Plantations of High Yield Eucalyptus Trees for Production of Fiber: The Alpha Case," *New Forests*, 17: 129–43.

—— Iannelli-Servin, C., Cardoso, N., Almeida, M., and Rosa, A. (2000), "Hidrojardim Clonal Champion: Uma otimização na produção de mudas de eucalipto," *Silvicultura*, 80: 42–6.

Cassiolato, J., Bernardes, R., and Lastres, H. (2002), *Transfer of Technology for Successful Integration in the Global Economy: A Case Study of Embraer in Brazil*, New York: UNCTAD.

Cimoli, M., and Katz, J. (2003), "Structural Reforms, Technological Gaps and Economic Development: A Latin American Perspective," *Industrial and Corporate Change*, 12(2): 387–411.

Costa, I., and de Queiroz, S. R. (2002), "Foreign Direct Investment and Technological Capabilities in Brazilian Industry," *Research Policy*, 31: 1431–43.

Dahlman, C., and Fonseca, F. (1978), "From Technological Dependence to Technological Development: The Case of the USIMINAS Steel Plant in Brazil," Working Paper 21, IBD/ECLA Research Program.

Dalcomuni, S. M. (1997), "Dynamic Capabilities for Cleaner Production Innovation: The Case of the Market Pulp Export Industry in Brazil," doctoral thesis, SPRU, University of Sussex, Brighton, UK.

De Assis, T. F. (2001), "Evolution of Technology for Cloning Eucalyptus in Large Scale," Proceedings of the IUFRO International Symposium on Developing the Eucalypt of the Future, Valdivia, Chile, September.

Evans, J., and Turnbull, J. W. (2004), *Plantation Forestry in the Tropics: The Role of Silviculture, and Use of Planted Forests for Industrial, Social, Environmental, and Agroforestry Purposes*, third edition, Oxford: Oxford University Press.

Figueiredo, P. N. (1999), "Technological Capability Accumulation and the Underlying Learning Processes in the Latecomer Context: A Comparative Analysis of Two Large Steel Companies in Brazil," DPhil thesis, SPRU, University of Sussex, Brighton, UK.

—— (2001), *Technological Learning and Competitive Performance*, Cheltenham, UK and Northampton, Mass.: Edward Elgar Publishing.

—— (2002), "Does Technological Learning Pay Off? Inter-firm Differences in Technological Capability-Accumulation and Operational Performance Improvement," *Research Policy*, 31: 73–94.

—— (2003), "Learning, Capability Accumulation and Firms Differences: Evidence from Latecomer Steel," *Industrial and Corporate Change*, 12(3): 607–43.

—— Silveira, G., and Sbragia, R. (2008), "Risk Sharing Partnerships with Suppliers: The Case of Embraer," *Journal of Technology, Management and Innovation*, 3(1): 27–37.

Frischtak, C. (1994), "Learning and Technical Progress in the Commuter Aircraft Industry: An Analysis of Embraer's Experience," *Research Policy*, 23: 601–12.

Grattapaglia, D. (2004), "Integrating Genomics into Eucalyptus Breeding," *Genetic and Molecular Research*, 30: 369–79.

Hay, D. A. (2001), "The Post-1990 Brazilian Trade Liberalization and the Performance of Large Manufacturing Firms: Productivity, Market Share and Profits," *The Economic Journal*, 111(July): 620–41.

Hira, A., and De Oliveira, L. (2007), "Take Off and Crash: Lessons from the Diverging Fates of the Brazilian and Argentine Aircraft Industries," *Competition and Change*, 11(4): 329–47.

Ikemori, Y. K. (1990), "Genetic Variation in Characteristics of Eucalyptus Grandis Raised from Micro-Propagation and Seed," unpublished PhD thesis, Oxford University, Oxford.

Kume, H. (1989), *A Proteção Efetiva Proposta na Reforma Tarifária*, Rio de Janeiro: Funcex.

Lall, S. (1990), *Building Industrial Competitiveness in Developing Countries*, Paris: OECD Development Center.

—— (2003), "Reinventing Industrial Strategy: The Role of Government Policy in Building Industrial Competitiveness," Trade and Industrial Policy Strategy (TIPS) Working Paper 9-2004.

Leite, L. (2005), *Inovaçao: O Combustível do Futuro*, Rio de Janeiro: Qualitymark.

Lim, C., and Lee, K. (2001), "Technological Regimes, Catching-Up and Leapfrogging: Findings from the Korean Industries," *Research Policy*, 30: 459–83.

Maxwell, P. (1981), "Technological Policy and Firm Learning Efforts in Less Development Countries: A Case Study of the Experience of the Argentina Steel Firm Acindar SA," unpublished DPhil Thesis, SPRU, University of Sussex, UK.

Meyer-Stamer, J. (1997), *Technology, Competitiveness and Radical Policy Change: The Case of Brazil*, London: Frank Cass.

Moreira, M. M., and Correa, P. G. (1998), "A First Look at the Impacts of Trade Liberalization on Brazilian Manufacturing Industry," *World Development*, 26(10): 1859–74.

Ocampo, J. A. (2001), "Structural Dynamics and Economic Development," Santiago: United Nations Economic Commission for Latin America and the Caribbean (CEPAL/ECLAC), mimeo.

Ramamurti, R. (1987), *State-Owned Enterprises in High Technology Industries*, New York: Praeger.

Reinhardt, N., and Peres, W. (eds.) (2000), "Latin America's New Economic Model: Micro Responses and Economic Restructuring," *World Development*, 28(9): 1543–66.

Rodrik, D. (2004), "Industrial Policy for the Twenty-First Century," Faculty Research Working Papers Series, RWP04-047, Harvard University, John F. Kennedy School of Government.

Sennes, R. (2008), "Intellectual Property and Innovation: An Assessment of Ten Brazilian Institutions," Presentation given at Woodrow Wilson Center, June 31.

Silva, O. (1999), *A Decolagem de um Sonho: A História da Criação da Embraer*, São Paulo: Lemos.

8

Argentina

Anabel Marin and Martin Bell

8.1. INTRODUCTION

This chapter examines the experience of Argentine manufacturing firms in accumulating innovative capabilities over the last two decades. It concentrates first on the patterns of innovative activity in manufacturing in the decade or so between the early 1990s and the early 2000s, and then explores more selective aspects of experience in subsequent years. That timing in the context of both changes in economic policy and instability in the economy inevitably places the main focus on issues of disruption, discontinuity, and transition. This is unusual for studies of innovative capability building in developing and emerging economies. These have much more often examined long periods of cumulative continuity running over two, three, or more decades. This has been especially so in the case of the large body of firm-level studies in Asian contexts—for example: Amsden (1989) on firms in Korea between the 1960s and 1980s; Kim (1997), again on firms in Korea, and tracking cumulative paths over a longer period until the 1990s; Hobday (1995), covering electronics firms in Singapore, Taiwan, and Korea over a 20- to 30-year period from the 1970s; or Mathews and Cho (2000), reviewing the development of the semiconductor industry in those countries.

Long-term continuity has been evident in such studies on two levels. On the one hand, the micro-level paths of capability development have typically proceeded fairly smoothly through successive stages of increasingly "deep" innovative activity. On the other, the policy and institutional contexts of those micro-level paths have also in broad terms involved fairly continuous evolution and relative stability—though in China that has run only since the mid to late 1980s. There have obviously been shifts and changes in important emphases of policy, and there have also been wider disruptions and crises in political and economic environments. But in the relatively small number of Asian countries where most of our understanding about long-term technological behavior in industrial firms has been generated, these have not been so disruptive that existing innovative capabilities were destroyed and dispersed—as happened, for example, in the socialist/centrally planned economies of Central and Eastern Europe. Consequently, the main trajectories of technological development were rarely disrupted in substantial ways, let alone truncated or reversed. Even the Asian financial crisis of 1997 was relatively benign in technological terms. Although it had far-reaching effects on the ownership of enterprises and on the diversity of their production activities, especially in countries like Korea and Thailand, most of the main trajectories of technological learning and innovation remained in place. Indeed, in several areas, the crisis seemed to have the effect of intensifying the investment made by Asian firms in strengthening their innovative capabilities and activities, while governments increased their investment in supporting infrastructure for their increasingly innovation-intensive economies.

Latin American experience has been very different. After a substantial period of cumulative, firm-level capability building in the context of relatively stable policy and institutional regimes during the period of import-substituting industrialization (ISI) between the 1950s and 1970s (e.g. Katz, 2001), disruption and instability in firms' environments became the norm. This occurred in two ways: (i) a fundamental reorientation of policy occurred as nearly all countries in the region moved though a phase of liberalization, privatization, and deregulation during the 1980s or early 1990s; and (ii) severe financial crises periodically disrupted most countries of the region. The first did not merely bring to a halt the period of progressive deepening of firms' innovative capabilities; it pervasively destroyed large proportions of the stocks of those capabilities that had been accumulated in private and public organizations. The second then disrupted the rebuilding and regeneration process.

We place that disruption at the center of our story about Argentina. We briefly review the experience of the preceding period and then concentrate on what has happened subsequently. Many other studies have already told that story, both for Latin America as a whole and for Argentina in particular (Katz and Bercovich, 1993; Katz, 2001, 2007; Cimoli and Katz, 2003; Chudnovsky et al., 2006). However, we tell the story in a somewhat different way. In most previous work, estimates of the damage to innovation capabilities arising from the disruption of the economic reforms have varied a little,[1] but they have all been substantially negative—though somewhat less so in the case of Chudnovsky et al. (2006).

---

[1] In part, this variation stems from different perspectives on the historical counterfactuals about what would have happened without the reforms (or with different kinds of reform). Would the path of deepening innovative capability accumulation in the ISI period have continued, or were there inherent limits on where those paths were going? We bypass the discussion of such "might-have-beens."

For sure, positive technology-related developments have been noted. In particular, rapid investment in improved production technology in several areas of the economy, especially in industries linked to the exploitation and processing of natural resources, has resulted in substantial increases in productivity and the narrowing of efficiency gaps with other economies. However, these advances have been identified as involving the application of advanced technology that is already embodied in imported capital equipment. But little of this investment has drawn on knowledge generated by innovative activity in the country. At the same time, the changing structure of economic activity has involved a rising proportion of natural resource-related manufacturing industries that have been characterized as inherently "low tech" or "mature" industries that draw little on innovative inputs such as R&D. In effect, the technology-related changes and advances have strengthened *production* capability in the country, but bypassed the country's already decimated *innovation* capabilities.

We wonder whether that remains the case. We have the advantage of being able to draw on data that, in comparison with the observations in many of the previous studies, cover a period in which more time has elapsed since the main phase of reforms. We therefore ask again whether new innovative capabilities are emerging? If so, how is this taking place? What is the sectoral ecology of the regeneration process? In particular, are innovative capabilities emerging in firms undertaking economic activities that are the same or different from those where they were previously concentrated? What kinds of firm are involved and what kinds of innovation-related interaction is there between them? Finally, can we discern anything about how the new patterns of innovative activity might further evolve?

Argentina is a particularly good context to explore these kinds of question about the regeneration of innovative capabilities following major disruption and discontinuity. Compared to other Latin American countries, the *apertura* was perhaps particularly destructive of the nascent innovative capabilities accumulated in the earlier period. At the same time, during that ISI period few "damage-resistant" organizational "islands" of exceptionally strong innovative competence had been created to carry forward the basis for innovative activity in the post-reform environment—in contrast, for example, to enterprises such as Petrobrás, Embraer, or USIMINAS in Brazil. In other words, while we obviously do not have a total *tabula rasa* with respect to innovation activities in Argentinean firms, we do have a fairly open context where, in principle, new innovative life forms may emerge in new and changing patterns.

One consequence of this approach is that, in contrast with the other chapters in the book, this one does not start from an a priori focus on particular sectors. Instead, the kinds of manufacturing industries that constitute our focus of interest will emerge from the analysis—we will identify them as those in which particularly innovative firms were concentrated during the relatively early stage of post-reform regeneration. We do this by drawing heavily on data from comprehensive innovation surveys of all manufacturing industry that were based on representative samples of approximately 1,600 firms that accounted for around 50–5 percent of all manufacturing sales and employment. This is an especially valuable data source as we are able to use multiple surveys to examine change over time through the 1990s. We do so by identifying a common subset of about 860 surveyed firms that were included in the samples for two surveys covering the periods 1992–6 and 1998–2001.

The structure of the chapter is as follows. In the next section we outline the historical context for the study, outlining both the development of innovative activity in the period before the 1980s and then sketching the post-*apertura* scene in the early 1990s. Then in Section 8.3 we explain the data sources and methods we used to examine the 1990s in more detail, and we indicate how we identified a group of particularly innovative firms that constitute the basis for the central analysis in the chapter. Section 8.4 provides the first set of results of that analysis by examining the sectoral distribution of those innovative firms, and it identifies the small group of manufacturing sectors in which they were particularly concentrated. In Section 8.5 we focus on the significantly innovative firms in those sectoral agglomerations, identifying their origins and background characteristics, their patterns of technological behavior relative to other firms, their innovation-centered linkages with other firms and organizations, and their economic performance. Section 8.6 elaborates on the basic picture by presenting selective case studies from within the group of sectors with concentrations of innovating firms. Section 8.7 discusses some implications and questions arising from the study.

8.2. THE CONTEXT: INDUSTRIAL AND TECHNOLOGICAL CATCHING UP IN ARGENTINA

It is customary to identify five periods in the process of industrial and technological catching up in Argentina: (i) the period of industrialization in an open economy—1880–1930; (ii) the period of import-substituting industrial growth—1930–75; (iii) the initial period of liberalization and opening—1976–90; (iv) the second period of liberalization and its immediate aftermath—from the early 1990s to the economic crisis in 2001; and (v) recent years. Our analysis in this chapter focuses on the emergence of innovation capabilities during the fourth and fifth periods, but this needs to be set in its earlier institutional and economic context.

8.2.1. From the Open Economy through Import-Substituting Industrialization

In the first phase between 1880 and 1930, despite the absence of specific industrial policies, the manufacturing sector grew remarkably, mainly linked to an agricultural boom and the export of primary products. Foreign companies started to participate in the economy mainly in the second half of the 1920s when the first wave of FDI arrived to exploit activities linked to the primary sectors, and to satisfy internal demand for final and intermediate products—including machinery (Villanueva, 1972; Kosacoff, 1999; Barbero, 2004).

The emergence of import-substituting industrialization

During the 1930s external conditions changed dramatically as multilateralism broke down and the degree of protectionism increased worldwide. Internally, the fragility of an economic model of growth based exclusively on primary goods export became evident to both academics and politicians and, as a consequence of a military coup in 1930, Argentina went from an open market system to a period of deep nationalism and an active industrial policy, "import-substituting industrialization" (ISI), began to be implemented. Also, as state institutions such as public credit institutions and public companies were created during the 1930s and 1940s, the state changed its role from being a facilitator and guarantor of market mechanisms to being the main engine of growth and a provider of public welfare. Between 1945 and 1955, during the *Peronista* government, ISI was oriented primarily to consumer goods for the internal market—a period that was later characterized as "simple industrialization" concentrated in the "easy" sectors of manufacturing such as food, textiles, clothing, and metal products.

Deepening ISI and the resurgence of FDI

The military coup of 1955 brought to power a new *"desarrollista"* (developmentalist) government that followed the recommendations of critics of mere "simple industrialization" and pursued a plan that sought the highest possible degree of self-sufficiency via the development of an integrated economic system with emphasis on basic goods and intensive exploitation of natural resources (Barbero and Rocchi, 2002). Import-substituting industrialization was pushed even further with the construction of capital-intensive plants in materials processing and capital goods industries that depended heavily on subsidy incentives. In addition, the role of FDI changed during this period. Between 1945 and 1953, in a context of relatively hostile internal policies toward FDI and a shortage of international capital supply, foreign participation in local industry had decreased substantially. But from the mid-1950s policies became more favorable and the international availability of capital increased. Consequently, FDI grew significantly, and MNC subsidiaries started to play a key role in the structure, evolution, and technological development of the manufacturing sector. Their participation in total manufacturing investment increased from 3 percent at the beginning of the 1950s to more than 30 percent by the beginning of the 1970s.

Catching up: the position by the mid-1970s

The period from 1964 to 1974 marked the highest uninterrupted expansion of Argentinean industry, with an average annual growth rate of 6.7 percent, and the ratio of manufacturing output to GDP rose from around 20 percent in the 1930s to 28 percent during the 1970s. The composition of manufacturing had also changed dramatically, and particularly significant were the automobile and associated metalworking sectors, which not only grew in magnitude but also became central to the process of knowledge generation and accumulation within the manufacturing sector. Thus, by the mid-1970s Argentina had developed a diversified and sophisticated industrial sector, and, it has been argued, the productive structure in the country had reached a level and complexity comparable to countries with income per capita at the level of Australia, Canada, and Italy.

But several major problems lay behind this substantial catching up in industrial production capacity. In particular, with heavy dependence on imported inputs and capital goods, together with weak export growth, recurrent balance of payments deficits characterized the whole ISI period, producing regular crises, instability, and inflation. Nevertheless, although manufactured exports had increased from less than 10 percent of total exports in 1959 to almost 25 percent in 1974, it was widely considered that the manufacturing sector had not managed to become internationally competitive. Part of the reason for this was the fact that the growth and diversification of industrial production capacity had not been matched by the growth in industrial innovative capability.

The process of technological learning during the ISI regime has been well studied in Argentina (Katz, 1976, 1987, 2001, 2007; and Katz and Kosacoff, 1989; Kosacoff, 2000a, 2000b), and the period is seen as a time when the manufacturing sector accumulated a substantial stock of technological, organizational, and managerial skills and knowledge. Nevertheless, important microeconomic features underpinned the problems faced in generating improvements in efficiency that would have been needed to export during the ISI period. Compared with international plants in similar industries, the firms in Argentina typically (i) were smaller, with diseconomies of scale, (ii) were excessively vertically integrated; (iii) were frequently outmoded, often with second-hand and home-made machinery and equipment, as well as old product designs and organizational technologies; and (iv) produced a wide product mix coupled with small production batches (Katz and Kosacoff, 2000). The relatively small scale, in conjunction with poor layout and old machinery, created a problem of productivity which the companies attempted to solve by developing sizeable *in-house* engineering departments. Drawing on the availability of "cheap" professionals in the local market, these generated substantial improvements in local products and processes and this had an important impact on productivity growth (Katz, 1976).

However, there was a major imbalance in this technological learning. The excessive vertical integration and limited specialization in engineering efforts, together with the abundant supply of skilled labor, led to a level of domestic effort in adapting and incrementally improving technologies that was excessive relative to investment in embodied technological change or R&D to develop significant cost reduction, new products, and more "radical" or "genuine" innovations (Teitel, 1981; Lopez, 1996). Correspondingly, R&D expenditures, and expenditure on royalties, patents, and franchising were very low by international standards (Katz, 1976), and it was also apparent that industry was falling behind the rapid advances in technology in the international economy associated with electronics and information technology.

In trying to explain the limited domestic innovative effort, most Latin American researchers also argued that the "excessive" import of externally developed technology limited local technological efforts to mere adaptation of these technologies, restricting the possibilities of endogenous development of technological change. The large role of FDI, along with imports and licenses, was commonly seen as a major contributor to this weakening of local innovative activity, but more recent analysis has been more positive in suggesting that, although it is clear MNCs did not come to the country to perform R&D or world-class innovation, they were an important channel through which new technologies diffused to the local economy (Katz, 2001; Lopez, 1996). MNC subsidiaries opened product design and process-engineering departments, developed local suppliers, created unique skills, and introduced norms of quality and procedures previously unavailable in the country (Barbero, 2004; Lopez, 1996). The relatively poor results in terms of moving from technology acquisition to technology development over the 40-year period since the 1930s should therefore be explained, it is argued, more in terms of the absence of appropriate regulations of the kind used in the more successful Asian experiences, and in the failure of the national system of innovation—or local institutions.[2] Both, it is argued, limited the possibilities for taking further advantage of externally developed technologies (Lopez, 1996).

---

[2] Some views also question the entrepreneurial attitude of company owners, and it is argued that during the ISI period a rent-seeking class of company owners obtained rents primarily from

8.2.2. From Liberalization through Crisis to a Managed Exchange Rate

Economic opening and liberalization in the mid-1970s

Prompted by an extreme economic crisis and a high level of social and political conflict following the return of Peron in 1973, plus external factors such as the oil crisis and the rise in international interest rates, a military government took power through another coup in 1976. In the context of a pervasive view that import-substituting industrialization had reached a dead end, the government drastically changed the policy regime, eliminating most of the regulations and subsidies introduced during the ISI period to protect the manufacturing sector, opening up the economy, and adopting a monetary approach to address the balance of payments and control inflation (Katz and Kosacoff, 2000). The combination of a massive increase in both imports of industrial goods and short-term investment produced an over-valuation of the domestic currency and a substantial increase in interest rates. Local firms acquired levels of indebtedness that exceeded the value of their assets and in 1982 the state took over most of the private debt. From then onwards the 1980s were characterized by permanent struggles and disequilibrium.

The consequence of all these changes was the deepest crisis in the history of Argentina's industrial sector and lasted until the beginning of the 1990s.[3] Between 1975 and 1990, manufacturing output fell by around 25 percent and its share of GDP decreased from 28 percent to 20 percent—a degree of industrialization that was no different from that of the 1940s (Kosacoff, 1996). Furthermore, the specialization of the sector changed dramatically, from metal mechanic industries to industrial commodities produced from processing natural resources, such as pulp and paper, petrochemicals, aluminum, and steel (Katz, 2001; Kosacoff, 1996). At the same time FDI decreased substantially, especially in manufacturing, and became concentrated primarily in services, especially the financial sector.

The 1990s—the second phase of liberalization and its consequences

After the long period of almost permanent macroeconomic instability (including two episodes of hyperinflation), and the economic and industrial

captive markets and from privileged contracts with the state, and therefore did not have the incentive to take the risks of innovative activities (Azpiazu, 1997). Arza (2005) demonstrated that, even in the 1990s, the companies in Argentina were more speculative than entrepreneurial in relation to their main investment decisions.

[3] This was not the only effect of the changes introduced by this military government, which also initiated the process of external indebtedness still present as one of the main problems of the Argentinean economy.

stagnation of the 1980s, a new government came to power in 1991. In a very similar fashion to others in Latin America, this government deepened the process of liberalization and deregulation that had been initiated in the mid-1970s, but with two novel features: the privatization of most public assets and companies, and the implementation of a rigid monetary policy, the Convertibility Plan.[4] In the short term, the main impact of all these changes was an end to inflation—one of the main problems of the Argentinean economy at that time. Also, in a context of substantial increases in international financing to the country, the main economic indicators responded very sharply and quickly. Between 1990 and 1994 industrial activity rose more than 30 percent, 7.8 percent per year, the highest growth rate of the previous 50 years. However, with the entire incentive regime and institutional system changing, the decade was characterized by five other substantial changes.[5]

(i) De-industrialization has been used to refer to the 1990s because both the manufacturing sector and the industrial sector as a whole reduced their share of GDP: between 1990 and 2000 the ratio of manufacturing to total value added fell from 19 percent to 16 percent, a trend that continued the persistent drop that had begun in 1970s.

(ii) Primarization refers to the change in the specialization pattern of industry in Argentina during this period, from the metal mechanic and chemicals sectors—the two most dynamic industries during the ISI period—to activities that process natural resources and industrial commodities, such as pulp and paper, iron and steel, and vegetable oils.

(iii) Increases in structural heterogeneity and concentration. Some firms, mostly large companies and MNC subsidiaries, substantially increased productivity and matched international best practice via major investments in equipment and far-reaching organizational changes in production. However a large number of firms, especially SMEs, were not able to introduce these changes and many of them disappeared, while others became mere survivors, achieving increases in productivity primarily by laying off employees. With a large numbers of firms disappearing and a relatively small number of newcomers joining the industrial structure, the levels of concentration increased at both industry and economy levels (Kosacoff, 1996, 2000a).

---

[4] The Convertibility Plan implied that the Central Monetary Authority (Banco Central) compromised by selling currency based on a fixed parity, and maintaining external assets of at least 80 percent of the monetary base. In general, the additional measures were intended to restrict the monetary supply. Additionally, it was not allowed to adjust contracts by using price indexes. The main short-term consequences of the policy were an abrupt fall in the interest rate, and in price indexes, and the long-term consequences led to the financial crisis of the 2001.

[5] Some of these transformations started earlier, during the first movement toward a more deregulated economy in the second half of the 1970s. Nevertheless, following the changes during the 1990s, they either persisted and/or intensified.

(iv) Closure of the productivity gap and internationalization of technology sources. The diminution of the technological gap with the international economy was the other face of the processes of concentration and primarization in manufacturing—as reflected in the fact that the share of Argentinean exports in world exports rose from 0.3 percent in 1985 to 0.51 percent in 1998. Two sectors improved their relative productivity particularly significantly. One was the automotive sector, which did not follow a process of opening up to international trade, being supported by ad hoc industrial policies and specific MNC strategies. The other was a group of industries based on static advantages associated with the processing of natural resources (industrial commodities such as iron and steel, pulp and paper, and vegetable oil) (Katz, 2001). However, associated with these changes in productivity, there was also a significant loss of employment, reflected in the substantial increase in unemployment during the decade. The main ways in which companies acquired new technological knowledge changed substantially as well. While channels such as international suppliers, licenses, and online technical assistance gained in importance, local suppliers of equipment, engineering firms, and domestic R&D labs became less so.

(v) Transnationalization. Although there were no specific incentives to attract FDI during the 1990s, Argentina became one of the main recipients of FDI in Latin America. As a result, foreign participation in total sales of the 200 largest manufacturing firms grew from 43 percent in 1994 to 69 percent in 1998 (Kulfas et al., 2002). Capital flows were mostly directed to the acquisition of existing assets—via privatization and mergers and acquisitions. Between 1990 and 1993, privatizations accounted for 40 percent of total FDI and mergers and acquisitions of existing assets constituted the main modality after 1994. Also, the main characteristics of the usual subsidiary in the 1990s were very different from those of typical subsidiaries in the ISI period. The latter, although typically operating behind the technological frontier, often made considerable engineering and localized development efforts to adapt processes and products to local conditions. In contrast, it is argued (although the evidence is partial and limited), that during the 1990s in the context of a more open economy subsidiaries produced less diversified product lines and were forced to operate closer to the international technological frontier. As a result, it is suggested, they tended to use more of the technological resources developed by the MNC parent, whilst reducing the level of local engineering and R&D—with fewer possibilities of technological externalities, via the development of local suppliers or demonstration effects (Kulfas et al., 2002; Chudnovsky and Lopez, 1997; Kosacoff, 2000a, 2000b).

Finally, however, cutting across these five transformations in the 1990s was a continuation of the macroeconomic instability that had characterized the previous period. While in 1991, 1992, and 1997 the rates of growth were as high as 10 percent, 12 percent, and 9 percent respectively, the years 1995, 1999, and 2000 registered negative growth rates. With instability being more pronounced after 1994, there was a distinct difference in growth between the two halves of the decade. While the average annual rate of growth of manufactured value added was 5 percent between 1991 and 1995, it was only 1 percent thereafter, and this was followed by the major economic crisis in 2001.

Views differ about the effect of this combination of economic transformation and turbulence on the development of innovative capabilities and activities. Some have argued, for example, that the heavy reliance on imported capital goods and the restructuring toward primary sectors reflecting static comparative advantages had a negative effect (e.g. Cimoli and Katz, 2003), as did the continued macroeconomic instability (Arza, 2005). Others have noted, however, that "unexpectedly" firms' R&D expenditures increased substantially (Chudnovsky et al., 2006: 268).

The main part of our analysis in the rest of the chapter takes another look at these features of the turbulent decade. In addition, case-study material later in the chapter explores how patterns of innovation have evolved in selected firms and industries since the crisis—a period during which the five main post-liberalization trends identified above have continued in an era of managed exchange rate stability.

8.3. DATA AND METHODS

8.3.1. Data

The empirical analysis reported here uses information provided by two innovation surveys in Argentina—collected by the National Statistical Council (INDEC). In the first innovation survey 1,639 firms were interviewed, and in the second 1,688.[6] In both cases, around 20 percent of the firms were MNC affiliates. Both samples were randomly selected from the National Economic Census (1992) and the Input Output Matrix survey (1997), so they constitute representative samples of manufacturing industry at the beginning of each survey period.

The first survey covers the period 1992–6, and the second, the period 1998–2001. The sample of firms changed from one survey to the other; nevertheless a group of 869 firms were interviewed in both periods. In this chapter we focus

---

[6] The difference is due to the rate of response, which changed from one survey to the other.

our analysis on this sub-sample for which we have information covering the period 1992–2001.

Following the broad framework of the OECD Manuals—Oslo (OECD, 1992 and 1997) and Frascati (OECD, 1994)—the Argentinean innovation surveys utilized a battery of alternative quantitative and qualitative questions to evaluate numerous aspects of the economic and technological behavior of the firms. Firms were asked to provide economic information such as size, age, added value, exports, imports, sales, employment, etc. and also, information about a wide range of technological activities at the firm level.

Although the first and second surveys differ slightly, the information covered by both is very similar. It can be classified in five main areas:

(1) General information about the firm and indicators of economic performance;
(2) Efforts to acquire externally developed technologies;
(3) Internal technological efforts and innovation-related interactions;
(4) Innovative output and strategy; and
(5) Others.

The main activity of the firm is also available from the surveys. The innovation survey and the industrial survey in Argentina use a classification of firms' activities similar to the industrial classification of economic activities in the UK (SIC). These classify manufacturing activities in 22 divisions, comprising divisions 15 to 36.

8.3.2. Method: Selecting Innovative Firms

The aim of the study is to focus on the firms that were at the "leading edge" of innovative activity in Argentinean manufacturing during the 1990s. This required us to identify among the 869 firms in the overlapping survey sample a sub-group of firms that were in some sense "particularly innovative." It was not appropriate to use for this purpose either of the two indicators most often used to measure firms' innovativeness, R&D expenditures and patents. Patent-based indicators of innovative output are inappropriate in less advanced contexts such as Argentina where firms rarely use patents to protect their new knowledge. For instance, in Argentina in 2003 only 98 firms took out 317 patents (Chudnovsky et al., 2006). R&D-based indicators reflect the efforts made by a firm to create knowledge, but do not show the effectiveness of the activity and, more important in this context, they tend to reflect inter-industry differences in R&D intensity rather than firm-specific differences in the intensity of innovative activity. They also tend to underestimate innovative activities closely related to production as well as information processing (Patel, 2000).

Alternative measures of innovativeness, based on data from innovation surveys (such as the European Community innovation studies), have been increasingly used over the last 15 years. The most popular of these have been measures based on the proportion of firms' turnover associated with the introduction of new or significantly improved products, and these have been used as indicators of the innovation performance of companies, industries, and countries. In principle, this is a good direct measure of innovation performance, but it discriminates against process innovation (particularly important in Argentina). We therefore used a different approach. Following the standard distinctions in the Oslo Manual (OECD, 1997), the Argentine Innovation Survey asked firms about the type of product or process innovation they had introduced during the survey period, giving the firms four different possible responses: (1) they did not introduce any product (or process) innovations, (2) they introduced product (or process) innovations that were new for the company, (3) they introduced product (or process) innovations that were new for the economy, or (4) they introduced product or process innovations novel for the world economy.[7]

We considered that a positive response to the last of these options in the 1998–2001 survey would indicate the more innovative Argentine firms. An obvious limitation is that responses are subjective, reflecting merely the opinion of the individual responding on behalf of the firm. In particular, therefore, responses claiming to have introduced this category of innovation may not reflect very precisely the occurrence of innovation that is truly "*new for the world market.*"[8] However, precision in that respect is not the main issue here since we are concerned primarily with the relative innovativeness of Argentine firms; and, given the possibility for respondents to select less novel kinds of innovativeness, we believe that in relative terms this category captures adequately for our purposes the "more significant" end of the distribution of innovative firms.

For convenience, we will in the rest of the chapter describe this group as "significant innovators"; and we will refer to the others simply as "non-innovators," even though they include the firms that claimed to have introduced innovations that were new for the company or for the economy. As shown in Table 8.1, 115 of firms in our sample (13 percent) are significant innovators. Among these less than one-third had introduced both product and process innovations that were "new to the world." Most of the group (63 percent) had introduced only product innovations of that type, and less than 10 percent had introduced only process innovations.

---

[7] For an explanation of these categories see the most recent version of the Oslo Manual (OECD, 2005: Section 6, pp. 57–8).

[8] For this reason we will use the term "new to world" to refer to this category of innovation, rather than alternatives like "world-leading" or "international frontier."

Table 8.1. Types of innovating firm in the sample

Types of innovating firm	Number of firms	Proportion (%)	
"Non-innovators"	754	86.7	
"Significant innovators"	115	13.2	
of which:			
Process innovations only	9		(7.8)
Product innovations only	72		(62.6)
Both product and process	34		(29.6)
TOTAL	869	100.0	(100.0)

Source: Author elaboration from database.

8.4. ANALYSIS I: THE SECTORAL DISTRIBUTION OF SIGNIFICANTLY INNOVATIVE FIRMS

A major purpose of the study is to identify where, in terms of their sectors within manufacturing industry, these significantly innovative firms are located. We therefore split the manufacturing sectors (at the three-digit level) into two groups—those that included at least one significantly innovative firm (38 sectors and 690 firms), and those that did not (17 sectors and 179 firms—about 20 percent of our whole sample). The latter are set aside here (shown in Appendix Table 8.A1), and we move on to concentrate on the sectors with significantly innovative firms.

A further central question is about whether these kinds of firm are concentrated (or agglomerated) in particular sectors and types of sector, so revealing what might be considered as actual or perhaps emerging areas of dynamic comparative advantage. We therefore identified as sectors with agglomerated significant innovators those in which significantly innovating firms accounted for 5 percent or more of all the significant innovators.

Table 8.2 shows the sectoral distribution of all the significantly innovative firms and also further distinguishes between domestic firms and MNE (multinational enterprise) subsidiaries. In total, these firms are widely distributed across 38 sectors; and (column 6) they account for 16 percent of all firms in these sectors—i.e. 84 percent of all the firms in these sectors are not significantly innovative in terms of our definition, suggesting that we have identified a relatively small group at the upper end of the distribution of firm innovativeness.

But these significantly innovative firms are not spread evenly across the 38 sectors. As shown in Table 8.2 they fall into two groups.

Group I: A small group of only five sectors with concentrations of significantly innovative firms (≥ 5 percent of all those firms);

Group II: A much larger group of 33 other sectors without substantial agglomerations of such firms.

The intra-sectoral agglomeration effect in Group I is striking in two ways.

First, the small number of sectors in Group I account for 45 percent of all the significantly innovative firms in all sectors (column 5). Moreover, they appear to be a fairly distinct group because there is a "break" in the distribution between the sectors in Group I and the others—the least agglomerated sector in Group I (the auto components sector) accounts for a substantially larger proportion of all the significantly innovating firms (6 percent) than the next sector in the ranking (plastic products with 4 percent).

Second, the Group I sectors appear to be more innovative in the sense that significantly innovative firms account for a substantially larger proportion of all firms in those sectors (24 percent—column 6) than is the case for the Group II firms (13 percent). Clearly there are within Group II sectors a number of individual sectors where significantly innovative firms account for larger proportions of the sector firms than in Group I. But these involve very small numbers of firms as isolated "islands" of innovative activity, not areas of sectoral agglomeration.

This is most evident in the case of sectors where single significantly innovative firms account for high proportions of all firms in the sector: coke oven products (231–100 percent), nuclear fuel processing (233–100 percent), lighting equipment/lamps (315–100 percent), and optical instruments/photographic equipment (332–67 percent).

In other words, there appears to be a substantial concentration of the leading edge of more significant innovative activity in Argentine manufacturing in the five sectors in Group I. We will therefore refer to the Group I significant innovators as "sectorally agglomerated innovators" (or agglomerated innovators for short),[9] and all the others are described from here on as "isolated innovators." Two further features of the Group I agglomerated innovator sectors are striking.

First, there is substantial co-location of domestically owned firms and MNE subsidiaries among the significant innovators in these sectors. The balance varies between the sectors, for example between agricultural machinery where nearly all the significant innovators are domestic, and agro-chemicals where MNE subsidiaries predominate. However, in contrast to many of the sectors in Group II, there is none in which one category or the other is absent.

It is also striking that four of the Group I sectors, accounting for 45 of the 52 significant innovators in the whole group, are associated through input-output

---

[9] We obviously refer here to sectoral, not regional, agglomeration. As we cannot identify the individual firms from the innovation survey data, we have no information about their spatial distribution.

Table 8.2. Distribution of significantly innovative firms across sectors (three-digit)

(1)	Sector description (2)	Domestic firms (3)	Sub-sidiaries (4)	% of total innovative (5)	% of total sector (6)
I	**Agglomerated innovators**				
151	meat products, fish, fruit/ vegetables, and vegetable oils/fats	6	4	9%	15%
154	Other food products*	6	2	7%	17%
242	Pesticides and other agro-chemical products	5	10	13%	22%
292	Agricultural and forestry machinery	11	1	10%	46%
343	Parts/accessories for motor vehicles and their engines	5	2	6%	27%
	Subtotal	(33)	(19)	(45%)	(24%)
II	**Non-agglomerated innovators**				
252	Plastic products	3	2	4%	13%
153	Grain mill products, starches, and animal feeds	2	1	3%	17%
222	Printing and service activities related to printing	2	1	3%	14%
269	Other non-metallic mineral products	3	1	3%	13%
293	Domestic appliances	2	1	3%	14%
191	Tanning and dressing of leather	3	0	3%	27%
291	General-purpose machinery	3	0	3%	12%
173	Knitted and crocheted fabrics	1	1	2%	10%
202	Veneer sheets; plywood, laminboard, other panel and boards	1	1	2%	17%
272	Steel tubes	1	1	2%	50%
289	Other metal products	1	1	2%	5%
312	Electricity distribution and control apparatus	1	1	2%	29%
172	Other textiles	2	0	2%	15%
281	Structural metal products	2	0	2%	15%
311	Electric motors, generators, and transformers	2	0	2%	20%
321	Electronic valves and tubes and other electronic components	2	0	2%	50%
332	Fabrication of optical instruments and photographic equipment	2	0	2%	67%
241	Basic chemicals	0	2	2%	13%
243	Man-made fibers	0	2	2%	29%
273	Casting of metals	0	2	2%	13%
171	Preparation and spinning of cotton-type fibers	1	0	1%	3%
210	Pulp, paper, and paper board	1	0	1%	4%
221	Publishing	1	0	1%	5%

231	Coke-oven products	1	0	1%	100%
233	Processing of nuclear fuel	1	0	1%	100%
261	Glass and glass products	1	0	1%	8%
315	Lighting equipment and electric lamps	1	0	1%	100%
361	Fabrication of furniture	1	0	1%	4%
313	Insulated wire and cable	0	1	1%	25%
322	Television/radio transmitters and telephone apparatus	0	1	1%	25%
323	Television/radio receivers, sound or video apparatus	0	1	1%	25%
341	Fabrication of motor vehicles	0	1	1%	25%
342	Fabrication of bodies for motor vehicles, trailers	0	1	1%	11%
Subtotal		41	22	55%	13%
TOTAL		74	41	100%	16%

Notes: * Includes bread, biscuits, sugar, cocoa, tea, yerba, etc.

Source: Author elaboration from database.

links with immediately natural resource-based industries, primarily agriculture. The exception is the sector producing automotive components (SIC 343). This sector is exceptional in several senses, apart from the fact that it is not natural resource (NR)-related industry. In particular, it is the residual of the flourishing automotive metal-mechanic industry that was fostered in the ISI period, and since the beginning of the 1990s it has been at the center of a special policy regime which includes a special trade regime with Brazil and various incentives for manufacturers. For these reasons, the sector is somewhat anomalous and we will set it aside in our analysis, concentrating on the four remaining "natural resource-linked" sectors.

These fall into two sub-groups. One we characterize as being "directly" related to NR exploitation and processing—e.g. engaged in processing meat, producing vegetable oils, or manufacturing food products like bread and biscuits. The other is "indirectly" related to NR exploitation and processing. In this case, they are upstream industries producing inputs for agriculture—pesticides, other agro-chemicals, and various kinds of agricultural machinery. In summary, therefore, we will use the following classification of the sectors within which the agglomerated innovators (Group I in Table 8.2 above) are located.

Group I Agglomerated innovators in natural resource-related manufacturing sectors

I.1 Directly related to NR-based industries—downstream processing
    (151) Meat products, fish, fruit/vegetables, and manufacture of vegetable oils/fats
    (154) Other food products (including bread, biscuits, sugar, cocoa, tea, yerba, etc.)
I.2 Indirectly related to NR-based industries — upstream inputs
    (242) Pesticides and other agro-chemical products
    (292) Agricultural and forestry machinery

We noted earlier two things about such directly or indirectly natural resource-related sectors: (i) they involve the kinds of production activity in which Argentina has had a historical competitive advantage, and (ii) much of the rationale of the ISI regime was about accelerating structural change *away* from these kinds of sector; partly because they were considered at that time to be "low-technology" sectors that would not help to embed more significantly innovative activities within the economy—especially in the more directly NR-related industries like 151 and 154 in Group I.1. We also noted earlier that this view has been prominent in more recent discussions in the post-1990 period about the implications of the structural characteristics of Latin American economies in general and of Argentina in particular. So, it is surprising to find such sectors as the locus of substantial agglomerations of significantly innovative firms in Argentina in the open economy context of the 1990s.

A little care is therefore needed to define what this observation actually is— or rather what it is not. There is no evidence in this data to suggest that NR-related manufacturing industries are *in general* acting as the leading innova-tive sectors of Argentine manufacturing industry. Quite the contrary, there is considerable evidence to suggest that is *not* the case.[10] For example, the pulp and paper industry is far down the ranking in Table 8.2, with a lone signifi-cantly innovating firm, constituting only 4 percent of the firms in its industry (the other 96 percent being non-innovators—at least in terms of our defini-tion). More striking is the fact that a considerable number of NR-related industries can be found in Appendix Table 8.A1, the list of our "reject" sectors that include no significantly innovative firms at all—for instance: dairy pro-ducts (152), beverages (155), footwear (192), sawmilling (201), and basic iron and steel (271). What our observation *does* suggest is that *several* closely NR-related manufacturing industries do seem to account for a large part of the more significant innovative activity in Argentine manufacturing. That alone, without any general comment about NR-related industries as a whole, is very surprising relative to common expectations. So, important questions emerge about these innovative firms.

- First, what are the general background characteristics of these firms? When were they created (e.g. before, during, or after the ISI period)? What is their size and their type of ownership?
- Second, what are the key features of their technological behavior? For instance, looking especially at those in the conventionally defined "low-tech" sectors in Group I.1, are they building up formal R&D facilities, investing in R&D, and employing highly skilled professionals in the same ways as firms in conventionally defined "high-tech" sectors, or compared

---

[10] Despite the fact that such a sector (grain milling and related products, 153) is the next in rank, just outside our Group I sectors in Table 8.3 below.

to other type of innovators, or do they fit the stereotype of "low-tech" firms? Do they generate linkages with other parts of the national innovation system, including other innovating firms, or are they more isolated compared with firms in so-called "high-tech" sectors?

- Finally, what is the economic performance of these firms compared with innovative firms in other sectors and with non-innovative firms?

We explore these kinds of question in the next section.

8.5. ANALYSIS II: THE CHARACTERISTICS OF SECTORALLY AGGLOMERATED INNOVATORS

8.5.1. Start-Up, Ownership, and Size

With respect to the timing of the start-up of firms, we do not observe that new firms dominate within the group of agglomerated innovators. On the contrary, as indicated in Table 8.3, their average age is more than 40 years and most of them (80 percent) were established during and even before the intensification of ISI. Moreover, in this respect the agglomerated innovators are quite similar to non-innovators in all industries. So, the innovative activity in these sectors in the 1990s does not reflect a process of destruction followed by the emergence of new, highly innovative firms. Instead, only a small proportion (20 percent) of the agglomerated innovative firms in 1998–2001 had been new entrants in the post-ISI period, while the majority had survived through the era of policy change and economic turbulence between the late 1970s and early 1990s. In other words, although we do not have information about the overall rate of firm survival through that period, the existence of these long-established firms as the dominant group among the agglomerated innovators suggests that there seems to have been a process of what we might call "creative accumulation"—i.e. old firms becoming, or continuing to be, innovative in the introduction of what they consider to be new-to-the-world products and/or processes.

We distinguish between three ownership categories: domestically owned business groups, independent domestic firms, and MNE subsidiaries. As shown in Table 8.4, about half of the agglomerated innovators were independent domestic firms; but they are under-represented among the agglomerated innovators (accounting for almost 70 percent of the total sample of firms in these sectors). On the other hand, MNE subsidiaries are over-represented—accounting for 37 percent of the agglomerated innovators and only 20 percent of the whole sample. There is, however, little difference in the ownership pattern between the two kinds of innovator firm—the distribution of firms in both categories between the three types of ownership was very similar.

Table 8.3. Categories of innovative firm—by time of establishment/age

	Agglomerated innovators in NR-related industries	Isolated innovators	Non-innovators in all industries	Total
Timing of establishment	Number of firms and proportions of column totals (%)			
Before/during ISI	41	43	509	593
	(80)	(72)	(69)	(70)
After ISI	10	17	231	258
	(20)	(28)	(31)	(30)
TOTAL	51	60	740	851
	(100)	(100)	(100)	(1000)
	Number of years in 2001			
Age	43.6	38.8	38.6	38.9

Source: Author elaboration from database.

Table 8.4. Categories of innovative firms—by type of ownership

	Agglomerated innovators in NR-related industries	Isolated innovators	Non-innovators in all industries	Total
Types of firm ownership	Number of firms and proportions of column totals (%)			
Domestic—business groups	8	8	88	104
	(15)	(13)	(12)	(12)
Independent domestic firms	25	33	536	594
	(48)	(52)	(71)	(68)
MNE subsidiaries	19	22	130	171
	(37)	(35)	(17)	(20)
TOTAL	52	63	754	869
	(100)	(100)	(100)	(100)

Source: Author elaboration from database.

Large firms (with $\geq$ 200 employees) are over-represented among the agglomerated innovators—accounting for more than 40 percent of the firms in this category, compared with only 22 percent in the whole sample—see Table 8.5 below. Reflecting this, the average size of the agglomerated innovators (nearly 420 employees) was almost twice the average size of all the sample firms. Nevertheless, a considerable proportion of the agglomerated innovators (nearly 60 percent) were SMEs (with less than 200 employees).

Table 8.5. Categories of innovative firm—by size

	Agglomerated innovators in NR-related industries	Isolated innovators	Non-innovators in all industries	Total
Size category	Number of firms and proportions of column totals (%)			
SMEs (< 200 employees)	30	43	608	681
	(58)	(68)	(81)	(78)
Large (≥ 200 employees)	22	20	146	188
	(42)	(32)	(19)	(22)
TOTAL	52	63	754	869
	(100)	(100)	(100)	(100)
	Number of employees			
Size	417	334	191	216

Source: Author elaboration from database.

One further background characteristic of the sectorally agglomerated innovators relates to how they organized their innovative activity. In particular, it focuses on whether they have a formally identified R&D laboratory. Table 8.6 indicates that only about half of all manufacturing firms have such a specialized organizational focal point for the technological aspects of their innovation—surprisingly high, and raising questions about the interpretation of this aspect of the innovation survey. As one might expect, agglomerated innovators with a formal lab (75 percent of all the agglomerated innovators) are over-represented. But it is interesting that as many as 25 percent of them undertake their "new-to-the-world" innovation without such an organizational arrangement. Since active innovating firms of this type are unlikely to under-report the existence of a laboratory, this suggests that a considerable amount of the innovative activity of these firms is undertaken by design and engineering capabilities that have mixed technological roles within the firm rather than specialized R&D responsibilities. This presumption is perhaps reinforced by the fact that firms *without* formal laboratories are especially over-represented in the sectors directly related to NR industries (engaged in food and vegetable processing, etc.), while innovators in the indirectly NR-related sectors are much more likely to have formally organized R&D labs.

In the next section we explore in more detail and more comprehensively issues concerning the nature of the innovative behavior of these firms.

8.5.2. Innovative Behavior

We explore the innovative behavior of the agglomerated innovators in two steps. First, we outline selected aspects of their behavior in the early 1990s,

Table 8.6. Categories of innovative firm—with formal R&D laboratories (2001)

Presence/ absence of formal R&D laboratory	Agglomerated innovators			Isolated innovators	Non-innovators in all industries*	Total
	All	Directly related to NR industries	Indirectly related to NR industries			
	Number of firms and proportions of column totals (%)					
With formal lab	34	11	23	40	330	438
	(75)	(61)	(85)	(63)	(44)	(49)
Without formal lab	11	7	4	23	412	457
	(25)	(39)	(15)	(37)	(56)	(51)
TOTAL	45	18	27	63	742	895
	(100)	(100)	(100)	(100)	(100)	(100)

Notes: * "Non-innovators" are defined here to include those that introduced innovations that were new to the firm and economy, but not new to the world.

Source: Author elaboration from database.

using data from the 1992 innovation survey. We deal quite briefly with this period as it relates to the same time as most of the studies discussed earlier, and we merely note some of the commonalities, and a few differences, between our material and the earlier studies. Then we examine in a little more detail how things changed during the 1990s, using data from the 2001 survey.

In both steps, we focus on three indicators of innovative behavior: (i) the R&D intensity of the firms (R&D expenditure as a proportion of total sales), as a reflection of knowledge creation in the firm; (ii) the intensity with which the firms employed skilled professional labor (the ratio of skilled professionals to non-professional employees), as a more general reflection of both the creation and use of knowledge in the firms; and (iii) the intensity of firms' investment in capital goods (expenditure on capital goods as a proportion of total sales), as a reflection of the type of innovation that involved the installation of capital-embodied technology that was probably originally created outside the firm.

We assess these aspects of innovative behavior of the agglomerated innovators by comparing them with other groups of firms. These include two general comparative groups: all the isolated innovators in other sectors and all manufacturing firms. This permits comment on the overall "innovativeness" of the agglomerated innovators relative to manufacturing industry in general in Argentina. They also include two more specific groups: firms in the "high-technology" industries as classified in the OECD system, and also MNE subsidiaries. These comparisons enable us to assess more specifically the "innovativeness" of the agglomerated innovators relative to groups of firms that are commonly thought to set benchmarks of more innovative behavior in emerging economies like Argentina.

(i) Innovative behavior in the early 1990s

Table 8.7 summarizes the information for 1992. The picture with respect to R&D conforms to what one might expect in the light of the studies of the early 1990s period. Although the R&D intensity of the agglomerated innovators was much more than the average for all manufacturing firms (0.6 percent compared to 0.2 percent), that difference depended entirely on the behavior of the innovators in the agro-chemical and agro-machinery firms which were indirectly linked to natural resource-based production. Consequently, these firms were much more R&D intensive than all the comparator groups (the ratios in rows G–K). In particular, it is striking that these indirectly NR-related innovators were (i) more R&D intensive than innovators in all other industries, (ii) more than five times as R&D intensive as firms in the "high-tech" industries, and (iii) considerably more R&D intensive than even the innovative firms in those industries. In contrast, the R&D intensity of the directly NR-related firms in the food product/vegetable oil industries was negligible, and they were considerably less R&D intensive than all the comparator groups.

This pattern is almost matched in reverse with respect to investment in capital goods. The intensity of investment was again much higher among the agglomerated innovators than in all manufacturing firms—(8 percent compared to 3 percent). But in this case the difference is almost entirely attributable to the directly NR-related food product/vegetable oil industries that had a very much larger investment intensity than the agro-chemical and agro-machinery industries. It was also much larger than in the comparator groups (the ratios in rows L–O). It was around four-to-six times larger than other innovators and all manufacturing firms, and massively larger than in the "high-tech" industries—even than the innovative firms in those industries.

The innovative behavior of the agglomerated innovators, as reflected in their employment of skilled professionals, falls roughly midway between these two patterns. Their intensity of such employment was considerably higher than on average in all manufacturing firms, but not dramatically so (15 percent compared to 10 percent). But in this case the difference between the directly and indirectly NR-related firms was minor—being slightly higher in the latter (the agro-chemical and agro-machinery firms). Consequently, both groups were noticeably more intensive in their employment of skilled professionals than most of the broader comparator groups. The exception in the narrower groups is the "high-tech" sectors. But it is striking that the agglomerated innovators were more professional-intensive on average than all firms in the "high-tech" industries, only being less intensive than the innovative

Table 8.7. Sectorally agglomerated innovators: aspects of technological behavior—1992

Types of firm: agglomerated innovators and others		R&D intensity	Skilled professionals (Mean values for firm types)	Capital investment
1. **Agglomerated innovators in sectors related to natural resources** Of which:		0.6%	15%	8%
1.1 Directly related to NR (food products)		0.0%	14%	17%
1.2 Indirectly related to NR (agro-chemicals and agro-machinery)		1.1%	17%	2%
2. All other innovators		0.4%	12%	4%
3. All firms in "high-tech" industries		0.2%	6%	1%
4. Innovative firms in "high-tech" industries		0.8%	33%	2%
5. All foreign subsidiaries		0.2%	23%	4%
6. Innovative foreign subsidiaries		0.2%	20%	12%
7. Non-innovators		0.1%	10%	3%
8. All firms		0.2%	10%	3%
Ratios				
All agglomerated innovators—relative to:				
A All other innovators	(1/2)	1.58	1.25	2.08
B All firms in "high-tech" industries	(1/3)	2.90	2.59	7.90
C Innovative firms in "high-tech" industries	(1/4)	0.75	0.45	4.01
D All foreign subsidiaries	(1/5)	3.41	0.65	2.03
E Innovative foreign subsidiaries	(1/6)	2.90	0.75	0.66
F All firms	(1/8)	3.34	1.50	2.72
Indirectly related to NR—relative to:				
G Directly related to NR	(1.2/1.1)	32.35	1.21	0.11
H All other innovators	(1.2/2)	2.99	1.42	0.47
I All firms in "high-tech" industries	(1.2/3)	5.50	2.93	1.80
J Innovative firms in "high-tech" industries	(1.2/4)	1.43	0.52	0.91
K All firms	(1.2/8)	6.33	1.70	0.62
Directly related to NR—relative to:				
L All other innovators	(1.1/2)	0.09	1.17	4.47
M All firms in "high-tech" industries	(1.1/3)	0.17	2.41	17.00
N Innovative firms in "high-tech" industries	(1.1/4)	0.04	0.42	8.63
O All firms	(1.1/8)	0.20	1.40	5.86

Source: Author elaboration from database.

firms in those industries. This is explained by the fact that there were only three innovative firms in those industries and one of them had an extremely high level of professional employment, so skewing the average for the very small group.

In summary, for the agglomerated innovators in the *directly* NR-related industries, this pattern corresponds almost exactly with the observations in previous studies of this period. Innovation consisted very largely of intensive investment in technology that was already embodied in capital goods, and as a consequence, production capability was being considerably strengthened. But there was almost no sign at all of R&D within the firms themselves, and knowledge-creating innovative capability was almost invisible. However, it was perhaps not totally invisible because these industries were relatively intensive employers of skilled professionals, and the borderline between knowledge-using and knowledge-creating is often very blurred for such workers.

However, it is striking that the kind of innovation in the *indirectly* NR-related industries was completely different. Here it was being driven by levels of in-house R&D activity that were higher than in any other manufacturing industries, even higher than in the innovative firms in the so-called "high-tech" industries and also higher than in innovative MNE subsidiaries. Clearly, even in the depths of the destruction of innovative capabilities in the late 1980s and early 1990s, the agricultural sector was sustaining a group of chemical and machinery suppliers that constituted a locus of agglomerated innovating firms that were the leading edge of knowledge-creating innovative activity in the Argentine manufacturing sector.

(ii) Change in innovative behavior during the 1990s

Our observations here, based on the average rate of change of the selected indicators over the period 1992 to 2001, inevitably reflect the financial crisis of 2001. This severely depressed economic activity at the time of the final survey date, and most of the absolute values of the scale of economic and technological activity therefore fell. We nevertheless use the same (relative) indicators of the intensity of innovative activities in order to show (as summarized in Table 8.8) what occurred over the full decade from 1992, despite (or because of) the short-term instability in the economy.

The sectorally agglomerated innovators increased their R&D intensity at an average annual rate of 5 percent over the decade, and this reached a level of more than 0.8 percent of sales by 2001. This was slower than among MNE subsidiaries and all firms in general, but it is interesting that the increase was particularly sharp in the last few years of the period, indicating a significant commitment to knowledge creation despite the economic instability. This commitment was reflected in the fact that the rate of growth of R&D intensity in these firms was more than three times faster than the rate among all other innovators and more than eight times faster than the typical rate among all firms in the "high-tech" sectors. More specifically, while the R&D intensity of the agglomerated innovators was rising, it was falling among the small number of innovators in the high-tech sectors (at an average rate of 10 percent per year).

Perhaps more striking, however, was the location of this rising intensity within the group of agglomerated innovators. It was concentrated among the innovators in the manufacturing sectors directly related to NR-based production—the sectors that had demonstrated insignificant R&D activity in the early 1990s. Consequently, albeit starting from a low base, the R&D intensity of this sub-group of firms grew at the extraordinarily rapid rate of 44 percent per year. As indicated by the comparative ratios in rows L to O, this was more than five times faster than for all manufacturing firms and far outstripped the rate among all other innovators and especially the firms in high-tech industries.[11]

But one must bear in mind that, despite the zero rate of growth of R&D intensity among the agglomerated innovators in the sectors indirectly related to NR-based production, they remained the most R&D-intensive group of firms among all those identified in Table 8.8. At more than 1 percent of sales, their level in 2001 was substantially more than twice as high as that of all other innovators, and more than five times higher than the rate among firms in high-tech industries.

Alongside their commitment to sustaining and deepening their R&D activity, the agglomerated innovators as a whole rapidly increased the professional skill intensity of their workforce—at an average annual rate of more than 25 percent. For the group as a whole, this was faster than the rate among all manufacturing firms and all the firms in high-tech industries, but it was somewhat slower than the rate among other innovators, especially innovators in the high-tech sectors (row C)—though the last comparison must again be qualified by the very small number of firms and the exceptional growth of professional employment intensity among them (more than 100 percent per year), especially in one firm.

Again it is striking that, among the sectorally agglomerated innovators as a whole, the growth of professional employment intensity was especially rapid in the sectors directly related to NR-based production. At 50 percent per year,

[11] The trend for this sub-group of agglomerated innovators was possibly part of a broader pattern in which there was a catching-up effect, in the sense that the groups with lower intensity in the early 1990s increased their intensity relatively rapidly—e.g. the non-innovators and all firms in general. Within that, it is striking that among all the groups that started the period with very low levels of R&D intensity, the agglomerated innovators in the sectors directly related to NR production increased particularly rapidly—(44 percent) compared with 8 percent and 10 percent.

Table 8.8. Agglomerated innovators: technological behavior—change: 1992–2001

Types of firm: agglomerated innovators and others		Average annual rate of change 1992–2001		
		R&D intensity	Skilled professionals	Capital investment
		(Mean values for firm types)		
1. Agglomerated innovators in sectors related to natural resources Of which:		5%	26.7%	−19.0%
1.1 Directly related to NR (food products)		44%	50.0%	−20.3%
1.2 Indirectly reacted to NR (agro-chemicals and agro-machinery)		0%	17.6%	−11.1%
2. All other innovators		1%	35.4%	−17.1%
3. All firms in "high-tech" industries— average		1%	14.7%	−18.5%
4. Innovative firms in "high-tech" industries		−10%	103.8%	−24.7%
5. All foreign subsidiaries		7%	14.1%	−19.2%
6. Innovative foreign subsidiaries		3%	51.3%	−19.2%
7. Non-innovators		10%	3.9%	−17.9%
8. All firms		8%	10.0%	−17.8%
Ratios				
All agglomerated innovators—relative to:				
A All other innovators	(1/2)	3.61	0.75	0.9
B All firms in "high-tech" industries	(1/3)	8.29	1.82	0.97
C Innovative firms in "high-tech" industries	(1/4)	−0.44	0.26	1.3
D All foreign subsidiaries	(1/5)	0.7	1.89	1.01
E Innovative foreign subsidiaries	(1/6)	1.38	0.52	1.01
F All firms	(1/8)	0.57	2.67	0.94
Indirectly related to NR—relative to:				
G Directly related to NR	(1.2/1.1)	0.00	1.41	0.46
H All other innovators	(1.2/2)	0.00	1.99	0.38
I All firms in "high-tech" industries	(1.2/3)	0.00	4.82	0.42
J Innovative firms in "high-tech" industries	(1.2/4)	0.00	0.17	2.23
K All firms	(1.2/8)	0.00	7.06	0.4
Directly related to NR—relative to:				
L All other innovators	(1.1/2)	34.89	1.41	0.84
M All firms in "high-tech" industries	(1.1/3)	80.00	3.41	0.91
N Innovative firms in "high-tech" industries	(1.1/4)	−4.25	0.48	1.22
O All firms	(1.1/6)	5.51	5.00	0.88

Note: Since all values are negative for the variable changes in capital investment, the ratios were calculated as the inverse and can therefore be interpreted in the same way as the others—i.e. "higher is better."

Source: Author elaboration from database.

this was about five times faster than among all firms, more than three times faster than firms on average in the high-tech industries, and roughly similar to other innovators.

The pattern with respect to capital investment is somewhat different. Across the board, there was a reduction in the intensity of investment from the relatively high levels at the start of the decade. For the agglomerated innovators as a whole, the average rate of reduction was 19 percent per year, and this was concentrated among firms in the sectors directly related to NR-based production where it had been so spectacularly high in 1992. In broad terms, however, these rates of reduction in investment intensity were similar across the different groups of firms shown in Table 8.8. Even in the case of the relatively rapid reduction among the agglomerated innovators in the directly NR-related industries, the difference compared to other groups of firms was slight (rows L–M).

In summary, the character of the innovation capabilities and activities of the agglomerated innovators appears to have changed considerably during the 1990s. Much of this change was concentrated among the 18 innovators in the sectors *directly* related to NR-based production—the group that had (i) depended heavily in the early 1990s on implementing innovation by investment in new technology that was already embodied in capital goods, and (ii) supported innovation by negligible levels of in-house R&D. In the subsequent decade, this group of firms increased their R&D intensity at extremely rapid rates. One must recognize the low base they started from, but by the end of the period the level of R&D intensity of these firms was becoming meaningful—slightly more than half the level for all other manufacturing firms, and nearly the same as the level for all firms in the high-tech industries. At the same time, they were also raising the professional intensity of their workforce at rates that were faster than most other groups of firms. In other words, they were not merely augmenting their production capability by using other people's technology; they were building a base of R&D activity and professional human capital to constitute their own significant stock of knowledge-creating innovative capability.

Alongside that, the 27 firms that were already R&D-intensive innovators in the sectors *indirectly* related to NR-based production sustained that earlier level of R&D intensity and further deepened the professional-intensity of their workforce. Taken together, the two groups of agglomerated innovators (45 firms in total) were coming to constitute a very substantial locus of knowledge-creating and knowledge-using innovative capability in Argentine manufacturing. This seems much more substantial and potentially significant than the much smaller pockets of innovative activity, typically less R&D-intensive and less professional-intensive, in other areas of manufacturing. This gap is especially wide, in terms of both numbers of significantly innovating firms and the quality of their innovative capability, when it is compared with the conventionally defined "high-tech" industries.

Table 8.9. Agglomerated innovators: innovation-related linkages with other agents (1998–2001)

Types of firm: agglomerated innovators and others		Intensity of links with:	
		All organizations	R&D institutes
1. Agglomerated innovators in sectors related to natural resources		**3.89**	1.60
Of which:			
1.1 Directly related to NR (food products)		3.61	1.60
1.2 Indirectly reacted to NR (agro-chemicals and agro-machinery)		3.86	1.50
2. All other innovators		3.58	1.40
3. All firms in "high-tech" industries—average		1.31	0.48
4. Innovative firms in "high-tech" industries		5.30	2.60
5. All foreign subsidiaries		3.78	1.10
6. Innovative foreign subsidiaries		4.60	1.8
7. Non-innovators		1.98	0.69
8. All firms		2.20	0.79
Ratios			
All agglomerated innovators—relative to:			
A All other innovators	(1/2)	1.09	1.14
B All firms in "high-tech" industries	(1/3)	2.97	3.33
C Innovative firms in "high-tech" industries	(1/4)	4.60	0.62
D All foreign subsidiaries	(1/5)	1.03	1.45
E Innovative foreign subsidiaries	(1/6)	0.85	0.89
F All firms	(1/8)	1.77	2.03
Indirectly related to NR—relative to:			
G Directly related to NR	(1.2/1.1)	1.07	0.94
H All other innovators	(1.2/2)	1.08	1.07
I All firms in "high-tech" industries	(1.2/3)	2.95	3.13
J Innovative firms in "high-tech" industries	(1.2/4)	0.73	0.58
K All firms	(1.2/8)	1.75	1.90
Directly related to NR—relative to:			
L All other innovators	(1.1/2)	1.01	1.14
M All firms in "high-tech" industries	(1.1/3)	2.76	3.33
N Innovative firms in "high-tech" industries	(1.1/4)	0.68	0.62
O All firms	(1.1/8)	1.64	2.03

Source: Author elaboration from database.

(iii) The agglomerated innovators' innovation-related interactions with other organizations

The 1998–2001 innovation survey asked firms about their interactions with other organizations in connection with their innovation activities. The 12 response options included parent companies and other affiliates, as well as local universities, technology centers, suppliers, consultants, and so forth.

Indicators of the intensity of these linkages have been calculated simply as the sum of all the "yes" answers to these options.[12] They are grouped into the two categories shown in Table 8.9: (i) links with all organizations—both national and international—indicating the general innovation-related interconnectedness of firms, and (ii) the subset of these consisting of links specifically with R&D institutes—again including both national and international institutes.

The agglomerated innovators' general innovation-related inter-connectedness is higher than that for the other groups. On average, they have links with almost four types of organization, and this is more intensive than all the other categories of firm except for innovative MNE subsidiaries. This is more or less the same for both sub-groups. This does not reflect a pattern of linkages with other firms simply for the acquisition and implementation of innovation that is already embodied in capital goods or other inputs. Instead, a substantial component of the general linkage intensity is concerned specifically with R&D institutes. Again the intensity of this kind of interaction is relatively high among the agglomerated innovators, and this is similar for both sub-groups. Thus, for both groups, the intensity is higher than among almost all the other types of firm. The exception in this case is the small group of innovative firms in high-technology sectors.

In other words, as well as having considerably strengthened their in-house knowledge-intensive activities and human resources, the agglomerated innovators were by the end of the decade deeply enmeshed in networks of innovation-related interaction with other organizations, including R&D institutes. Indeed, in comparison with most other areas of Argentinean manufacturing industry, they were more strongly embedded in such networks.

8.5.3. Economic Performance

As before, we proceed in two steps. First, we concentrate on performance in the early 1990s and then we analyze evolution over the 1990s. We focus on three indicators:

- *export intensity*, as a reflection of economic performance in world markets (measured as exports as a proportion of total sales—percent);
- *market share*, as a reflection of economic performance in the domestic market (measured as sales of firms as a proportion of total sales in their five-digit sector);

---

[12] Strictly speaking, they do not measure the "intensity" of interaction for each firm in the sense of the frequency of links with specific kinds of organization. Instead, they indicate the existence of at least one link with each type of other organization. These are summed across firms and shown here as the average per firm for the various categories of firm.

- *size*, as a reflection of general economic importance and, when analyzed in terms of change over time, as a commonly used indicator of the success of firms (measured simply in terms of the number of employees).

(i) Economic performance in the early 1990s

It is striking that, as indicated in Table 8.10, by the beginning of the 1990s the agglomerated innovators were already much more export intensive than any other group of firms. They were three times as export intensive as all firms on average and as firms in "high-tech" industries (both all of them and the significant innovators among them); and almost twice as export intensive as innovators in all other industries. However, as might be expected, the high level of export intensity was particularly pronounced for the agglomerated innovators in the sectors directly related to NR-based production. These were almost three times as export intensive as all other innovators, four times as export intensive as the average firm in all manufacturing industry, and almost five times as export intensive as firms in "high-tech" sectors.

The superiority of the agglomerated innovators is also evident with respect to the indicator of general economic importance, size. Their average size of 440 employees was larger relative to all manufacturing firms, other innovative firms, and, and high-tech firms in general. These gaps were particular pronounced in the case of the larger agglomerated innovators in the sectors *directly* related to NR-based production (nearly 700 employees). However, both the agglomerated innovators in general and even this sub-group were smaller than the small number of large innovative firms in "high-tech" industries and than foreign subsidiaries in general.

Given their high level of export orientation, it is perhaps not surprising that the agglomerated innovators performed relatively poorly in terms of their share of the domestic market. They performed better than the average manufacturing firm and the average "high-tech" firm; but worse than other groups—in particular, the innovative firms in the "high-tech" industries.

(ii) Change in economic performance during the 1990s

As indicated in Table 8.11, our group of agglomerated innovators clearly outperformed all other groups with respect to change in size (by employment). However, this was an issue about *reducing* size less than the others. In the context of a general reduction of employment across all manufacturing in Argentina during the 1990s, the agglomerated innovators reduced employment least—by only 1.5 percent per year. This was three times less than the average firm in manufacturing and the non-agglomerated other innovators. More strikingly, it was between four and five times less than in foreign

Table 8.10. Agglomerated innovators: aspects of economic performance—1992

Types of firm: agglomerated innovators and others		Export intensity	Market share	Size—number of employees
			(Mean values for firm types)	
		%	%	Number of employees
1. **Agglomerated innovators in sectors related to natural resources** Of which:		21	5	444
1.1 Directly related to NR (food products)		29	4	684
1.2 Indirectly related to NR (agro-chemicals and agro-machinery)		16	5	331
2. All other innovators		12	5	420
3. All firms in "high-tech" industries		6	2	184
4. Innovative firms in "high-tech" industries		6	10	1330
5. All foreign subsidiaries		12	6	584
6. Innovative foreign subsidiaries		19	7	1012
7. Non-innovators		5	3	232
8. All firms		7	3	259
Ratios				
All agglomerated innovators—relative to:				
A All other innovators	(1/2)	1.75	0.83	1.06
B All firms in "high-tech" industries	(1/3)	3.5	1.88	2.41
C Innovative firms in "high-tech" industries	(1/4)	3.28	0.45	0.33
D All foreign subsidiaries	(1/5)	1.75	0.75	0.76
E Innovative foreign subsidiaries	(1/6)	1.11	0.64	0.44
F All firms	(1/8)	3	1.32	1.71
Indirectly related to NR—relative to:				
G Directly related to NR	(1.2/1.1)	0.55	1.25	0.48
H All other innovators	(1.2/2)	1.33	0.93	0.79
I All firms in "high-tech" industries	(1.2/3)	2.67	2.08	1.8
J Innovative firms in "high-tech" industries	(1.2/4)	2.5	0.5	0.28
K All firms	(1.2/8)	2.29	1.47	1.28
Directly related to NR—relative to:				
L All other innovators	(1.1/2)	2.42	0.74	1.63
M All firms in "high-tech" industries	(1.1/3)	4.83	1.67	3.72
N Innovative firms in "high-tech" industries	(1.1/4)	4.53	0.4	0.51
O All firms	(1.1/8)	4.14	1.18	2.64

Source: Author elaboration from database.

subsidiaries, and six times less than in the innovative "high-tech" firms. The difference was especially striking for the agglomerated innovators in the sectors that were indirectly related to NR-based production—the suppliers of chemical and machinery inputs to agriculture. They reduced employment by only 0.5 percent per year—three times slower than the innovators in the sectors that were directly related. Particularly striking is the fact that this was eight and 16 times less than in "high-tech" industries in general and in innovative "high-tech" firms in particular—industries frequently identified as the potential basis for labor absorption and employment growth in Latin America.

Turning to market share, agglomerated innovators in general increased their internal market share over the period by 9.2 percent per year. This increase is superior to the one registered by almost all the other groups; except all other innovators, and innovative foreign subsidiaries, which achieved slightly higher participation in the domestic market during the period than our group of agglomerated firms.

Comparisons within the group of agglomerated innovators indicate that agglomerated innovators directly related to natural resources increased their share in local markets by twice as much as agglomerated innovators in sectors linked indirectly to NR. Thus, when compared with other groups, this sub-group increased its participation in local markets by four times as much as the average firm in manufacturing and almost twice as much as highly innovative firms within the "high-tech" sector.

Finally, agglomerated innovators increased export intensity more than their share in domestic markets. Their export intensity increased on average by 14 percent per year during the period. In general, as before, with respect to this indicator they outperformed all other groups of firms, with the exception of two: all other innovators and all firms. However, given the high values with which they started the period relative to all the other groups, they ended up in 2001 still having an export intensity that was almost three times higher than the average firm, and 1.5 times higher than all the other innovators.

Strikingly, agglomerated innovators indirectly related to NR increased their export intensity seven times more than the group of agglomerated innovators in sectors directly related to natural resources and twice as much as other "high-tech" companies. As a consequence of this evolution, they ended 2001 with an export intensity very similar to that registered by the agglomerated innovators in industries directly related to NR (around 33 percent), the highest among all the groups. In the next section, we turn to examine in more detail the emergence of this group of increasingly export-intensive innovators that were indirectly related to natural resource-based production, focusing in particular on agricultural machinery producers.

Table 8.11. Agglomerated innovators: economic performance—change: 1992–2001

Types of firm: agglomerated innovators and others		Export intensity	Market share (Mean values for firm types)	Size—number of employees
		%	%	Number of employees
1. Agglomerated innovators in sectors related to natural resources Of which:		14.3	9.2	−1.5
1.1 Directly related to NR (food products)		3.4	13.1	−1.4
1.2 Indirectly related to NR (agro-chemicals and agro-machinery)		25	6	−0.5
2. All other innovators		27	14.4	−5.1
3. All firms in "high-tech" industries—average		12.5	−2.1	−4.3
4. Innovative firms in "high-tech" industries		−16	7.5	−8.5
5. All foreign subsidiaries		12.5	8.3	−5.7
6. Innovative foreign subsidiaries		6.6	14.3	−7.9
7. Non-innovators		20	−1.6	−4.3
8. All firms		18	4.4	−4.2
Ratios				
All agglomerated innovators—relative to:				
A All other innovators	(1)/(2)	0.53	0.64	3
B All firms in "high-tech" industries	(1)/(3)	1.14		3
C Innovative firms in "high-tech" industries	(1)/(4)		1.22	6
D All foreign subsidiaries	(1)/(5)	1.14	1.1	4
E Innovative foreign subsidiaries	(1/6)	2.17	0.64	5
F All firms	(1/8)	0.8	2.08	3
Indirectly related to NR—relative to:				
G Directly related to NR	(1.2)/(1.1)	7.25	0.46	3
H All other innovators	(1.2)/(2)	0.92	0.42	10
I All firms in "high-tech" industries	(1.2)/(3)	2		8
J Innovative firms in "high-tech" industries	(1.2/4)		0.8	16
K All firms	(1.2)/(6)	1.4	1.36	
Directly related to NR—relative to:				
L All other innovators	(1.1)/(2)	0.13	0.91	4
M All firms in "high-tech" industries	(1.1/3)	0.28		3
N Innovative firms in "high-tech" industries	(1.1/4)		1.75	6
O All firms	(1.1)/(6)	0.19	4.14	3

Notes: All indicators are average yearly rate of change.

Source: Author elaboration from database.

8.6. TRANSFORMATION IN AGRICULTURE: NEW OPPORTUNITIES FOR INNOVATION IN RELATED SECTORS

8.6.1. Transformations in the Agricultural Sector

During the 1970s and 1980s, in a macroeconomic scenario of high instability and depressed economic activity, and after years of unfavorable internal relative prices, the agricultural sector in Argentina performed poorly. It grew less than the rest of the economy, with the total volume of output in 1990 being little higher than it had been in the 1960s, and it was very slow in adopting the new technologies and organizational arrangements associated with the Green Revolution. However, in the 1990s, in association with the openness and deregulation of the economy, and with the increasing exposure of the Argentinean economy to international competitive pressures, the sector recovered its economic dynamism of previous periods. Between 1990 and 2005 the production of the sector grew by 5.7 percent per year on average (while GDP growth was 3.4 percent per annum), and the total production of grains (mainly soya, maize, and wheat) more than doubled, from around 30 million tons at the end of the 1980s to around 70 million tons.

Besides this economic dynamism, however, the sector acquired during this period a technological dynamism that differed from anything in the recent past (Bisang and Kosacoff, 2006). Several transformations occurring in parallel contributed to this technological dynamism. These included in particular the massive diffusion of agro-chemicals and transgenic seeds; the expansion of the agricultural frontier; the emergence of a new actor, professional contractors; and the rapid diffusion of "precision agriculture." However, the most dramatic technological change in the 1990s, interacting with all the other transformations, was the massive adoption of the radically novel zero tillage (ZT) technology. In 1990 the proportion of the area cultivated under ZT was almost negligible; in 2000 it was applied to 50 percent of the total cultivated area; and in 2005–6 it had reached 70 percent. This had enormous implications for both the agricultural sector itself and for its suppliers:

In narrow terms, ZT involves planting crop seeds in previously unprepared soil. However, more broadly, it involves a complete farm management system covering planting practices, plant residue management, weed and pest control, and other activities through to harvesting. In Argentina, as elsewhere, such as in Brazil, it has also been closely associated with the use of genetically modified seeds that are resistant to herbicides. It is therefore a technological "package" that requires the close integration of several components. Moreover, a particularly important feature of this package is that it is very sensitive to ecological conditions, and its individual component parts require substantial integrated adaptation for small variations in local conditions (Ekboir, 2003). Interestingly, therefore, the technology (or management system) encourages networks of close collaboration by farmers, professional contractors, scientific and extension institutions, and suppliers of biotech and chemical products (seeds, pesticides, and herbicides), as well as suppliers of the machinery component of the package—in particular, the specialized seed planters, sprayers, and equipment for residue management. We explore in more detail below the paths of localized innovation associated with selected components of this package.

8.6.2. Emerging Localized Innovation in Seeds

Although international seed suppliers drawing on innovation undertaken largely outside Argentina captured a large part of the seed market opened up by this transformation of the sector, a striking feature of the last decade has been the emergence of significant localized innovation in the seeds industry. The leading firm in this development has been Nidera—a trading and agribusiness company with strong roots in Argentina and the Netherlands. Its main activities include the procurement, conditioning, and export handling of grains and oilseeds; the manufacture and refining of vegetable oils; research, development, and production of agronomic seeds; and the sale and distribution of a wide variety of agricultural inputs to the farm sector. Since the beginning of 2006, Nidera has also been active in the bio-energy market, and since 2007 it has moved further toward the energy market by becoming active in the green power industry. The company has foreign affiliates in 15 countries, including Brazil, France, the United Kingdom, Germany, Russia, Italy, and Australia.

Nidera concentrates its main innovative efforts in the area of agronomic seeds in Argentina. Despite operating in a highly concentrated market, dominated mostly by a few large multinational corporations (today, the top ten MNCs control half of the world's commercial seed sales), the company has managed to capture a leading market share in soybean, sunflower, and maize seeds. This has been supported by an extensive proprietary germplasm base and a strong applied genomics competence. This market position is globally significant because Argentina, with 21 percent of world soybean grain production, in third place after the United States (32 percent) and Brazil (28 percent), is one of the main world markets for soybean seeds.

The main innovations of the company in the area of seeds have been developed largely on the basis of strategic alliances with other companies. One important example is the BASF/Nidera new CLEARFIELD sunflower trait (CLHA-Plus)—a new genetic trait for the CLEARFIELD sunflower production system which was developed by Nidera in alliance with

BASF. Weed control is often one of the most limiting factors for global sunflower production, and this production system is an innovative agronomic solution that matches carefully selected hybrid seeds with custom-designed BASF imidazolinone herbicides.[13] CLHA-Plus makes it easier for seed companies to breed tolerance to BASF imidazolinone herbicides in high-yielding sunflower hybrids. This, combined with the fact that the new gene, CLHA-Plus, was developed in high-performing sunflower germplasm, will result in superior sunflower hybrids in the future.

8.6.3. The Agricultural Machinery Industry in the 1990s and 2000s

Agricultural machinery was first produced in Argentina at the end of the 19th century by immigrants with the technical capacities to satisfy the needs of the country's successful producers of primary goods. They were protected at that time not only by high transport costs and their closeness to the users, as were many other industries in Argentina at that time. Also important was the early mechanization of agriculture in the country. This was similar in several respects to the USA and, for example, in 1929 the sector in Argentina patented the first self-propelled harvester in the world, and in 1944 launched the first harvester for sunflower seeds (Baruj et al., 2005).

However, it was not until the 1950s and 1960s that the number of companies and locally produced models expanded substantially, after the government declared the sector a national priority (Dec. 20056/2952). During this period, within the framework of the ISI regime, high protective tariffs and other specific policies such as import quotas were introduced to preserve the domestic market for domestically produced products. As a result, major MNCs such as John Deere were attracted to Argentina, and a large number of domestic producers started to produce tractors, seeding machines, harvesters, and other types of agricultural implements, mainly copying designs of machinery produced in advanced countries. The sector developed to satisfy domestic demand but did not reach the levels of competitiveness and innovation necessary to penetrate external markets.

The first period of openness and liberalization in the mid-1970s therefore had a significant negative effect on the sector. Several types of equipment previously produced locally were replaced by imports, and many companies

---

[13] The CLEARFIELD Production System has been used extensively since 1995. The system matches carefully selected advanced seed varieties/hybrids with custom-designed imidazolinone herbicides. All CLEARFIELD varieties and hybrids are recognized as non-genetically modified by international authorities. At the present time, BASF possesses the world's largest portfolio of non-genetically modified imidazolinone-tolerant traits and has established relationships with over 100 seed companies throughout the world.

exited the market unable to face the increasing competitive pressure. The second period of openness and liberalization initiated in the 1990s was followed again by an increase in the share of imports and the exit of national companies. However, this time the transformations were associated with a phase of technological and economic dynamism in the agricultural sector which benefited specific parts of the industry. This had only a little to do *directly* with the changed policy context.[14] Instead, it was shaped primarily by an impressive combination of technological and economic transformations in the agricultural sector that opened up a set of new opportunities for particular types of agricultural machinery producer.

The rapid and widespread diffusion of ZT technologies provided new opportunities for the agricultural machinery sector. This was not simply a consequence of the general scale and growth of demand, which in any case generally favored imports more than the domestic production of machinery. Probably more important was the emergence of particular market niches that favored the evolution and emergence of specific producers of agricultural machinery. More specifically, it opened niches for the evolution of only certain types of firm within the sector because not all types of agricultural machinery were similarly affected.

As shown in Figure 8.1, the favored segments were the manufacturers of relatively specialized self-propelled sprayers (c) and seeding machines (or planters) (d), as well as producers of other knowledge-intensive implements and associated inputs for agriculture.[15] In contrast, in the case of more generally applicable tractors (a) and harvesters (b), the share of the domestic market held by local producers was substantially reduced in the 1990s. The favorable position of seeding machinery and self-propelled sprayers can be explained by the combination of two factors. First, ZT technologies require complex and precise planters and related equipment, including spraying machines, which have to be closely adapted to the local ecological and organizational characteristics of their operational conditions. Second, Argentina, together with Brazil, was a pioneer in the diffusion of ZT technologies.[16] These two conditions meant that these kinds of equipment were not available as imports at the time they were required by innovative agricultural producers. Some domestic producers, in association with agricultural technology institutes such as Instituto Nacional de Tecnología Agropecuaria-/NTA (National Agricultural Technology Institute), responded very well to this challenge by timing the

---

[14] Although trade policy reforms permitted tariff-free imports of agricultural machinery, there were also compensatory payments to local machinery manufacturers, as well as other tax allowances under competitiveness programs (Bisang, 2003: 8).

[15] For instance, one sector for which we do not have systematic data, but which is emerging and growing, is the sector producing satellite software and hardware for precision agriculture.

[16] Although ZT research and extension programmes have been implemented in more than 40 countries, massive adoption only occurred in a few regions, such as Argentina and Brazil, where strong networks for participatory research and extension already existed (Ekboir, 2003).

development of product innovations to meet the requirements of producers incorporating ZT managements systems. Indeed, several observers of the diffusion of ZT in Argentina and Brazil have argued that the rapid diffusion of this technology would not have been possible in these countries without the active participation of these specialized suppliers of machinery.

When looking at the export side of this story, however, it might be argued that this segment of machinery production, tailored to the specific needs of local agricultural producers, would have limited opportunities in external markets. Indeed, export data might seem at first sight to support such a view. As can be seen in Figure 8.2, the share of exports in total production of seeding machines has not increased to the extent attained by tractors and harvesters, which started to recover after 2003 with rising shares of exports in production. However, as we illustrate in the cases below, these statistics hide a different process of connecting to external markets that is taking place in the producers of more specialized equipment: the internationalization of production. Having accumulated substantial capacities to satisfy the demands of innovative agricultural producers in Argentina, those companies that were pioneers in the massive adoption of ZT technologies are in a strong position to produce machinery adapted to other ecological conditions by setting up production in the context of those conditions in other countries. As is often the case with any process of internationalization, this has started in neighboring countries, in this case Uruguay and Brazil. In principle, though, this might also evolve toward more distant countries to which these producers have already started to export, such as Russia and South Africa. However, as it is too early to know the next phase of this story, this is mere speculation.

8.6.4. The Experience of Two Selected Firms

Case 1: PLA SA—a leader in the market segment for self-propelled sprayers

PLA started as a private family company in 1975, and became a public company in 1995. At the moment, it has 400 employees and is positioned 546th in the ranking of Argentinean companies with respect to sales. In the early stages, the company produced a varied range of machinery, equipment, and parts. However, in the 1990s it became specialized in agricultural implements: in particular, sprayers and planters. The company has been able to develop world-leading innovations in these products and these have received numerous national and international prizes.

Its more innovative products are different types of self-propelled sprayers (e.g. self-propelled inter-seeders and sprayers controlled by computer and satellite), and several systems for variable dosage of herbicides and fertilizers.

(a) Tractors

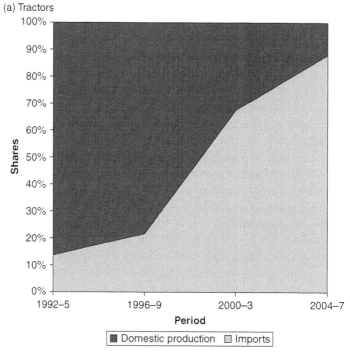

(b) Harvesters

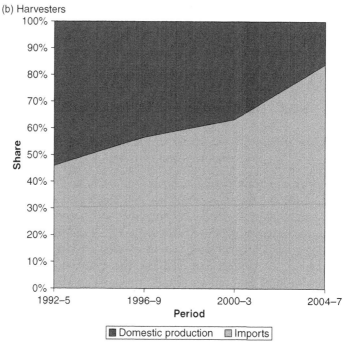

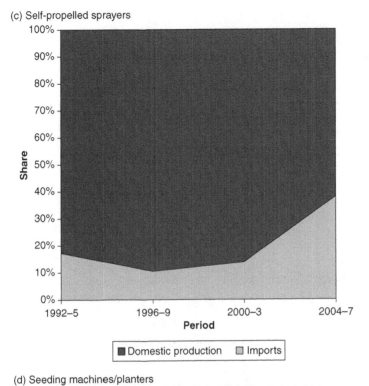

(c) Self-propelled sprayers

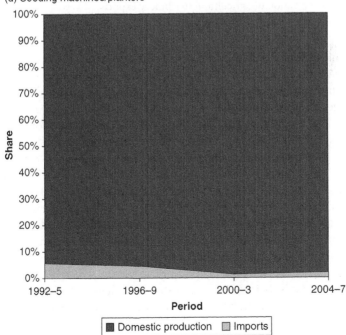

(d) Seeding machines/planters

Fig. 8.1. Agricultural machinery: shares of domestic demand

Note: Own elaboration, based on data from Camara Argentina Fabricantes de Maquinaria Agricola (CAFMA).

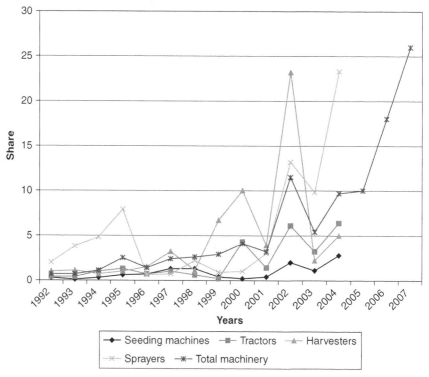

Fig. 8.2. The evolution of agricultural machinery exports

Note: Own elaboration, based on data from CAFMA.

As a result of these innovations in the sprayer segment, PLA is the leader in Argentina, with 30 percent of the market. But the company does not serve only the Argentinean market. It has recently started to internationalize by setting up production in other countries in Latin America, opening production plants in Brazil, Paraguay, Uruguay, and Bolivia with the purpose of serving the markets in these countries. It also exports to distant locations such as Russia, Ukraine, Kazakhstan, and South Africa. In this last group of countries, the company has exclusive distribution points, which also provide after-sales services, and are used to identify specific characteristics of the demand in local agricultural contexts. Owing to the expansion that this incipient process of internationalization has encouraged, the company has broadened its innovative efforts to include not only product innovation, but also process innovations, which allow increases in productivity and scale.

In the view of the company, two things have been crucial in explaining its success. The first is its intensive use of strategic alliances with other suppliers such as Profertil and Petrobrás, which provide pesticides and fertilizer, with the aim of jointly developing and proving technological packages. The second has been the extensive use of national programs supporting innovation. In particular, since 2000 the company has used five programs administered by FONTAR, a national technology funding agency, to contribute to the costs of R&D activities.[17] In 2006, for instance, the company obtained from FONTAR a matching grant of half of the total cost (Arg$570,000) of developing a family of sprayers for international markets; and in 2007 it obtained 23 percent of the total cost of more than $1 million to develop a flexible multi-purpose carrier. The company also invests a considerable amount of resources, including time, in developing close connections and links with clients. These are crucial in a sector in which the main form of technical change is not the launching and marketing of radically new products, but continuing trajectories of incremental improvements and innovations to existing products, based on specific demands from clients.

Case 2: Agrometal SA—a leader in the market segment for seeding machines

Agrometal SA was created in 1950 as a cooperative of 46 entrepreneurs in the province of Cordoba. The company produces agricultural soil breaking and seeding machinery (or planters). It fabricated its first planter in 1957. In 1961 it became a public company. In 1981 Agrometal was a pioneer in incorporating French origin pneumatic suction deflectors in its equipment; and in 1983 it was the first Argentinean company to introduce double disks with twinned limiting wheels which result in reduced soil damage.

As early as the 1980s, Agrometal started to invest and innovate to meet the needs of ZT. As a result, since then the company has developed several innovations which have been key in the rapid diffusion of this technology in Argentina: (i) in 1985 it developed machinery to allow fertilizer to be spread to deeper parts of the soil, (ii) in 1992 it developed fine and coarse seed planters, (iii) in 1995 it developed a technology which facilitated early sowing, the star-shaped crop residue sweeper disks, (iv) in 1996 it introduced a turbo blade in the machines, offering a solution for the removal of excessive and wet-crop residues in non-resistant soils, (v) in 1998 it developed jointly with Monsanto an inter-sowing system, and (vi) in 2004 it developed precision seeders for mixed seed types, with the unique capability to perform wheat-soya inter-sowing. As a result of all these innovations and product developments, Agrometal has become the leading company in seeding machines in Argentina. It has 20 percent of the market and exports not only to countries in Mercosur, but also to distant markets in countries such as Italy, Spain, and Russia. Since 2000,

[17] FONTAR (El Fondo Tecnologico Argentino) is a funding body managed by the National Agency for Scientific and Technological Promotion (ANPCYT) under the Ministry of Science, Technology and Productive Innovation.

in order to support its increasing production, the company has also focused on improving its productive capacity. In 2004, for instance, it opened a new plant that increased capacity by 50 percent. Another recent reflection of its success is the fact that in 2008 the company bought for $4.5 million 60 percent of its competitor in Brazil, Fankhauser.

8.7. CONCLUSIONS

Argentina, after several decades of import-substituting industrialization, during which it accumulated substantial technological capabilities, has been a rather unstable country for firms. Many studies have analyzed the erosion and destruction of industries, firms, institutions, and technological capabilities that occurred as a consequence of this instability, after the initial step of liberalization, privatization, and deregulation in the mid 1970s and its deepening at the beginning of the 1990s. In this chapter we have taken a different route. We acknowledged the destruction, as well as the general patterns identified in most of the previous studies. However, we explored a different issue: whether there was any subsequent resurgence of innovative capacity in manufacturing industry and, if so, how the sectoral "direction" of that resurgence evolved.

We did so in two ways: first, by an aggregate analysis of innovative firms in manufacturing sectors, and then by examining in more detail the experience of resurgent innovative activity in industries supplying seed and machinery inputs to agriculture. We review these two parts of the chapter separately below, and then pull both together in the concluding comments.

(i) The aggregate analysis of innovative firms and sectors

The aggregate analysis provided a number of interesting results.

First, we found that highly innovative firms in Argentine manufacturing are agglomerated in a few sectors; five accounted for 45 percent of total innovators in our sample.

Second, we found that there is substantial co-location of domestically owned firms and MNE subsidiaries among the significant innovators in these sectors. The balance varies between the sectors, for example between agricultural machinery, where nearly all the significant innovators are domestic, and agro-chemicals, where MNE subsidiaries predominate. However, in contrast to most other sectors, there is none in which one category or the other is absent.

Third, we found that four of these five manufacturing sectors with agglomerated innovators were linked to other sectors producing goods based on natural resources. One we characterize as being "directly" related to natural resource (NR) exploitation and processing—e.g. engaged in processing meat, producing vegetable oils, or manufacturing food products like bread and biscuits. The other is "indirectly" related to NR exploitation and processing. In this case, they are upstream industries producing inputs for agriculture—pesticides, other agro-chemicals, and various kinds of agricultural machinery.

Fourth, however, while the sectors with high concentrations of innovators were almost all NR related in these two ways, it was not the case that a high incidence of firms with significant innovative activity was a general characteristic of all manufacturing sectors linked to other sectors engaged in the primary production of natural resource-based products. On the contrary, many such manufacturing sectors had low numbers of relatively innovative firms, and many of them had none at all.

Fifth, we found that in general the agglomerated innovators in the NR-related industries performed much better than any other group of firms with respect to both the level of innovative activity at the beginning of the period (the 1990s) and its subsequent evolution. This gap, in terms of both the numbers of significantly innovating firms and the quality of their innovative capability, was especially wide when comparisons were made with firms in the conventionally defined "high-tech" industries or with foreign subsidiaries—two groups of firms that are commonly thought to set benchmarks of more innovative behavior in emerging economies like Argentina.

Sixth, we find interesting differences between the two groups of agglomerated innovators:

- On the one hand, we found that those in the *directly* NR-related industries conformed in the early 1990s to common expectations—in that: (i) they depended heavily on implementing innovation by investment in new technology that was already embodied in purchased capital goods, and (ii) they supported innovation by negligible levels of in-house R&D. However, our analysis of the evolution of technological activity in these firms showed that in the subsequent decade they increased their R&D intensity and skills at extremely rapid rates that were faster than those in most other groups of firms. In other words, contrary to what is commonly expected, they were not merely augmenting their *production* capability by using other people's technology; they were building a base of R&D activity and professional human capital to constitute their own significant stock of *knowledge-creating innovative capability.*
- Contrasting with this pattern, firms in *indirectly* NR-related industries started the period with levels of in-house R&D activity that were higher than in other manufacturing industries, even higher than both innovative MNE subsidiaries and innovative firms in the so-called "high-tech" industries. Besides that, over the period analyzed they sustained their level

of R&D intensity and further deepened the professional-intensity of their workforce during the 1990s. As a result, they ended the period with the highest R&D intensity among all the groups.

(ii) The case-study explorations

Our more detailed examination of selected agricultural input suppliers illuminated aspects of the innovative behavior contributing to those broad patterns of resurgent innovative activity, especially the second. A number of speculative generalizations seem warranted.

First, the paths of resurgent innovative activity in these firms do not seem to have been examples of widely generalized micro-responses to macro-level changes. Those macro changes (different real exchange rates, increased competition, and, over recent years, somewhat greater economic stability) were indeed important in contributing to the rapid growth of agricultural production and closely related downstream processing (e.g. vegetable oils) primarily for export. But this stimulus did not work its way evenly through the system. As we noted earlier, it did not stimulate a general increase in innovative activity in all input- and output-related manufacturing sectors; only in some. Similarly, even within a single manufacturing industry like agricultural machinery, it also did not give rise to a generalized increase in demand and a pervasive stimulus for innovation. Instead, something much more selective seems to have taken place. The changes in macro conditions were accompanied by a technological transformation of the agricultural sector that opened up niches for new kinds of inputs, not just a greater demand for more of the same kinds of inputs as before. Thus, the opportunities that opened up were at least initially *particular kinds of niche market* generating associated *demands for technological novelty*. It appears to have been the case that responses to this combination could be much better made by particular kinds of firm—for example, within the agricultural machinery industry, by relatively specialized, low-volume producers rather than high-volume suppliers of general-purpose products like tractors and conventional grain harvesters.

Second, however, among the firms we examined, a further component of firm-related particularity seems to have been important in responding to the new opportunities—a significant degree of "technological preparedness." As the opportunities opened up, those firms appear to have already possessed an existing base of "innovation readiness." For example, Agrometal, already an innovator in the early 1980s, seems to have been a very early entrant into the production of specialized, innovative equipment for use in ZT systems. PLA also moved very quickly from its existing base in "conventional" agricultural machinery into the production of innovative, specialized equipment for ZT-related applications. In the area of seeds inputs for the new kinds of opportunity in agriculture, Nidera quite rapidly built its trajectory of innovation on a strong competence in genomics, coupled with an established germplasm base accumulated in large part from its experience in "conventional" plant breeding.

Third, in considering other components of the basis that was available for responding to the selective, novelty-demanding opportunities opened up by the new agricultural economy, we should note a "non-observation" in our exploratory case studies. This concerns the role of public science, technology and innovation institutes, and policy mechanisms. We did note that PLA made extensive use of public funding from FONTAR for its own R&D activities. However, we do not know whether other firms made similar use of such funding support for innovation. Nor do we know about the role of links to public science and technology institutes and universities—and hence whether flows of people or R&D-derived knowledge from such sources were important.[18]

Fourth, however, we were able to throw a little more light on two aspects of the firms' innovation trajectories in responding to the new opportunities. One of these is about the cumulative and largely incremental nature of the innovation process. This is a common and fairly well-recognized feature of innovation paths, but it merits highlighting again—not least because it helps to illustrate how the sharp distinction that is commonly made between "radical" and "incremental" innovation can often be unhelpful. The firms whose experience we explored did not simply develop specific new types of equipment or seed in the form of one-off "inventions." They engaged in cumulative paths of innovation in which there was a mixture of relatively large "steps" and smaller incremental advances. Certainly, by 2000 when ZT systems were applied to about 50 percent of the cultivated area in Argentina, one could identify ZT technology as a new technical system that was widely used and "radically" different from the preceding mode of agricultural production. One might also have identified some of the components of the system as amounting to "radical" innovations compared with the technologies used in agriculture some 30 years before—for example, perhaps self-propelled inter-seeders controlled by computer and satellite would qualify as radical innovations. But those were not innovations in the form of one-off, step-jump advances that had subsequently diffused through the agriculture industry to reach 50 percent adoption by 2000. Instead, they had been arrived at cumulatively over nearly 20 years via continuous sequences of incremental (and not so incremental)

---

[18] The information about linkages provided earlier in Table 8.9 sheds only very limited light on this issue—showing that, for agro-chemical and agricultural machinery firms in 1998–2001, innovation-related links with R&D institutes were identified as less important than innovation-related links with other organizations, primarily other firms.

steps of advance. That cumulative process subsequently continued after 2000 until the present, and it will no doubt continue into the future.

Fifth, a second aspect of those trajectories is about the international sources of technology that contributed to the cumulative paths of innovation being pursued by the firms. For example, in developing its innovations, PLA not only interacted with other local firms such as Profertil (a chemical fertilizer producer), but also with international companies such as Petrobrás. Agrometal developed new technologies with Monsanto, and Nidera made use of alliances with international companies like BASF. In other words, the boundaries of the sectoral innovation systems that generated the paths of innovation in these industries were not simply intra-national. However, the *inter*-national channels in these systems carried flows of technology that were quite different from the types of "imported technology" that are commonly discussed in the context of industrializing economies. They were not "ready-to-use" final technologies that were acquired for immediate application in production. Instead, they involved cross-border flows of knowledge into localized *innovative* activity. The networks and alliances through which these "technology imports" flowed were therefore components of *innovation* systems, and not just of production systems. These were "national" in the sense of the location of much of the innovative activity, but they were also internationally "open" in terms of the contributing actors and knowledge sources.

(iii) An overview: from static to dynamic advantage

In seeking to pull together the different strands in this chapter, it is useful to start by returning to our analysis of the economic performance of manufacturing sectors in Section 8.5. This showed that the agglomerated innovators in NR-related sectors already performed substantially better than any other group at the beginning of the 1990s. This suggests, somewhat speculatively, that the achievement of relatively high levels of economic performance might have preceded the raising of innovative performance for these firms. Manufacturing firms linked to primary natural resource industries, which were in a relatively strong economic position given the pattern of comparative advantage, seem to have moved through two phases of investment. They were able to invest first in new production capacities needed to compete successfully in international markets; then, second, they invested in deepening their innovative capacity. This second phase was perhaps both a consequence of their strong position in international markets[19] and a necessary basis for sustaining that position. Consequently, if something like that

[19] Recall from Table 8.11 that these firms increased their export intensity during the 1990s at high rates and to very high levels.

process did indeed occur, we may have observed what could be called "creative accumulation": a transition from static to dynamic advantages within firms and within sectors, rather than more simply a reallocation of resources across sectors that have inherent differences in their technological characteristics.

There have, of course, been numerous other studies of this kind of creative accumulation within manufacturing sectors. Most of these have reflected East Asian experience—for example, experience in the industries examined in Linsu Kim's study of Korea's transition, *From Imitation to Innovation* (Kim, 1997), and many others covering especially electronics industries in Korea and Taiwan. However, there were several sharp differences between the paths followed in the manufacturing sectors explored in this chapter and those examined in most East Asian studies.

First, the firms and industry cases examined here have not been about a transition to dynamic advantage that started from an initial base of static advantage associated with abundant low-cost labor. In this case, the initial static advantages were rooted in endowments of natural resources.

Second, the cases here were not rooted in an initial phase of acquisition of well-established "ready-to-use" technologies from the advanced economies, followed by successive stages of assimilation and deepening of innovation capability until, perhaps three or four decades later, innovation was undertaken close to, or at, the international technological frontier. Instead, innovation-based dynamic advantages underpinning both rising exports and the internationalization of production were built up largely on the basis of localized innovative activities—though these drew some of the needed knowledge inputs from international sources.

Third, that technologically creative process was not centered primarily on what Lee and Lim (2001) have called *"path-following"* trajectories of innovation and catching up with the international technological frontier—paths that constituted the dominant experience of industries in economies like Korea, Taiwan, and Singapore between the 1960s and 1990s.[20] Instead, the process in Argentina was largely centered on *"path-creating"* trajectories of innovation—i.e. trajectories in which the firms explored their own paths of technological development that were to a significant extent directionally different from paths already pursued by global innovation leaders in agricultural technology. Moreover, the path-creating dimension seems to have been involved at an early stage in these trajectories of local innovation. In contrast, in the East Asian case, this type of trajectory was relatively rare, and it usually occurred at a relatively late stage of "catching up"—i.e. when latecomers turned to new

---

[20] Such "path-following" trajectories involve the cumulative deepening of localized innovation that follows broadly the same direction of technological development already pursued by world-leading firms in the same industries.

directions of technological development after having followed the path of global forerunners for a considerable period.

Thus, it is striking that this Argentine experience of transition from static to dynamic advantage appears to have occurred in a very different way from what has often been seen as the benchmark model for such processes—the experience of industries and firms in economies like Korea and Taiwan. But it is also striking that, according to one line of argument about Latin American experience, it should not have occurred at all.

This is because the transition occurred in and around a natural resource-based industry—agriculture—and, since at least the time of Prebisch in the 1940s, an important strand of opinion in Latin America has considered NR-based industries to be inherently "non-dynamic" in a technological sense. Consequently, it has been argued, specialization in such industries over the longer term locks economies into technologically non-dynamic paths of development. In broad terms, therefore, policy should seek to influence the allocation of investment and other resources such that the structure of the economy diversifies away from NR-based specialization and toward entry into more dynamic types of industry. Such industries have been identified in changing ways over time—very roughly, they were seen as manufacturing industries in general in the 1950s and 1960s, more specifically as capital goods (especially machine tools) in the 1970s and early 1980s, and as ICT-related industries in the late 1980s and 1990s. Diversification of the economy by entry into such industries would, it was argued, open the door to more technologically dynamic futures as firms and industries pursued trajectories of path-following learning and deepening innovation activities as per East Asia.[21]

The story we have sketched in this chapter, somewhat speculatively in places, does not fit that model at all. On the one hand, it does not fit the Latin American view about specialization in NR-based production. It is *not* a story about specialization in agriculture that locked an important segment of the Argentinean economy into a long-term future of technological stagnation

---

[21] Even as a very broad simplification, this last point is a bit inaccurate about one issue. At earlier stages in the development of such arguments, notions about learning and the cumulative deepening of innovative capabilities were not really recognized. The idea of technological dynamism was seen more as something that was inherent in the particular industrial activities. Thus, for example, the machine tool industry was not just technologically advanced in terms of the complexity of the technology it *used*. It was also inherently innovative in the sense that engaging in the production of machine tools would necessarily also involve engaging in innovation in machine tools. It was only after the research on Latin American industries by Jorge Katz and colleagues during the 1970s that the distinction between production capability and innovation capability began to be teased open, with the consequent recognition that, if significant innovative activity was to be undertaken, entry into production in an industry had to be followed by various explicit learning efforts to create the necessary innovative capabilities.

and an inability to earn innovation-related rents in international markets. Instead, it is a story about changing the structure of the economy by increasing the production and export of knowledge-intensive goods and services in sectors related to agriculture and by the internationalization of their production via outward foreign direct investment. On the other hand, however, the story does not fit the East Asian model either. Diversification into these areas of increasingly knowledge-intensive production was not achieved by entering into *production* in new sectors and then *subsequently* learning to *innovate*. It seems more appropriate to see it as having been achieved by an interlinked process of learning to innovate within existing sectors and so creating the capabilities to capture opportunities to expand and diversify production and exports of new kinds of goods and services in and around those sectors.[22] In technological terms, therefore, this diversification of the structure of production and exports emerged "organically" out of the existing structure. The areas of new technology were cumulatively created in the context of the existing technology, not "bolted on" as external acquisitions and then assimilated.

Two kinds of question arise. The first is about whether our interpretation of this Argentinean experience of "creative accumulation" is reasonably accurate. If the answer to that is adequately positive, the second set of questions is about the generalizability of this experience of transition from static NR-based advantages toward significant innovation-based competitiveness in international markets. Was this feasible in only the very specific conditions of agriculture in Argentina in the 1990s and subsequently? Even within those bounds, what is the potential scope for this agriculture-related transition to influence in the longer term the evolution of the broader economy as a whole? Under what conditions can one expect similar patterns of transition to occur around this or other NR-based industries in this or other industrializing economies? We hope others may be interested in exploring such questions much more intensively than seems to be the case at present.

---

[22] This perspective is similar in many ways to the ideas of Hausmann, Rodrik, and colleagues who have identified "self-discovery" (Hausmann and Rodrik, 2003) or "local cost discovery" (Hausmann et al., 2007) as an important process underlying diversification in the structure of developing economies. Perhaps the main difference is that we stress the importance of a much more technologically active and creative form of process. The entrepreneurs running firms like PLA, Agrometal, and Nidera were not merely exploring the underlying cost structure of the economy (Hausmann et al., 2007: 2) and "discovering" what they would be good at producing within that structure (Hausmann and Rodrik, 2003: 605). They were *creating* new spaces within the cost structure and developing the means to exploit them.

Appendix Table 8.A1. Distribution of non-innovative firms in non-innovative sectors

	Sector	Domestic firms	Subsidiaries
152	Manufacture of dairy products	6	3
155	Manufacture of beverages	34	5
160	Manufacture of tobacco products	0	2
181	Manufacture of wearing apparel and accessories, except leather	19	0
192	Manufacture of footwear	6	1
201	Sawmilling and planing of wood, impregnation of wood	14	0
232	Manufacture of refined petroleum products	2	3
251	Manufacture of rubber products	15	2
271	Manufacture of basic iron and steel	7	2
314	Manufacture of accumulators, primary cells, and primary batteries	1	0
319	Manufacture of electrical equipment not elsewhere classified	6	2
331	Manufacture of medical surgery equipment and orthopedic appliances	6	3
351	Building and repairing ships and boats	2	0
352	Manufacture of railway and tramway locomotives and rolling stock	2	0
353	Manufacture of aircraft and spacecraft	4	1
359	Manufacture of other transport equipment	4	0
369	Miscellaneous manufacturing not elsewhere classified	5	2
Total		133	26

Source: Author elaboration from database.

REFERENCES

Amsden, A. H. (1989), *Asia's Next Giant: South Korea and Late Industrialization*, New York and Oxford: Oxford University Press.

Arza, V. (2005), "Technological Performance, Economic Performance and Behaviour: A Study of Argentinean Firms during the 1990s," *Innovation: Management, Policy and Practice*, 7(2–3): 131–51.

Azpiazu, D. (1997), "El Nuevo perfil de la elite empresaria," *Realidad Económica*, 145: 7–43.

Barbero, M. (2004), "Impacto de la inversión extranjera directa en la industria argentina en la década de 1920: Estrategias empresariales y sus efectos sobre el sector productivo local," *Revista do Centro de Estudos Interdisciplinares do Século*, 20(4): 201–22.

—— and Rocchi, F. (2002), "Industry and Industrialization in Argentina in the Long Run: from its Origins to the 1970s," in G. Della Paolera and A. Taylor, *The New Economic History of Argentina*, Cambridge: Cambridge University Press, 261–94.

Baruj, G., Giudicatti, M., Vismara, F., and Porta, F. (2005), "Situación productiva y gestion del cambio tecnico en la industria Argentina de Maquinaria agrícola," mimeo, Project Redes-Cepal-Secyt: Sistema Nacional y Sistemas Locales de Innovación, Estrategias Innovativas Empresarias y Condiciones Meso y Macroeconomicas, August.

Bisang, Roberto (2003), "Diffusion Process in Networks: The Case of Transgenic Soybean in Argentina," paper read at Conferência Internacional sobre Sistemas de Inovação e Estratégias de Desenvolvimento para o Terceiro Milênio, November 2003, in Brazil.

—— and Kosacoff, B. (2006), "Las redes de producción en el agro argentino," document presented at the 14th annual congress of AAPRESID, Rosario, Argentina.

Chudnovsky, D., and Lopez, A. (1997), "Las Estrategias de las Empresas Transnacionales en Argentina y Brasil: Qué Hay de Nuevo en los Años Noventa?" CENIT, Documento de Trabajo No. 23, Buenos Aires.

—— —— and Pupato, G. (2006), "Innovation and Productivity in Developing Countries: A Study of Argentine Manufacturing Firms' Behavior (1992–2001)," *Research Policy*, 35: 266–88.

Cimoli, M., and Katz, J. (2003), "Structural Reforms, Technological Gaps and Economic Development," *Industrial and Corporate Change*, 12(1): 387–411.

Ekboir, J. (2003), "Research and Technology Policies in Innovation Systems: Zero Tillage in Brazil," *Research Policy*, 32: 573–86.

Hausmann, R., and Rodrik, D. (2003), "Economic Development as Self-Discovery," *Journal of Development Economics*, 72: 603–33.

—— Hwang, J., and Rodrik, D. (2007), "What You Export Matters," *Journal of Economic Growth*, 12: 1–25.

Hobday, M. (1995), *Innovation in East Asia: The Challenge to Japan*, Aldershot: Edward Elgar.

Katz, J. (1976), *Importación de Tecnología, apprendizaje e industrialización dependiente*, Mexico: Fondo de Cultura Económica.

—— (1987), "Domestic Technology Generation in LDCs: A Review of Research Findings," in J. Katz (ed.), *Technology Generation in Latin American Manufacturing Industries*, Basingstoke: Macmillan.

—— (2001), "Structural Reforms and Technological Behaviour: The Sources and Nature of Technological Change in Latin America in the 90s," *Research Policy*, 30: 1–19.

—— (2007), "Cycles of Creation and Destruction of Production Capacity and the Development of New Export and Technological Capabilities in Latin America," in T. Grosse and L. Mesquita (eds.), "Can Latin American Firms Compete," *Oxford Scholarship Online Monographs*, 16(October): 66–81.

—— and Bercovich, N. A. (1993), "National Systems of Innovation Supporting Technical Advance in Industry: The Case of Argentina," in R. R. Nelson (ed.), *National Innovation Systems: A Comparative Analysis*, New York and Oxford: Oxford University Press.

—— and Kosacoff, B. (1989), "El proceso de industrialización en la Argentina: evolución, retroceso y prospectiva," mimeo, CEPAL, Buenos Aires.

Katz, J. and Kosacoff, B. (2000), "Import-Substituting Industrialisation in Argentina, 1940–1980: Its Achievements and Shortcomings," in E. Cardenas, J. A. Ocampo, and R. Thorp (eds.), *An Economic History of Twentieth-Century Latin America; Volume 3: Industrialization and the State in Latin-America: The Postwar Years*, Basingstoke: Palgrave, 283–313.

Kim, L. (1997), *Imitation to Innovation: The Dynamics of Korea's Technological Learning*, Boston, Mass.: Harvard Business School Press.

Kosacoff, B. (1996), "Estrategias Empresariales en la Transformación Industrial Argentina," Documento de Trabajo, No. 67, CEPAL.

—— (1999), "Las multinacionales argentinas," in D. Chudnovsky, B. Kosacoff, and A. López (eds.), *Las multinacionales latinoamericanas: sus estrategias en un mundo globalizado*, Buenos Aires: Fondo de Cultura Económica.

—— (ed.) (2000a), *Corporate Strategies under Structural Adjustments in Argentina: Responses by Industrial Firms to a New Set of Uncertainties*, Basingstoke: Macmillan.

—— (2000b), *El desempeño industrial argentino más allá de la sustitución de importaciones*, Buenos Aires: CEPAL.

Kulfas, M., Porta, F., and Ramos, A. (2002), "Inversión extranjera y empresas transnacionales en la economía Argentina," Serie Estudios y Perspectivas 10, Buenos Aires: CEPAL.

Lee, K., and Lim, C. (2001), "Technological Regimes, Catching-Up and Leapfrogging: Findings from the Korean Industries," *Research Policy*, 30(3): 459–83.

Lopez, A. (1996), "Las ideas evolucionistas en economía: una visión de conjunto," *Revista Buenos Aires Pensamiento Económico* (RBA), 1: 93–154.

Mathews, J., and Cho, D.-S. (2000), *Tiger Technology: The creation of a Semiconductor Industry in East Asia*, Cambridge: Cambridge University Press.

OECD (1992, 1997, 2005), *The Measurement of Scientific and Technological Activities: Guidelines for Collecting and Interpreting Innovation Data—The Oslo Manual*, first, second, and third editions, Paris: Organisation for Economic Co-operation and Development.

—— (1994), *The Measurement of Scientific and Technological Activities: Proposed Standard Practice for Surveys on Research and Experimental Development—The Frascati Manual*, fifth edition, Paris: Organisation for Economic Co-operation and Development.

Patel, P. (2000), "Technological Indicators of Performance," in J. Tidd (ed.), *From Knowledge Management to Strategic Competence: Measuring Technological, Market and Organisational Innovation*, London: Imperial College Press, 129–54.

Teitel, S. (1981), "Towards an Understanding of Technical Change in Semi-Industrialized Countries," *Research Policy*, 10: 127–47.

Villanueva, J. (1972), "El origen de la industrialización argentina," *Desarrollo Económico*, 12(47), October–December: 452–76.

Part III

Comparative Conclusions

9

Conclusions

Edmund Amann and John Cantwell

9.1. SETTING THE SCENE

In this chapter we will not provide a simple summary of the earlier chapters of the book, but rather we develop some analytical conclusions that in our view follow from the earlier findings. We develop here an evolutionary and institutional approach to firm-level capability building in the tradition of Teece, Pisano, and Shuen (1997), Dosi, Nelson, and Winter (2000), and Teece (2009). This draws upon some of the features of an evolutionary approach to the firm in an emerging market context that we discussed in Chapters 1 and 2 (Bell and Pavitt, 1995; Lall, 1992). However, in this chapter we emphasize two further elements of an evolutionary approach. First, we recognize that firm-level capability building should be analyzed mainly as a process over time which reflects a continual change and transformation in the nature of both the actors and their environment. Second, an evolutionary approach helps us to better understand the variety of complex ecosystems in which innovative firm capability building can take root, and how such capability building co-evolves with other elements in the system of which it is part. In particular, what is apparent from the earlier studies in this book is the much greater variety of contexts in which innovative capability building now occurs. Not only are more actors from emerging market economies now involved in this process, as well as firms from mature industrialized countries, but we have also seen that the emerging market contexts themselves are often quite different from one another.

Connected to these aspects of an evolutionary approach to firm capability building, a major influence on our subject in recent years has been the steadily rising globalization of the technological knowledge base, the internationalization of epistemic and professional communities of practice and related science (Mazzoleni and Nelson, 2007), as well as the increased international interconnectedness of business relationships. This trend toward a greater international integration in the processes of firm-level capability building has meant that all the nationally specific ecosystems such as those we have examined in the earlier chapters have been shifting substantially over the past 20 years. In the more dramatic cases, this has been associated with a process of radical institutional reforms such as in China, India, Brazil, and Argentina. These reforms are designed to avoid exclusion from the potential advantages of international relationships.

In the evolutionary approach that we are proposing, we emphasize that the environment within which firms operate is complex and systemic in character and in continual flux. Hence, firm capability building co-evolves with other features of such ecosystems. Evolutionary systems are known to exhibit strong aspects of the cumulativeness and path dependency of economic and social processes (Nelson and Winter, 1982; Dosi, 1982; Mokyr, 2005; and David, 1985). This reinforces the specificities of both national systems of innovation and the firm-level processes that arise within them, since cumulative paths lead to local distinctiveness. Consequently, many of the institutional features of a national system of innovation are inherited from historical antecedents in each country (Nelson, 1993).

It should be noted that a crucial implication of our evolutionary approach—which goes beyond our immediate topic of firm-level capability building—is that it enhances the potential for social science analysis. In the conventional social sciences, as they have developed especially since the 19th century, processes are treated mechanically such that simplifying assumptions are made that enable the scholar to focus upon outcomes rather than underlying processes. For example, in economics a rational actor responds to received signals from the environment while in sociology a social group responds to its environment in some broadly predictable fashion. This enables the application of mechanical principles similar to those used in 19th-century physics and renders the subject capable of analysis within a deterministic framework.

In contrast, the evolutionary approach to economic, social, and cultural change is inherently more interdisciplinary in nature, since the focus is on understanding the evolution of an ecosystem in its entirety as opposed to the actions of one part of that system in isolation. In order to better appreciate the co-evolution of actors and their environment over time we need to draw on elements of different disciplines in a more synthetic fashion. This also suggests that multi-method approaches are appropriate and desirable for social science research, since we need to combine the insights on processes that can be obtained from qualitative analysis with the benefits of generality that can be gained from quantitative methods. Our book can be seen as an illustration of this approach, since many of our chapters combine qualitative and quantitative evidence on firm-level capability building.

In the remainder of this chapter, we elaborate upon this institutional and evolutionary approach to our subject. In the next section (Section 9.2), we examine the processes of firm-level capability building that lie at the heart of our book and current argument. Then, in Section 9.3, we move on to consider the inter-organizational relationships that are most often associated with firm-level capability building in different contexts. Finally, in Section 9.4, we discuss the wider institutional context of the environment for innovative firms, including the role of policy and relationships between firms and policy-makers.

9.2. CONSIDERATIONS AT THE FIRM LEVEL

In this book we have argued that traditional approaches toward technological and economic catch-up have tended to disregard the firm level and to focus attention on certain key features of the macro or industry-level environment of economies that are beneficial to closing the gap with mature industrialized economies. Here, instead, we have concentrated on firm-level capability building in its own right. In an evolutionary approach, what matters critically is the goodness of fit of different firm types with their respective environment. This goodness of fit varies substantially with two related features of that environment: first, the institutional context and, second, the form of international connectedness.

An evolutionary approach, as derived from the pioneering study of Nelson and Winter (1982), allows for an active role for individual agency. This is true whether we treat the individual agent in the sense of the firm as a whole as the actor, or we think of the active contribution of the individual manager within a firm. In our book we have developed more the study of the role of the firm as opposed to the individual, although we have come across a few illustrations of the role of certain key entrepreneurial figures. This evolutionary approach in a social setting steers a mid course between blind evolution, such as in the processes of random natural selection on the one hand, and carefully calculating rational actors with perfect foresight on the other. In the analytical framework that we are proposing here, and which is implicit in our earlier studies, the firm and the individual co-evolve with their respective environments. Thus, because different firms in a roughly equivalent situation choose different paths depending in part on their own past histories and knowledge, processes are essentially non-ergodic and do not give rise to neat predictions of unique outcomes. Thus, we have to understand the progressive interaction in the evolution of the firm with its environment and how this unfolds over time, as opposed to attempting to explain it with reference to received outcomes.

As we have indicated, a critical feature of our approach is that the development of innovative capabilities and, indeed, of firms themselves can be understood as an evolutionary process. Agency, as opposed to the interplay of impersonal forces, exercises a central function in all of this. In this regard, the systemic context for innovation at firm level is likely to be strongly influenced by internal management structure, culture, and the influence of key individuals whether entrepreneurs, technologists, or managers. For example, the Indian pharmaceutical and automotive enterprises reviewed in Chapter 4 highlight just how significant the internal dynamics of leadership and organization can be in driving innovative success. The evidence suggests clearly that certain entrepreneurial and management approaches proved more suited than others to coping with (and shaping) the evolving external environment whether in terms of policy, external business partnerships, or technology suppliers.

Evidence from the Brazilian steel industry also indicates that particular managerial and entrepreneurial cultures may be better suited to certain business environments than others. Thus, despite similar sectoral and policy environments, CSN and USIMINAS have experienced contrasting success in managing the transition between capability levels. Equally, in the South Korean context, Samsung, LG, Daewoo, and Hyundai, despite similar patterns of ownership and (conglomerated) organization, have experienced sharp differences in their abilities to successfully manage rapid capability building in the electronics sector. Again, the lesson appears to be that the internal management and organization characteristics of firms have a critical bearing on whether constructive co-evolution with the external environment occurs.

As already indicated, a central preoccupation of this book is the relationship between any given firm type in a particular national context and the ability of an individual firm to build up capabilities. To repeat, what matters critically is the goodness of fit of different firm types with their respective environments. It follows from this—and indeed is borne out in the country studies—that no one firm type can be associated with the most innovative firms across all national contexts. Thus, taking one example at random, it is simply not the case that multinational corporation (MNC) subsidiaries form the cadre of the most innovative enterprises, that is, firms associated with advanced capability levels, in all countries; but they do in some. Where one does find an association between a particular firm type and particular capability levels, this tends to be in a specific country, or, indeed, sectoral context. This once again suggests that the drivers of innovation are complex and systemic in nature, that this systemic context varies by country and sector, and that there can be no automatic association between firm type and capability level.

As we have argued, the goodness of fit of a firm with its environment varies substantially with two related features of that environment. These features comprise the institutional context and the prevalent form of international connectedness. Some further examples from earlier chapters will help to bear out these points. Perhaps the most obvious case of the specificity of the institutional and international connectedness and its link with the best suited firm type centers on South Korea. In the very particular context of that country, diversified conglomerates known as *Chaebol* have proven highly effective at building up technological capability. This has allowed *Chaebols* to operate at the frontier in some technologies, while also expanding into new, more challenging areas.

No one would pretend that enterprises of this conglomerate type have powered capability building across all emerging market economies. Still, they have proven very effective in South Korea. Why might this be? The institutional context of South Korea for much of the post-war period comprised an export-focused, centralized industrial policy regime committed to restricting the role of foreign capital, in particular inward direct investment. In this context, the emergence of a few large, domestically owned business groups with strong links to the state forged connections between industries, proved amenable to policy-makers, and was suited to the task of achieving rapid industrialization in a planned and sequential manner in the specific world economic environment of the early post-war period.

The highly nationalistic character of the industrialization context may also privilege the emergence of enterprise forms which seek to gain access to technologies through joint venture partnerships (as, for example, in the Chinese case). Instead, international interconnectedness in the Korean context has involved extensive external licensing arrangements and, to an increasing extent, the acquisition of technologies through outward direct investment. Just as a particular national context has helped to favor the emergence of Korean business groups, so these enterprise forms have contributed toward the development of a distinctive ecosystem around them. Thus, we have seen the rise of a specialized policy regime and a series of close relationships with outside research organizations whether these be domestic public sector institutes or foreign MNCs.

In other national and sectoral contexts, quite different enterprise types have emerged having proven highly able to build capability. Thus, for example, entrepreneurial software companies, often with arm's length international business connections, have been well suited to the Indian business environment. Conversely, international joint ventures with strong connections to both a foreign parent company and an indigenous country base have been well placed to benefit from institutional reform in China. To some extent, a similar pattern may be noted in the situation of Malaysia.

In the Brazilian case, where, as in China but unlike South Korea, the initial industrialization process was more outward looking (in the specific sense that inward direct investment was a vital component), we find success in capability building across a mixture of MNC subsidiaries, domestic business groups, and former state-owned enterprises (SOEs). Enterprises in all these categories have proven able to successfully co-evolve with their surrounding environments as the associated processes of institutional reform and market liberalization have unfolded. Similarly, in the case of Argentina, it is clear that a variety of enterprise forms have proven able to innovate within a rapidly evolving institutional context. As in the case of Brazil, modalities of international interconnectedness have proven rather diverse across the range of enterprises surveyed. Whereas some innovative firms draw on direct equity participation from foreign MNCs, others have engaged in licensing, while a select few (mainly in the Brazilian case) have been able to reinforce capabilities accumulation through outward direct investment.

While no one firm type is associated with the most innovative firms across all national contexts, given the variety of national institutional environments that we observe, we might still ask whether there is any association between a transition in capability levels and firm type. This, after all, was one of the key questions posed at the outset in Chapter 1. The evidence presented in this book offers a mixed picture in terms of the potential association between firm internationalization and the attainment of certain capability levels. One might expect, at least from the perspective of the Eclectic Paradigm,[1] that firms able to progress up the hierarchy of capability levels would possess an increasingly rich capacity to generate ownership advantages. Such advantages could potentially form the basis for subsequent internationalization and attainment of MNC status through outward foreign direct investment (OFDI). As the internationalization of the firm occurs, this will undoubtedly affect the process of capabilities accumulation in the enterprise as a whole both through the adaptation of existing capabilities used abroad and through the acquisition of new capabilities from foreign partners.

What is immediately apparent is that the innovative domestic enterprises surveyed in this volume that did become MNCs happen to be strongly concentrated in three countries: Brazil, India, and South Korea. Their sectoral focus embraced a broad range of activities, including more technologically intense components of the manufacturing and natural resource-based product sectors.

In the case of Indian pharmaceutical enterprises such as Dr Reddy's, internationalization has clearly built on advanced process capabilities attained in cost-effectively manufacturing drugs developed originally by European and North American MNCs. Thus, it might be argued that asset-exploiting behavior is a critical aspect of internationalization here. On the other hand, and still in India, the case of Tata Motors is illustrative of an enterprise striving to achieve world-leading process and product-design capabilities through international asset acquisition. In this regard, the recent purchase of the UK's Jaguar Land Rover is a case in point. There are echoes here of the Chinese automotive producer, SAIC's, internationalization strategy. This has involved purchasing the plant and intellectual property of Rover Cars (also in the UK).

---

[1] John Dunning's classic framework, which is widely used to explain both the underpinning motivations and the ways in which firms internationalize. For a comprehensive explanation of the Eclectic Paradigm, see Dunning and Lundan (2008), chapters 4 and 5.

In the case of Brazil, the evidence tends to suggest that the transition to MNC status has also been associated with upward progression in capability levels. Thus, Embraer and Gerdau—to cite but two examples from the product- and process-intensive sectors—witnessed a strong association between internationalization through OFDI and increasing technological virtuosity. What seems notable about the Brazilian case, however, is that asset-acquiring behavior has not been a prime initial motive for OFDI. This, perhaps, testifies to the effectiveness of the local systemic context for innovation in which these firms are embedded, although there may be positive international technology feedback effects to Brazil in due course.

The internationalization of the Korean business groups, the *Chaebols*, also provides some evidence of basic and intermediate capability thresholds being crossed as a prelude to internationalization. As noted, the creation of these capabilities depended, to an extent, on knowledge transfers from foreign MNCs with whom licensing or contract manufacturing agreements had been reached. Despite the undoubted expansion in indigenous capability that has occurred, it remains the case that some *Chaebol* ODFI has had from the outset asset-augmenting motivations. In the electronics sector, LG, Samsung, Daewoo, and Hyundai have all established R&D facilities in the US. In the case of LG, for example, its acquisition of Zenith Inc. in 1995 was partly driven by the desire to gain access to the venerable US television manufacturer's proprietary technology.

Contrary to the experience of Korean investment in the US, however, *Chaebol* investment in Europe appears to be targeted more at establishing market presence than gaining access to technology. Thus, the Korean case underscores our general conclusion that the relationship between capability building, internationalization, and change in firm type is complex, firm-specific, and dependent on the institutional environment of home and host countries and prevalent modes of international interconnectedness.

We have argued that success in innovative terms will be strongly related to a firm's goodness of fit with its surrounding environment. Still, however good this fit may be, if the wider environment imposes sufficiently severe constraints on enterprises, then it is unlikely that innovative behavior will result. In particular, if the broader environment faced by firms is characterized by stagnant demand, inadequate or costly availability of inputs, and structural obstacles to export, then, no matter how well molded to its surroundings, a firm is less likely to be innovative. This points to the obvious conclusion that the sector in which any firm finds itself will have a critical bearing on capabilities building. For example, in sectors characterized by rapidly expanding demand and underlying cost-related comparative advantages—such as the Brazilian pulp and paper sector, the Chinese automotive sector, or the Indian software sector—we have seen that highly innovative enterprises can emerge. However, the literature is replete with cases where such sectoral dynamics (in particular, demand dynamics) have not been present, with the result that capabilities have atrophied rather than been accumulated. The work that Katz (2001) has done on Latin American enterprises illustrates this possibility.

9.3. CONSIDERATIONS OF INTER-ORGANIZATIONAL AND INTERNATIONAL BUSINESS RELATIONSHIPS

Just as the goodness of fit of any specific firm type with its environment depends upon the national institutional setting, so too we can understand the variety of inter-organizational relationships that we have observed in our different country chapters through their goodness of fit with the relevant national system. Those inter-organizational relationships that are most conducive to firm-level capability building can vary markedly with the characteristics of the specific ecosystems in which they are observed. Thus, for example, the role of the relationships of an innovative firm with universities or public research institutes plays out quite differently in each of the countries we have studied.

Likewise, the form of international business relationships reflects the requirements of any given national industrial structure or system of innovation. The form of international business connections that are most typical for the domestic firms of a country helps to condition both the nature and the extent of international technology transfer. Another feature to which our various country studies draw attention is that these international business relationships have been in the process of substantial change in recent years. This is also a consequence of the global diffusion of the technological knowledge base to which we referred earlier in the chapter.

Given their centrality to our argument, it is worth dwelling on these two points a little further. First, let us consider the issue of inter-organizational relationships. In many of the cases analyzed, interaction with universities or public research institutes has played a critical role in the acquisition of capabilities. For example, enterprises in the Indian pharmaceuticals sector and the Brazilian aerospace and pulp and paper sectors have drawn extensively on public sector research laboratories as they have sought to upgrade capability levels. Indeed, in the case of Embraer, the enterprise was originally established as a spin-off from a publically funded research institute.

In the case of Korean *Chaebols* operating in the electronics sector, interaction with public research institutes has also proved a recurrent feature in their technological upgrading, transition into new product areas, and capabilities acquisition. This has also been the case among Malaysian electronics enterprises, though less obviously so in relation to the firms surveyed in the Chinese and Argentinean manufacturing sectors. However, in the Chinese case we know that some university-originated or university-owned firms have played a significant role in innovation, which could be added to the story of foreign-domestic partnerships on which we have focused.

Reviewing the evidence, it appears the case that an association may well exist between the relative importance of links with public sector research institutes and the presence of enterprises in certain sectors. In particular, the preponderance of such links appears more marked in the electronics, aerospace, and pharmaceutical sectors than it does in other sectors such as steel, automobiles, and agricultural machinery. However, this is not to dismiss the long-standing state-sponsored efforts to build up capability in natural resource-based sectors, as shown, for example, by extensive university-industry linkages in Brazilian agriculture. The recent emphasis on non-traditional activities is likely to reflect in part the strategic priorities of policy-makers, who, in many Asian and Latin American economies, have increasingly displayed a bias in favor of supporting innovative firms in high-profile emerging sectors. Such prioritization might be viewed as evidence of an aggressive desire to position economies in sectors where the prospects for long-term market growth appear most promising. It reflects as well the composition of sectors in which technology is closer to science and R&D intensity is higher, so linkages with public research facilities are more likely to bear fruit.

Having considered inter-organizational links, we turn now to the changing nature of international business relationships. Accentuated by trade, investment, and financial market liberalization, accelerating FDI flows have increasingly enabled enterprises operating in emerging market countries to participate in cross-border knowledge-sharing inter-firm networks. These have taken on a variety of forms, their character reflecting the modalities of direct investment involved. Thus, international joint ventures have arisen naturally within the Chinese context and have formed a central plank in the networks which have evolved. In the Argentinean case, by contrast, the role of wholly owned subsidiaries has assumed greater relative importance. The Malaysian semiconductor sector has been built up through knowledge transfers between MNC parent companies and their subsidiaries.

The internal transfer of knowledge to facilitate capability building in newly established subsidiaries also turns out to be a hallmark of the Indian and Korean business groups surveyed in this volume. Enterprises such as India's Tata or Korea's Samsung are large industrial conglomerates with established research facilities and what amounts to a well-developed internal capital market. This has allowed sequential diversification into new product areas, with the new activities drawing on capabilities, and financial and managerial resources from elsewhere in the organization.

The scope of international business connections extends much beyond investment relationships and embraces links which firms may have established as suppliers or contract manufacturers. In particular, across a range of countries in East and Southeast Asia, considerable capabilities have been developed as a consequence of firms engaging in original equipment manufacturer (OEM) and original design manufacturer (ODM) relationships with foreign enterprises. The case of the Brazilian aerospace sector, too, illustrates how the inclusion of enterprises in increasingly global production networks can form the basis for fruitful knowledge creation and transfer.

The presence of foreign MNCs in such networks offers a means through which domestically owned enterprises can gain access to the key knowledge and resources needed to build capability. There is an increasing variety of organizational forms of international business networks that sustain the coordination and exchange of capabilities. The growing phenomenon of emerging market MNCs only serves to underline how the character of such inter-firm linkages is only likely to become more international (as opposed to purely national) in scope. There is already much evidence for this in the case of OFDI realized by Korean, Chinese, and Indian MNCs in the electronics, automobile, and pharmaceuticals sectors.

What then becomes very clear from a survey of the firm experiences analyzed in this volume is the fact that (increasingly international) external relationships are highly important in determining the technological trajectories of firms. Indeed, they form the bedrock of the systemic context in which innovation occurs. However, the character and configuration of these linkages varies quite widely from one home country to another and from firm to firm. This heterogeneity in turn reflects the fact that the most effective forms of inter-organizational and international business relationships will vary according to the nature of the technological ecosystem in which firms are embedded.

9.4. CONSIDERATIONS OF THE WIDER ENVIRONMENT

As we have argued here, we examine in an evolutionary setting a process of progressive interaction between the levels of individual agency on the one hand and the change or transformation in the environment on the other. In other words, in the wider context we need to pay attention to the co-evolution of the different elements of an ecosystem. As we noted above, we claim that this helps us to resolve some of the older longer-standing debates in the social sciences which reflected a notion of passive actors responding deterministically to certain features of their environment. For example, some have argued that free markets are more conducive to innovative enterprise, while others have claimed that more regulated and structured environments are more helpful to innovative enterprise. Regardless of where one stands on such debates, for us instead, what matters most is the progressive interaction over time between innovative firms and their environment, whatever the nature of that environment. Hence, the kinds of firms that are more likely to thrive in a free market setting are different from the kinds that are likely to prosper in a more regulated setting. In each case, the advantages and constraints upon innovation arising in that environment are distinct and lead to a specific form of interaction with innovative firm capability building.

Therefore, our perspective on the role of policy is very different from that stemming from more traditional viewpoints. In the traditional type of argument, policies are seen in the manner of exogenous shocks to firms to which they should react. Instead, in our evolutionary approach, policies must be understood as merely part of a broader structure of an environment within which firms are operating and upon which they also have some effect over time. Hence, the focus of attention needs to be on the progressive interaction between firm-level capability building and policy-making as a process, as opposed to a set of isolated actions.

Moreover, with the globalization of knowledge, communities of practice, and business activity, as outlined earlier, and the greater presence of local firm capability building in a wider range of countries, policy has increasingly migrated from the macro-level to the micro-level. We believe that this change in the policy context is at least as important as the more widely discussed transition to liberalization. It entails a far greater interchange than in the past, of a continuous nature, between policy-makers and business management, especially those responsible for aspects of innovative capability building. Various managers have commented on this shift in the international environment that now involves much more detailed negotiations with policy-makers and official agencies in countries in which they have ambitions to develop innovative capability-building enterprises.

In this context, Ozawa (2011) has discussed the changing contribution of multinational firms to industrialization processes in host economies as a reflection of a shift from the infant industry protection arguments associated with import-substitution industrialization regimes (ISI) toward environments in which the direct presence of multinational firms helps to precipitate industrial and technological catch-up. To understand this shift in the international policy context, we need to appreciate the increasing role of international knowledge interconnectedness and the internationalization of communities of practice which have rendered policies of national economic isolation effectively redundant. Thus, the forms of catch-up strategy used so effectively in the past by Japan and Korea, which built entire national industrial systems behind a protective wall, are no longer viable. Reflecting this, China's recent industrialization has been far more open and globally interconnected in character. China has taken advantage of the desire of multinationals to participate in its strong market growth to leverage technology and facilitate combinations of

Chinese and international technology as a means of enhancing and consolidating national economic development.

The key question that stems from this ongoing transformation in the wider environment centers on its implications for the systemic context within which firms innovate and, by extension, the impacts that may have been visited on firm-level trajectories of learning and capability building. It might be expected, a priori, that the implications of the globalization of knowledge, communities of practice, and business activity are likely to be profound and, in many, but not all, instances, favorable. It is certainly the case that the new environment we have described has the potential to stimulate firm-level efforts to improve capability levels to meet the challenge of international competition. Still, this must be set against the possibility that the challenge is met through intensified passive reliance on external (in all likelihood, foreign) sources of technology.

Dependent on the mode of technology transfer, and the learning efforts of firms, it may well be the case that firms' own capabilities are much improved as external sources of technology are tapped. This tends to occur as the degree of international business connectedness intensifies. Still, if the pace of international integration were too great, the competitive and financial pressure on firms may be such that in-house efforts directed at learning and capability building are deliberately scaled down. Another possibility is that increased market openness raises the likelihood that innovative domestically owned firms become the focus for foreign takeovers. It may sometimes be the case that existing domestic technological capabilities are eroded as a new parent company eliminates cross-border duplication of innovative facilities.

The ability of the public sector to counteract these pressures on firm-level capability building may be limited. In particular, such attempts are likely to be constrained by tight fiscal policy, itself the macroeconomic hallmark of liberalization drives associated with the globalization agenda. Indeed, the negative connotation of policy liberalization for firm-level capabilities creation tends to be a recurring theme in some of the literature. This is especially true where the experience of firms in Latin America is concerned. However, this narrative is often overly pessimistic.

The evidence presented in this volume has suggested instead that the implications of the new and more internationally integrated environment are on balance positive and not negative. In the case of Argentina, while it was acknowledged that capabilities destruction had characterized some sectors, firms in other sectors, notably those related to natural resource-based products (NRBP) had navigated the wrenching transition from ISI, not only surviving but intensifying their in-house learning efforts, a process which had led to the building up of capabilities. This finding stands in marked contrast to the conclusions of much of the work centering on the experiences of Argentinean or, indeed, Latin American firms in transition (see e.g. Katz, 2001). Reconciling what, at first sight, appears to be a glaring discrepancy in findings involves discarding the traditional narrow focus on policy liberalization. Instead, we concentrate on the finer details of firm-specific systemic contexts for innovation.

In many respects, Argentina stands as a paradigmatic case of crash liberalization whether one places the focus on trade reform, privatization, or internal market deregulation. However, the survival—and, indeed the enhancement—of innovative capabilities among some firms (notably in certain NRBP-related (especially agriculturally related) clusters) reflect the particularities of the market and the innovative environment in which they were embedded. In the new environment, both domestic and international inter-organizational and inter-business linkages have been strengthened as market demand for natural resource-based products has soared. It has also been the case that increasing inward and outward direct investment has opened up new sources of technology for Argentinean firms. This has helped foster effective capabilities building. This advantageous context also provided a springboard for the increasingly effective participation of these innovative firms in international markets.

In the case of Brazil and India, the pace of institutional investment and trade reform was rather slower than in Argentina. Still, many enterprises in these economies struggled to cope with the transition to the new environment and capabilities were sometimes lost as restructuring, closure, and takeovers occurred. Despite this, there has been a flowering of innovative capabilities across a large range of firms, many of which operate in sectors other than natural resources. To understand these experiences it is once again of prime importance to reflect on the specificities of the systemic context for innovation facing firms and not just the fact of policy liberalization. Equally, it is important to think in terms of a progressive interaction between firm-level capability building and policy-making: policy should not be considered as some kind of independent exogenous shock.

In the case of Brazil's Embraer, for example, significant capabilities had been built up during the ISI period thanks to targeted technology policy initiatives, the establishment of a tight network of suppliers, significant domestic demand, and technological interaction with the military. The abandonment of import-substitution industrialization and the privatization of Embraer in 1994 generated significant incentives—and opportunities for exports. However, the success that was eventually realized here depended on continued capabilities building in order to make the product transition to passenger jets. Despite privatization and the demise of ISI policies, support for capabilities building continued to be drawn from the public sector, whether through public laboratories, research subsidies, or official lines of credit. Also, the opening of Embraer to foreign investment following privatization gave rise to new international business connections, in particular with

France's Dassault. This relationship has given rise to substantial knowledge flows in both directions. Here, policy appears to have co-evolved in a
constructive manner, with Embraer providing a sound foundation on which
capability could be built.

In this regard, there are strong parallels with the experiences of Indian
pharmaceutical and automotive firms. Here, the transition to a more open
market setting has accompanied broadly successful attempts to build capabilities through enhancing inter-organizational links whether with public sector
research enterprises or foreign enterprises. In regard to the latter, the rise of
asset-seeking behavior by Indian MNCs has played a critical role. For Indian
pharmaceutical enterprises, the environment for learning and capabilities
building has proved especially auspicious, thanks to the watering down of
intellectual property legislation in the late 1970s. This has allowed domestic
enterprises scope to reverse engineer pharmaceuticals developed overseas, the
product then being targeted at the domestic market. Again, progressive and
constructive interaction between firms and policy-makers appears to have
played an important role.

Similar evidence of constructive co-evolution between firms and policy-
making can also be witnessed in the case of South Korea. As elsewhere, the
past two decades have witnessed significant market opening and growing
international competitive pressure. Consequently, *Chaebols* such as Samsung
and LG have been obliged to intensify their international market presence
through sequential product upgrading. Far from falling off, capability building in the reform period has continued. Firm capability building has been
supported by an interlocking network of public sector research entities,
official finance, and domestic and international suppliers. At the same time,
the opening up of key sectors to foreign participation (in particular, the
automobile sector) has created new channels for knowledge transfer. The
key point here is that, while the pursuit of reform may have accentuated
competition and recalibrated the role of the state, it did not adversely impact
the "micro climate" for innovation faced by the *Chaebols*. In particular, the
public sector continued to play a constructive role, while firms were able to
more effectively leverage opportunities for gaining access to critical foreign
technologies.

In the case of Malaysia, the change in broad policy context is probably the
least marked of all the countries surveyed, by virtue of the long-standing
openness of that country's development model. Nonetheless, Malaysian enterprises, as a consequence of multilateral trade reform, have been obliged to
compete in an increasingly fiercely contested marketplace. As in the case of the
Korean *Chaebols*, Malaysian semiconductor firms have been obliged to build
up further capabilities, engaging in sequential product and process upgrading.
In doing so, they have been able to draw on a legacy of capabilities accumulation. They have also benefited from the persistence—despite the crisis of

the late 1990s—of effective and interactive public sector engagement with the innovative process.

The Chinese case invites strong parallels with that of India in this respect: capability building, by and large, has tended to be concentrated inside firms whose activities are generally quite far removed from the manufacture of NRBP. The highly particular character of the liberalization process in China has been associated with distinctive patterns of learning and capabilities accumulation. While limited capabilities had been built up at the firm level in the pre-reform period, these generally did not prove adequate for coping with the pressures of progressive insertion into the international economy. This was particularly true when it came to the need to export. The signing of joint ventures with foreign MNCs across a range of sectors has proved an effective means of building capabilities through knowledge exchange and learning.

The ability of Chinese firms to engage in a meaningful process of learning and capabilities accumulation as a consequence of their participation in joint venture agreements cannot be considered a casual or automatic consequence of the formation of such partnerships. Rather, as is commonly recognized in the growing literature on inward investment in China, joint venture agreements have tended to be quite closely scrutinized by the authorities. This has been done with a view to ensuring that genuine opportunities will be created for learning, knowledge transfer, and capabilities accumulation. Thus, while at one level, the boom in inward FDI can be considered the product of a long-standing and profound market-reform drive, it can be argued that the opening up of China to foreign investment has also been a managed process, resting on a significant degree of progressive interaction between firms and policy-makers.

Thus, the interaction between the firm and its environment is playing out in a situation in which the state generally continues to have an active role, but a changed one that reflects the opportunities for capability building associated with a greater ease of international knowledge flows and connections. Consequently, the state and policy-making have been co-evolving with firm-level capabilities in each of the emerging market economies. Nonetheless, as we have explained earlier, the forms of international business connection that are most conducive to local industry development have tended to vary quite markedly across different national institutional contexts.

The change in global context we have just discussed has given scope for the emergence of technological capabilities outside the traditional centers of Europe, North America, and North Asia. It might be tempting to believe that distinctive (or even contrasting) models of capability building apply according to whether a firm originates in a mature industrialized country or in an emerging market economy. It is already well known that in the mature industrialized country case there are varieties of capitalism (Hall and Soskice, 2001; Whitley, 1998) in which national institutional structures differ considerably and, hence, so do some of the characteristics of innovation systems.

What we have found in this book is that there are equally varieties of capitalism across different emerging market economies. These variations matter a
good deal in terms of the kinds of firms that are most innovative. Hence, for
the purpose of this analysis, it is not terribly useful to simply argue that
institutions in emerging market economies tend to be less well developed
than they are in the mature industrialized economies. What are more important are the finer-grained detail of these institutional arrangements in practice
and the inherited structure of firm-level capabilities from each country's past.
To return to where we began in this chapter, this underlines the significance of
path dependence in evolutionary social systems. While the variety of potential
paths may be constrained, or, indeed, as we have shown, transformed by the
character of the global environment, in the new environment too there are still
a variety of paths to capability building. In this evolutionary process, it may
not be possible to predict in advance the exact nature of a successful path or
the form that it will take. However, we can be sure that alternative paths to
capability building will continue to exist alongside each another and that, just
as in the natural world, we may be able to classify common species or families
of structure associated with innovative capability building.

REFERENCES

Bell, M., and Pavitt, K. (1995), "The Development of Technological Capabilities," in I. ul
    Haque (ed.), *Trade, Technology and International Competitiveness*, Washington, DC:
    The World Bank.
David, P. (1985), "Clio and the Economics of Qwerty," *The American Economic
    Review*, Papers and Proceedings of the 97th Annual Meeting of the American
    Economic Association, 75(2), May: 332–7.
Dosi, G. (1982), "Technological Paradigms and Technological Trajectories:
    A Suggested Interpretation of the Determinants and Directions of Technical
    Change," *Research Policy*, 11(3), June: 147–62.
——— Nelson, R., and Winter, S. (eds.) (2000), *The Nature and Dynamics of Organiza-
    tional Capabilities*, Oxford and New York: Oxford University Press.
Dunning, J. H., and Lundan, S. M. (2008), *Multinational Enterprises and the Global
    Economy*, Cheltenham, UK: Edward Elgar.
Hall, P., and Soskice, D. (eds.) (2001), *Varieties of Capitalism: The Institutional
    Foundations of Comparative Advantage*, Oxford: Oxford University Press.
Katz, J. (2001), "Structural Reforms and Technological Behaviour: The Sources and Nature
    of Technological Change in Latin America in the 1990s," *Research Policy*, 30(1),
    January: 1–19.
Lall, S. (1992), "Technological Capabilities and Industrialisation," *World Development*,
    20(2): 165–86.

Mazzoleni, R., and Nelson, R. R. (2007), "Public Research Institutions and Economic Catch-Up," *Research Policy*, 36(10): 1512–28.

Mokyr, J. (2005), "Is There a Theory of Economic History?" in K. Dopfer (ed.), *The Evolutionary Foundations of Economics*, Cambridge: Cambridge University Press.

Nelson, R. (ed.) (1993), *National Innovation Systems: A Comparative Perspective*, New York: Oxford University Press.

—— and Winter, S. (1982), *An Evolutionary Theory of Economic Change*, Cambridge, Mass.: Harvard University Press.

Ozawa, T. (2011), "The Role of Multinationals in Sparking Industrialization: From 'Infant Industry Protection' to 'FDI-Led Industrial Take-Off'," *Columbia FDI Perspectives*, No. 39, June: 1–3.

Teece, D. (2009), *Dynamic Capabilities and Strategic Management: Organizing for Innovation and Growth*, Oxford: Oxford University Press.

—— Pisano, G., and Shuen, A. (1997), "Dynamic Capabilities and Strategic Management," *Strategic Management Journal*, 18(7): 509–33.

Whitley, R. (1998), "Internationalization and Varieties of Capitalism: The Limited Effects of Cross-National Coordination of Economic Activities on the Nature of Business Systems," *Review of International Political Economy*, 5(3): 445–81.

Index

This Index refers principally to persons, countries and organisations mentioned in the main body of the text. Reference to individual companies and particular industries are indexed under the headings "companies (named)" and "industries (named)"

DATE DUE